COMPETITION LAW AND ECONOMIC REGULATION

Niamh Dunne undertakes a systematic exploration of the relationship between competition law and economic regulation as legal mechanisms of market control. Beginning from a theoretical assessment of these legal instruments as discrete mechanisms, the author goes on to address numerous facets of the substantive interrelationship between competition law and economic regulation. She considers, amongst other aspects, the concept of regulatory competition law; deregulation, liberalisation and 'regulation for competition'; the concurrent application of competition law in regulated markets; and relevant institutional aspects including market study procedures, the distribution of enforcement powers between competition agencies and sector regulators, and certain legal powers that demonstrate a 'hybridised' quality lying between competition law and economic regulation. Throughout her assessment, Dunne identifies and explores recurrent considerations that inform and shape the optimal relationship between these legal mechanisms within any jurisdiction.

NIAMH DUNNE is a lecturer in Law at King's College London.

COMPETITION LAW AND ECONOMIC REGULATION

Making and Managing Markets

NIAMH DUNNE

CAMBRIDGE
UNIVERSITY PRESS

CAMBRIDGE
UNIVERSITY PRESS

University Printing House, Cambridge CB2 8BS, United Kingdom

Cambridge University Press is part of the University of Cambridge.

It furthers the University's mission by disseminating knowledge in the pursuit of education, learning and research at the highest international levels of excellence.

www.cambridge.org
Information on this title: www.cambridge.org/9781107070561

First published 2015

A catalogue record for this publication is available from the British Library

Library of Congress Cataloging-in-Publication Data
Dunne, Niamh, 1984- author.
Competition law and economic regulation : making and managing markets / Niamh Dunne.
pages cm
Includes bibliographical references and index.
ISBN 978-1-107-07056-1 (Hardback)
1. Competition, Unfair. 2. Competition, Unfair–United States. 3. Competition, Unfair–European Union countries. 4. Antitrust law. 5. Antitrust law–United States. 6. Antitrust law–European Union countries. I. Title.
K3850.D86 2015
343.2407'23–dc23 2014042970

ISBN 978-1-107-07056-1 Hardback

CONTENTS

ACKNOWLEDGEMENTS

This work started life as a doctoral research project exploring one of the apparent transatlantic divergences that continue to exist within competition law, namely the differing approaches to the issue of a regulated margin squeeze adopted by the EU and US antitrust systems. It soon became clear, however, that the concurrent application of competition law and economic regulation is merely a single aspect of their broader interrelationship. Thus, the focus of research shifted to providing a more systematic account of the interface between these instruments than could be found in the existing literature. This book provides an updated and slightly expanded version of that original research project.

Given its origins, primary thanks must go to my wonderful doctoral supervisor, Albertina Albors Llorens, for getting this project from proposal to PhD, to ultimate publication. Her advice, support and kindness during my three years of research was utterly invaluable. My examiners, Rosa Greaves and Angus Johnston, provided helpful feedback and much-appreciated encouragement to develop the original thesis into a monograph. The manuscript also benefitted from thoughtful comments from Bill Allan, plus useful criticisms and suggestions for improvement from three anonymous referees. Peter Dunne provided eagle-eyed editing skills at the doctoral stage, while the editorial team at Cambridge University Press has been fabulous in bringing my initial proposal to polished reality. I am grateful for support of a more material kind from the UK's Arts & Humanities Research Council and the Competition Authority of Ireland. (My interest in the relationship between competition law and regulation is perhaps more understandable given my past life in competition enforcement in a small Member State.) Corpus Christi College, Cambridge and the Faculty of Law at the University of Cambridge each provided generous funds for research activities. While writing this work, I benefitted from research stays at Harvard Law School and the Max Planck Institute for

Comparative and International Private Law. Finally, apologetic thanks must go to the friends and family members who endured much over-excited (and occasionally under-excited) antitrust and regulatory chat over the past few years, and who put up with me in good humour nonetheless.

TABLES OF CASES

European Cases

Commission Decisions

Commission Decision of 8 July 2009 in Case COMP/39.401 – *E.ON/GDF* (OJ C248/5, 16.10.2009), 252

Commission Decision of 4 May 2010 in Case COMP/39.317 – *E.ON Gas* (OJ C278/9, 15.10.2010), 111, 113–4, 136

Commission Decision of 3 December 2009 in Case COMP/39.316 – *Gaz de France* (OJ C57/13, 9.3.2010), 113–4, 223

Commission Decision of 26 November 2008 in Case COMP/39.388 – *Germany Electricity Wholesale Market* and Case COMP/39.389 – *German Electricity Balancing Market* (OJ C36/8, 13.2.2009), 111, 113–4, 223

Commission Decision of 14 January 1998 (IV/34.801 *FAG – Flughafen Frankfurt/Main AG*) (OJ L72/30, 11.3.98), 73

Commission Decision of 13 December 2011 in Case COMP/C-3/39692 – *IBM Maintenance Services* (OJ C18/6, 21.2.2012), 115, 126

Commission Decision of 10 February 1999 (IV/35.767 – *Ilmailulaitos/Luftfartsverket*) (OJ L69/24, 16.3.1999), 74

Commission Decision of 13 May 2009 in Case COMP/C-3/37.990 – *Intel* (D(2009)3726 final), 309

Commission Decision in Case COMP/39.386 – *Long-term contracts France* (OJ C133/5, 22.5.2010), 111, 113

Commission Decision of 19 December 2007 in Cases COMP/34.579 – *MasterCard*, COMP/36.518 – *EuroCommerce* & COMP/38.580 – *Commercial Cards*, summary at 2009 OJ (C 264), 75

Commission Decision of 16 December 2009 in Case COMP/C-3/39.530 – *Microsoft (tying)* (OJ C 36/7, 13.2.2010), 115

Commission Decision of 6 March 2013 in Case COMP/39.530 – *Microsoft (Tying)* breach decision (OJ C 120/15, 26.04.2013), 82

Commission Decision of 21 January 2010 in Case COMP/M.5529 – *Oracle/Sun Microsystems* (OJ C 91/7, 9.4.2010), 96

Commission Decision of 10 February 1999 (IV.35.703 – *Portuguese Airports*) (OJ L69/31, 16.3.1999), 74

Commission Decision of 9 December 2009 in Case COMP/38.636 – *Rambus* (OJ C30/17, 6.2.2010), 110–1, 259

Commission Decision of 18 March 2009 in Case COMP/39.402 – *RWE Gas Foreclosure* (OJ C133/10, 10.12.2009), 111, 113–4, 136, 223

Commission Decision of 23 July 2004 in Case COMP/A.36.568/D3 – *Scandlines Sverige AB* v. *Port of Helsingborg*, 125

Commission Decision of 26 July 2000 (*Spanish Airports*) (OJ L208/36, 18.8.2000), 74

Commission Decision of 15 November 2011 in Case COMP 39.592 – *Standard & Poor's* (OJ C31/8, 4.2.2012), 110–1, 126

Commission Decision of 14 April 2010 in Case 39.351 – *Swedish Interconnectors* (OJ C142/28, 1.6.2010), 111, 113–4, 118

Commission decision of 22 June 2011 in COMP/39.525 – *Telekomunikacja Polska* (OJ C324/7, 9.11.2011), 136, 214, 219–20, 232, 242, 247, 250, 260

European Court of Human Rights

US Cases

International Salt Co. v. *United States* 332 US 392 (1947), 98
Lorain Journal Co. v. *United States* 342 US 143 (1951), 131
Maryland v. *United States*, 460 US 1001 (1983), 63
MCI Communications v. *AT&T Corp.* 708 F.2d 1081 (7th Cir. 1983), 131
Otter Tail Power Co. v. *United States*, 410 US 366 (1973), 131, 204
Pacific Bell Telephone Co., d/b/a AT&T California et al. v. *linkLine Communications, Inc., et al.*, 555 US 438 (2009), 192, 209, 243, 248
Pan American World Airways, Inc. v. *United States*, 410 US 366 (1973), 254
Parker, Director of Agriculture, et al. v. *Brown*, 317 US 341 (1943), 199, 200
Rambus, Inc. v. *FTC*, 522 F.3d 456 (D.C. Cir. 2008)259, 310–1
Rice, Director, Department of Alcoholic Beverage Control of California v. *Norman Williams Co.*, 458 US 654 (1982), 199
Silver, d/b/a Municipal Securities Co. et al. v. *New York Stock Exchange*, 373 US 341 (1963), 204
Southern Motor Carriers Rate Conference, Inc., et al. v. *United States*, 471 US 48 (1985), 200
Standard Oil Co. of NJ v. *United States*, 221 US 1 (1911), 124
Theatre Enterprises v. *Paramount Film Distribution Corp.* et al., 346 US 537 (1954), 178
Town of Concord, Massachusetts v. *Boston Edison Co.*, 915 F.2d 17 (1st Cir. 1990), 209–10, 230
United Mine Workers v. *Pennington*, 381 US 657 (1965), 200
United States v. *Aluminum Co. of America (Alcoa)*, 148 F.2d 416 (2d Cir. 1945), 22, 124
United States v. *Armour & Co. et al.* 402 US 673 (1971), 100–1, 103
United States v. *ASCAP*, 1940–1943 Trade Cases ¶56,104 (S.D.N.Y. 1941), 106
United States v. *ASCAP*, 1950–1951 Trade Cases ¶62,595 (S.D.N.Y. 1950), 106
United States v. *AT&T*, 552 F. Supp. 131 (DDC, 1982), 62–4, 107, 157, 257
United States v. *Armour & Co. et al.* 402 US 673 (1971), 100–1, 103
United States v. *BMI*, 1940–1943 Trade Cases ¶56,096 (E.D. Wis. 1941), 106
United States v. *BMI*, 1996–1 Trade Cases ¶71,378 (S.D.N.Y. 1994), 106
United States v. *BMI*, 426 F.3d 91 (2nd Cir. 2005), 107
United States v. *Borden Co. et al.*, 308 US 188 (1939), 203
United States v. *Colgate & Co.*, 250 US 300 (1919), 130
United States v. *General Dynamics Corp.*, 415 US 486 (1974), 159
United States v. *ITT Continental Baking Co.*, 420 US 223 (1975), 103
United States v. *Microsoft Corp.*, 56 F.3d 1448 (1995), 95, 98–9
United States v. *Microsoft Corp.*, 231 F. Supp. 2d 144 (DDC, 2002), 118
United States v. *National Association of Securities Dealers, Inc.*, 422 US 694 (1975), 204–5, 238, 247
United States v. *Philadelphia National Bank et al.*, 374 US 321 (1963), 204, 277
United States v. *SBC Communications, Inc. and AT & T Corp.* 489 F.Supp.2d 1 (DDC, 2007), 99
United States v. *Swift & Co. et al.* 286 US 106 (1932), 102

UK Cases

Australian Cases

1

Introduction

Ever tried. Ever failed. No matter. Try again. Fail again. Fail better.

Samuel Beckett, *Worstward Ho* (1983)

Market-based economies are ubiquitous throughout the world. Whether motivated by ideology, experience or the discipline of economics, there is a general – though not universal – acceptance of the market mechanism as an integral element in the organisation of society. Adam Smith's striking vision of 'the invisible hand of the market'[1] underlines a widely accepted tenet of the functioning of market systems: namely, that markets work best when unencumbered by government intervention. Yet history, both distant and recent, tells us that neither markets nor economists are infallible in this respect. The well-functioning market, bringing the wealth of society to its highest and best uses, may be a thing of beauty in the abstract realms of economic theory. Quite disobligingly, however, real-life markets often fail to live up to the promise of their impeccable archetype. Governments thus not infrequently intervene in dysfunctional markets in order to correct persistent market failures or to advance alternative non-economic goals. Competition law and economic regulation are both components of the State's arsenal of market regulatory tools that facilitate the legal function of market regulation – what one might, somewhat cynically, describe as the task of enabling markets to 'fail better'. The operation of and interactions between these legal instruments comprises the subject of this work.

Markets are everywhere, and increasingly so. Particularly with respect to the State-owned enterprise and regulated monopoly sectors, 'privatisation' and 'liberalisation' have been (somewhat loaded) buzzwords for decades. As we will discuss in Chapter 3, the latter half of the twentieth

[1] Smith (1776:293).

century witnessed a prolonged attack against the perceived inefficiencies of much existing economic and social regulation, which led to a notable paring back of purported regulatory burdens. This politically motivated embrace of a purer form of free markets has led to decidedly mixed results. Few would dispute that certain market-based reforms have been largely beneficial; think, for example, of deregulation of the cossetted airline industry, which brought about a dramatic reduction in airfares and has made air travel possible for a much broader section of society. Other developments are more controversial, particularly those involving the marketisation of public-service provision; recent efforts to partially 'privatise' the UK's National Health Service provide a clear example in this regard.[2] The Global Financial Crisis offers a trite but still potent example of how markets can go very badly wrong, and the negative consequences – both economic and social – that may follow. The phenomenon of globalisation has, amongst other things, led to the emergence of a globalised marketplace, and encouraged the broader adoption of market-based principles in many developing economies. Frustration with unthinking 'market fundamentalism'[3] has led to a backlash in many areas, however: from prominent anti-globalisation protests in Seattle and London, for example; to the (still largely untapped) vigour of the Occupy movement; to increasing disillusionment with and rejection of the so-called 'Washington Consensus' by developing nations.[4] Rising levels of inequality, in particular, provide an increasingly urgent rebuke to the ascendancy of markets-focused thinking.[5] Generally, it might also be said that there is a growing realisation, to quote Cass Sunstein, that 'markets should be understood as a legal construct to be evaluated on the basis of whether they promote human interests, rather than as a part of nature and the natural order, or as a simple way of promoting voluntary interactions'.[6]

The very concept of 'free' markets is, to an extent, a fallacy – what Sunstein calls the 'myth of *laissez-faire*'.[7] While this idea may appeal to notions of autonomy and freedom from State oppression, all markets depend, to a degree, on law for their existence and operation. It is essentially impossible to think of any market that does not, in some way, rely upon legal rules that regulate, for example, contracts, tort or criminal penalties (for instance, controlling financial crimes such as

[2] See the Health and Social Care Act 2012.

[3] The phrase is most closely associated with the work of economist Joseph Stigliz.

[4] Williamson (1990). [5] Piketty (2014). [6] Sunstein (1997:5). [7] Ibid.

fraud). Thus, the 'invisible hand' is both facilitated and constrained by law, even in markets that look, at first glance, to be wholly unencumbered by regulation. Moreover, it is naïve to view State involvement solely as an obstacle to the operation of markets; put simply, markets don't always work well in practice. The operation of the market mechanism may be hampered in a way that means it produces, ultimately, a sub-optimal distribution; or the market itself may work fine, but it produces an outcome that, although efficient, seems deeply unfair. In such circumstances, there is likely to be a *prima facie* case for government intervention in the wider public interest. The stated mission of the UK's former competition authority, the Office of Fair Trading, comes to mind at this juncture: namely, 'to make markets work well for consumers'.

At a very general level, therefore, this book concerns the means by which law intervenes in markets to secure a better outcome for society. The potential breadth of this formulation is readily apparent, however, and even a cursory consideration of this topic in full would fill many volumes. Instead, this study focuses upon two particular instruments for State market supervision, competition law and economic regulation, considering the uses of and interface between these legal tools. Our focus is thus upon economic problems of a more micro-than macro-economic nature. In brief, competition law seeks to strengthen the workings of the market mechanism by prohibiting certain forms of anticompetitive behaviour by firms that, alone or acting in concert, have the ability to exercise market power. Economic regulation, as the concept is conceived for our purposes, generally involves a State-directed, positive, coercive alteration of or derogation from the operation of the free market in a particular sector, typically undertaken in order to address market failure, to be distinguished from regulation that pursues a predominantly 'social' aim. In essence, this conception of regulation involves an overreaching of the market mechanism, whereas competition law seeks to reinforce its operation. Our enquiry is premised upon the starting assumption that competition law and economic regulation are, in large part, separate mechanisms for market supervision, but that these instruments have overlapping scopes of application, so that, in practice, there can be considerable substantive interaction between these legal tools. Consequently, although competition law and economic regulation may comprise discrete mechanisms, there is no clear and absolute distinction between them; instead, this relationship is more intricate and multifaceted. The aim of this work is, broadly, to unpick and analyse the complexities of this relationship at a substantive level.

The question of the interface between competition law and regulation has become increasingly pertinent, and increasingly pressing, as the liberalisation of former monopoly industries has created markets where partial regulation coexists alongside competitive segments. The apparent transatlantic division over approaches to the vexed question of concurrent application of competition law in regulated sectors – compare the decision of the US Supreme Court in *Trinko* to the holding of the Court of Justice of the European Union (CJEU) in *Deutsche Telekom*,[8] both considered in Chapter 4 – provides perhaps the clearest example of on-going controversy over this question. There are numerous additional dimensions to this relationship, nonetheless, each of which presents challenging legal and policy questions. Can or should competition law be used as a form of quasi-regulation, for example to control exploitative behaviour or fill gaps in a regulatory framework, an issue that is explored in Chapter 2? Given the persistent criticisms advanced by advocates of deregulation, considered in Chapter 3, why and when would regulation be the preferred mechanism by which to control anticompetitive firm behaviour? Moreover, while we focus on the substantive legal interactions between competition law and regulation that might arise, there are certain related, and problematic, institutional matters that must be must be considered, specifically concerning the division of labour between competition authorities and regulators. These questions are explored in Chapter 5. These analyses of overlaps in practice are complemented by a more abstract consideration, in the remainder of this chapter, of the concepts of competition law and economic regulation, both individually and in comparison. In the overarching treatment of these interrelated issues, the objective here is to produce a taxonomy of sorts that probes the actual and potential functional overlaps between competition law and economic regulation, and thus allows for a cohesive description of this interface as a whole.[9]

This book is not unique in addressing the relationship between competition law and economic regulation; generally speaking, however, existing work has considered the relationship only with respect to a specific regulatory regime – for example, the interface between competition law and telecommunications or energy regulation – or in relation to

[8] *Verizon Communications, Inc.* v. *Law Office of Curtis V. Trinko*, 540 US 398 (2004), and Case C-280/08 P *Deutsche Telekom AG* v. *Commission*, EU:C:2010:603.

[9] For discussion of the roles and benefits of taxonomy in law, see, e.g., Sherwin (2005) and Low (2009).

one facet of the interface – for example, the problem of concurrency, or the application of competition law as quasi-regulation. The aim here, instead, is to develop a more objective, systematic and holistic exposition and analysis of the interface between these legal instruments, with a particular focus on substantive rather than procedural interactions. Having first clarified and classified the various interactions that may arise, this book will, moreover, engage in a normative exercise aimed at demonstrating the policy implications of a State's market intervention choices. We do not purport to provide a definitive answer to all interface conflicts that may arise, or even, in many instances, to advocate any preference between competition law and regulatory approaches to market supervision. The very existence of competition law or economic regulation within a system indeed reflects policy choices of some variety, and inevitably involves trade-offs, thus requiring political rather than purely legal decision-making. Moreover, the precise requirements and market effects of any scheme of economic regulation, and to a lesser extent antitrust, which condition the relationship between these legal instruments, can vary considerably from sector to sector and between jurisdictions, thus limiting the utility of any 'broad brushstroke' assessment of these issues.[10] Nonetheless, the detailed exposition and analysis provided in this work allows for the identification of recurrent themes and issues of potential concern. Our aim is, ultimately, to undertake the more modest task of assisting in the identification of socially beneficial market regulatory policies, and, furthermore, to understand the full implications of such policy choices.

This is not a politically charged work: it neither advocates for nor against a greater or lesser place for markets in societal organisation. It does, however, sound a sceptical note regarding the power and benefits of unbounded markets, recommending, amongst other things, that where the untamed operation of the market mechanism would work against the public interest, States should not be reluctant to constrain or even replace the market. In this regard, although a predominant focus of this book is the role for competition law, it differs from many other works on this topic insofar as it proposes a more direct acknowledgement of the benefits, and often the necessity, of more traditional forms of economic regulation (in contradistinction to competition law) to address certain market defects.

[10] O'Donoghue & Padilla (2013:45).

I. Market failure and the pursuit of efficiency

We begin by examining competition law and economic regulation, separately, as legal instruments for market supervision. The primary purpose of both is, as noted, to address weaknesses (howsoever these may be conceived) within the market system. It is necessary, therefore, to consider the functioning of the market mechanism prior to any assessment of the mechanics of these legal instruments. Neoclassical economic theory – which is not without its critics, it will be acknowledged – posits that free markets are the engines of progress and function as efficient allocators of resources.[11] The free-functioning of the market thus puts the resources of society to the 'best' (i.e., most efficient) uses – Smith's 'invisible hand'.[12] Consequently, the State should, where possible, abstain from direct market intervention.[13] Yet, embracing a free-market model does not require that a State abstain entirely from market intervention. In particular, the persistence of market failures – or market absences, where no effective market exists – creates a need for State corrective action, for example through competition law or regulatory instruments.[14]

The ascendency of market-based economics, with its preference for free markets over central planning, is evident in practice throughout the contemporary developed world. Yet the robustness of the neoclassical approach has been challenged more recently by, amongst other things, developments in behavioural economics,[15] while the effects of the Global Financial Crisis have emphasised again the inadequacy of this model, particularly at a macro-economic level, in accounting for recurrent economic crises.[16] Thus, its teachings are now viewed rather more sceptically, at least outside the academy.[17] Nonetheless, neoclassical thinking about markets remains at the forefront of regulatory policy-making. We shall, accordingly, take its conventional explanations of how markets work, and how they fail, as the departure point for our broader discussion of the relationship between the market-supervisory instruments of competition law and regulation. This discussion comes with an acknowledged 'health warning' – these theories are not infallible, and may indeed fail to reflect important real-world concerns – as well

[11] Scherer (2008:31); Majone (1996:28); McKie (1970:6). [12] Smith (1776:293).
[13] Coase (1960). [14] Baldwin et al. (2011:15).
[15] See, e.g., Sunstein (2000); Reeve & Stucke (2011); Armstrong & Steffen (2011).
[16] See, e.g., Posner (2009); Stiglitz (2010); Mixon (2010); Sandel (2012).
[17] See, e.g., Colander et al. (2009).

as a disclaimer that the choice of market theory in this instance is pragmatic rather than ideological. Efforts will be made throughout to highlight limitations within the existing model, in particular relating to its emphasis on *efficiency* in a world where *equity* is an equally compelling consideration. Moreover, a central idea within this book is the unavoidable need for State supervision of market functioning in many circumstances; the more complex question is how best this can be achieved.

In essence, within a market system firms produce products. The channels by which products reach purchasers constitute the market.[18] Market theory assumes that firms attempt to maximise profits, and, in doing so, select factor combinations for production that minimise total costs, as well as output levels that maximise net revenue.[19] Each individual firm stands in a relationship of rivalry to other firms, which conditions the actions of each; this setting comprises the industry in which firms operate. The prices that a firm achieves for its products are determined by supply and demand, which dictates market structure.[20] Generally, demand for a product increases as price falls, while supply increases as prices rise. The Keynesian notion of 'effective demand' links creation of demand, at the *micro*economic level, to a strong role for the State in maintaining *macro*economic stability, through full employment and stimulation of investment. The market-equilibrium price is then determined by the interaction of supply and demand on a commodity within a competitive market. This is, in theory, the 'market-clearing' price, namely the price for each good at which consumer demand is fully satisfied and supply exhausted.[21]

Market theory indicates that this market-clearing process achieves the most efficient allocation of society's resources. As each individual seeks to maximise his or her own utility, in aggregate the sum of total welfare reaches its highest value.[22] Efficiency, or wealth maximisation,

[18] Generally, Coase (1937); Clark (1961).

[19] Samuelson (1983:8); Gelhorn (1975:6).

[20] Carstensen (1983:493–7). The concept of demand measures the desire of consumers to purchase a product at each of several different alternative price levels, while supply measures the quantities of a product that producers are willing to offer for sale at different price levels.

[21] Gelhorn (1975:7–22); Vickers (1995:1).

[22] Smith (1776:293); Williamson (1977:722). At a technical level, competitive markets are assumed to satisfy the requirements of Pareto efficiency, whereby there is no more efficient allocation of resources that can be achieved without making some individual worse off: Bator (1958:351).

is the standard concept used in economics to measure an industry's performance of its economic task in society's interests.[23] Efficiency, in this context, comprises two aspects that are not wholly complementary.[24] *Static efficiency* concerns the allocation of resources with a given state of technology; it is a measure of total surplus, meaning consumer surplus (the difference between the consumer's valuation of the good and the effective price he pays for it) and producer surplus (the sum of all profits made by producers in the industry).[25] Static efficiency has two components: allocative efficiency involves matching production to consumer demand, while productive efficiency measures avoidance of wastage of resources.[26] *Dynamic efficiency*, also known as technical progress, measures innovation: namely, improvements in production methods and the quality levels of products.[27] Conflicts can arise between these elements in practice, requiring a trade-off between present and future welfare, which is a recurrent tension within economic regulatory policy.

Achieving efficiency in a market is not a given, however, as market theory incorporates numerous assumptions that condition its operation.[28] Becker suggested three such criteria: that individuals act rationally, maximising utility; that they have stable, ordered preferences, which inform their maximising behaviour; and that markets clear, meaning supply and demand reaches equilibrium.[29] Additional requirements may include sufficient information for actors to make rational choices, an absence of externalities that impede the market-clearing process, and a need for competitive markets.[30] Where one or more of these assumptions does not hold true – which, it should be emphasised, occurs with considerable frequency – the operation of a market may not achieve an efficient allocation of resources. This is 'market failure': namely, 'the failure of a more or less idealized system of price-market institutions to sustain "desirable" activities or to estop "undesirable" activities'.[31] Market failures may exist, *inter alia*, where buyers or sellers lack sufficient information to act efficiently,[32] for public goods,[33] for moral

[23] Viscusi et al. (2005:79); Motta (2004:18). [24] Vickers (1995:4).
[25] Viscusi et al. (2005:66); Motta (2004:18). [26] Gelhorn (1975:1); Motta (2004:40–52).
[27] Viscusi et al. (2005:67), Motta (2004:19). [28] Dempsey (1989:11).
[29] Becker (1976:5). [30] Ogus (1994:23–4, 30). [31] Bator (1958:351).
[32] Majone (1997:266).
[33] Public goods are non-rivalrous and non-excludable, meaning that any individual's consumption does not affect the consumption of others and nobody can be excluded from consuming the good: Bator (1958:369–71). For example, clean air and traffic lights

hazards,[34] or when externalities such as pollution are not factored into transaction costs. Notably, for our purposes, monopoly *may* cause market failure if market power leads to a restriction of output or excessive prices, but it does not necessarily do so.[35] It has even been argued that distributional failures comprise a form of market failure inasmuch as existing market structures fail to secure an acceptable allocation of income.[36] While such an approach is difficult to square with economic conceptions of efficiency, concerns of justice and fairness have, as we shall see, frequently provided a legitimate rationale for market intervention. Given understandable concerns regarding the priority accorded in conventional discourse to market-focused problems in comparison with rights- or solidarity-based objections,[37] a more neutral formulation for this broader conception of dysfunctional markets is that of market 'defects'.[38]

Generally, economists schooled in neoclassical theory tell us that, where efficiency is the aim, the State should refrain from interference in the workings of the market, because the market itself secures a more efficient allocation of society's wealth than State-directed economic policy can achieve. Under market failure, however, the unencumbered free market produces a sub-optimal result, and so there is a *prima facie* case for State intervention to achieve a more desirable allocation.[39] The State has two principal mechanisms available to address market failures.[40] First, it can use price incentives – most obviously taxation – to encourage or discourage certain types of market behaviour.[41] Whilst important in practice – think, for example, of tax relief on pension contributions, or high taxes on cigarettes – such State action falls outside the scope of this work. Second, the State may attempt directly to control market behaviour through regulatory policy mechanisms, which prohibit or, conversely, require certain market conduct.

are public goods. Under a strict market-based approach, public goods are typically undervalued and underproduced.

34 Moral hazard involves excessive risk-taking in circumstances where the risk-taker does not incur the costs of an unsuccessful gamble, a typical example being the decreased incentives of health insurance holders to minimise their medical bills because they do not pay the bill ultimately.

35 Viscusi et al. (2005:2–3).

36 Stewart (1988:111); see also New (1999:65).

37 Prosser (2004:38).

38 Breyer (1987:1006).

39 Majone (1996:54), for example, identified the three main functions of government in the socio-economic sphere as income redistribution, macroeconomic stabilisation, and regulation comprising efforts to correct market failures.

40 Viscusi et al. (2005:3).

41 Jarass (1988:77–81).

Competition law and sector-specific economic regulation both fall within the broad rubric of this latter category.

The economic models of market equilibrium and market failure, outlined earlier, provide a simplified (and not uncontroversial) explanation of the functioning – and shortcomings – of the market mechanism. This book is concerned, primarily, with circumstances where the market itself fails, in whole or part, thus prompting corrective intervention of a legal nature. In translating economic theory to legal rules and public-policy choices, however, several important qualifications must be added.

First, efficiency as an economic concept is unconcerned with questions of equity. The balance between consumers and producers within an income distribution is irrelevant to the question of whether a total distribution is efficient;[42] accordingly, 'the transformation of benefits from one form (consumers' surplus) to another (profit) is treated as a wash'.[43] Strictly speaking, the efficiency standard is compatible with very great inequality within society. Although efficiency is routinely used as a proxy for utility (societal happiness) in economics, the two concepts are not synonymous.[44] In particular, the notion of an economically optimal outcome fails to account for the critically important role that non-commodity values play in society.[45] Economists advocate a total welfare standard for economic analysis,[46] arguing, not without some basis, that the wealth of producers often returns to society through dividends, pension funds and taxation; consumers benefit from increased innovation; and wealth redistributive decisions belong, instead, within the political sphere.[47] Nonetheless, to the extent that markets are viewed, instrumentally, as a mechanism to serve society, efficiency as an end result is not always optimal. Consequently, although the market often provides the best outcome, in cases where non-economic values are better served by derogating from the market – so that total utility rather than total wealth is maximised – the latter outcome should be preferred.[48]

When economic theory is applied as a *legal* framework for market regulation, moreover, the adequacy of efficiency as a *normative* goal for a legal system becomes more pressing. The question is whether efficiency is

[42] Vicusi et al. (2005:66–7), Motta (2004:18); Bork (1978:90).
[43] Williamson (1977:711).
[44] See Posner (1979:111–35) for a strong critique of equivalent uses of efficiency and utility.
[45] Stewart (1983). [46] Motta (2004:18–21); Viscusi et al. (2005:9).
[47] Motta (2004:21). [48] See, e.g., Bator (1958:378–9); Prosser (2004:17–38).

a sufficiently close proxy for utility so as to provide a morally significant foundation for law, or whether the pursuit of efficiency is merely an instrument by which to achieve more compelling normative goals. In order to defend the pursuit of efficiency as a normative activity in itself, two interrelated arguments might be advanced: a 'greater good' claim, which emphasises the overall maximisation of resources to be distributed; and a 'political responsibility' claim, which stresses the role of political choices and economic institutions, such as progressive taxation and social welfare provision, in arriving eventually at a fair distribution of these resources. In the well-known Posner-Dworkin-Calabrese debate, Posner furthermore argued that efficiency is supported by the principles of autonomy and consent, given that it underpins a system that permits individuals to pursue autonomous, utility-maximising behaviour.[49] Moreover, he saw altruism within the market system insofar as producers generate more than they consume,[50] which enables a 'capitalist conception of justice'.[51]

Criticisms of a pure efficiency standard abound, nonetheless, particularly amongst more liberal scholars or those who place greater emphasis on rights-based concerns. One recurrent objection to efficiency as a normative goal is its single-mindedness: that is, the exclusion of non-economic values such as justice from efficiency's utilitarian assessment. Sen, surveying more conservative scholarship promoting efficient markets to realise freedom of choice, argued that efficiency could be compatible with freedom but that this might be 'deeply unattractive' from an equity perspective.[52] Similarly, Dworkin, rejecting the arguments advanced by Posner outlined earlier, denied that efficiency is a social value in itself. At most, Dworkin argued, efficiency is valuable only where its pursuit is instrumental in achieving some separate, morally significant value such as justice – a position he grounded in a theory of 'deep equality'.[53] In the same debate, Calabrese, whilst more receptive to the notion that 'an appropriate blend' of efficiency and distribution could be instrumental towards achieving a just society',[54] nonetheless recognised that justice operates as an absolute veto on unjust distributions and so cannot entirely be traded off against efficiency.[55] A further repeated criticism of efficiency is its inherent bias in favour of those already in

[49] Posner (1980:491–7). [50] Posner (1980:496); Posner (1979:123).
[51] Posner (1979:136). [52] Sen (1993).
[53] Dworkin (1980b), defending arguments in Dworkin (1980a).
[54] Calabrese (1980:558). [55] Calabrese (1980:557–8).

positions of wealth or power within society. Thus, Sunstein noted that, to the extent that efficiency reflects private willingness to pay, it inevitably favours the wealthy who can, of course, pay more.[56] Prosser expressed this idea with particular passion:

> Above all, markets are a seriously inadequate means of protecting rights to equal citizenship because we do not come to markets as equals. Our market power as consumers is determined by the existing distribution of wealth in which we are placed, and this determines our ability to satisfy our preferences in a market system. In the absence of a Dworkinian redistribution to ensure equality of resources, competitive markets are likely to defeat the equal allocation of rights because of the radically unequal power of different market actors.[57]

The adoption of efficiency – an abstract and essentially amoral economic concept – as a goal or value for a legal system, along with the normative implications that such a choice implies, thus requires some reflection and justification. For example, as discussed later in this chapter, there is a consensus – established in the US, emerging in the EU – that efficiency comprises at least the primary goal of modern competition law. Even if we accept that efficiency is a socially desirable phenomenon, however, the question arises as to why efficiency should be compelled by the State in this context – that is, why efficiency justifies intrusion into individual freedom of action – whereas inefficiency is tacitly tolerated in other areas. By contrast, while efficiency is an acknowledged value in the realm of economic regulation, not infrequently regulators make policy choices that focus wholly or predominantly on advancing only the consumer surplus aspect of the efficiency equation, or which are motivated primarily by considerations of paternalism or social-justice-oriented wealth redistribution.[58] Indeed, another recurrent idea throughout this book is the necessity of economic regulation in certain instances to realise important non-market goals.

Second, the conventional supply and demand model used in microeconomic analysis is static, assessing a given state of affairs. Yet, efficiency also has a dynamic component that focuses on innovation rather than simple price reductions. Schumpeter famously described market competition as a process of 'creative destruction',[59] which Baumol explained as 'churning equilibria…with firms frequently being born and both incumbents and entrants dying off with about equal

[56] Sunstein (1997:344). [57] Prosser (2004:29). [58] New (1999:65).
[59] Schumpeter (2010:83).

frequency'.[60] Static models of competition may therefore fail to encapsulate the whole process.[61] Economic theory is also somewhat equivocal about the role of market concentration in facilitating innovation.[62] Even if we accept that efficiency provides a valid goal for economic policy, there remains a question as to whether static or dynamic efficiency should be preferred. Contemporary competition and regulatory policy must accommodate the often contrasting objectives of preventing and controlling monopoly, while simultaneously fostering innovation. Moreover, the line between efficient and inefficient conduct can be somewhat 'fuzzy'.[63] In determining whether to intervene in apparently inefficient markets, States run the risk of incurring two forms of error: false positives, or Type I errors, which involve prohibition of efficient conduct, and false negatives, or Type II errors, which involve permitting inefficient conduct. For reasons perhaps more concerned with ideology than law or even economics, the extent to which Type I or Type II errors are viewed as less objectionable has tended to have a significant impact on the shape and strength of systems of market control.

Third, in any event the static model of market equilibrium and efficiency represents an idealised state of affairs that cannot be realised in the real world. Thus, there is a problem of 'second best': namely, how to identify and secure the next best outcome, given that the optimal is unachievable.[64] Policy-makers must decide whether to pursue the most efficient market-based allocation achievable in the circumstances, which may have significant imperfections, or whether instead to opt for some non-market-based regulatory solution that secures the distribution that society considers optimal in the circumstances, but with the risks that accompany interference with the market process. A key feature of second-best solutions is that a single deviation from the optimal conditions for the functioning of a market is likely to have an impact on each of the other market assumptions. Consequently, there is no *a priori* means by which to choose between different solutions to market imperfections.[65]

The problem of market defects or 'failures', and particularly the legal response to such difficulties, thus lies at the heart of this book. In order to counter the negative societal consequences that may result from an inefficient or otherwise unsatisfactory distribution, States have a variety

[60] Baumol (2002:172). [61] Clark (1961:70–2); Hildebrand (2002:8). [62] See p. 16.
[63] Posner (2001:267). [64] Bator (1958:378–9); Lipsey & Lancaster (1956).
[65] Lipsey & Lancaster (1956:11–2); Viscusi et al. (2005:559–60).

of legal and fiscal market-supervisory mechanisms at their disposal. Having identified the limitations of the market mechanism, both in economic and non-economic terms, we turn to examine competition law and economic regulation as two such legal instruments by which to address market defects that may arise. We consider, first, the theory and structure of each instrument individually. The latter half of the chapter then assesses, at a theoretical level, the relationship between competition law and economic regulation, laying the groundwork for the more concrete exploration of their actual and potential interactions to follow.

II. Mechanisms to address market failure (I): the concept of competition law

Competition law can be understood as a mechanism of market supervision that addresses a particular variety of market failure, namely the problem of monopoly.[66] The market system assumes that the free market is competitive; if captured by monopoly power, however, the market outcome may be sub-optimal. Competition law imposes a series of competition-focused proscriptions on the behaviour of market actors, which, broadly speaking, aim to prevent the illegitimate acquisition of market power and, where market power is already accumulated, to control its exercise. In order to understand why accumulations of market power are disfavoured, it is necessary, first, to consider the economic theories of competition and monopoly.

(i) Theories of competition and monopoly

Perfect competition, as a market structure, describes a market in which a single seller's sales would plummet if it raised its prices above those charged by other sellers. It is premised on the existence of a number of structural requirements: a large number of buyers and sellers, a homogeneous product, perfect information, freedom of entry into the market, and where the quantity of products traded by any buyer or seller is so small relative to the total traded that changes in these quantities leave market prices unaffected.[67] A firm operating in a competitive market is merely a quantity-adjuster, deciding only its output level, whereas the market determines the price it receives.[68] At a technical level, the

[66] Posner (2001:1) [67] Gelhorn (1975:24–5). [68] Gelhorn (1975:29).

competitive price is equal to marginal cost, meaning the cost the firm incurs to produce an additional unit of the product. Because, in the longer term, marginal-cost pricing is both unsustainable and undesirable,[69] a more realistic expression of competitive price is where market price is equal to the cost of making and selling the product, cost being defined to include a reasonable return on capital.[70] In a perfectly competitive market, the consumer is 'sovereign'.[71] Consumer wealth is thus maximised as the consumer acquires the desired good for the lowest price that the producer will take, rather than the highest price that the consumer will pay. The difference between these two amounts is the consumer surplus, which in a competitive market accrues to the consumer.

At the other end of the spectrum we find a monopoly market, in which a single seller has sufficient market power to alter price unilaterally, either by increasing output to drive down price, or by reducing output to raise price. Monopoly, too, is premised on the existence of various structural factors: a single seller occupying the entire market, selling a unique product, with substantial barriers to entry and imperfect market knowledge in the industry.[72] When compared to competition, the primary effects of monopoly are reduced output, higher prices and a transfer of income from consumers to producers.[73] Unlike within competitive markets, a monopolist that reduces its output has sufficient market power to drive up the market price, whereas other market participants have no individual power to influence prices. The consumer can obtain the desired product only by paying the (typically inflated) price that the monopolist can insist upon charging. Although the monopolist may suffer reduced sales, because some consumers switch to inferior substitutes and others simply do without, that loss is outweighed by the increased profits that accompany higher prices. Producer wealth is therefore maximised, at the expense of consumer wealth. This scenario might still be efficient, albeit inequitable, if total wealth was nonetheless maximised. A 'deadweight loss' can arise in monopoly markets, however, whereby some benefits that would accrue to consumers in a competitive market fail to transfer to the monopolist and thus are lost to society.[74] Furthermore, the struggle by producers

[69] Marginal cost makes no allowance for fixed costs or a fair rate of return on investments, and therefore provides no incentives to innovate: Samuelson (1983:241–2).

[70] Posner (2001:10). [71] Clark (1961:12). [72] Gelhorn (1975:29–30).

[73] Gelhorn (1975:34). [74] Gelhorn (1975:35); Viscusi et al. (2005:82–3).

to achieve a monopoly, in anticipation of the supra-competitive returns that follow, may generate 'rents' that are also considered a cost of monopoly.[75] Monopoly is therefore disfavoured both on efficiency and equity grounds: it can lead to inefficient distributions, and it requires consumers to subsidise producers.

Monopoly is not, however, an unambiguously negative phenomenon. Dynamic efficiency prioritises innovation rather than short-run wealth maximisation, meaning that, when dynamic considerations are taken into account, monopoly may be the most efficient way to structure an industry.[76] The extent to which, in practice, monopoly leads to innovation is disputed.[77] The Schumpeterian viewpoint holds that market concentration fosters innovation, as larger firms funded by supra-competitive profits innovate more than smaller ones.[78] The contrasting Arrowian perspective hold that firms which already enjoy monopoly profits have fewer incentives to innovate than firms under competition, which are motivated by the prospect of elevated returns.[79] As Hicks memorably observed, '[t]he best of all monopoly profits is a quiet life'.[80] Hovenkamp thus identified an innovation paradox of sorts: while firms under competition have short-run incentives to innovate to reduce costs, they may have insufficient resources to do so; whereas monopolists typically have sufficient resources to innovate, but may not face sufficient competitive pressures.[81] Empirical research suggests that the relationship between innovation and competition assumes an inverted U-shape, so that innovation is greatest in markets with moderate levels of competition.[82] Accordingly, while competition enforcement can play a useful role in strengthening competition in concentrated markets, particularly by protecting new entrants from incumbents, it cannot be assumed that more competition always means greater social welfare.[83]

Additionally, some markets are subject to 'natural monopoly', meaning that production of the total output of the goods or service by a single

[75] Viscusi et al. (2005:89–90). Rent-seeking involves expenditure of resources in an effort to acquire greater economic opportunities. It is undesirable because it constitutes a cost of production that is not manifested in improvements in the final product; consumers thus pay higher prices for no extra value: see Krueger (1974).

[76] Samuelson (1983:253). [77] Viscusi et al. (2005:94–5); OECD (2006:42–52).

[78] Schumpeter (2010). [79] Arrow (1962). [80] Hicks (1935:8).

[81] Hovenkamp (2005:25). In categorising monopolists as output-restrictors, Hovenkamp (2005:13) measured 'output' by both quantity and innovation.

[82] Scherer (1967); Aghion et al. (2005); OECD (2006:46–7). [83] Segal & Whiston (2007).

producer minimises total cost (subadditivity) and is most efficient.[84] Natural monopoly is distinct from economies of scale, where average production costs decline with increased output, although many natural monopoly markets display scale economies.[85] Fixed-line telecommunications services, railways, and gas and electricity distribution networks have, for example, each displayed natural monopoly characteristics historically. Monopoly may, accordingly, be a desirable and even unavoidable industry structure in such circumstances, yet competition problems can still arise. The natural monopolist lacks the downward pressure on prices and the incentives to innovate faced by firms under competition,[86] and/or the monopolist may attempt to leverage its market dominance into adjacent non-natural monopoly segments.[87] In natural monopoly markets, the public-policy dilemma is to secure the social benefits of least-cost production (which requires single-firm production) without suffering from inefficient monopoly behaviour.[88]

Finally, antitrust scholars of a more conservative bent tend to emphasise the inherently self-destructive nature of monopoly: the presence of inflated returns encourages entry, and the resulting competition causes profits to drop.[89] Even where monopoly is undesirable, goes the argument, markets can self-correct, which renders government intervention unnecessary. Some would even argue that intervention is more harmful than unrestrained monopoly, because markets self-correct eventually whereas anticompetitive regulation does not.[90] There is significant danger, however, of overstating the case in this instance. Because self-correction is premised on new entry, the existence of high barriers to entry into a market is liable to hinder and delay the self-correction process. Such barriers may be structural (e.g., scale economies), legal (e.g., licensing requirements) or behavioural (e.g., anticompetitive conduct by the incumbent firm) in nature.[91] Barriers to entry render monopoly more durable and may justify increased competition law or regulatory scrutiny.

Between pure competition and monopoly, there is an intermediate theory of oligopoly, or monopolistic competition. Oligopoly occurs in concentrated markets with few sellers, where each recognises their

[84] Viscusi et al. (2005:401–6). [85] Baumol (1977); Viscusi et al. (2005:405–6).
[86] Viscusi et al. (2005:401). [87] Motta (2004:362); Viscusi et al. (2005:266–7).
[88] Viscusi et al. (2005:401).
[89] Easterbrook (1984:2); Burton (1997:160), discussing the Austrian School of economics.
[90] Easterbrook (1984:2–3). [91] Viscusi et al. (2005:168–73).

substantial interdependence. Consequently, each seller takes into account the reactions of its rivals when making output and pricing decisions.[92] There is an assumption that firms in an oligopolistic market act less competitively, insofar as they anticipate that efforts to reduce prices or improve quality will lead to a similar response by rivals, cancelling out any competitive advantage and leading to an overall deterioration in market conditions for all firms. Oligopoly presents a particular problem for competition law: while, typically, the conduct of firms falls within neither the competition rules regulating coordinated conduct nor unilateral behaviour, consumers nonetheless fail to reap the full benefits of a competitive market.

(ii) The structure of competition law: the US and EU systems of competition

Theories of perfect competition and monopoly are extremes, and, generally, neither structure arises in real market situations.[93] The economist J.M. Clark thus argued for a theory of 'workable competition',[94] later redefined as 'effective competition',[95] being the best *im*perfect competition achievable in a market. This pragmatic approach is followed within competition law. Generally, a dominant or even monopoly market position acquired through competition on the merits is not prohibited as such. Moreover, competition law does not prescribe permissible categories of market behaviour, but, instead, provides a residual mechanism of market control by proscribing certain types of anticompetitive behaviour, while otherwise allowing economic actors to compete as vigorously as they choose or the market demands. Broadly speaking, the objective of competition law is to prevent the anticompetitive accumulation of market power and to control its exercise, so that the typical benefits of competition – lower prices, greater choice, higher quality – are realised fully.

In effect, competition law amounts to a pre-commitment by the State to the unfettered functioning of competitive markets. Such regimes do not exist in every State, although progression towards a more globalised coverage of competition law can be discerned.[96] The precise parameters

92 Gelhorn (1975:38); Viscusi et al. (2005:106); Stigler (1964).
93 Bork (1978:101); Vickers (1995:7). 94 Clark (1940). 95 Clark (1961:ix).
96 For discussion of global developments in competition law, see Gerber (2010) and Dabbah (2010).

of the prohibitions imposed by competition law also vary between jurisdictions. Nonetheless, three broad categories of potentially anticompetitive conduct are addressed by most competition systems: (i) exploitative or exclusionary unilateral conduct by dominant firms; (ii) collusion between two or more firms, which generates or seeks to acquire greater market power; and (iii) mergers that have a detrimental effect on competition, either because the merged entity gains significant market power or the post-merger market structure facilitates collusion. We now turn to examine the structure of the two most prominent and influential of competition jurisdictions – namely, the US and the EU – in order to illustrate how such prohibitions can be translated into legally binding rules.

The Sherman Act, introduced into US federal law in 1890, is amongst the earliest competition statutes[97] and is arguably the most renowned. The Act was intended to provide a specific legislative solution to the so-called 'trust problem':[98] the phenomenon of large industries combining as trusts or looser arrangements to control pricing and output, and which were presumed to have the effects of squeezing suppliers in upstream markets and inflating prices in downstream markets.[99] Hence, US competition law is commonly called 'antitrust'; both terms are used in this work when discussing this area of law. In structure, the Sherman Act rejected a corporate regulatory model, which would have granted the federal government substantial power to correct market failures by directly controlling the behaviour of firms. Instead, the Act prohibits specific anticompetitive concerted and unilateral conduct by firms, adopting a crime-tort model that proscribes certain 'bad acts'.[100] This approach contrasts with the sector-specific regime for direct federal regulation of railroads introduced three years previously under the Interstate Commerce Act of 1887;[101] its more constrained

[97] The Sherman Act was preceded by various state antitrust regimes, enacted in the late 1880s, and a Canadian competition statute in 1889: Thorelli (1954:155–6); Stigler (1985). The Act was passed under the Commerce Clause (Article I, Section 8, Clause 3, Constitution of the United States), which empowers the federal government to regulate commerce amongst the various states.

[98] See Thorelli (1954:12–53); Dewey (1955); and Stigler (1985) for discussion of the common law doctrines that prefigured US antitrust, and the extent to which these foreshadowed the emergence of 'common law' antitrust following adoption of the Sherman Act.

[99] Thorelli (1954:63–85); Fox (1981:1146–55).

[100] Crane (2008:14–15).

[101] Thorelli (1954:229–30). The establishment of a federal regulatory agency, the Interstate Commerce Commission, followed the Supreme Court decision in *Wabash, St. Louis &*

scope has been linked to persistent ideas of anti-federalism in the early US government.[102]

Thus, Sherman Act, §1, prohibits anticompetitive coordinated conduct: 'Every contract, combination in the form of trust or otherwise, or conspiracy, in restraint of trade or commerce among the several States, or with foreign nations, is declared to be illegal. Every person who shall make any contract or engage in any combination or conspiracy hereby declared to be illegal shall be deemed guilty of a felony'.[103] Subsequent case law distinguished two categories of agreements under §1. *Per se* violations involve conduct that is 'manifestly anticompetitive', such as price-fixing; these are always prohibited.[104] Conversely, non-*per se* violations are subject to a contextual rule-of-reason assessment, during which the court 'weighs all of the circumstances of a case in deciding whether a restrictive practice should be prohibited as imposing an unreasonable restraint on competition'.[105] Additionally, Sherman Act, §2, prohibits anticompetitive unilateral conduct by monopoly firms: 'Every person who shall monopolize, or attempt to monopolize, or combine or conspire with any other person or persons, to monopolize any part of the trade or commerce among the several States, or with foreign nations, shall be deemed guilty of a felony'.[106] The Sherman Act prohibitions are complemented by a merger control framework under the Clayton Act. Enacted in 1914 and amended in 1950, the Clayton Act addressed the growing number of mergers that occurred in order to avoid the antitrust rules. It prohibits mergers where 'the effect of such acquisition may be substantially to lessen competition, or to tend to create a monopoly'.[107] A framework for pre-merger notification and assessment by public antitrust authorities was established under the Hart-Scott-Rodino Act of 1976.[108] It is misleading, however, to view US antitrust as exclusively statute-based. Given the broad and rather abstract nature of the Sherman Act prohibitions,[109] essentially the whole

Pacific Railway Company v. *Illinois*, 118 US 557 (1886), which held that state regulation of inter-state railroads violated the Commerce Clause.

102 That is, the notion that the federal government, as opposed to the states, 'should have no direct regulatory power over corporations qua corporations for purposes of effectuating national industrial policy': Crane (2008:3). See also Thorelli (1954:571–2).

103 Now 15 U.S.C. §1.

104 *Continental T.V. Inc., et al.* v. *GTE Sylvania Inc.* 433 US 36 (1977), 50.

105 Ibid, 49.

106 Now 15 U.S.C. §2.

107 Now 15 U.S.C. §18.

108 Now 15 U.S.C. §18a.

109 Kovacic & Shapiro (2000:43) asserted that the Sherman Act is 'unequalled in its generality' amongst statutes regulating commerce in the US.

of the law's substantive content was developed judicially. Antitrust, therefore, is effectively common law.[110] Moreover, the attitude of US courts to the scope of antitrust has varied widely during the century-plus following enactment of the Sherman Act,[111] as will be shown when we examine the purposes of competition law.

Competition law also lies at the heart of the EU legal framework for the creation and supervision of the internal market. Treaty provisions regulating unilateral and coordinated conduct were contained in the original Treaty of Rome of 1957, while formal merger control rules were added in 1989. There had been national competition laws in several European States from the inter-war years, and, following World War II, the US authorities implemented antitrust rules within the Occupied German Territories.[112] Another key influence was the work of German Ordoliberal scholars, also known as the Freiburg School,[113] which saw the role of competition law as, effectively, regulation of competition.[114] Although US antitrust was not the principal influence behind the adoption of the EU rules, nonetheless the shape of the provisions as adopted mirrors broadly the crime-tort model contained in the Sherman Act.[115] Thus, like US law, EU competition law prohibits individual anticompetitive conduct, rather than providing a mandate for direct market regulation to address competition problems.

The principal EU competition provisions are now contained in Articles 101 and 102 of the Treaty on the Functioning of the European Union (TFEU) and the Merger Control Regulation.[116] Article 101 TFEU addresses anticompetitive coordinated conduct. Thus, Article 101(1) prohibits 'as incompatible with the internal market': 'all agreements between undertakings, decisions by associations of undertakings and concerted practices which may affect trade between Member States and which have as their object or effect the prevention, restriction or distortion of competition within the internal market'.[117] Article 101(2) declares such agreements automatically void. Unlike the approach under Sherman Act, §1, there is no scope within Article 101(1) for any contextual rule-of-reason analysis of the restraint; to the extent that coordination

110 Hovenkamp (2005:44); Crane (2011:20). 111 Kovacic & Shapiro (2000).

112 See generally Gerber (1998). 113 Gerber (1998:257–65); cf. Akman (2009).

114 Gerber (1998:233–55); Möschel (2001). 115 Giocoli (2009:765–6).

116 Council Regulation 139/2004 of 20 January 2004 on the control of concentrations between undertakings (OJ L24/1, 29.01.2004).

117 Article 101(1) provides an illustrative but non-exhaustive list of prohibited practices.

prevents, restricts or distorts competition, it is prohibited.[118] Article 101(3) nonetheless provides an express savings clause for *prima facie* prohibited agreements, where, in essence, the agreement is defensible on efficiency grounds.[119]

Article 102 TFEU regulates unilateral conduct by firms with appreciable market power, providing that: 'Any abuse by one or more undertakings of a dominant position within the internal market or in a substantial part of it shall be prohibited as incompatible with the internal market in so far as it may affect trade between Member States.'[120] The express scope of Article 102 TFEU is noticeably different from that of Sherman Act, §2. Article 102 TFEU applies to firms that hold a 'dominant position', a concept that is interpreted to require a considerably lower market share than the monopoly concept utilised in US law.[121] Conversely, while Sherman Act, §2, applies both to conduct intended to acquire a monopoly and to maintain it, EU law formally applies only to anticompetitive conduct by firms *already* in possession of market dominance.[122] Certain categories of

[118] Case T-112/99 *Métropole television et al.* v. *Commission*, EU:T:2001:101, paras. 72–8. This approach is endorsed by Whish & Bailey (2012:134–6); cf. Nazzini (2006); Marquis (2007).

[119] The savings clause applies where all four elements of a cumulative legal test are satisfied, namely where the agreement or concerted practice:

> contributes to improving the production or distribution of goods or to promoting technical or economic progress, while allowing consumers a fair share of the resulting benefit, and which does not:
>
> (a) impose on the undertakings concerned restrictions which are not indispensable to the attainment of these objectives;
>
> (b) afford such undertakings the possibility of eliminating competition in respect of a substantial part of the products in question.

[120] Like Article 101(1), Article 102 provides a non-exhaustive list of practices that may amount to abuse of dominance.

[121] In *United States* v. *Aluminum Co. of America (Alcoa)*, 148 F.2d 416 (2d Cir. 1945), 424, Justice Hand held that a market share of 90 per cent 'is enough to constitute a monopoly; it is doubtful whether sixty or sixty-four percent would be enough; and certainly thirty-three per cent is not'; this position was endorsed by the Supreme Court in *American Tobacco Co.* v. *United States*, 328 US 781 (1946), 813-4. Under EU competition law, a market share of 50 per cent or higher creates a presumption of dominance (Case C-62/86 *Akzo* v. *Commission*, EU:C:1991:286, para. 60), and dominance can be found where the market share falls below this level if other factors support the finding (see Case C-95/04 P *British Airways plc.* v. *Commission*, EU:C:2007:166, where a market share of 39.7 per cent sustained a finding of dominance).

[122] Hovenkamp (2010:244–9), however, demonstrated that the differences in scope between these provisions are less significant in practice.

dominant/monopoly abuses have also, historically, received rather different treatment under EU and US antitrust, albeit the move towards a more economic focus in Article 102 TFEU may narrow this divergence. Yet, the core prohibition under both §2 and Article 102 TFEU is largely the same, namely, proscription of anticompetitive (exclusionary) conduct by individual firms with significant market power.[123]

The Merger Control Regulation establishes a pre-notification and assessment regime for 'concentrations with a [Union] dimension', defined as mergers reaching specified turnover thresholds in several Member States.[124] Like the Clayton Act, such mergers are permitted where they do not significantly impede effective competition in the internal market by creating or strengthening dominance.[125]

EU law also contains a number of quasi-competition provisions that are more or less unique. These include Article 106 TFEU, which regulates public undertakings and undertakings granted special or exclusive rights, and also provides certain derogations from the competition prohibitions for provision of services of general economic interest.[126] Articles 107–9 TFEU govern State aid: that is, support (monetary or otherwise) granted by Member States to economic operators. Finally, the 'duty of loyalty' under Article 4(3) of the Treaty on European Union (TEU), applied in conjunction with Article 3(1)(b) and Articles 101 or 102 TFEU, may prohibit Member States from enacting or maintaining in force measures that render the competition rules ineffective.[127]

As this discussion demonstrates, in both the US and EU, competition law comprises various open-textured prohibitions of anticompetitive coordinated conduct or unilateral monopolistic conduct by firms, and mergers with significant anticompetitive effects. The 'victims' of competition infringements can be conceptualised in two categories. In general terms, *all* consumers suffer due to the overall diminution in market

[123] See, generally, Abbott (2011), discussing the relationship between US and EU unilateral conduct regulation, following the European Commission's 2008 Guidance on its Enforcement Priorities in Applying Article 82 EC (OJ C45/7, 24.2.2009) and withdrawal in May 2009 of the DOJ's 2008 guidance on single-firm under Sherman Act, §2, which had espoused considerably more restrictive standards within US law.

[124] Article 1, Regulation 139/2004.

[125] Article 2, Regulation 139/2004.

[126] See also Commission Decision of 20 December 2011 on the application of Article 106(2) of the Treaty on the Functioning of the European Union to State aid in the form of public-service compensation granted to certain undertakings entrusted with the operation of services of general economic interest (OJ L7/3, 1.11.12).

[127] Case 13/77 *GB-Inno-BM* v. *ATAB*, EU:C:1977:185.

competition. Concurrently, certain *individual* consumers may suffer specific distinct and quantifiable harms attributable directly to the breach. Mechanisms for competition enforcement reflect this duality, potentially encompassing both public sanctions – administrative fines and/or criminal penalties – and private damages actions.

US antitrust law adopts a wide-ranging approach to enforcement.[128] Private parties who suffer losses due to Sherman Act violations can bring actions for damages against infringing firms, under a plaintiff-friendly system that features generous discovery rules, civil jury trials, treble damages, contingency fee arrangements and one-way fee-shifting.[129] The US is unique amongst competition jurisdictions insofar as levels of private enforcement much exceed public enforcement.[130] Public enforcement is undertaken by two federal agencies, alongside state prosecutors in local matters.[131] The Antitrust Division of the US Department of Justice (DOJ) is entrusted with criminal and civil enforcement of the Sherman Act and the merger control framework. Additionally, the Federal Trade Commission (FTC) is an independent government agency, enacted under and with responsibility for enforcing the provisions of the Federal Trade Commission Act (FTCA), also of 1914. The FTC has concurrent jurisdiction with the DOJ over the merger control provisions of the Clayton Act, and it has primary responsibility for enforcing FTCA, §5, which prohibits, *inter alia*, 'unfair methods of competition'.[132]

Enforcement mechanisms for EU competition law have undergone a seismic shift in the past decade. Historically, enforcement of Articles 101 and 102 TFEU consisted of, effectively, a tightly centralised public-enforcement system administered by the Commission. Under the original procedural framework of Regulation 17,[133] any agreements that might breach Article 101(1) TFEU yet which could potentially be exempted under Article 101(3) TFEU had to be notified to the Commission for pre-approval. With expansion of the EU, the administrative burden of the notification procedure became unmanageable, while the

128 See, e.g., Baer (2014).
129 15 U.S.C. §15; see also Crane (2009:125); Cavanagh (2010:640).
130 Over 90 per cent of US antitrust suits are brought by private plaintiffs: Lande (2010:4); Crane (2011:163).
131 Enforcement of state antitrust is undertaken by each state's attorney general.
132 We consider the §5 power in detail in Chapter 5.
133 Regulation 17 of 1962 (OJ 13/204, 21.2.1962), hereafter 'Regulation 17'.

distance that the system created between the Commission and national authorities and courts was deemed politically unacceptable.[134] Consequently, the modernising Regulation 1/2003 entered into force in 2004.[135] It abolished the notification system, and not merely empowers but indeed requires national competition authorities to apply EU competition law in appropriate domestic cases.[136] At the EU level, the Commission has the power to impose fines for breaches of the competition rules,[137] and it has pursued an aggressive fining policy in recent years. Although there is no criminalisation of competition infringements at the EU level, various Member States have adopted criminal sanctions for enforcement of the competition rules.[138] Premised on the *Courage* v. *Crehan* ruling,[139] the Commission has also adopted a proactive policy aimed at encouraging and facilitating private enforcement of EU competition law at the national level.[140] Although levels of private enforcement within the EU remain low,[141] this may change with the adoption of a EU-level Directive on damages actions, which seeks to harmonise procedures for antitrust redress across the EU alongside provisions aimed at recalibrating the relationship between public and private enforcement.[142]

[134] See European Commission, *White Paper on Modernisation of the Rules Implementing Articles 85 and 86 of the EC Treaty*, COM(99)101 final, published 28 April 1999; Hawk (1995) and Ehlermann (2000).

[135] Council Regulation 1/2003 of 16 December 2002 on the implementation of the rules on competition laid down in Articles 81 and 82 of the Treaty (OJ L1/1, 4.1.2003), hereafter 'Regulation 1/2003'.

[136] Regulation 1/2003, Articles 1 & 3.

[137] Regulation 1/2003, Article 23. See also European Commission, *Guidelines on the method of setting fines imposed pursuant to Article 23(2)(a) of Regulation 1/2003* (OJ C210/2, 1.09.2006).

[138] See e.g. the UK's Enterprise Act 2002, s.188, and Ireland's Competition Act 2002, ss.6&7. For consideration of the potential for criminalisation at the EU level, see Wils (2005).

[139] Case C-453/99 *Courage* v. *Crehan*, EU:C:2001:465.

[140] See the European Commission's Green Paper, *Damages actions for breach of the EC antitrust rules*, COM(2005)672, published 19 December 2005; its White Paper, *Damages Actions for Breach of the EC antitrust* rules, COM(2008)165, published 2 April 2008; and the *Proposal for a Directive of the European Parliament and of the Council on certain rules governing actions for damages under national law for infringements of the competition law provisions of the Member States and of the European Union* (COM(2013)404 final), published 11 June 2013. The Directive on Antitrust Damages Actions was formally signed into law on 26 November 2014.

[141] Connor (2010:17); Vrcek (2010:279).

[142] See fn. 140.

This complementary duality of public and private enforcement is encouraged precisely to improve the effectiveness of competition law, directly securing compensation for victims while indirectly deterring future anticompetitive conduct.[143] Yet this overlap in enforcement mechanisms is potentially problematic insofar as the competition rules apply uniformly, regardless of whether they are enforced by a public agency to correct market distortions or by a private firm seeking compensation or merely to hamstring a rival. As Crane has argued, institutions matter, particularly in the competition enforcement context.[144] A theme that will be developed throughout this work is the impact of public versus private antitrust enforcement and its role in shaping the interface between competition law and regulation.

(iii) *The goals of competition law: outcomes or processes?*

The competition laws of the US and EU are ostensibly very broad in scope, potentially applying to (and possibly prohibiting) almost every agreement, contract, large merger and the exercise of market power by dominant firms. Taken to this extreme, these laws would impede whole swathes of economic life that are necessary (e.g., contracts), unavoidable (e.g., natural monopolies) or desirable (e.g., innovation by dominant firms). Instead, ideas of 'competition' and 'anticompetitive' behaviour are applied as filters, thus bringing within the ambit of antitrust only those activities detrimental to the competitive process. Emphasis must therefore shift to the meaning of these ideas as term of arts within competition law.[145] The characterisation of competitive (or anticompetitive) conduct is crucial insofar as it defines the parameters of competition law. Both the US and EU rules provide a legal framework for protection of competition and advancement of competition policy, but neither offers clear guidance as to what these concepts should be taken to mean. Easterbrook thus described the Sherman Act as a 'blank cheque' without set policy objectives, to be filled in instead by scholars,

[143] See Commission White Paper COM(2008)165, p. 3. Lande (2010:7–8) argued that private antitrust enforcement generates 'tremendous benefits' for the wider US economy in terms of compensation, deterrence and saved public-enforcement costs; while Connor (2010:12) argued that optimal deterrence principles imply that public fines, private settlements and individual criminal penalties are complementary responses.

[144] Crane (2011:128); cf. Wils (2009:23–5).

[145] Under a 'plain meaning' interpretation, a broad range of understandings of competition are possible: Bork (1978:58–61); Fox (1986b:578).

practitioners or courts,[146] while the EU provisions arguably provide a comparable opportunity to the Commission and CJEU.

It is difficult to do justice, in the space permitted, to the breadth of arguments that have been advanced regarding the purpose or goals of competition law. First, a means-end division can be discerned: a key question is whether competition is a matter of *outcome* or *process.* Outcome-focused conceptions of competition law emphasise the socially desirable distribution that competitive markets are presumed to yield. Process-focused conceptions, by contrast, aim to facilitate the functioning of the market mechanism to the fullest extent, albeit on the implicit assumption that this secures a desirable outcome eventually. These conceptions are not mutually exclusive: the optimal market result may well be the same under both. What differs is the extent of the role for competition law in securing the specific parameters of the preferred outcome.

A focus on outcomes typically relates to issues of efficiency and equity within the resulting distribution. The persistence of outcome-focused thinking is attributable to the legacy of Chicago School antitrust scholarship, which stressed the pivotal role of economic theory, and in particular the efficiency criterion, in constructing the parameters of antitrust. A critical question is whether the efficient outcome is one that maximises total surplus (that is, consumer plus producer surpluses, considered in aggregate) or merely consumer surplus.[147] A purist Chicagoan would argue that the sole legitimate goal of competition law is improvement of total welfare efficiency, meaning that the wealth of society as a whole is maximised.[148] Equity considerations are rejected, although proponents of a total efficiency standard argue that other policy instruments are available to achieve non-efficiency goals.[149] Moreover, by prioritising dynamic efficiency considerations, and preferring Type II errors over Type I errors under an error-cost assessment,[150] such a perspective reduces significantly the perceived benefits of, and thus the need for, antitrust intervention.[151]

As explored previously, however, a total efficiency standard is reconcilable with great inequality, thus rendering it unpalatable from a

[146] Easterbrook (1986:1702); see also Kovacic & Shapiro (2000:43); Kovacic (2007:11,16).
[147] Orbach (2011:137–8). [148] Bork (1978); Easterbrook (1984); Posner (2001).
[149] Williamson (1977:734); Bork (1978:70); cf. Monti (2007:16).
[150] First proposed by Easterbrook (1984), and now adopted as a central tenet of Chicagoan thinking: Huffman (2012:107).
[151] Kolasky (2004:42); Weiser (2005: 554–7).

public-policy and distributive-justice perspective. Indeed, the transfer of wealth from consumers to producers permitted by this approach has been likened to theft or extortion.[152] A more acceptable outcome-focused formulation is the protection of consumer welfare. A clarification of terminology is useful at this juncture. Robert Bork, provocatively, used the phrase 'consumer welfare' while advocating, effectively, a total welfare standard in his competition polemic, *The Antitrust Paradox*.[153] Recent formulations have tended to adopt a more plain meaning interpretation, however, by requiring that at least some benefit accrue to consumers alongside any benefits for producers.[154] It is insufficient merely that a total distribution is efficient; additionally, the distribution itself must respect some principle of justice, equality or fairness. Efficient wealth transfers from consumers to producers, in particular, are disfavoured.[155] Others go further in identifying legitimate non-efficiency outcome goals for competition law. Some commentators would, for example, attribute to competition law an explicitly political role, rebalancing the division between private and public power in society.[156] Most controversial are arguments that competition law should proactively effect wealth redistribution from rich to poor or from producers to consumers,[157] or protect small businesses from the creative destruction inherent in the competition process.[158]

The alternative viewpoint is that competition law is concerned, primarily, with protecting the process of competition.[159] This approach focuses upon securing an environment favourable to vigorous rivalry – the process of the 'invisible hand' – it being presumed that such an environment is most conducive to efficiency and progress.[160] The focus

[152] Kirkwood & Lande (2008:196,202).
[153] Bork (1978); sharply criticised by Skitol (1999:249) as counterintuitive, and Kirkwood & Lande (2008:199) as an 'Orwellian term of art'. Orbach (2011) argued that Bork's own conception of 'consumer welfare' was confused, conflating distinct economic concepts without identifying a single operational standard for analysis.
[154] See, e.g., Hovenkamp (2005:1): 'Few people dispute that antitrust's core mission is protecting consumers' right to the low prices, innovation, and diverse production that competition promises.' Also Pitofsky (1979).
[155] Lande (1982); Kirkwood & Lande (2008).
[156] Amato (1997); Thorelli (1954:568); Clark (1961:11); Fox (1981:1152–3); Fox (1986a: 1715–16); Pitofsky (1979:1053–54).
[157] Considered by Hovenkamp (2001:269); Pitofsky (1979:1058).
[158] Discussed by Bork (1978:49); Posner (2001:25–6); Pitofsky (1979:1058); Kovacic (2007:51–64); *contra* Kirkwood & Lande (2008:233–6); Schwartz (1979).
[159] Fox (1981:1191); Fox (1986b:578); Breyer (1987:1006); Burton (1997:160).
[160] Fox (1981:1169).

here is whether the practice hinders or degrades the market mechanism.[161] Efficiency can function as a useful yardstick, insofar as it frequently corresponds to the promotion of the competitive process, but it is merely indicative of a means to an end (competition), rather than the end in itself.[162] Clark emphasised this aspect by defining competition as business discipline: the struggle to secure the customer's favour forces the profit-minded firm to become production-minded.[163] Gelhorn, too, put the idea succinctly: competition is 'the regulator that supervises the orderly working of the market'.[164] Thus, competition is a process that results in the wealth of society being put to its highest uses rather than dictating a specific outcome, while competition law is concerned with protecting this process. Post-Chicago approaches to competition law similarly place greater emphasis on problems of strategic behaviour (e.g., raising rivals costs) or apparently irrational conduct by firms.[165] Although such market conduct might not be condemned under a pure efficiency analysis, it may nonetheless harm or inhibit the competitive process.

The process approach is attractive: in theory, having reinforced the process of competition, the State can revert to its supposed *laissez-faire* approach on the assumption that a well-functioning market is both self-policing and likely to secure the most desirable allocation. In markets with structural barriers to competition, however, merely strengthening the competitive process is unlikely to secure a socially beneficial outcome. Protection of the competition process may also require direct or indirect protection of competitors, in order to ensure that there are rivals remaining in the market actually to compete, again a highly controversial goal for antitrust.

An alternative viewpoint on the competition-as-process argument is offered by German Ordoliberalism, which provided much of the intellectual foundations for EU competition law.[166] Ordoliberalism emphasises the importance of economic freedom as a value in itself. Competition law protects the right of individuals to participate in the economy, regardless of whether their participation is efficient.

161 Fox (2002:372). 162 Fox (1981:1179–80); cf. Posner (2001:28–9).

163 Clark (1961:9). 164 Gelhorn (1975:22). 165 See, e.g., Reeve & Stucke (2011).

166 Considered generally by: Gerber (1998:232–65); Moschel (2001); Akman (2009:273–7); and Giocoli (2009:768–75). Fox (1981:1149) argued that freedom of economic opportunity was also a central theme in the passage of the Sherman Act, albeit this rationale is less prominent today.

Competition policy is shaped by the rule of law: there is a strong role for the State in preserving the prerequisites of the market system, but State intervention in the market is disfavoured. While the Ordoliberal vision is similar to the goal of protecting the competitive process, insofar as both seek to protect opportunities for competitors to enter markets and participate in trade, the crucial concern for advocates of the economic freedom approach is to vindicate the right of individuals to participate in economic life.

The task of identifying concretely a single purpose or goal for either US or EU competition law is probably impossible. The primary purpose of the Sherman Act, at the time of its enactment, was to protect small businesses from the full rigours of competition.[167] This objective is also seen in the much-criticised Robinson–Patman Act, enacted in 1936, which we consider further in Chapter 5. As antitrust matured, this initial aim has been discarded; instead, US law has embraced micro-economic theories and methods that did not exist when the Sherman Act was conceived originally. Three schools of economic thought have progressively shaped the evolution of these legal rules:[168] the Harvard School, which focused on industry structure and performance;[169] the Chicago School, which shifted the emphasis to ideas of dynamic efficiency and antitrust scepticism;[170] and post-Chicago approaches, which invoke Game Theory and behavioural economics to challenge the rational actor assumptions underlying neoclassical models.[171] Over time there has been significant refinement of, and convergence between, these various intellectual schools.[172] There is now a (fairly) general consensus that US antitrust law aims to secure efficiency, albeit tempered by considerations of equity which place consumers at the centre of antitrust's mission.[173] Despite quixotic attempts to argue that the framers of the Sherman Act actually intended such a central role for efficiency,[174] in practice the adoption of this standard within US antitrust probably reflects a more pragmatic policy consensus about

167 Thorelli (1954:227); Hovenkamp (2005:39–42). 168 Hovenkamp (2005:31).

169 Carstensen (1983). 170 Bork (1978); Easterbrook (1984); Posner (2003).

171 Reeves & Stucke (2011); Huffman (2012:120–7). Behavioural economics was, however, strongly criticised by Wright & Stone (2012) as failing to provide any relevant contribution to assessment of antitrust liability.

172 Crane (2012); Huffman (2012). Thus, Dogan & Lemley (2009:696–7) suggested that nowadays US antitrust scholars are merely 'tinkering at the margins', with few polarising doctrinal conflicts remaining.

173 Weber Waller (1997). 174 Bork (1966).

the need to discipline the case law,[175] and to identify a single legislative objective amongst competing alternatives.[176]

An even broader spectrum of goals can be identified in the context of the EU competition framework.[177] Historically, EU competition law was criticised for its perceived formalism, excessive interventionism and a lack of consistency in its application, at the expense of efficient outcomes.[178] Ordoliberal influence on the development of EU competition law is important, insofar as the economic freedom approach may be incompatible with an efficiency-focused conception of competition law, given that Ordoliberalism perceives individuals as ends in themselves rather than a means to general welfare.[179] More recently, the European Commission has sought to rationalise and increase the economic coherence of EU competition law while simultaneously embracing an explicit commitment to consumer welfare,[180] an approach endorsed (more or less) by the CJEU.[181] Illustrations of the effects-based approach are seen, for example, in the refinement of the rules governing vertical agreements,[182] and the use of an 'as-efficient competitor' calculation in

175 Orbach (2011). 176 Eisner & Meier (1990:271–2).

177 See, e.g., Odudu (2006); Townley (2009); Parret (2010).

178 Korah (1986); Odudu (2010:600–1); Jones (2010:787–8). Sidak (2008:295) equated the EU approach to a 'Potemkin village of "managed competition"'.

179 Akman (2009:276). Although the orthodox viewpoint is that Ordoliberalism has heavily informed EU competition law (e.g., Gerber (1998:263–5), Moschel (2001)), Akman (2009) argued, by reference to the *travaux préparatoires* of the Treaty of Rome, that its drafters were concerned primarily with advancing efficiency rather than economic freedom. According to Giocoli (2009:777–8), Ordoliberalism's greatest influences arose *after* the adoption of the Treaty provisions, insofar as enforcement in the early years was substantially informed by Ordoliberal proponents and ideas.

180 See European Commission, *A proactive Competition Policy for a Competitive Europe*, published 20 April 2004 (COM(2004) 293), p. 7; also European Commission, *Guidelines on the application of Article 81(3) of the Treaty* (OJ C101/97, 27.4.2004), and European Commission, *Guidance on the Commission's enforcement priorities in applying Article 82 of the EC Treaty to abusive exclusionary conduct by dominant undertakings* (OJ C45/7, 24.2.2009). For discussion of the effects-based approach within EU competition law, see Jones (2010).

181 Compare e.g. Case C-202/07 P *France Télécom SA* v. *Commission*, EU:C:2009:214, where the CJEU rejected Advocate General Mazák's recommendation that recoupment should comprise an element of the test for predatory pricing, with Case C-209/10 *Post Danmark A/S* v. *Konkurrencerådet*, EU:C:2012:172, where the Court accepted an effects-based approach to price discrimination.

182 Contained in Commission Regulation 330/2010 of 20 April 2010 on the application of Article 101(3) of the Treaty on the Functioning of the European Union to categories of vertical agreements and concerted practices (OJ L102/1, 23.4.2010) and European

assessing abuses under Article 102 TFEU.[183] Nonetheless, the CJEU has emphasised that pursuit of economic efficiency cannot comprise the sole aim of EU competition law.[184] Single market integration is another key goal,[185] which distinguishes the EU rules from US antitrust, and indeed integration was arguably the primary objective in the law's earlier stages.[186] The pursuit of market interpenetration may also explain some of the more questionable uses of EU competition law that we will consider, particularly in the context of markets undergoing liberalisation.

Outside the context of the US and EU systems, the goals of antitrust may become more fragmented. Efficiency is a goal pursued within most systems, to a greater or lesser extent.[187] Yet divergent cultural norms,[188] the influence of national circumstances, both historical and contemporary,[189] and the potential strategic application of antitrust mechanisms to achieve, for example, social goals,[190] can result in significant variation in terms of the aims and application of competition law across different systems, particularly with respect to developing economies. Indeed, the urgency of any need for the adoption of 'global' standards in antitrust, over and above the elimination of actively harmful or counterproductive rules, has been questioned.[191] The increasing pervasiveness of economic analysis within competition law may nonetheless provide a common analytical language of sorts across dozens of antitrust jurisdictions worldwide; assuming, of course, that economics can identify a single optimal answer to the legal question at issue.

We have seen that systems of competition law typically address three broad categories of anticompetitive behaviour: concertation, unilateral conduct, and mergers. This book will focus on the first and second categories – what the European Commission, perhaps somewhat confusingly, describes as 'antitrust' rules as opposed to competition law more broadly. Mergers are largely excluded from our assessment, for several

Commission, *Guidelines on Vertical Restraints* (OJ C130/1, 19.5.2010); see also Jones (2010).

183 European Commission, *Guidance on the Commission's enforcement priorities in applying Article 82 of the EC Treaty to abusive exclusionary conduct by dominant undertakings* (OJ C45/7, 24.2.2009); see also Peeperkorn & Viertiö (2009); Monti (2010).

184 Case C-509/06 P *GlaxoSmithKline*, EU:C:2009:610, paras. 62–3.

185 Monti (2007:39–44); see also cases like *GlaxoSmithKline* and Joined Cases C-403/08 & C-429/08 *Football Association Premier League*, EU:C:2011:631, in which contract provisions that prevented the sale of goods or services in other Member States were held to constitute restrictions of competition by object under Article 101(1) TFEU.

186 Amato (1997); Giocoli (2009).

187 Sokol (2012:87).

188 Cheng (2012).

189 Lewis (2013).

190 Pena (2012).

191 Monti (2012:347).

reasons. First, the temporal element of merger control is substantially different from that of the other competition rules: while the latter are applied *ex post* against past breaches, merger control (like regulation) is a forward-looking enterprise, which considers the market situation in the future and so addresses competition concerns *ex ante*.[192] Second, merger control is, essentially, voluntarily triggered by the actions of firms that choose to acquire or merge with different businesses. Conversely, the other competition rules regulate, effectively, the ordinary business conduct of the firm, rather than the more extraordinary business of merger. The rules against anticompetitive concerted and unilateral conduct are thus considerably more likely to overlap with regulation of a firm's market activities than the merger control rules, justifying closer scrutiny of this relationship. Third, building upon the first two distinctions, in a sense the rules on merger control, antitrust and economic regulation each provide alternative mechanisms by which to address market contraction. Merger control aims to prevent a monopoly market position from being acquired initially; if unsuccessful, the State may need to impose *ex ante* regulation, or punish anticompetitive conduct *ex post* through use of competition law. Thus, the exclusion of merger control does not compromise the coherence our assessment.

III. Mechanisms to address market failure (II): the concept of economic regulation

Next, we turn to economic regulation, considering, specifically, its conceptualisation and use as a discrete legal instrument separate from competition law. As legal rules, the antitrust provisions are easily identifiable; disagreements tend to arise instead regarding their purpose and scope. The concept of regulation, by contrast, is much broader and rather amorphous in nature; the question of what it comprises is complex and unsettled.[193] This section considers the literature on regulation and builds a functional definition of the concept for the purposes of our analysis. The objective here is primarily to identify and explain those instances of regulation that are likely overlap, in substance, with the operation of

[192] Bavasso (2004:103); Cave & Crowther (2005:487).

[193] Morgan & Yeung (2007:3). In many accounts of regulation or deregulation, the concept is not defined, but is simply assumed to be understood: Jarass (1988:76). Both Ayres & Braithwaite (1992) and Sunstein (1990), for example, failed to define the concept in their treatises on the nature of regulation.

competition law, which, in practice, tends to be sector-specific economic regulation. This definitional exercise is not intended to exclude or challenge broader or competing conceptions of regulation as such; rather, we are simply defining the scope of enquiry for the purposes of this work.

We begin by considering the varying conceptions of regulation that have been advanced. Regulation as a concept within politics or social science is construed broadly. A common departure point is the formulation advanced by Selznick, of 'sustained and focused control exercised by a public agency over activities that are valued by a community'.[194] This provides an expansive and rather abstract definition. More generally, regulation can be viewed as any conscious ordering of activity, meaning the act of controlling, directing or governing according to a rule, principle or system.[195] Regulation, in this sense, is a synonym for State action intended to influence or control behaviour. It encompasses all forms of State market supervision, as well as contract and criminal law, and even soft law institutional arrangements.[196] This conception of regulation is, however, too broad and insufficiently precise for our purposes, insofar as it fails to address the qualitatively different impact that certain forms of market regulation have on firm behaviour, in contradistinction to competition law's impact.

Narrowing the definition, the 'core conception' of regulation has been described as State intervention into the operation of markets.[197] Regulation, thus construed, comprises State activity to remedy market failures or defects. Jarass refined the notion of market intervention: if regulation and public enterprise are separated, regulation means State intervention into the economic conduct of private enterprises.[198] Ogus suggested that this rationale of market failure marks regulation as a 'collectivist' enterprise, in contradistinction to law implementing 'the market system',[199] although few would claim that the mere presence of regulation within a market wholly displaces the latter. While this approach comes closer to our notion of regulation as a mechanism to remedy market defects, it cannot, however, account for the distinction between competition law and other forms of market supervision.

Under this narrower conception, a subdivision into different categories of regulation can be made, typically into economic regulation and social

[194] Selznick (1985:365). Cited by, e.g., Ogus (1994:1), Baldwin et al. (2011:2–3); Black (2001:133); Veggeland (2009:1).

[195] Prosser (1997:4); also Stewart (1988:100).

[196] Veggeland (2009:2–4, 9).

[197] Prosser (1997:4–5).

[198] Jarass (1988:77–81).

[199] Ogus (1994:1).

regulation.[200] Stewart thus identified a primary distinction between types of regulation: sector-specific economic regulation of competition in particular industries through some combination of entry, service and price controls; and social regulation, comprising environmental, health, safety, anti-discrimination and consumer protection regulation through uniform standards applying to many or all industries.[201] Ogus argued that both categories address types of market failure: economic regulation is a substitute for competition in industries with monopolistic tendencies, whereas social regulation corrects information inadequacies in transactions between individuals and firms plus externalities or spill-over effects.[202] Although, in practice, competition law can interact and even conflict with social regulation,[203] competition enforcement is rarely deployed to remedy the types of market failure that fall within the purview of social regulation.[204] Since there is limited substantive overlap between the scope of application of competition law and social regulation – that is, generally these two forms of market regulation are deployed to address different market problems and cannot be considered interchangeable in terms of application – only economic regulation is considered in this work.

Scholars of regulatory economics typically view economic regulation as a relatively narrow concept, limited, in effect, to conventional forms of public utilities regulation. Such regulation has four distinguishing components: control of entry; price-fixing; prescription of quality and conditions of service; and universal service obligations.[205] Unlike competition law, which provides a residual mechanism of market supervision applicable in most sectors, economic regulation is sector-specific in nature, and tends to prescribe particular market conduct, rather than merely proscribing broad categories of anticompetitive conduct. Yet often the market difficulties to be remedied through economic regulation stem from the same problem that is addressed by competition law: namely, excessive market power. Economic regulation thus provides a

200 Cf. Breyer (1982:7) who expressly adopted a broad conception of economic regulation, as encompassing not only issues of price and entry, but also health, safety, and the environment.

201 Stewart (1988:115–6).

202 Ogus (1994:4–5).

203 See, e.g., Kingston (2011) on environmental regulation; Camesasca & Van den Bergh (2000) and Kahn (2009) on labour rights.

204 Although, increasingly, market-based approaches are used in social regulation, particularly environmental controls: Stewart (2000), Kingston (2011).

205 Kahn (1988:3/I).

substitute of sorts for the market discipline of competition by emulating the competitive outcome.[206] Kahn accordingly described the essence of economic regulation as 'the explicit replacement of competition with governmental orders as the principal institutional device for ensuring good performance'.[207] Economic regulation as a discrete category of State supervision aimed at controlling market power has been repeatedly recognised by economic policy-makers.[208] Within regulatory economics, moreover, competition law has been identified as a third facet in alongside economic and social regulation.[209] Accordingly, it is possible to discern a notion of economic regulation that is distinct from, yet has overlapping spheres of application with, competition law, creating a potential for cumulative application of these mechanisms. This possibility is explored later in this work.

The focus on market defects as the rationale for regulation leads some commentators to advance a functional definition, framed in terms of what is to be remedied or achieved.[210] Prosser favoured that approach, arguing that it provides a fuller account of what regulators do or should do.[211] Considering Yeung's claim that '[t]he aim of any form of regulation is to modify the behaviour of those subject to regulation in order to generate a desired outcome',[212] the functional approach to regulation should encapsulate ideally both the desired outcome and the means to achieve it. It is necessary, therefore, to give some consideration to the purpose of regulation in order to understand the concept more fully.

The question as to why regulation is enacted can be answered from at least two distinct perspectives: an 'interest theory' viewpoint, which focuses on the causes or political motivations for regulation, or a 'normative justificatory' viewpoint, which focuses on the social or economic problem to be remedied or other regulatory task that legitimises the imposition of regulation.[213] At this juncture, our focus is on the latter, because we are primarily concerned with the substantive issue of the use of regulation to address market defects rather than the political question of why regulation is implemented initially. Interest theory questions remain relevant, of course, given that the motivation behind a regulatory framework may dictate its structure, efficiency and the extent to which

[206] Sappington & Weisman (2010:229); Tardiff (2010:958). [207] Kahn (1988:20/I).
[208] See, e.g., OECD (2001:9); DTI (2006:6). [209] Viscusi et al. (2005); Prosser (1997:5–6).
[210] Stewart (1988:110). [211] Prosser (1997:5–6). [212] Yeung (1999:40).
[213] Breyer (1982:9).

it prioritises special interests over general interests. Broadly, two interest theories are discernible, focusing on public interests and private interests (also known as public choice), respectively, while alternative conceptualisations of regulation address institutional aspects or transaction costs.[214] These theories are considered further in Chapter 3. Unsurprisingly, where regulation is enacted at the behest of special interests, it is likely to favour those interests rather than society in general. In such circumstances, the *ex post* application of competition law to correct the resulting sub-optimal distribution may be more likely. Thus, the question arises, which is considered in Chapter 4, of the extent to which competition law can and should be deployed to correct regulatory failures.

Considering the second dimension – the normative justificatory viewpoint – a standard explanation for economic regulation is to correct inefficiencies that result from market failure.[215] Yet, economic efficiency is not the sole imperative, and often not even the primary objective, in regulatory policy-making. In fact, the various rationales for regulation – described by Yeung as the 'collective goals justifying regulatory intervention'[216] – might be divided, roughly, into two categories. The economic rationale for regulation prompts intervention to maximise economic efficiency, correct spill-over costs or address information inadequacies. The social rationale focuses on distributional issues, seeking to avoid undesirable distributions of wealth or opportunity.[217] It is important to emphasise that the division between economic and social rationales for regulation is not coextensive with concepts of economic and social regulation, considered earlier. Rather, Prosser pointed to a distinction in terms of regulatory goals that is more akin to the division between efficiency and equity, considered previously. Hence, for example, considerations of a social nature can inform the necessity for and content of economic regulation. In practice, furthermore, while some justifications

[214] Baldwin et al. (2011:40–65); Ghertman (2009:352–5).

[215] Nicolaïdes (2005:25).

[216] Yeung (2004:30).

[217] Prosser (1997:11–3). Baldwin et al. (2011:15–23) identified a more extensive, substantive list of rationales for regulation: to control monopoly and natural monopoly firms; to redistribute windfall profits; to counter or internalise externalities; to address information inadequacies; to ensure continuity of service; to prevent anticompetitive behaviour; to share the costs of public goods and moral hazards; to counter unequal bargaining power; to deal with scarcity and rationing of scarce commodities; rationalisation and coordination of declining industries or for standard-setting purposes; planning for future generations or altruistic concerns; alongside human-rights- and social-solidarity-based rationales.

for regulation conform to the economic/social divide (control of monopoly firms as an example of the former, continuity of service issues as the latter), others may contain aspects of both (e.g., internalising externalities may have distributive and economic aspects.) It is important to note, additionally, that the question of the substantive policy goals pursued by regulation is distinct from (although, of course, not unrelated to) the issue of whether that regulation is effective at achieving those goals, an issue considered further in Chapter 3.[218]

The role of non-commodity or social values within the regulatory sphere is widely accepted, even within the realms of economic regulation. Insofar as regulation has social functions, it may therefore serve social ends that even perfectly functioning competitive markets cannot achieve.[219] Bator, who viewed market failure as a static institutional problem, nevertheless suggested that market efficiency is 'neither sufficient nor necessary for market institutions to be the "preferred" mode of social organisation'. Assuming that 'markets might be ends as well as means', it might be the case that alternative political, social and/or organisational values are so much better served by non-efficient market institutions as to require selection.[220] Thus, Stewart argued that regulation may legitimately reflect a variety of non-commodity values, such as aspiration, diversity, mutuality, civic virtue, distributional equity, condemnation of behaviour viewed as morally wrong, access to justice, legitimate expectations and certainty.[221] In distilling guiding principles for regulation, Sunstein applied the Rawlsian 'original position' to derive two criteria – welfare and autonomy – in an approach that is clearly at odds with pure efficiency-focused wealth-maximisation.[222]

Moreover, a regulatory regime may promote non-commodity values even while it addresses an ostensibly 'economic' problem, such as regulation of a natural monopoly. For example, regulated utilities are often subject to universal service obligations, under an equity rationale, in addition to regulatory requirements that aim more directly at remedying the problem of monopoly, such as rate regulation or mandatory access requirements.[223] Indeed, Areeda and Hovenkamp argued that the

[218] See also Yeung (2004:30). [219] Grenfell (1999:232). [220] Bator (1958:378–9).
[221] Stewart (1983:1568); Stewart (1988:113–14). [222] Sunstein (1990:34).
[223] Universal service obligations (USOs) require operators to serve certain categories of customers that a normal profit-making firm would not necessarily serve, and generally involve cross-subsidies from low-cost customers to high-cost customers: O'Donoghue & Padilla (2013:46), Laffont & Tirole (2000:217–64). Examples include requirements that

primary objective of much economic regulation is the prevention of consumer exploitation,[224] an approach that blurs the boundary between avoiding the inefficiencies of monopoly and securing distributive justice. The primary difficulty is that, by introducing non-economic goals into the equation, this complicates and can sometimes even work against realisation of the economic principles that underlie many regulatory regimes.[225] Non-commodity values might, therefore, introduce considerable indeterminacy into regulatory analysis.[226]

The parameters of regulation as a legal or economic term of art are inherently unsettled.[227] Insofar as this work considers the substantive legal relationship between competition law and regulation as mechanisms of market control, it focuses upon economic regulation alone, because it is within this area where questions of substantive overlap typically arise. Yet a precise definition of economic regulation as a legal construct remains elusive, principally because, in practical terms, economic regulation is imposed on a case-by-case basis in many different market sectors to solve individual market failures. The elements contained within a particular regulatory regime are therefore dictated by the specifics of the market problem to be addressed, as well as the political environment and societal disposition towards market intervention. A broad range of potential regulatory strategies or techniques exist: from, for example, classical 'command and control' approaches such as centralised price-setting, or licensing requirements that set entry and/or services standards within the market; to incentive-based regulation such as emissions trading schemes that seek to induce efficient or desirable conduct by market actors; to disclosure obligations intended to address information asymmetries; and even self-regulatory or 'meta-regulatory' approaches. Moreover, as will be discussed in Chapter 3, recent decades have seen a concerted effort to improve the quality and effectiveness, howsoever this is defined, of much economic as well as social regulation. The choice of regulatory instrument can be of central importance to the success of the regulated outcome, and thus is of relevance for our purposes, insofar as ineffective regulation may prompt calls for

fixed line telephone services must be extended to all properties, and that mail be delivered to and from all areas within a State for the same price.

224 Areeda & Hovenkamp (2006:¶221d4, p. 58).

225 Kahn (1988:182–3/I).

226 Stewart (1988:115).

227 See, e.g., Tombs (2002:113), noting 'the sheer *range* of activities, functions and processes that have come to be subsumed by the label "regulation"' (emphasis in original).

deregulation or the concurrent application of competition law in regulated markets. A detailed account of the full range potential regulatory strategies approaches available is, however, beyond the scope of this work.[228]

In order to accommodate, at a definitional level, the complexities inherent in the concept of regulation, Black therefore suggested that it should be treated as a 'cluster concept': that is, composed of a broad range of elements none of which is essential, where there is 'regulation', where a significant number are present, and where these elements themselves may be complex concepts.[229] Economic regulation as a synonym for State market intervention is too vague for our purposes; it is necessary to construct a narrower and more precise conception that distinguishes regulation from competition law as a market-supervisory mechanism. Defining a cluster concept of economic regulation is helpful, insofar as it allows for identification of the typical components of an economic regulatory regime, without rendering these elements *a priori* requirements. A number of recurrent components emerge from the literature, which function to structure our definition, namely: (i) the central role of the State; (ii) the coercive or directive nature of regulation, as opposed to 'soft' law or self-regulation; (iii) its positive nature, placing specific obligations on regulated parties, rather than merely proscribing certain conduct; (iv) the sector-specific nature of regulatory rules; and (v) the use of regulation to correct markets in difficulty, meaning deliberate intervention in and derogation from the free market. For our purposes, therefore, economic regulation is any State-imposed, positive, coercive alteration of or derogation from the operation of the free market in a sector, typically undertaken in order to correct market defects of an economic nature, and to be distinguished from regulation that pursues a predominantly 'social' aim. Competition law and economic regulation may thus be viewed as separate mechanisms of market supervision: regulation supplants the market, whereas competition law supplements it.[230] As we shall see, however, in reality the dividing line between these mechanisms tends to be rather more ambiguous.

The conceptualisation of regulation advanced here is broad but not unlimited. Under this definition non-commodity values may be relevant, although of primary interest for our purposes is the extent to

[228] For further discussion see Breyer (1982); Ogus (1994); Morgan & Yeung (2007:79–146) and Baldwin et al. (2011).

[229] Black (2001:141). [230] Kahn (1988:1/II).

which regulation, whatever its objective, affects the functioning of the market. Of course, regulation also occurs outside the purview of the market, typically in order to pursue socio-cultural values. As our concern is the intersection between competition law and regulation, however, further references to 'regulation' denote economic regulation unless indicated.

IV. A comparison of competition law and regulation

Having considered competition law and regulation as discrete legal instruments to address market failures – defining, as far as possible, the purposes and parameters of each – we now turn more directly to the core issue to be considered: namely, the relationship between these mechanisms. A central idea within this work is that the exact parameters of this relationship are fluid and elusive, and perhaps even impossible to delineate conclusively. Both competition law and regulation involve, to a greater or lesser extent, derogation from the presumed default position of unencumbered free markets. When viewed at an abstract level, therefore, these instruments may appear broadly similar or even equivalent, insofar as both comprise State-imposed legal mechanisms for market supervision or control, necessitated by the presence of market defects. As is implicit from the title of this work, however, and reinforced by the preceding discussion, our starting point acknowledges that distinct conceptualisations of these instruments as separate and discrete mechanisms for market supervision can nonetheless plausibly be identified. In particular, the scope and means of application of these mechanisms, as well as the market outcomes achievable, begin to distinguish one from the other. This work aims, therefore, to provide a more balanced account of the interactions between competition law and regulation that may arise, premised on the assumption that, in reality, these instruments are neither identical nor wholly distinct.

The spheres of application for competition law and regulation are neither entirely co-extensive nor mutually exclusive. Certain forms of market failure can be addressed effectively only by competition law mechanisms; others can be remedied only through regulation; and some market failures are susceptible to both competition law and regulatory intervention, albeit the outcome might vary depending on the mechanism selected. Of the five categories of market failure justifying regulation that were identified by Breyer – control of monopoly, rent control, excessive competition, inadequate information and compensation for spill-overs[231] – the first three might potentially be addressed, alternatively, through competition law. Certain information deficits are also susceptible to antitrust solutions, for example where increased competition within a sector forces firms to improve the quality of information available to consumers in order to distinguish their product and compete harder. Conversely, externalities such as pollution generally demand a regulatory remedy, because even a perfectly competitive market cannot deliver the optimal outcome. Where the desired result is to free the market of monopoly, in the absence of natural monopoly or insurmountable barriers to entry competition law is the appropriate mechanism. Competition law is also well tailored to achieve market solutions that utilise the process of competition, for example by fostering innovation,[232] which regulation struggles to provide.[233]

The decision whether to regulate involves a balancing of 'the market and all its failings' against 'regulation and all its failings',[234] so that the optimal solution must negotiate a path between the risks of 'private opportunism and government overreaching'.[235] Similarly, while markets might be strengthened or corrected by competition law, this too has limitations. Something of a consensus exists that competition law solutions should be preferred where possible, so that State intervention is restricted to strengthening the market mechanism rather than prejudging its operation.[236] Potential benefits of the competition law approach include its across-the-board nature, lower levels of intrusion into the internal decision-making of firms, the likelihood of creating lower barriers to entry than sector-specific regulation, and a lighter enforcement burden for the State through greater use of private action.[237] In some market circumstances regulation remains indispensable, however, insofar as it provides the State with control over problems where competition law has only limited or tangential jurisdiction.[238] Competition law thus tends to be less effective at addressing competition problems that result from structural market difficulties, involve exploitative rather than exclusionary conduct, or necessitate quasi-regulatory remedies requiring on-going implementations and monitoring. In deciding whether to regulate, the aim is to identify the most effective

[231] Breyer (1982:15–29). [232] Baumol (2002); Baldwin et al. (2011:452).
[233] Jarass (1988:89). [234] Baldwin et al. (2011:23). [235] Epstein (2005:336).
[236] Baldwin et al. (2011:452–3). [237] Baldwin et al. (2011:115).
[238] Carstensen (1983:523).

mechanism to achieve the desired result, with the lowest potential for undesirable consequences.

While competition law and regulation can address some of the same market problems, these mechanisms operate by different means and, typically, generate different outcomes. Six conventional distinctions between competition law and regulation can be identified, which relate to (i) the sectoral scope of application, (ii) the temporal nature of enforcement, (iii) the roles of the principles of efficiency and distributive justice, (iv) the nature of the legal obligations imposed, (v) the dynamic-versus-static quality of these rules, and (vi) the qualitative nature of any infringements. While certainly not incontrovertible, these somewhat imprecise yet well-recognised dichotomies provide a useful departure point for a more refined consideration of the interactions between competition law and regulation in theory and practice to follow.

First, competition law is generally applicable across all markets, unless a sector is expressly or impliedly exempted. Once enacted, competition law provides an economy-wide residual mechanism for market supervision. Regulation, by contrast, is enacted on a sector-by-sector basis, usually to address identified and discrete failures within particular markets.[239] This means, for example, that regulation implemented in the telecommunications sector does not affect the structure or functioning of other markets, such as the energy sector, except perhaps to strengthen political arguments for further regulation to address equivalent market failures and/or provide empirical evidence of regulatory successes or failures. Another consequence of this 'generalised-versus-specialised' divergence is that regulators tend to have greater technical market expertise and institutional resources relating to the sectors under their control, whereas competition authorities have specialist expertise in competition law and economics.[240]

Second, the temporal nature of enforcement is a key distinction. Regulation is, typically, viewed as a prospective phenomenon, imposed *ex ante*, which creates a structural framework intended to prevent market failures from occurring. With the exception of merger control, competition law is retrospective in application, utilised *ex post* once competition problems arise or anticompetitive behaviour is identified.[241] A corollary

239 Larouche (2000:401).

240 Larouche (2000:401–2); Laffont & Tirole (2000:278); Weiser (2005:558–9).

241 Posner (2003:383); Bloom (1999:243); Ogus (1994:28); Hellwig (2009:212); Laffont & Tirole (2000:277–8); Laguna de Paz (2012:79).

is that competition intervention tends to be piecemeal, whereas regulation of a sector provides a systemic solution.[242] *Ex ante* solutions offer legal certainty by laying down clear ground rules, and may more effectively prevent rather than merely punish or remedy market failures.[243] Yet criticisms of much prospective regulation abound, on grounds of inefficiency, unresponsiveness to the dynamic nature of markets, vulnerability to capture by regulated entities, and, conversely, as constituting unnecessary (and illegitimate) interference in private commercial freedom.[244] The Chicagoan assumption that markets self-correct whereas government regulatory failures have no self-correcting mechanism is central to these criticisms. By contrast, retrospective competition enforcement can harness and strengthen the automatic power of the market to right itself, intervening in the competitive process only to the extent necessary to correct particular market failures.[245]

The distinction between *ex ante* and *ex post* enforcement is disputed. Thus, it has been argued that the development of more detailed competition rules through case-law precedent and statutory guidelines imposes what are *de facto* prospective obligations on firms.[246] The process of clarifying legal rules of general application, which is inherent in a system based on precedent, is, however, substantially different from the imposing of obligations for firms within a sector that are intended to modify private behaviour in the future. In addition, it has been noted that most regulation is enacted in markets with existing competition problems, rather than on the hypothesis that such problems might occur.[247] In this sense the enactment of regulation is essentially *ex post*, insofar as it is triggered by the existence of the market defect that provides its rationale; whereas the enactment of competition law occurs *ex ante*, insofar as such laws provide a means to address market problems that may subsequently occur. Nevertheless, enforcement of competition law is generally *ex post*, against identified breaches of its proscriptions, whereas regulation typically directs the market actors' behaviour going forward, in order to eliminate anticompetitive conduct *ex ante*. The distinction between *ex ante* and *ex post* enforcement is considered further in the next chapter.

Third, the principles of efficiency and distributive justice play different roles in shaping the structure and enforcement of competition law when

[242] Hellwig (2009:212–15). [243] Geradin & O'Donoghue (2005:412).
[244] Ayres & Braithwaite (1992). [245] Ogus (1994).
[246] Ibáñez Colomo (2010:265–8); Glachant et al. (2008:1603). [247] Smith (2004:62).

compared to regulation. Regulation certainly might pursue efficiency,[248] but it frequently also or alternatively incorporates express redistributive goals. Universal service obligations, for example, may entail wealth transfers from urban to rural customers.[249] Redistribution is not, however, generally accepted as a goal in the context of competition law,[250] although such rules may function to prohibit exploitative wealth transfers from consumers to producers.[251] Fundamentally, competition law takes as given the wealth distribution within an economic system, and focuses on ensuring that monopoly, broadly defined, does not distort the functioning of the market in the further allocation of resources. Indeed, many would argue that competition law would provide a relatively unsuitable vehicle to achieve wealth redistribution even if required.[252] Regulation, by contrast, can effect alteration of both the original allocation of resources *and* the current or future allocation, in order to achieve the most desirable policy outcome. To the extent that a regulatory regime incorporates redistributive goals, efficiency alone is an insufficient measure of whether those aims are achieved.[253] An unsurprising result of this divergence is that standards for intervention generally differ under competition law and regulation.[254]

Fourth, the conventional view is that competition law and regulation impose qualitatively and quantitatively different obligations on economic actors.[255] Competition law merely proscribes certain broad categories of anticompetitive exercise of market power, and otherwise allows the market mechanism to function unhindered. Regulation, by contrast, prescribes the desired outcome for the market, and, to that extent, oversteps the market mechanism entirely. In this sense, the obligations imposed by competition law are negative or reactive (prohibitions on certain conduct), while obligations under regulation are positive or proactive (the economic actor is required to perform certain functions).[256]

248 It has been argued that with deregulation, considered in Chapter 3, regulation increasingly pursues efficiency as its primary objective: Hausman & Sidak (1999:451).

249 Hovenkamp (2005:229–30); Crampton & Facey (2002:39); Laffont & Tirole (2000:276–7); Geradin & O'Donoghue (2005:363); Dempsey (1989:23–5).

250 Pitofsky (1979:1058), Hovenkamp (2001:269); Faella & Pardolesi (2010:266); Laffont & Tirole (2000:277); Geradin & O'Donoghue (2005:362–3).

251 Lande (1982).

252 Hovenkamp (2005:45–8); Crampton & Facey (2002:30); Laguna de Paz (2012:78).

253 Baldwin et al. (2011:25–38).

254 Auf'mkolk (2012:153).

255 O'Donoghue & Padilla (2013:46); Rab (2009:506).

256 Hovenkamp (2005:15); Hellwig (2009:211); Geradin & O'Donoghue (2005:362).

Typically, the negative obligations imposed by competition law are broadly and somewhat imprecisely drawn, creating significant scope for ambiguity and argument regarding their exact parameters; whereas regulation can impose more precise, detailed and demanding obligations.[257] This creates a corresponding need for regulatory agencies to hold strong monitoring and sanctioning powers to ensure compliance with regulatory duties. The close and on-going nature of the relationship between the sector regulator and regulated firms also creates an increased risk of regulatory 'capture', or the adoption of a firm-centric perspective by regulators, when compared with the more detached competition authority.[258] The assumption that competition law merely proscribes rather than prescribes has been challenged;[259] the extent to which competition law can and should become prescriptive will be considered in the following chapter.

Fifth, the nature of the obligations imposed by competition law renders it a dynamic tool, by buttressing the market mechanism to solve market defects. Regulation, at least conventionally, is more static in nature, providing a concrete solution to defined market problems. This leads to criticism of some examples of regulation as inflexible and ill-suited to adapt to market changes. Thus, in theory, competition law is an indirect or facilitating mechanism, which assists the market process to arrive at the most efficient outcome, whereas regulation directly imposes its solutions within the market, bypassing the market process itself. This divergence explains some of the difference in scope in terms of the forms of market problems that can be addressed through either mechanism. The dynamic nature of competition law enables it to provide innovative solutions, harnessing the 'creative destruction' of the competitive process.[260] By contrast, empirical evidence suggests that regulation struggles to promote innovation, which cannot be produced by order, although the State may induce or stimulate innovation by alternative methods.[261] Regulation can, nonetheless, address problems that cannot be remedied by a well-functioning market mechanism – particularly those of a structural or distributional nature – by allowing the regulator to tailor a specific solution to market defects that cannot self-correct. Since the regulatory regime is a static solution imposed in a dynamic environment,

[257] Geradin & O'Donoghue (2005:361); Larouche (2000:401).
[258] Laffont & Tirole (2000:278). [259] Ibáñez Colomo (2010:268–76).
[260] See pp. 12–3. [261] Jarass (1988:89).

however, as the market itself changes the outcome generated may be less efficient than intended.

Sixth, the qualitative nature of regulatory and competition law violations also differ: the latter arguably falls within the category of offences that are *mala in se*, whereas the former is merely *mala prohibita*. It is generally acknowledged that regulatory breaches, even where they attract punitive fines,[262] do not fall within the category of conduct that is *mala in se*, meaning conduct that is 'wrongful in itself' and thus treated as 'criminal' throughout various societies with different social and economic values. Instead, regulatory offences are typically *mala prohibita* conduct, that is, conduct that cannot be characterised as inherently unlawful, and which is instead the subject of specific legal proscription.[263] Within the regulatory sphere strict liability is common, thereby dispensing with the necessity of any mental element to establish breach.[264] This conception of regulatory offences accords with the characterisation of regulation as an inherently political enterprise:[265] regulation reflects political choices about the optimal structure of markets and society more generally, to which firms must then adhere. This creates a concomitant need for sufficient accountability with the process of regulation to legitimise such choices.

Conventionally, statutorily created white-collar (occupational) offences have also been considered to fall within the *mala prohibita* category.[266] However, the role of competition law within modern economies can, arguably, be distinguished from the regulatory archetype of white-collar crime, bringing competition law towards a *mala in se* conception. The earliest competition statutes originated in common law doctrines, suggesting that prohibitions on abusive exercises of market power are founded in general legal principles rather than purely political decision-making.[267] Consequences for competition violations are, moreover, often severe: for example, very high fines imposed by the European Commission, punitive treble damages available to private litigants in the

[262] Baldwin et al. (2011:249–51).

[263] Ogus (1994:79); see generally Wells & Quick (2010:661–73).

[264] Ogus (1994:79).

[265] Hovenkamp (2005:228); Clarke (2000:3–4).

[266] Newman (1958:737–8); Green (2004:502) noted an 'ambiguity' within many white-collar offences regarding whether the alleged violation should be considered *morally* wrong.

[267] Notably, Newman (1958:738) invoked the fact that white-collar offences are generally legislatively created and often derogate from common-law principles to support the assertion that white-collar crimes are *mala prohibita* in nature. Conversely, the Sherman Act originated in the common-law restraint of trade doctrine: see p. 19, fn. 98.

US, and criminal sanctions imposed by many jurisdictions for cartel activity. The rhetoric of public enforcement, particularly against cartels, also tends to analogise competition breaches as a form of theft, which is clearly a *mala in se* offence.[268] Accordingly, while competition economics may conceptualise the discipline in pure efficiency terms, in practice competition law incorporates a significant *moral* element,[269] which distinguishes antitrust violations from regulatory ones.[270]

Two interesting process issues for enforcement arise as a result of this divergence, which are noteworthy for our purposes. The first is that greater emphasis is placed on competition enforcement as a judicial procedure, rather than simply an administrative one. This has consequences in terms of, for example, the levels of protection afforded to rights of defence in competition law versus regulatory proceedings, and the degree of decision-maker independence required. Second, to the extent that regulation tends to represent not merely objective legal adjudication but also more subjective political choices, there is a much greater role for stakeholder participation to inform and even legitimise regulatory decision-making.[271]

V. Conceptualising the interface between competition law and regulation

From this perspective, competition law and regulation might be regarded as sufficiently distinct in their operation and effects to comprise wholly separate legal instruments, albeit both can be used to address certain forms of market defects. When considered broadly, therefore, two alternative theoretical conceptions of the relationship between competition law and regulation emerge: that is, as separate and divergent market-supervisory mechanisms, or as varying manifestations of the same phenomenon, namely market intervention. The choice between these differing notions has significant implications in terms of the permissible parameters of the concepts of competition law and regulation, as well as the interactions between these mechanisms. Although this book aims to

[268] See, e.g., the statements of former US Assistant Attorney General for Antitrust Klein (2000): '[t]he perpetrators of [cartel] conspiracies are, quite literally, stealing money out of the pockets of American businesses and consumers', and former EU Competition Commissioner Neelie Kroes (2005): 'when we break up cartels, it is to stop money being stolen from customers' pockets'.

[269] MacCulloch (2007:358); Whelan (2007:29–30).

[270] Cf. Parker (2012).

[271] Prosser (2004:106); Yeung (2012:337).

provide a more nuanced and comprehensive account of this relationship, such an enterprise is necessarily located between these polarised conceptions of competition law and regulation as wholly separate or as one and the same mechanisms of market control. It is instructive, therefore, to first consider these abstract boundaries, which each represent the outer limits of any possible understanding of the relationship between competition law and regulation. We do so primarily by reference to the existing literature addressing this question, in order to provide a solid theoretical grounding for the analysis to follow. Much of the existing scholarship tends to presume, rather than to probe from first principles, the parameters of this relationship as falling within one of these two dichotomous models. Essentially, the distinction between these conceptions turns upon the core question of whether competition law and regulation should be viewed as substitutes or complements. The approach of this book is not to argue in favour of one conceptualisation or other as more accurate or appropriate, but to suggest that the overall relationship between competition law and regulation is more subtle and complex than either of these categorical viewpoints. It remains useful, nonetheless, to consider how these varying conceptions of the interactions between competition law and regulation have been manifested within the scholarship to date, which also provides a provocative departure point for the substantive chapters that follow.

(i) Competition law and regulation as substitutes

The first conceptualisation of the relationship between competition law and regulation envisages these instruments as entirely distinct mechanisms for the organisation of economic activity. Both competition law and regulation are instruments of economic policy, broadly defined.[272] Although both provide a means by which to remedy market failures, however, the fundamental distinction is the notion that competition law works *within* the market system by strengthening its operation, whereas regulation occurs entirely *outside* the market system by overreaching its operation. The market mechanism itself constitutes the dividing line between these conceptualisations. By implication, the absence of the

[272] See, e.g., Daintith (1988:3), defining economic policy as 'all purposeful governmental action whose actual or professed primary objective is the improvement of the economic welfare of the whole population for which the government is responsible or of some segment of that population'.

market mechanism precludes the application of competition law within any industry subject to sector-specific regulation.

Under this approach, competition law applies within the boundaries of the market system, attempting to correct flaws in its operation to allow it to function as effectively as possible. Competition law relies fundamentally on the premise of the 'competitive paradigm', whereby the most desirable result for society follows from the 'invisible hand' of the competitive process.[273] In particular, competition law proscribes anti-competitive behaviour by private actors that enables firms to exercise monopoly power, and by strengthening the competitive process, the antitrust solution is thus one of 'forcing competition'.[274] Having freed the market of monopoly, the market mechanism operates more effectively. Critically, the continued presence and operation of the market mechanism as the basic organising principle for economic activity is an integral element of the operation of competition law. Regulation, by contrast, amounts to State acknowledgement that the market mechanism cannot correct a particular form of market failure – it provides 'a heroic cure reserved for a serious disease'.[275] Thus, the State steps outside the market mechanism to correct the market defect at issue. To the extent that the State removes the sector from the purview of the market mechanism, that sector is also removed from the scope of competition law, because the functioning of the competitive process is a key assumption of the application of competition law. While regulation can be extended to activities currently within the purview of the market mechanism, doing so removes any scope for continued application of competition law. Deregulation, or the reintroduction of the market mechanism as the organising principle for a particular economic activity or sector, again opens up that activity to antitrust enforcement.

This model therefore views competition law and regulation as opposing instruments of market control. Ogus encapsulated this distinction succinctly: competition law serves to reinforce the market system, whereas regulation seeks to overreach it entirely.[276] Kahn further developed this basic dichotomy. Within private competitive sectors of the economy, although the State has important functions (e.g., enforcing contracts), it operates essentially at the periphery of the market. Thus, the role of the State is one of 'maintaining the institutions within whose framework the free market can continue to function, of enforcing,

[273] Loevinger (1966:108).
[274] Hovenkamp (2001:293–4).
[275] Breyer (1987:1007).
[276] Ogus (1994:30).

supplementing, and removing the imperfections of competition – not supplanting it'.[277] Within sectors in which competition remains the organising principle, market conduct and firm performance are governed by the pressures of the competitive process, and the State may intervene only to strengthen or reinforce the market mechanism through competition laws that proscribe and sanction anticompetitive conduct.[278] Conversely, Kahn described the essence of regulation as the explicit replacement of competition with State planning as the principal institutional device for organising economic activity.[279] In exchange for the limitations placed on their individual commercial freedom, regulated firms receive some insulation from the forces of creative destruction driving the competitive process.[280] Thus, Kahn saw the relationship between competition law and regulation as alternative systems of social control that are 'essentially competitive rather than complementary'.[281]

This substitutionary or exclusionary understanding of the relationship between competition law and regulation finds further support within existing scholarship. Easterbook expressed the idea forcefully: '[r]egulation displaces competition. Displacement is the purpose, indeed the definition, of regulation'.[282] Breyer similarly conceived of competition law and regulation as alternative legal instruments.[283] More precisely, he viewed unregulated markets as the alternative to regulation, and the function of competition law as being to make unregulated markets competitive.[284] Competition law seeks to create or maintain the conditions of competitive markets, whereas regulation tries to replicate the results of competition or correct for defects within competitive markets by replacing the market mechanism with affirmative governmental requirements.[285] At its core, Breyer argued, competition law relies upon the assumption that a workably competitive marketplace is achievable where private impediments to competition are removed, yet where this assumption fails, supra-market governmental intervention, like regulation, becomes necessary.[286] Carstensen argued that, although competition law and regulation both constitute what he described broadly as 'economic regulatory systems', each aiming to achieve an efficient allocation of resources, they reflect fundamentally different perceptions of how

[277] Kahn (1988:2/I). [278] Kahn (1988:115/II). [279] Kahn (1988:114–5/II).
[280] Kahn (1988:46/II); Loevinger (1966:122). [281] Kahn (1988:1/II).
[282] Easterbook (1983:23); also Laguna de Paz (2012:79).
[283] Breyer (1982:157–8); Breyer (1987:1006–7). [284] Breyer (1982:161).
[285] Breyer (1982:157). [286] Breyer (1982:158).

optimal market performance should be achieved.[287] Similarly, Loevinger suggested that, although competition law and regulation are separate and distinct, they are not alternatives because they do not achieve the same ends by different means.[288] Competition law utilises the competitive paradigm, a dynamic process rooted in the activities of private economic operators driven by the profit motive, whereas regulation is a static process, imposed by governmental actors driven by a power-seeking motive.[289] Moreover, Loevinger's reasoning suggests that competition law produces only market-based solutions, whereas regulation produces only extra-market solutions.

From this viewpoint, competition law is general and residual in nature, being the default mechanism by which to police markets. Regulation is specific, and applies only if the State takes the deliberate step of removing a particular sector or activity from the purview of the market mechanism, and, consequently, of competition law.[290] Unlike competitive sectors governed by the market mechanism, every regulated industry is to an extent *sui generis*.[291] Insofar as regulation has been enacted, it becomes the primary mechanism by which the sector or activity is structured or supervised. The competitive process and competition law are fall-back options in the event of deregulation. A corollary of this divergence is that regulation becomes the province of specialisation and experts who are well-versed in the peculiarities of an industry and best-placed to address sector-specific problems. Competition law, by contrast, comprises legal rules of general application, with the attendant advantage of increased legal certainty by virtue of the development of a comprehensive body of legal precedent defining the method and parameters of its enforcement.

This approach accords with the view that competition law should encompass only economics-based objectives. Under this view, competition law operates in tandem with the market mechanism, which functions to secure the most efficient allocation of resources. This model can also accommodate the antitrust objective of protecting the competitive process,[292] compared with the regulatory decision to step outside this process. Competition law is, accordingly, a purely economics-focused phenomenon. Competition law prohibits firms from engaging in anticompetitive conduct in order to control

[287] Carstensen (1983:506). [288] Loevinger (1966:131–9).
[289] Loevinger (1966:118–22). [290] Klein (1998:48). [291] Kahn (1988:115/II).
[292] Fox (1981).

monopoly power or prevent it from arising, but does not require firms to perform intrinsically unprofitable activities. Regulation, conversely, may be used to achieve social or redistributive functions.[293] Bork argued that antitrust is wholly prohibitory and passive in nature, and thus 'unable to serve values that must be implemented by requiring affirmative conduct which the self-interest or capabilities of private persons do not cause or permit them to undertake'.[294] Conversely, regulation may explicitly impose or perpetuate a monopoly or sponsor what amounts to a cartel,[295] but such a protected position typically brings onerous market obligations that firms in competitive industries avoid.[296] This model echoes Ogus's conception of regulation as 'the law which implements the collectivist system',[297] in contrast with competition law, which is the principal instrument by which the functioning of the *market* system is improved.[298]

Arguably, however, the binary nature of the assumptions underlying this conceptualisation of the relationship between competition law and regulation present difficulties for its practical application: namely, the idea that an economic activity or sector is either wholly competitive, thereby subject to competition law, or not at all. In modern economies, where many purportedly 'competitive' industries are subject to considerable governmental regulation, this stark dichotomy is unhelpful, even unrealistic. In an attempt to answer this criticism, it may be necessary to introduce a caveat to this conceptualisation. Where an industry is partially regulated, this model explains which activities in that sector are subject to competition law (those governed by the market mechanism) and which activities are outside the purview of competition law (those from which the market mechanism has been removed). As an industry becomes subject to more intensive regulation, however, there may come a 'tipping point' where, despite remaining vestiges of market influence, in reality the influence of supra-market governmental regulation is so predominant as to remove the whole sector from the application of antitrust.[299] There can be no *de minimis* principle with respect to regulation, however: regulating any activity removes it from the purview of competition law, even where the majority of the sector remains governed exclusively by the market mechanism.

293 Grenfell (1999:221). 294 Bork (1978:70). 295 Hovenkamp (2001:293–4).
296 Grenfell (1999:232). 297 Ogus (1994:2). 298 Ogus (1994:30).
299 Hayek (1944:64).

(ii) Competition law and regulation as complements

An alternative conceptualisation of the interface between competition law and regulation views these mechanisms as different aspects, or intensities, of the same phenomenon: namely, State intervention in the otherwise free market. Competition law and regulation are again conceived as mechanisms to address market failure and supervise the economy. Under this conceptualisation the emphasis lies, not on their different modes of operation, but rather on the degree to which each represents a divergence from, or realisation of, the two poles of economic organisation described by Hayek as 'individualism' and 'planning'. Both competition law and other economic regulation can thus be viewed as species of regulation in a looser sense, as 'all interventions by government to steer the economy'.[300] The difference between these concepts is one of form or degree, but in substance they are essentially the same.

From this viewpoint, the economic system represents a spectrum in which the State intervenes to a greater or lesser extent in economic activity. At one end lies individualism, or the unrestricted free market. Under this principle of economic organisation, private economic actors have maximum commercial freedom, with the role of the State limited solely to enforcement of contracts and prevention of fraud: the *laissez-faire* approach.[301] At the other end lies the wholly centrally planned economy, where the State dictates all aspects of the economic system, such as inputs, outputs and prices: the *interventionist* approach. The conventional starting assumption is that the market represents the default means by which to organise economic activity,[302] although, of course, markets-focused thinking is not unchallenged.[303] Where one or more of the key premises of the market system is not satisfied, however, the market fails to provide an economically optimal outcome. Moreover, as the market system says nothing about the correctness of the original resource allocation, an alternative means of organisation may be preferred where the redistribution of societal resources is desirable. State intervention in the free market then becomes necessary or appropriate. The more intensively a State intervenes in the process of competition, however, the more it risks derogating from its presumed position

[300] Scott (2003:xi).

[301] Loevinger (1966:104–5) and Stewart (1988:106) both argued, however, that the market itself is an artefact of government action.

[302] McKie (1970:6); Kahn (1988:250/II).

[303] Discussed generally at pp. 1–3.

of neutrality as between the plurality of conceptions of the good that are supposed to exist, and may impose a particular conception of the good on all citizens.[304]

Competition law and regulation represent different strengths of market intervention, and, hence, derogation from the market mechanism. Competition law constitutes, generally, a weaker form of intervention that functions by strengthening the market mechanism itself through the overlay of a series of legal prohibitions on certain behaviour; this has been described as derogation from *laissez-faire* in order to preserve the broader free-market approach.[305] This viewpoint accords with the notion that competition law aims to protect the competitive process, as the (supposed) superior supervisor of markets.[306] Where competition law is insufficient to tackle market failure, or where the problem simply cannot be addressed through the market mechanism, the State may need to intensify its intervention in the form of more prescriptive regulation. Operation of the market mechanism declines further and further as greater numbers of sectors are regulated. The opposing pole is reached when no aspect of the economic system is controlled by the market mechanism, but instead every element is dictated by the State.

Viewed from a markets-focused perspective, when faced with market imperfections competition law is the option of first resort, regulation the option of second resort, and comprehensive central planning the path of last resort.[307] Although competition law and regulation are different species of market-supervisory mechanisms, they are of the same genus: namely, State intervention. Competition law and regulation therefore apply in tandem to the extent that economic activity falls within the scope of both. A broad interpretation of the concept of regulation is central to the argument that competition law and regulation are essentially the same; with the effect that competition law is effectively subsumed within the latter concept.[308] Under Yeung's definition of regulation as governmental action that aims to modify behaviour to generate a desired outcome, competition law is viewed as regulation

[304] Stewart (1983). [305] Bork (1978:418). [306] Fox (1981:1154).

[307] Schwartz (1979:1978). This progression from free markets to central planning risks oversimplification, however, as more intensive forms of competition enforcement – such as the excessive-prices or refusal-to-deal cases – may involve greater intrusion into the functioning of markets than less prescriptive regulation.

[308] Hovenkamp (2005:7–13).

aiming to control commercial behaviour.[309] Similarly, under Stewart's broad conception of regulation as 'governmental standards and commands, backed by coercive sanction, requiring private persons to undertake or refrain from specified conduct', competition law is a species of regulation.[310] Competition law and regulation are therefore complementary: they operate in the same sphere of economic activity; they can address the same problems; and the use of one mechanism does not preclude application of the other to the same circumstances.[311]

In accordance with this approach, Ayres and Braithwaite argued that market intervention is a question of degree, taking place 'between the Scylla of full-industry regulation and the Charybdis of *laissez-faire* policies'.[312] Context is everything: the optimal regulatory strategy – where a State should position itself between those extremes – cannot be dissociated from its historical context. Rather, its appropriateness is contingent upon the legal, constitutional and cultural context.[313] This viewpoint echoes the work of Fox, who emphasised competition law's role in the struggle between control of public and private power in society.[314] The choice between alternative configurations for market control is, essentially, a socio-political preference, so that selection of the assumptions underlying operation of the market governs the economic analysis, rather than vice versa.[315] Unlike our first conceptualisation, which reflects conceptions of microeconomics, this second approach is based in principles of political economy and, where a particular market structure is advanced, political philosophy.[316] This approach therefore exposes the overtly political nature of competition and regulatory policy, in contrast to the economics-focused approach of the first model. It is unnecessary, even for the purposes of this second model, to choose between differing philosophies regarding the proper role of the State within the market, as the principal concern is the plane within which that discussion occurs. At most, it is necessary to consider the ordinal issue of where a particular legal system lies on this spectrum, insofar as this reveals the interface between competition law and regulation within a system, rather than the cardinal question of the optimal role

[309] Yeung (1999:39–40) [310] Stewart (1988:100).
[311] Supporting the view that antitrust and regulation are 'complements', see, e.g., Bavasso (2004:87); Schwartz (1987:1051); Varney (2011:784); Klotz (2009a:108).
[312] Ayres & Braithwaite (1992:133). [313] Ayres & Braithwaite (1992:101).
[314] Fox (1986b:573–4). [315] Fox (1986b:574–88).
[316] Fox (1981:1156–7); Sunstein (1990:41); Dempsey (1989:3–7).

for government. Consideration of the variety of possible arrangements is nonetheless useful to illustrate the range of choices that can be accommodated.

At one extreme, conservative and libertarian scholars advocate minimal State intervention in order to protect the individual freedom that is associated with economic freedom. Hayek, for example, argued that society should make as much use as possible of 'spontaneous forces', and as little use as possible of coercion.[317] Although advocating use of the competition process as the sole organising principle for economic activity where viable, Hayek nonetheless accepted that State intervention may be necessary to create a system where competition works more beneficially.[318] The Chicago School applied Hayekian ideas to competition law, construing it as a form of regulation, which, although useful in certain narrow circumstances,[319] imposes substantial economic costs.[320] From a Chicagoan perspective, the market is robust and self-correcting, whereas inefficient State regulation has no such in-built safety net. Thus, the smallest degree possible of State intervention is preferable.

By contrast, modern liberals tend to distrust large aggregations of private power, while a redistribution of resources may be favoured where the original allocation is perceived as capricious or unfair.[321] Accordingly, State intervention is necessary to avoid or modify adverse outcomes that result from the uncontrolled or unfettered functioning of the market.[322] Amato interpreted competition law as a battleground for the division between conflicting desires to control public and private power in society, where advocates of strong competition laws fear accumulation of private economic power, whereas critics of competition law fear the threat posed by strong public powers to individual freedoms.[323] This reasoning is equally applicable to perceptions of regulation and its role, with the caveat that regulation may also be considered desirable to achieve other non-economic goals, and not merely the control of private power. More radically, both socialist and fascist perspectives would criticise the notion that the free market should provide the organising principle for society, instead advocating approaches that are closer to the centrally planned model – albeit, it must be emphasised, to profoundly different social ends.

317 Hayek (1944:17). 318 Hayek (1944:18). 319 Bork (1978:406).
320 Kauper (2008:46); see, generally, Bork (1978).
321 Fox (1981); Sunstein (1990:36–45). 322 Przeworski (1990); Sunstein (1990:45).
323 Amato (1997).

By locating the antitrust/regulation question within a broader debate about the appropriate division of powers within a democratic society, this second approach accounts for the substantial policy aspect of the formation and enforcement of competition and regulatory law and policy. Moreover, it can explain why free marketeers and advocates of the minimal State criticise the perceived inefficiency of contemporary competition law, viewing it as unnecessary interference in markets. Unlike our first conceptualisation, which emphasises the role of the market within the process of competition law, the second approach presents competition law as derogation from the neoclassical economic norm of unrestricted markets. Nevertheless, competition law might be preferred over more interventionist approaches, such as sector-specific regulation, which represent further derogation from the free-market model. Between competition law and regulation, the libertarian viewpoint favours the former, even using competition law to cure the deficiencies of regulation if necessary.[324] The second approach also explains the evolving nature of regulation, in response to the deregulation and 'better regulation' movements of recent decades, which are considered further in Chapter 3. In particular, it envisages a variety of options for the State in structuring the economic system, which may incorporate a complementary mixture of both competition-based and regulatory elements rather than a strict dichotomy between these two mechanisms, and this mixture may evolve over time. The optimal solution may therefore involve a bundled approach, with the mix determined by the market defect to be remedied. Thus Baldwin et al. and Sunstein both viewed competition law and regulation as complementary phenomena, with each compensating for any shortcomings of the other. Competition law is preferred where an indirect approach to market intervention is effective, whereas regulation is utilised when competition law cannot provide successful solutions.[325]

This model finds further support in theories regarding the complexities of drawing clear boundaries between regulated and competitive sectors. McKie described the challenges of delineating the parameters of regulation, including the task of determining what activities should fall within the regulation itself, and the difficulty of securing an efficient outcome for regulated activities when the unregulated sector remains free to misallocate resources: a second-best problem.[326] Unlike our first conceptualisation, which envisages a clear dividing line between

[324] Bork (1978:407). [325] Baldwin et al. (2011:116); Sunstein (1990).
[326] McKie (1970).

competition law and regulation – namely, the market mechanism – our second employs a gradual approach. Thus, it can account for situations where the division between regulation and competition (and, consequently, the scope for competition law) is less obvious. Moreover, because this model does not posit competition law and regulation as separate and discrete phenomena, it is better placed to address the problem of second best.[327] By locating these instruments within the same spectrum of mechanisms for market intervention, it exposes their interconnected nature and the ways in which application of one may influence the other. Gerber, for example, described how many European competition laws emerged from wartime price regulation, illustrating the often-blurred dividing line between a regime of proactive government regulation and a 'behind-the-scenes' antitrust-based approach.[328]

Finally, this second approach may find some support in economic scholarship albeit of a more indirect nature. Stigler viewed regulation as an example of the coercive power of the State, involving a 'compelled universality' that he argued was fundamentally different from the market process.[329] Peltzman, too, focused on the emphasis of regulation on commonality or uniform treatment when compared with a free enterprise model.[330] Clark equated the market, or 'free private enterprise', with freedom, which he construed as 'a good thing in itself'.[331] Such freedom is to be preferred over prescriptive rules organising production: that is, economic regulation. Yet, the limits imposed by competition law on the economic freedom of individuals are necessary in order to preserve the freedom of others: individuals can make choices for their own business, but should not accumulate sufficient economic power to make choices for society as a whole.[332] Ordoliberal theory can also be interpreted in a manner compatible with this model. Under Ordoliberalism, competition law is a means to regulate competition. Not dissimilarly to a libertarian perspective, individual economic freedom is the key value to be protected by the economic system. Yet, Ordoliberalism exhibits less reticence than libertarianism in according a strong role to the State to protect this freedom. As the unsupervised free market is inadequate to secure individual economic freedom, competition law is required to regulate the competitive process in order to secure greater freedom in the longer run. Competition law is an integral part of the framework

[327] Lipsey & Lancaster (1956); see also p. 13.
[328] Gerber (1998).
[329] Stigler (1971:4).
[330] Peltzman (1976).
[331] Clark (1961:85).
[332] Clark (1961:86).

of the economic system, a conceptualisation that fits comfortably with the model of competition law as part of a spectrum of techniques for market intervention. Although Ordoliberals were less enthusiastic about regulating outcomes, such reservations indicate merely a political preference for a particular economic structure that can be accommodated within the spectrum of possibilities under our second approach.[333]

VI. The interface in practice: the evolution of US telecommunications regulation

In reality, of course, these contrasting conceptualisations present an essentially artificial dichotomy, illustrating the potential (but unrealised) absolute boundaries of the relationship between competition law and regulation. The substitutes-complements distinction is necessarily narrow, static and over-inclusive. More nuanced, alternative formulations have viewed competition law as providing 'a beneficial supplement [to] even if it is not a full substitute' for regulation,[334] or envisage regulation as 'a surrogate for competition' that attempts to replicate the effects of competitive markets.[335] A notable example of the latter, in the context of environmental regulation, is the EU's emissions trading scheme, which commoditises the right to pollute in an effort to use market forces to reduce industrial greenhouse gas emissions.[336]

Indeed, some scholars have conceptualised competition law and regulation as potentially both substitutes *and* complements. Carlton and Picker suggested that a substitutionary relationship arises in fully deregulated markets, where competition law replaces regulation as the mechanism of control; whereas a complementary relationship arises in partially deregulated markets, where competition law supervises the functioning of deregulated segments and the regulatory framework covers the remainder of the field.[337] Alternatively, Laguna de Paz argued that competition law and regulation comprise complements, and can be applied cumulatively, where they pursue different market objectives, but should be viewed as substitutes, with regulation displacing competition

[333] Möschel (2001). [334] Shelanski (2011:719). [335] DTI (2006:13).

[336] Directive 2003/87/EC of the European Parliament and of the Council of 13 October 2003 establishing a scheme for greenhouse gas emission allowance trading within the Community and amending Council Directive 96/61/EC (OJ L275/32, 25.10.2003); see generally Baldwin et al. (2011:195–224).

[337] Carlton & Picker (2006:22–5).

law, where the substantive scope of these rules overlaps.[338] For Hovenkamp, while competition law and regulation may compete at the margins because the boundaries between these mechanisms are unclear, they are complementary at their core.[339] Given the evolving nature of the concepts of competition law and regulation and their respective roles within modern economies, moreover, the relationship between these legal instruments is a dynamic, fluctuating one. Thus, Hovenkamp furthermore suggested that, with deregulation, the general perception of this relationship moves away from more absolutist visions in line with our first model, premised on a theory of regulatory 'completeness', towards a more disorganised, interlinked vision that corresponds more closely with the second approach.[340]

Despite the nuanced nature of the interface between competition law and regulation in practice, the more polarised archetypes just discussed nonetheless help to explain competing impulses towards convergence or divergence. Understanding why one or other paradigm might be preferred is useful insofar as the relationship between competition law and regulation tends to be complex and even contradictory in practice. Although it is probably impossible to define unequivocally an overarching relationship between competition law and regulation, we can explore and hopefully explain the individual elements of this interaction that may arise. To illustrate these complexities, we examine the regulatory history of US telecommunications, which demonstrates an intricate relationship between the use of antitrust and more direct regulatory mechanisms to control and shape market evolution. This sets the scene for the substantive analytical exploration of these issues in the following chapters, which seeks to chart systematically and account for, *inter alia*, the range of interactions illustrated by the US telecommunications example.

The technology of telephony emerged in the USA in the late 1870s, eventually superseding the then-dominant telegraph system.[341] US telephony markets developed initially as a series of unregulated local monopolies, some operated by the Bell Company, while others were independent systems intended to provide services for their immediate community.[342] The Bell Company, through its subsidiary, the American Telephone and Telegraph Company (AT&T), also undertook the development of a series of 'long lines' to link its discrete local systems.[343]

338 Laguna de Paz (2012:78–9). 339 Hovenkamp (2005:277).
340 Hovenkamp (2011:772). 341 Wu (2010:17–32). 342 Wu (2010:45–50).
343 Wu (2010:32).

Although AT&T, as the Bell Company became known, initially tolerated the presence of independent systems, from 1907 onwards it promulgated the idea of a single telephony monopoly, and actively sought to drive independents from the market.[344]

AT&T's efforts at consolidation, unsurprisingly, attracted the attention of antitrust enforcers. Instead of fighting the antitrust charges levelled against it, however, AT&T actively courted government regulation. It agreed to divest its (dying) telegraph business, to act as common carrier for independent systems, and to refrain from acquiring local rivals. This compromise, known as the 'Kingsbury Commitment', effectively permitted AT&T to continue its progress towards monopoly, albeit in the guise of a regulated public utility.[345] The Kingsbury Commitment also embraced the Mann-Elkins Act of 1910, which extended the jurisdiction of the Interstate Commerce Commission to cover telecommunications regulation. In parallel, additional layers of telecommunications regulation were developed at the state level.[346] In 1921, Congress passed the Willis Graham Act, which replaced the Kingsbury Commitment by recognising telephone systems as natural monopolies and removing barriers to AT&T's acquisition of its remaining system rivals.[347] Finally, the Communications Act of 1934 created a dedicated telecommunications regulator, the Federal Communications Commission (FCC).

Despite these growing regulatory controls, by 1949 the DOJ considered it necessary to pursue further antitrust action against AT&T. This second suit alleged breaches of Sherman Act, §§1 and 2, relating to the markets for telephony equipment, and as a remedy the government sought the divestiture of AT&T's telephone equipment manufacturing business, Western Electric. Notably, however, the DOJ's suit was opposed by another government entity, the Department of Defence, which claimed that a strong integrated AT&T was essential to national security.[348] In 1956, the case was eventually concluded by consent decree, a negotiated settlement procedure considered further in Chapter 2 as an example of regulatory antitrust. The terms of the decree precluded AT&T from engaging in any business apart from the provision of common-carrier

[344] Wu (2010:50–4). [345] Wu (2010:55–7); Weber (2008:22).

[346] In 1902, only one US state had a regulator with authority to regulate telephony; by 1913, 39 states had such regulators: Wallsten (2006:1).

[347] Wu (2010:59).

[348] *United States* v. *AT&T*, 552 F. Supp. 131 (DDC, 1982), 136–7. Wu (2010:160) described AT&T's relationship with the federal government as 'a uniquely intimate entanglement of interests'.

communications services, prohibited Western Electric from manufacturing equipment except for use by the Bell system, banned AT&T activity in the nascent computing sector and required royalty-free licensing of certain AT&T patents.[349] The company nonetheless retained its regulated monopoly status and integrated infrastructure.

From the late 1960s onwards, the FCC began to shift telecommunications regulation from a regulated monopoly model towards a competition-focused approach, in line with a broader deregulatory movement that will be considered in Chapter 3. Accordingly, the FCC permitted competitive entry into the market for long-distance calls, and it allowed for the first time the use of consumer equipment not manufactured by AT&T.[350] AT&T resisted these efforts to dismantle its end-to-end monopoly through a series of non-compliance strategies that made it practically impossible for new entrants to operate within newly competitive market segments.[351] In addition to violation of regulatory obligations, the possibility that such 'regulatory gaming' can constitute an antitrust offence is explored in Chapter 4. The FCC, however, lacked the regulatory powers and practical ability to enforce regulatory competition effectively on AT&T in response.[352]

Instead, AT&T's effective refusal to comply with its regulatory obligations – namely, to support competition in the long-distance and telecommunications equipment markets – as well as use of cross-subsidies from monopoly markets to subsidise competitive activities, became the subject of another antitrust suit brought by the DOJ in 1974. Although again opposed by the Department of Defence,[353] the DOJ was supported the FCC.[354] After almost a decade of litigation, and strong resistance from AT&T, this case was again concluded by a consent decree, under which the company agreed to divest ownership of its various local Bell operating companies (BOCs).[355] The consent decree worked from the premise that the local systems continued as natural monopolies.[356] Accordingly, the BOCs, which were divested as seven regional 'Baby Bells', were forbidden from entering competitive markets, such as long-distance,

[349] *United States* v. *AT&T*, 135–8.

[350] Wu (2010: 187–90); Weber (2008:22–4); Cudahy (2001:162–3).

[351] Wu (2010:192); Shelanski (2011:715).

[352] *United States* v. *AT&T*, 168, 223.

[353] Posner (2008:16).

[354] Posner (2008:14).

[355] *United States* v. *AT&T*, affirmed sub nom. *Maryland* v. *United States*, 460 US 1001 (1983). The decree took effect from 1 January 1984.

[356] *United States v. AT&T*, 224.

and were subject to strengthened regulatory controls.[357] AT&T retained its long-distance infrastructure (where, however, it faced competition from firms that utilised microwave technology) and its research and development and manufacturing divisions. It was also permitted to enter the computing sector, which it attempted, unsuccessfully, to do.[358] The magnitude of the AT&T antitrust divestiture should not be underestimated: at the time of its break-up, AT&T was the largest company in the world.[359]

The impact and effectiveness of the 1982 consent decree is disputed.[360] In any event, the configuration of competition envisaged did not survive long when subjected to the unpredictable forces of creative destruction – and the equally unpredictable preferences of the legislature. Subsequent mergers reduced the number of regional BOCs from seven to three,[361] while most of the long-distance companies, including AT&T itself, failed to survive in an intensely competitive marketplace. The original AT&T company was later acquired by one of its 'babies', formerly Southwestern Bell, which then re-emerged as a renewed 'AT&T'.[362] In 1996, the Telecommunications Act was passed, replacing the 1982 consent decree, which sought to overhaul, and specifically to make more competitive, telecommunications markets – a 'tectonic shift' in the existing regulatory paradigm.[363] In essence, the 1996 Act permitted BOCs to enter competitive segments in exchange for relinquishing local monopolies, that is, permitting access by competitors to local networks. In practice, however,

[357] Weber (2008:26); Wu (2010:194); Krouse et al. (1999:61–2). [358] Wu (2010:194).

[359] Measured both by revenue and asset value: see *United States* v. *AT&T*, 151–2.

[360] Shelanski (2011:715). The immediate impact was a decline in service quality together with increased prices as the sector reorganised: Wu (2010:161,195); Hausman & Sidak (1999:429). Krouse et al. (1999:83) nonetheless identified significant efficiency savings resulting from the divestiture and accompanying regulatory reforms, while Wu (2010:195) argued that, by ending AT&T's stranglehold on innovation, the break-up facilitated significant advances in telecommunications and information technology. Weber (2008:29), conversely, argued that such innovation would have occurred regardless, and emphasised the substantial monetary costs that divestiture imposed. An interesting divergence of opinion is discernible between two prominent conservative scholars: while Posner (2001:111) described the consent decree as 'the most successful antitrust structural remedy in history', Epstein (2007:58) criticised it as suffering 'from an excess of ambition and from a lack of focus and finitude'.

[361] Weber (2008:26). [362] Wu (2010:248–9).

[363] Rubin (2005:727); see also Speta (2003:102). In *Verizon Communications Inc. et al.* v. *Federal Communications Commission et al.*, 535 US 467 (2002), 488, the Supreme Court described the 1996 Act in terms of 'uprooting the monopolies that traditional rate-based methods had perpetuated'.

a similar problem to that which prompted the AT&T break-up emerged, namely, strategic resistance by BOCs to access obligations in order to exclude new entrants and maintain local monopolies. Again, the FCC has encountered difficulties in enforcing regulatory duties against infrastructure monopolists,[364] as well as the more fundamental task of actually setting regulations.[365] The 1996 Act is generally seen as a failure, therefore, inasmuch as it has been unsuccessful in its objective to introduce effective competition into local markets.[366]

Much like the DOJ has done throughout AT&T's history, many potential new entrants turned to antitrust litigation as a means to access the BOCs' essential infrastructure.[367] The 2004 decision of the US Supreme Court in *Trinko*, examined in Chapter 4, appears largely to have foreclosed the possibility of using antitrust to address anticompetitive conduct regulated under the 1996 Act, however. Indeed, this decision would arguably have barred the DOJ's successful suit initiated three decades earlier.[368] Echoing the language of the dichotomous conceptions of the interaction between competition law and regulation described earlier, it has been argued that the jurisprudential shift discernible between the decisions in *US* v. *AT&T* and *Trinko* reflects a concomitant movement from viewing competition law and regulation as complements to substitutes.[369] An unresolved question is the potential use of specialised public-enforcement tools, such as §5 of the FTCA, to escape the apparent limitations placed on antitrust litigation by *Trinko* and later cases.[370] In Chapter 5, we consider the potential expansion of §5 FTCA as such a 'hybridised' mechanism of market control.

VII. Concluding remarks

At a conceptual level, it is possible to posit competition law and regulation as either wholly separate mechanisms of market supervision, or as different manifestations of, essentially, the same legal phenomenon, both

364 Speta (2003:103–4).

365 Shelanski (2011:722–4). In *AT&T* v. *Iowa Utilities Board*, 525 US 366 (1999), for example, the Supreme Court struck down the FCC's rules on unbundling as overbroad.

366 Economides (2005:399); Faulhaber (2008:40–1); Weber (2008:28); cf. Epstein (2005:336), arguing that the 1996 Act's primary failure was to mandate conditions for interconnection rather than voluntary contracting.

367 Speta (2003:106).

368 Brennan (2005:639–40); Shelanski (2011:714–18).

369 Brennan (2008:142).

370 Kovacic & Winerman (2010:948).

being components of the State's overall regulatory arsenal. Reality is rather more nuanced, however, than a blunt substitutes-or-complements dichotomy. A market might be subject to successive waves of competition enforcement, regulation and deregulation; competition law may be applicable in regulated markets, or conversely, wholly or partly excluded by the presence of regulation; competition law may function as a substitute for regulation or *vice versa*; or recourse may be had to legal powers of a hybridised nature that are designed precisely to escape the limitations of the antitrust and regulatory models. As our brief market history of the US telecommunications sector demonstrated, moreover, all of these elements might be present within a single market at certain points. In the following chapters, we turn to consider the various interactions between competition law and regulation that might arise in practice, which blur the dividing line between these discrete but interrelated legal mechanisms.

Given the potential breadth of this topic, it is useful to clarify, as a final preliminary issue, what this book does not cover as well as what it does. First, our enquiry focuses on the *substantive* relationship between competition law and regulation as mechanisms of market supervision. This book therefore concentrates upon issues regarding the content and mode of operation of each of these mechanisms, and, in particular, how each can impact upon and, conversely, is influenced or affected by the operation of the other. This question must be distinguished from the related-but-separate issue of institutional concurrency between competition law and regulation, which has two dimensions. There is the question of what functions are performed by a competition authority in addition to its competition enforcement activities: for example, whether it also functions as a consumer protection agency, like the UK's Competition and Markets Authority or the US's FTC, or acts as a sector regulator, like Australia's Australian Competition and Consumer Commission (ACCC), or holds hybridised competition law-regulatory powers that extend beyond the parameters of the conventional antitrust rules. Additionally, in regulated sectors, there is a question of whether competition law should be enforced by the generalist competition authority, or by the sector-specific regulator, or both under some concurrency arrangement.[371] The appropriate 'division of labour'[372] between public-enforcement agencies relates to, in large part, an administrative law issue

[371] Rab (2009); Dabbah (2011). [372] Dabbah (2011:132).

of allocation of powers rather than the substantive relationship between these powers, and thus lies largely outside the scope of this work. It is impossible to draw an absolutely rigid distinction between substantive and institutional issues in practice, however, and for this reason relevant institutional aspects will be explored in Chapter 5. Furthermore, this work does not consider concurrency between different antitrust regimes that may apply within a single jurisdiction, for example, concurrency between enforcement of EU competition law and the national competition laws of Member States,[373] or between US federal and state antitrust law.[374]

Second, although this book examines the application of legal rules to address economic problems, it is not a work of law and economics in the methodological sense.[375] Competition law and economic regulation provide, typically, legal solutions to market problems, and so concepts and questions of economics are unavoidable. To the extent that such concepts are invoked or discussed here, the purpose is to explain and test the soundness of the legal frameworks under examination. It must be emphasised again that it would be naïve to accept, in an uncritical manner, all economics-based arguments that have been made in this area. The objective of this book is not to use economics to critique the legal framework; rather, it is to produce a legal assessment of various State-implemented solutions to economic problems.

Third, although we will discuss legal rules and case examples from a number of different jurisdictions, this is not a work of comparative law in the sense that this likewise implies adoption of any particular methodological approach. A key objective here is to distil general principles regarding the relationship between competition law and economic regulation, which, to the greatest extent possible, are applicable without reference to a particular jurisdiction. The plentiful use of examples throughout the text is intended to illustrate the breadth and potential contours of the interface between these legal instruments. Readers may discern an apparent bias for examples taken from the European Union, in particular, alongside the US. This preference is explainable by reference to the long histories and rich jurisprudence concerning the application of competition law within both systems, and, in the context of the

373 Cf. Nazzini (2004),

374 Cf. Hovenkamp (1983). For a comparative consideration of concurrency approaches in both jurisdictions, see e.g. Hawk & Laudati (1996); Bergeron (2001); Cengiz (2012).

375 See, e.g., Posner (2003).

EU, the close interrelationship between competition law and economic regulation that has arisen in pursuit of internal market integration. Of course, it cannot be assumed that the requirements of or principles for applying these legal mechanisms are identical across different legal systems, and attention must be paid to the technical distinctions as well as the underlying policy context in which the examples considered have arisen. Within EU law, the recurrent use of competition enforcement to further the distinctive aim of market integration may also serve to distinguish this jurisdiction, to a degree, from other competition systems. We would argue, nonetheless, that the EU antitrust framework is not so unique as to render any comparative exercise meaningless, particularly in view of its recent adoption of a conventional 'more economic approach' to competition enforcement, alongside the enthusiastic efforts of the European Commission to encourage new competition jurisdictions to adopt and develop their antitrust systems in line with the EU model. Given the presupposition that this is an area of the law where public-policy decisions abound and are perhaps preeminent, it is hoped that value may be derived from an account of past practice and resulting broader implications, alongside an accompanying theoretical and analytical framework.

2

Competition law as regulation

We begin our overview of the interface between competition law and economic regulation by reference to circumstances in which the former may begin to resemble the latter, namely the idea of 'regulatory competition law'. This concept embraces, in essence, situations where the use or operation of antitrust shifts away from its paradigmatic or conventional 'core' conception, considered in the preceding chapter, and moves towards a regulatory archetype. The crime-tort model of competition law – adopted by the US, the EU and other antitrust jurisdictions – involves, in theory, a series of discrete prohibitions that forbid firms from engaging in certain proscribed activities, with a liability structure that holds firms directly and individually accountable if they breach these proscriptions. Regulatory competition law, by contrast, implies a meaningful departure from this standard model, whether it relates to the temporal or on-going nature of enforcement, the grounding of remedial powers in findings of breach, or the identification of individual anti-competitive behaviour to trigger liability. The application of competition law in a quasi-regulatory fashion is a well recognised – but also a much criticised – phenomenon. In this chapter, we aim to explore whether and when competition law takes on such claimed 'regulatory' characteristics, and why this might be so, and we also seek to understand and assess certain criticisms of this approach to competition enforcement.

As Chapter 1 demonstrated, competition law can be considered as simply another form of regulation or State market control when viewed at an abstract level. Accepting the posited distinction between competition law and regulation, the notion of competition law-*as*-regulation can imply either a descriptive *functional* characterisation, or a substantive *doctrinally significant* one. At a descriptive level, regulatory competition law designates the use of competition law as an alternative to, or substitute for, sector-specific regulation. Although such regulation is neither necessary nor appropriate in every market, often it is required in industries with structural competition problems, or, as we shall discuss further in Chapter 3, where non-market goals are at issue. In the absence of a market-wide regulatory scheme, the residual nature of competition law might render it the default control mechanism available. The use of competition law as a substitute for regulation arises, most frequently, where there has simply been a failure to enact regulation within a sector or where existing regulation has gaps in coverage, rather than any decision against regulation as such. Such use can, on the other hand, represent a more positive ideological choice by policy-makers to defer to competition law and the market mechanisms, and thus to address all market failures stemming from monopoly through antitrust rather than through sector-specific regulation. Depending on the nature of the market problem, competition law may be more or less successful in these gap-filling or substitutionary roles.

The concept of regulatory competition law may, alternatively, denote a substantive shift within antitrust doctrine itself: away from the supposed norm of competition law as a proscriptive, *ex post* conduct-focused instrument of market control, and towards a more interventionist regulatory conception of competition law's role. The use of competition law in a quasi-regulatory manner has, perhaps, been most contentious in this context. As we shall see, the adaptation and application of competition law in this way, whether strategically oriented or largely inadvertent, can generate significant immediate benefit in terms of effectiveness, providing a more focused and potent tool by which to solve existing market defects. The longer-term implications of shifting antitrust from a legalistic to regulatory enterprise, however, may be more equivocal.

Two qualifications are necessary at the outset. First, in practice there can be significant intersections between functional and substantive notions of regulatory competition law. Unsurprisingly, where competition law is applied in lieu of regulation or to plug gaps in an existing regulatory framework, the antitrust doctrines applied and remedies imposed often exhibit a distinct 'regulatory' flavour. Although we consider these aspects separately for analytical purposes, both may arise in tandem, and in particular, the functional use of competition law as a substitute for regulation tends to necessitate a more regulatory-style application of the competition rules in substance. Our concern, in this chapter, is to provide an assessment of each dimension, considered both individually and in tandem. Second, the concept of regulatory competition law must be distinguished from the quite separate notion of 'regulatory competition'. The latter refers to a rivalry between governments for regulatees, whereby legislators select and deselect regulatory rules through the process of competition, aiming to provide the most attractive regulatory offering within their jurisdictions. Regulatory competition is linked to the idea of regulatory arbitrage, whereby regulated entities seek to take advantage of the most favourable conditions between a number of regulatory regimes, which may prompt preventive action by legislators in less favoured jurisdictions.[1] While there can be overlap in practice between the use of competition law as regulation and the phenomenon of regulatory competition – the former may be prompted, for example, by a political decision to 'roll back' *ex ante* regulatory constraints within a jurisdiction in order to attract or retain investment – the concept of regulatory competition, as such, lies outside this work.

I. Competition law as substitutionary or gap-filling regulation

The overlaps that exist in terms of scope of application between competition law and economic regulation mean that, where the latter is absent, competition law might provide an alternate mechanism to address market defects.[2] Once enacted, competition law provides a residual market control mechanism of general application unless expressly or impliedly excluded.[3] The continuing latent availability of competition law to address new competition problems contrasts with regulation, which must be enacted specifically within a market. Competition law is, by default, available for *ex post* enforcement, including in markets not yet subject to sector-specific regulation. Usually, a market remains unregulated because regulation is unnecessary: that is, there are no persistent market problems that require on-going positive State intervention. It is nevertheless possible that market failure may occur and yet (ostensibly necessary) regulation is not implemented. Such absence may be unintentional or due to legislative tardiness. More unusually, it may reflect a deliberate policy choice to reject more interventionist approaches to market supervision. In either instance, competition law might be deployed to buttress the imperfect market and provide a remedy – whether temporary or more permanent – to continuing market difficulties.

We consider first the use of competition law as an improvised or temporary form of quasi-regulation, in the (non-deliberate) absence of

[1] Gabor (2013:3–4). [2] See also Breyer (1982:158–61). [3] Hovenkamp (2005:10).

sector-specific regulation in markets with on-going competition problems. This is, essentially, a 'gap-filling' function. Almost by definition, competition law aims to provide a legal framework to address discrete market problems that arise due to the conduct of individual firms. Consequently, certain types of market failure, particularly those related to structural issues such as exploitation of natural or legal monopolies, are not optimally addressed through competition enforcement. In the absence of any more appropriate sector-specific regulatory alternative, however, antitrust may provide a reasonably effective second-best solution to such problems. Recurrent competition law complaints or investigations may also highlight the existence of market-wide problems, which may subsequently prompt adoption of a more comprehensive regulatory solution. The use of competition law within airport markets in the EU provides a good illustration of its role as a temporary substitute mechanism of market control. In these cases, discrete but recurrent instances of antitrust enforcement functioned as a precursor to enactment of generally applicable sector-specific regulation addressing structural market issues.

Liberalisation of EU air transport markets began with the *Nouvelles Frontières* judgment, which confirmed the applicability of competition law in the sector, but required implementing legislation for direct application of (now) Articles 101 and 102 TFEU.[4] Between 1987 and 1992, the Commission introduced a series of progressively liberalising regulations.[5] These measures concerned air transport activities (e.g., airline market access and air-fares) but not airport infrastructure or ancillary activities such as ground-handling services provided at airports (e.g., check-in, baggage-handling, fuelling and catering). The latter remained subject to competition law,[6] but were not expressly liberalised. Accordingly, while legal monopolies for air transport were dismantled by regulation, the legal and natural monopolies existing in airport markets remained unchallenged and unregulated.

At the time, ground-handling services at many European airports were provided exclusively by airport operators or designated providers. The quality of services was comparatively low, in general, and prices were comparatively high.[7] In the absence of any EU regulation requiring

[4] Joined Cases 209–213/84 *Ministère Public* v. *Lucas Asjes* EU:C:1986:188.

[5] Giemulla & Weber (2011:143–53)

[6] Confirmed in Case C-82/01 P *Aéroports de Paris* v. Commission EU:C:2002:617, paras.16–19.

[7] Giemulla & Weber (2011:159).

competition, ground-handling customers (i.e., airlines) resorted to competition enforcement in order to improve the functioning of the market. By 1993, the Commission was investigating ten formal complaints from airlines alleging breaches of competition law, particularly Article 102 TFEU, relating to ground-handling services.[8] The Commission took the view that these similar and recurrent complaints highlighted a deeper structural issue. While individual instances of abuse of dominance may have occurred, the fundamental cause of these problems was the monopolies granted for ground-handling provision.[9] In tandem with its antitrust investigations, therefore, the Commission sought to produce a market-wide regulatory solution. The Directive on ground-handling was enacted in 1996, requiring Member States to open ground-handling markets at larger airports to third-party providers and self-handling by airlines, albeit with several substantial reservations.[10]

The intention of the Directive was to provide a prospective market-wide solution to access problems in the ground-handling sector. The Commission nonetheless continued to pursue individual cases under Article 102 TFEU in this area. In *FAG*,[11] the Commission held that the refusal of the owner-operator of Frankfurt Airport to permit third-party ground-handling and airline self-handling constituted an abusive extension of its monopoly in airport services into the ground-handling market. Although Germany invoked exemptions contained in the ground-handing Directive to exclude Frankfurt Airport from its application for a three-year period, this exemption did not immunise the operator from application of competition law. In *Aéroports de Paris*,[12] the operator of the Paris-area airports had permitted self-handling and third-party handling, but charged higher access fees for the latter. This policy was held to be discriminatory and abusive under Article 102 TFEU because it favoured the airports' largest airline customers. Soames has argued

[8] European Commission Press Release IP/93/714, 'Statement by Mr Van Miert on Ground-Handling Services for Air Transport', published 25 August 1993.

[9] Ibid.

[10] Council Directive 96/67/EC on access to the ground handling market at Community airports (OJ L272/36, 25.10.1996). See Monti (2007:235–7); Soames (1997).

[11] Commission Decision of 14 January 1998 (IV/34.801 *FAG – Flughafen Frankfurt/Main AG*) (OJ L72/30, 11.3.98).

[12] Commission Decision of 11 June 1998 (IN/35.613 – *Alpha Flight Services/Aéroports de Paris*) (OJ L230/10, 18.8.98); confirmed in Case T-128/98 *Aéroports de Paris* v. *Commission* EU:T:2000:290 and Case C-82/01P *Aéroports de Paris* v. *Commission*.

convincingly that the Commission's strategic decision to continue these individual actions was motivated primarily by a need to place pressure on Member States for rapid agreement of the liberalising legislation.[13] This demonstrates how a gap-filling use of competition law can have a political as well as a merely practical role. The instrumental use of competition law to further regulatory objectives, such as liberalisation of ground-handling markets, is a more controversial issue, however, which is discussed later in this chapter.

A similar gap-filling or precursory role for competition law is discernible in the related airport charges cases. Although air transport liberalisation enabled airlines to enter new markets, the regulatory framework imposed no express requirements regarding equal treatment of airline customers by airports. In the years following liberalisation, the Commission faced an emerging problem of discriminatory airport charges that favoured national airlines, which, again, it addressed initially through competition enforcement. Infringement decisions were thus adopted under Article 102 TFEU against the airport operator in *Finnish Airports*,[14] and against the responsible Member States under Article 106(1) applied in conjunction with Article 102 TFEU in the *Brussels Airport*,[15] *Portuguese Airports*[16] and *Spanish Airports*.[17] The preponderance of Article 106(1) TFEU decisions indicates the significant role of government policy in the airports context, which complicates any competition analysis. Moreover, the competition abuse alleged in these cases – price discrimination based on nationality – is amongst the more controversial when judged from an economic perspective, because price discrimination is frequently efficient, but is nonetheless considered inimical to EU competition law's parallel objective of protecting development of the internal market.[18] Unsurprisingly, the Commission subsequently sought to include regulation of airport charges within the codified liberalisation framework. After several earlier setbacks,[19]

13 Soames (1997:85–6).

14 Commission Decision of 10 February 1999 (IV/35.767 – *IlmaL/Luftfartsverket*) (OJ L69/24, 16.3.1999).

15 Commission Decision of 28 June 1995 (*Brussels National Airport*) (OJ L216/8, 12.9.95).

16 Commission Decision of 10 February 1999 (IV 35.703 – *Portuguese Airports*) (OJ L69/31, 16.3.1999).

17 Commission Decision of 26 July 2000 (*Spanish Airports*) (OJ L208/36, 18.8.2000).

18 See generally Motta (2004:491–9).

19 European Commission, *Proposal for a Council Directive on airport charges* (COM (97) 154), published 12 November 1997.

a Directive on airport charges was enacted in 2009.[20] It imposes obligations of non-discrimination, transparency and consultation, as well as quality requirements upon operators of larger airports within the EU. Like in the ground-handling context, there has accordingly been a movement from gap-filling antitrust enforcement to subsequent market-wide regulation.

It is also useful to consider, in this context, the Commission's recurrent use of competition law as a means to 'regulate' costs within payment card systems in the absence of formalised EU-wide controls. These efforts included a time-limited exemption granted to Visa under Regulation 17, which was premised upon a substantial reduction in fee levels,[21] plus an infringement decision against MasterCard, which prohibited its interchange fees but permitted the association a six-month grace period to reform its fee structure.[22] More recently, the Commission reached settlements with Visa in respect of its debit and credit card fees,[23] pursuant to its relatively novel quasi-regulatory commitment procedure, which we examine later. Acknowledging the inadequacy of such 'ad hoc' supervision in the longer term,[24] however, the Commission has proposed the enactment of EU-level regulation to cap interchange fees, which will apply across all Member States, and to all payment systems that provide certain financial products.[25]

Reliance upon competition law as the sole or predominant mechanism of market supervision does not, necessarily, imply a precursory failure to enact *ex ante* regulation to correct market defects, however. Rather,

[20] Directive 2009/12/EC of the European Parliament and of the Council of 11 March 2009 on airport charges (OJ L70/11, 14.3.2009).

[21] Commission Decision of 24 July 2002 in Case COMP/29.373 – *Visa International – Multilateral Interchange Fee* (OJ C 318/17, 22.11.2002).

[22] Commission Decision of 19 December 2007 in Cases COMP/34.579 – *MasterCard*, COMP/36.518 – *EuroCommerce* & COMP/38.580 – *Commercial Cards*, summary at 2009 OJ (C 264); confirmed by the General Court in T-111/08 *MasterCard* v. *Commission*, EU:T:2012:260

[23] Commission Decision of 8 December 2010 in Case COMP/39.398 – *Visa MIF* (OJ C79/8, 12.3.2011) and European Commission Press Release IP/14/197, 'Antitrust: Commission makes Visa Europe's commitments to cut inter-bank fees and to facilitate cross-border competition legally binding', published 26 February 2014 (no decision yet published).

[24] European Commission, *Introductory Remarks on Proposal for Interchange Fees for Cards, Internet and Mobile Payments, Speech by Vice President Joaqúin Almunia*, SPEECH/13/660, published 24 July 2013.

[25] *See* European Commission, *Proposal for a Regulation of the European Parliament and of the Council on interchange fees for card-based payment transactions*, COM(2013) 550 final, published 24 July 2013.

the use of competition law to address market problems that are more typically tackled through economic regulation may instead represent a deliberate policy choice to favour market-oriented solutions. Such an approach often reflects a degree of political scepticism regarding the utility or effectiveness of sector-specific regulation more generally, an issue considered further in the Chapter 3. The initial liberalisation of German electricity markets, and New Zealand's general approach to market regulation in the years following enactment of the Commerce Act 1986, both provide illustrations of how such a hands-off approach to regulation might operate in practice.

We consider first the more circumscribed German example. Electricity markets contain significant natural monopoly segments, relating to transmission and distribution activities. Even where certain segments of electricity markets are opened to competition, such as generation or retailing, regulation typically remains necessary in order to ensure access for competitors to non-competitive segments. When Germany liberalised its electricity sector in 1998 in order to implement the EU's First Electricity Directive,[26] however, it did so not by imposing new *ex ante* regulatory requirements but simply by removing the then-existing exemption from competition law for electricity contracts.[27] In effect, Germany opted for self-regulation by the electricity industry in the form of negotiated access agreements, to be supervised by competition law.[28] In the absence of a specific electricity regulator, the German competition authority acquired a *de facto* regulatory role. In addition to *ex post* enforcement against discrete instances of anticompetitive conduct, the authority played a quasi-*ex ante* role under national competition law, with the ability to veto industry-wide access agreements deemed anticompetitive.[29] This hands-off approach to regulation ended in 2005, when a federal regulator, the Bundesnetzagentur, was established with responsibility for numerous sectors (electricity, gas, telecommunications, postal and rail), with corresponding developments at the state (*Länder*) level.[30] Interestingly, this development was largely attributable to the requirements of the EU's second package of energy directives and the shift from a negotiated third-party access model to a

[26] Discussed p. 112. [27] Glachant et al. (2008).
[28] Glachant et al. (2008:1603); von Danwitz (2006:440–1).
[29] Glachant et al. (2008:1603).
[30] See von Danwitz (2006:445–8) for discussion of the amended electricity regulatory scheme.

regulated access model this entailed,[31] rather than dissatisfaction with the existing approach as such.

The New Zealand experience was more radical. In the mid-1980s, economic policy for New Zealand was overhauled entirely. The aim was to move the economy from a substantially State-regulated and controlled system to one that vigorously embraced free-market ideas, in order to increase international competitiveness and stimulate economic development.[32] Accordingly, the government adopted, *inter alia*, a policy of 'light-touch' regulation for all markets, including utilities sectors, such as telecommunications and energy, which elsewhere continued to be subject to residual sector-specific regulation even after liberalisation.[33] The New Zealand approach to market regulation relied, instead, almost exclusively on market mechanisms and general competition law – the newly enacted Commerce Act 1986 – in an approach described as an 'extreme experiment in the utility of undiluted competition law'.[34] While the government retained the ability to impose sector-specific regulation under Part 4 of the Commerce Act 1986,[35] this option was disfavoured, and functioned principally as a (purported) deterrent to anticompetitive behaviour.[36] In practice, however, this *laissez-faire* approach failed to generate a socially optimal outcome, as the general competition rules proved inadequate to address exploitative behaviour by incumbent firms, such as price-gouging, which in other jurisdictions is controlled by sector-specific regulators.[37] From the late 1990s onwards, the New Zealand government began a process of reviewing and revising its regulatory regimes, enacting sector-specific regulation for the telecommunications, electricity and gas industries, which moreover has been progressively strengthened over time.[38]

The wider implications of the German and New Zealand experiences are somewhat disputed. While New Zealand's blanket rejection of sector-specific regulation is largely judged to be a failure,[39] the initial German

[31] See pp. 112–3.
[32] Sumpter et al. (2010:348); Bollard & Pickford (1995); Laffont & Tirole (2000:33–4).
[33] Howell (2010:265). [34] Brunt (2003:18).
[35] See Sumpter et al. (2010:345–67) for discussion of the Part 4 power.
[36] Sumpter et al. (2010:348–9); Bollard & Pickford (1995:418); Adhar (1995:219).
[37] Adhar (1995); Adhar (2010:54–9); Brunt (2003: 19–22); Geradin & Kerf (2003:334).
[38] Brunt (2003:22–4); Sumpter et al. (2010:346–9); Adhar (2010:59–61).
[39] Brunt (2003:21–2); cf. Howell (2010).

approach to electricity liberalisation was viewed more positively.[40] The subsequent decision in Germany to implement a specific regulatory body for the sector was indeed informed primarily by EU requirements, rather than any domestic conclusion that reform was necessary. Undoubtedly, a generalised policy of reliance upon antitrust alone to address competition problems within a market, including structural issues, is likely to prove inadequate to secure an efficient outcome in every market. In certain circumstances, however, it seems possible that self-regulation, policed by competition law, may be sufficient to achieve a relatively well-functioning market, even in utilities sectors such as energy and telecommunications.

II. Doctrinal regulatory competition law: procedural and substantive dimensions

These functional substitution cases, and particularly the competition doctrines applied to remedy market problems arising in the absence of regulation, hint at our second category within regulatory competition law: namely, the doctrinal shift towards competition law-as-regulation at procedural and substantive levels. Under this latter conception, competition law is viewed 'more as policy and less as law'.[41] The contention that enforcement of competition law has become a regulatory endeavour implies both a distinct vision of the standard (non-regulatory) conception of competition law, as well as a marked and perhaps questionable departure from this archetype under the quasi-regulatory model. Although the shift towards regulatory competition law is usually considered in broadly homogeneous terms, two divergent strands emerge – procedural and substantive – that raise certain different issues. We consider these strands concurrently nonetheless, partly because of the considerable overlap in terms of the issues involved, and partly because both feed into the broader question of whether competition law should depart from its purported archetype.

40 Glachant et al. (2008:1609); von Danwitz (2006:440–1); cf. Joskow (2008:25), who argued that the German and New Zealand decisions to commence liberalisation without a regulator were 'clearly a mistake', and Hellwig (2009:212–13), who emphasised the time-consuming and belated nature of competition enforcement as a means to address market failures.

41 First (1995:9).

(i) *Distinguishing regulatory competition law from competition law's established core*

To suggest that forms of competition law are 'regulatory' makes sense only insofar as this description serves to distinguish those examples from other, perhaps more typical, applications of competition law. Chapter 1 considered the conventional core distinguishing features of competition law when compared with the archetype of regulation. At least formally, the antitrust model adopted by the Sherman Act premises liability in a crime-tort structure requiring identification of anticompetitive conduct by defendant firms, rather than a corporate regulatory mechanism permitting more generalised intervention to address market failure.[42] This approach is replicated within EU competition law. The development of a regulatory conception of competition law represents, in effect, a corresponding departure from this conventional model. Accordingly, competition law becomes regulatory in nature when it incorporates certain procedures or substantive characteristics more typically associated with regulation. A number of recurring elements of this shift towards competition law-as-regulation can be identified: administrative/technocratic rather than adversarial/judicial implementation; *ex ante* enforcement; detailed positive obligations on firms; static, regulatory-type remedies that require on-going monitoring; and a focus on achieving best outcomes rather than merely preventing anticompetitive behaviour. Each of these developments will be examined in turn, although in practice the categories overlap and can be mutually reinforcing. The extent to which the characteristics of a particular system align with the archetypal model might also vary between jurisdictions, as considered later in this chapter.

a. Administrative/technocratic enforcement

The use of administrative-technocratic enforcement processes is posited as a central element of regulatory competition law.[43] The conventional enforcement model is premised on individual cases litigated before an independent trier of fact and law under an adversarial procedure, which results in a concrete finding of breach that constitutes an authoritative statement of competition law.[44] In some systems, such as enforcement by the US's DOJ, the general civil or criminal court system is tasked with decision-making. In other systems, such as enforcement by the European

[42] Crane (2008); see also pp. 19–20.

[43] Crane (2011); First (1995); Larouche (2000).

[44] Larouche (2000:119–24).

Commission and the US's FTC, decisions are taken by an administrative decision-making body, generally incorporated within the enforcement agency. Even the latter systems, however, typically utilise adversarial procedures, grant protection for rights of defence, and result in a formal finding of breach that can be appealed before ordinary courts.

By contrast, the regulatory model of competition enforcement is premised on bureaucratic rather than legalistic processes.[45] Two administrative tools or procedures are viewed as being forefront to this approach: namely, the use of negotiated settlements to conclude public-enforcement activity, and the issuance of guidelines and statements of enforcement practice by competition authorities. Negotiated settlements involve, typically, consensual agreement between the public enforcer and defendant firm regarding prospective alternation of the firm's behaviour or structure. Although rooted in some theory of competition infringement, such settlements generally contain neither any admission nor formal finding of liability. Negotiated settlements cannot, therefore, amount to a formal statement of competition law, and as such, might be criticised as creating uncertainty as to the parameters of the law, particularly where novel case theories or controversial theories of harm are advanced. Such settlements often impose, nonetheless, obligations on firms that go considerably beyond the remedial duties or penalties that might be imposed following a formal finding of breach. Accordingly, the use of negotiated settlements is considered to facilitate the pursuit of broader regulatory objectives by public-enforcement agencies, in contrast with the circumscribed parameters of conventional competition enforcement against identified harmful acts.[46]

Similarly, the publication by competition authorities of guidelines, enforcement procedures and statements of future enforcement priorities, which are distinct from formal statements of competition law that emerge from litigated cases, is viewed as shifting the mode of enforcement from an adversarial to an administrative model.[47] In contrast to negotiated settlements, which prioritise problem solving for markets in difficulties, the aims of administrative guidance are, generally, to increase transparency and legal certainty for firms in the context of competition

[45] First (1995:9).

[46] Weber Waller (1998:1409–17); Weiner (1995); Melamed (1995); Ibáñez Colomo (2010:286–7) Epstein (2007); Geradin & Kerf (2003:15); Ginsburg & Wright (2013).

[47] Varney (2011:780); Weber Waller (1998:1400–8); Larouche (2000:127–8); Geradin & Kerf (2003:15).

enforcement. Although such guidance may not purport to alter or even authoritatively represent existing law, in practice it can have a significant impact on both the general understanding of competition law in the future and the behaviour of regulated firms. Competition authorities generally conduct future enforcement activity in accordance with these statements, and indeed principles of legal certainty and legitimate expectations may require authorities to adhere closely to these guidelines.[48] Firms often tailor their own behaviour to act in conformity, because, regardless of whether such guidance accurately represents the settled law, compliance may avoid public enforcement or provide a plausible defence in private actions. In this manner, the driving force behind the development of competition law shifts from a judicial 'case-bound'[49] approach to one determined, to a greater or lesser extent, by policy preferences of the competition agency.[50]

b. *Ex ante* enforcement

The conventional distinction between *ex ante* regulatory and *ex post* antitrust enforcement is recurrent though not undisputed.[51] In parallel with the adoption of more bureaucratic public-enforcement mechanisms, another element of regulatory competition law is a perceived shift in the temporal nature of enforcement from conventional *ex post* implementation towards an *ex ante* framework.[52] Bureaucratic enforcement is viewed as a forward-looking enterprise that focuses on the optimal structure and operation of the market, rather than on the identification and prosecution of past anticompetitive conduct.[53] Accordingly, regulatory competition law aims to control in advance the market activity of firms in the future, and is, in this sense, closer to the prescriptive (rather than proscriptive) model of regulation.

Negotiated settlements and administrative guidance again each play a pivotal role within this temporal switch. Settlement permits competition authorities to influence the future behaviour and/or structure of individual firms, as firms might accept positive obligations that bind them prospectively. Moreover, negotiated settlements often do not contain

[48] For general consideration of the role of 'soft law' instruments in the context of EU competition law, see Stefan (2012).

[49] Larouche (2000:122).

[50] Weber Waller (1998).

[51] See pp. 43–4.

[52] Ibáñez Colomo (2010:264–8); Monti (2008:139–41); Weber Waller (1998:1394); Cave & Crowther (2005).

[53] First (1995:9).

definitive conclusions about the legality of past behaviour, but instead are limited to the determination of adequate prospective solutions for existing problems. Administrative guidance influences more broadly the pattern of future public (and, indirectly, private) enforcement. Such guidance serves to clarify and develop the general competition rules, thus providing firms with a clearer and more detailed understanding of their on-going, though residual, obligations under competition law. The increasing use of economic analysis may also contribute to this *ex ante* enforcement model, insofar as it requires a prospective analysis regarding the future best performance of markets.[54] In each instance, the effect is essentially the same: shifting the focus of enforcement efforts from *ex post* censure to *ex ante* improvement.

This shift in emphasis has a number of noteworthy practical consequences. The competition agency may find that it not only has to identify problematic firm behaviour or structures, but also has to devise appropriate substitute arrangements, which, furthermore, must be sufficiently sensitive yet robust to remain effective as the market evolves. The extent to which this empowers enforcers to impose 'best' market outcomes is considered later. In any event, the competition agency may then be required to 'pick winners' in such circumstances, a task that is anathema to conventional antitrust approaches, as well as one that is fraught with practical difficulties and arguably even vulnerable to abuse, as public-choice scholars would contend.[55] The existence of enumerated obligations for a firm that agrees a negotiated settlement can also change the emphasis of future competition scrutiny, whereby compliance is measured by reference to the settlement terms rather than the underlying competition rules.[56] Similarly, the presence of *ex ante* administrative guidelines provides an additional yardstick for *ex post* scrutiny of allegedly anticompetitive business behaviour.[57]

c. Prescriptive competition law doctrines

The emergence of regulatory competition law has challenged the assumption that antitrust imposes only proscriptive duties on a firm by

[54] Melamed (1995:15); Ibáñez Colomo (2010:293).

[55] Considered in detail in the next chapter, p. 145.

[56] Consider the approach of the European Commission in imposing a fine for non-compliance with the *Microsoft (Tying)* commitment decision (OJ C 120/15, 26.04.2013).

[57] See, again, Stefan (2012).

prohibiting discrete forms of anticompetitive behaviour, whereas prescriptive or affirmative obligations of market conduct must be imposed through sector-specific regulation. In practice, certain antitrust doctrines involve the imposition of what are, effectively, affirmative obligations, particularly in respect of unilateral conduct by firms with market power. Prescriptive theories of competition law can therefore result in quasi-regulatory outcomes, even in the context of private enforcement. A tacit link between procedural and substantive aspects of competition law-as-regulation can also be discerned, insofar as negotiated settlement procedures are used not infrequently to conclude antitrust investigations concerning novel or more controversial case theories, a point we consider further later.

The clearest examples of such prescriptive competition doctrines are the regulation of anticompetitive refusals to deal, including the 'essential facilities' doctrine,[58] and the prohibition on excessive prices. Under the former, a dominant firm can be required to transact with competitors in order to resolve market bottlenecks, whereas antitrust prohibitions of very high prices tend to replicate the traditional rate-setting functions of sector-specific utilities regulators. Notably, such quasi-regulatory obligations are imposed via the substance of competition law, and are not merely an ancillary outcome of enforcement. Perhaps unsurprisingly, such competition theories are controversial, particularly to the extent that they seek to 'level the playing field' of competition by requiring a dominant firm to positively seek to assist competitors, or again oblige competition adjudicators to pick winners amongst rivals. Claims for mandatory access or regulation of high prices are, arguably, more readily accommodated within an explicit market regulation framework, and, in this regard such theories may represent the boundaries of competition law.

d. Regulatory remedies

As a corollary of the argument that competition law can impose positive regulatory-type obligations on firms, corresponding quasi-regulatory remedies may be required to administer such duties. Typically, the conventional antitrust model uses a remedial framework that involves a mixture of compensatory (e.g., private damages), punitive (e.g., public

[58] Hellwig (2009:211): '[a] rule that forbids the denial of access is not really a prohibition. The objective of this rule is to induce the granting of access, that is, to prescribe a specific behaviour'. See also Ibáñez Colomo (2010:268–76).

fines or exemplary damages), and prohibitive (e.g., cease-and-desist obligations) elements. Conversely, remedies that require on-going implementation or monitoring, which might be appropriate within sector-specific regulation, have, conventionally, been viewed as incompatible within competition enforcement.[59]

Linked to the greater use of prescriptive competition doctrines, however, and facilitated by consensual settlement procedures, the application of quasi-regulatory remedial obligations is another recurrent theme of the shift towards competition law-as-regulation. Where, for example, an affirmative duty to deal is imposed, a detailed remedial scheme is usually required to ensure that resulting access rights are realisable in practice. Even competition rules that, in theory, merely prohibit anticompetitive conduct may require on-going remedies. Rules that prohibit excessive prices, for instance, typically require the competition adjudicator to determine a 'reasonable' price for the future, and possibly to monitor the defendant's future pricing practices to verify compliance. Courts are often loath to undertake such a regulatory role, and thus delegate, where permitted, to any available sector-specific regulator.[60] Negotiated settlements create the possibility that a defendant may, voluntarily, agree to assume quasi-regulatory market obligations, as well as, potentially, the establishment of a regulator-like monitoring body.[61] The interconnectedness of the regulatory shift within competition law is again discernible, as the arguably greater scope for the application of more prescriptive competition theories within the context of negotiated settlement proceedings further increases the need for (and capacity to craft) regulatory-type remedies.

e. Mandating 'best' solutions

Finally, the conventional model of competition law addresses, ostensibly, discrete instances of anticompetitive private behaviour. Certain commentators have argued, however, that legal standards employed to assess the compatibility of firm behaviour under a more regulatory conception of competition law may, in some instances, require the *most*

[59] Areeda & Hovenkamp (2006: ¶325a,p. 8). [60] Speta (2003:133–5).

[61] A well-known example is the AT&T consent decree of 1982, considered at pp. 63–4, which required on-going monitoring by federal courts until replaced by the Telecommunications Act of 1996.

procompetitive market outcome, rather than the simple prohibition of indisputable anticompetitive behaviour.[62] In the United States, this viewpoint is expressed most forcefully by Devlin, who argued that adoption of a 'least restrictive alternative' standard under the rule-of-reason analysis within US antitrust requires courts to search for the single most efficient market outcome possible, as opposed to permitting any welfare-enhancing arrangements.[63] He concluded that such an approach is regulatory rather than antitrust-focused.[64] Within EU competition law, Monti suggested that theories of antitrust liability such as the rules against excessive prices and refusals to deal effectively compel competition-enhancing behaviour by dominant firms, rather than merely prohibiting anticompetitive conduct.[65] He acknowledged the often-laudable aims of substantive regulatory competition law – to ensure the greatest possible benefits to consumers – but argued that this goes beyond the purpose of competition law as such, namely, to deter firms from acting unlawfully.[66] Similarly, Lianos criticised the disjuncture that can arise between the theory of competition harm deployed and the remedies imposed – invoking the Birksian concept of 'discretionary remedialism'[67] – as incompatible with the principle of proportionality. Where more robust solutions are required, either a more closely aligned theory of antitrust harm or a wholly different legal instrument such as regulation should be used instead.[68]

For the purposes of this work, of greatest interest is the search for 'best' solutions, but also, potentially, at its most contentious, where regulatory antitrust overlaps with existing regulatory structures. We saw earlier how, in the absence of effective economic regulation in the airports and payment card system sectors, the Commission applied competition law to similar effects, leading, subsequently, to calls for more formalised regulatory structures within these markets. Arguably more problematic, however, is the application of competition law to overreach or usurp the existing regulatory framework, an issue considered in detail in Chapter 4, and also touched upon later in this chapter in the context of the strategic deployment of antitrust commitment decisions by the Commission to restructure EU energy markets.

[62] Devlin (2012); Melamed (1995); Ibáñez Colomo (2010); Larouche (2000:319).
[63] See also Feldman (2009). [64] Devlin (2012:830). [65] Monti (2007:216–17).
[66] Monti (2007:243). [67] Lianos (2012:197). [68] Lianos (2012).

f. Regulatory competition law: jurisdictional variations

Accordingly, competition law becomes regulatory in nature when it incorporates certain procedural or substantive elements that are more closely associated with regulation. Regulatory competition law does not, typically, dispense entirely with antitrust's conventional objectives of securing competitive markets and efficiency; what differs is the manner in which competition law is deployed to achieve these, and perhaps other, goals. The extent to which this identified shift has materialised may differ between jurisdictions and modes of enforcement. The adoption of an administrative enforcement model by competition authorities renders public enforcement more vulnerable to this regulatory turn than private enforcement, for example, albeit the latter is usually concluded through private contract (settlement) rather than through comprehensive litigation. Conversely, quasi-regulatory case theories, such as the essential facilities doctrine, provide private plaintiffs with powerful legal mechanisms by which to restructure markets for personal benefit. Criminal competition enforcement remains the exception to this regulatory shift, generally retaining a wholly legalistic enforcement framework and standards of proof.[69]

The notion that competition law has moved towards a regulatory paradigm is also perhaps more novel, and controversial, in the US than in the EU context. From its origins, US antitrust enforcement was a predominantly judicial enterprise, with both private and DOJ enforcement occurring through the courts, supplemented by the administrative FTC procedure. The EU competition model, by contrast, has historically utilised centralised administrative enforcement procedures, albeit incorporating an adversarial decision-making process. At a doctrinal level, moreover, EU law may appear rather more regulatory in character than US antitrust, particularly towards unilateral conduct. Article 102 TFEU is largely unconcerned with creation of dominance, for example, and instead prefers to regulate dominance when acquired.[70] EU competition law also incorporates an important additional, non-efficiency-focused objective: development of the internal market.[71] Nonetheless, such distinctions ought not to be overstated. Recent reforms within EU law have decreased its regulatory impulses, including efforts to increase private enforcement,[72] abolition of the notification system and the

[69] Crane (2011:120–1). [70] Fox (2002:393); Hovenkamp (2010:241).
[71] Larouche (2000:353–6); Amato (1997). [72] See p. 25.

decentralisation of enforcement more generally,[73] and the movement towards a greater economic focus with an implicit diminished scope for integration concerns to trump efficiency.[74] Within the USA, the impact of the *Trinko* decision,[75] considered in Chapter 4, may represent a shift away from regulatory competition law in doctrinal terms,[76] although the decision says little about the procedural regulatory turn within public enforcement. The substantive legal framework of both EU and US competition law moreover remains the same, with each formally requiring identification of individual acts of anticompetitive conduct to ground liability. Such an approach stands in clear contrast to the archetypal regulatory enquiry, which, in theory, seeks to remedy identified market problems without attribution of liability. Thus, claims (and criticisms) of a modern 'regulatory turn' arise in both the US and EU systems.[77] Within each jurisdiction, the use of certain public-enforcement procedures plus adoption of quasi-regulatory enforcement standards, case theories and remedies have blurred the ostensible line, to a greater or lesser extent, between competition law and the regulatory enterprise. We turn now to a critical question: whether this is a positive, or at least benign, development.

(ii) The pros and cons of regulatory competition law

Plausible arguments can be advanced in favour of regulatory competition law, alongside rather robust criticisms of this approach. We consider, first, the two principal justifications that might be invoked: pragmatism and effectiveness. The *pragmatic* justification acknowledges that competition law, as it has been enforced, applied and interpreted in the EU and US and other jurisdictions, has developed as a body of law with certain quasi-regulatory characteristics that supersede its legalistic foundations. The mere fact that, for example, competition law can be enforced *ex ante* or imposes affirmative obligations says nothing, in and of itself, about the legitimacy or value of the market-supervisory enterprise.[78] As explained in Chapter 1, from a legal perspective the competition rules are broadly

[73] See pp. 24–5. [74] See pp. 31–2.

[75] *Verizon Communications, Inc.* v. *Law Office of Curtis V. Trinko*, 540 US 398 (2004).

[76] Weber Waller (2009:24–5); Barnett (2009:33).

[77] For a US perspective, see, e.g., First (1995); Melamed (1995); Weber Waller (1998); Devlin (2012). For a EU perspective, see, e.g., Larouche (2000); Monti (2008); Ibáñez Colomo (2010).

[78] Ibáñez Colomo (2010); see also Robertson (2009:111).

and abstractly drawn. The drafters of the Sherman Act, and latterly the Treaty of Rome, allowed considerable scope and a large margin of discretion for the development of the content of these rules through their application. US antitrust is treated largely as common law,[79] and has evolved almost beyond recognition over the decades of its existence. Although the more textually prescriptive nature of Articles 101 and 102 TFEU limits EU competition law's scope for radical reform,[80] adoption of the 'more economic approach' in recent years, for instance, demonstrates its potential for progressive development.[81] Given that the appropriate content of these rules cannot be determined *a priori* from their underlying legal structure, policy choices are unavoidable in formulating or fleshing out the content of these rules. Under this approach, regulatory competition law becomes an artefact of legal evolution rather than a policy prescription.

Additionally or alternatively, the *effectiveness* justification suggests that incorporation of quasi-regulatory elements within competition law might be seen, in itself, as a positive phenomenon. Given the abstract nature of antitrust, the policy choice to incorporate regulatory components is not merely defensible but commendable, insofar as this provides the most effective means by which to address market problems that comprise its core concern. A distinction must be made between regulatory public enforcement, and quasi-regulatory duties and remedies in this regard. The use of quasi-regulatory procedures by competition agencies arguably facilitates more efficient public-enforcement practices. Both firms and enforcement agencies favour negotiated settlements on grounds of procedural economy and as a mechanism for managing risk. Administrative guidelines similarly contribute to legal certainty, and may function as an *ex post* restraint on the enforcement discretion of competition authorities.[82] Negotiated settlements and administrative guidance both have their origins in established competition law and practice; therefore, at most these practices represent an explication or progressive development of existing law. To the extent that regulatory competition law is confined to public-enforcement activity, this minimises the risk that private interests might hijack expansive conceptions of competition law. Moreover, the 'expert' nature of the public antitrust agencies arguably counterbalances the absence of judicial scrutiny: the adversarial

[79] Hovenkamp (2005:44). [80] See, e.g., the discussion on excessive prices at pp. 124–5.
[81] See pp. 31–2. [82] Robertson (2009:112); First (1995:11); Larouche (2000:127–8).

procedure is more readily dispensable because, quite simply, public enforcers are more likely to get the antitrust assessment right.

These limiting safeguards are not available in relation to our second category of quasi-regulatory competition doctrines and remedies. The elaboration of more demanding antitrust duties might be justified, nonetheless, on the basis that it increases the ability of the law to reach and provide solutions for market failures such as natural monopolies and exploitative abuses. Here, too, considerations are pragmatic. Such market problems might be more appropriately addressed through sector-specific regulation. Yet, in the absence of a regulatory solution or perhaps even the political capacity to enact one, general welfare is better protected by a regulatory deployment of antitrust rather than by allowing market problems to persist. Under this view, regulatory competition law is a second-best solution, but at least it provides a solution of sorts.

Yet regulatory competition law finds few defenders amongst antitrust scholars. Four broad objections have been advanced, focusing on respect for the separation of powers, problems of legitimacy and maintenance of the rule of law, fears of error costs in analysis, and the risk of politicisation of competition law, which we will consider in turn.

a. Separation of powers

The separation-of-powers doctrine has been invoked as a threshold objection to regulatory competition law.[83] The determination of whether breach of the competition rules has occurred is properly considered a judicial or adjudicative function, whether performed by the ordinary courts, by specialist competition tribunals, or by an administrative body, such as the European Commission or FTC, with quasi-judicial powers. The enactment of regulation is, by contrast, a legislative task, whereas its implementation is, typically, a delegated executive function. In formulating regulation, the legislature makes political choices regarding the desired content; these choices are incorporated within the substance of the regulatory regime, and from this the regulator derives its policy-focused mandate for action. Thus, it has been argued that competition authorities or other adjudicative bodies enforcing competition law should not apply or sanction its use to create *de facto* regulation, given that this is a legislative task rather than an executive or judicial function. This objection is essentially constitutional: the executive and judiciary

[83] Easterbrook (1987:33); Malone & Sidak (2007:485–9); Werden (2009:75); Epstein (2007:36).

should not usurp the prerogatives of the legislature. In particular, it is feared that competition law-as-regulation permits one branch of government to gain an advantage over another,[84] either to circumvent a decision to replace market competition with regulation,[85] or to regulate through competition law in the absence of sector-specific regulation.[86] This objection is an absolute one: the executive and judiciary cannot regulate, therefore they cannot, *inter alia*, regulate through competition enforcement.

Criticisms of regulatory competition law on this basis have tended to occur, most forcefully, in the context of US antitrust,[87] where, particularly with respect to public enforcement by the DOJ, there is a relatively distinct division of labour between the legislature, executive and judiciary. In the EU context, the separation-of-powers question is complicated by the broad array of functions performed by the Commission. In addition to its prosecutorial and adjudicative functions under competition law, the Commission possesses the right of legislative initiative, including with respect to sector-specific regulation that might alter the functioning of markets, or even provide an alternative to competition enforcement. The Commission tends to deploy its powers in a holistic manner to mutually reinforcing effect. With respect to ground-handling services, as we saw, the Commission initially pursued a policy of competition enforcement against airport operators in order to generate political support for subsequent EU-wide regulation of such services.[88] When competition enforcement against very high roaming charges for mobile telephone services proved untenable, the Commission opted instead, with approval of the Parliament and Council, for direct price regulation, an approach explored in the next chapter.[89] This apparent complementarity becomes more problematic, however, if the subsequent application of competition law undermines the regulatory accord, an objection that may be levelled against the EU's energy sector commitment decisions, considered later in this chapter. While the separation of powers might not provide a compelling, wholly unqualified objection to regulatory competition law, it nonetheless casts doubt upon its enforcement in a manner that effectively subverts the democratic process.

[84] Easterbook (1987:33).
[85] Monti (2008:141); Larouche (2000:356–8); Breyer (1987:1044).
[86] Werden (2009:75); Sidak (2008:279). [87] See p. 89, fn. 83. [88] See pp. 73–4.
[89] See pp. 179–85.

b. Legitimacy and the rule of law

Regulatory competition law is also challenged in substantive terms. First, it has been argued that the development of competition law beyond its abstract general prohibitions is legitimised by the 'case-bound' nature of the law-making process.[90] Competition law is made through litigation, in essence, which involves an adjudicative procedure with strong rights of defence, a duty to state reasons for decision-making, and a right of judicial review. These limits constrain the otherwise substantial discretion granted to the decision-maker by the open-textured nature of antitrust, while the adversarial procedure subjects case theories to rigorous scrutiny to ensure realistic decision-making and the emergence of good law.[91] The antitrust rules that emerge from regulatory public-enforcement mechanisms, such as negotiated settlements and administrative guidance, are not, however, subject to such disciplining, and consequently legitimising, processes.[92] The (usual) absence of an adversarial hearing,[93] and the generally constrained scope for appeal against such determinations, limit opportunities to test the legal robustness and economic coherence of promulgated rules. The transparency of decision-making is furthermore compromised by the opacity of the administrative process.[94] Compliance with the rule of law cannot be verified, therefore, and the legitimacy of the resulting law is compromised.

The legitimacy of regulatory competition law case theories and remedies has also been challenged. When applying such theories, competition adjudicators are required to make what are, effectively, regulatory determinations. This is, arguably, an inappropriate activity for institutions that performs what is, essentially, a judicial function.[95] The complex, market-dependent data and resource-intensive nature of regulatory decision-making is well recognised, meaning that courts and even competition authorities are not particularly well-equipped to perform these functions,[96] although public consultation or

[90] Larouche (2000:122). [91] Larouche (2000:119–23).

[92] Larouche (2000:127–8); First (1995:11);

[93] As considered later in this chapter, negotiated settlements may be concluded after a merits hearing in a competition investigation, which alleviates somewhat this concern. Similarly, where proposed administrative guidelines are subjected to public scrutiny under a consultation procedure, this serves to test the viability and desirability of proposed rules, although it provides a weak proxy for the contextualised rigours of an adversarial procedure.

[94] First (1995:11); Larouche (2000:401). [95] Larouche (2000:318–19).

[96] Larouche (2000:401–2); Laffont & Tirole (2000:278).

market-testing may go some way towards resolving these information deficits. In addition, although the ability of regulators to exercise discretion in making such determinations is generally restricted by the regulatory mandate, competition authorities or courts that exercise regulatory antitrust powers are not subject to these limitations.[97] To the extent that regulators are permitted or required to take account of non-efficiency considerations, moreover, these powers derive from their regulatory mandate.[98] No equivalent authority can be derived from competition law, and so competition adjudicators lack a democratic mandate for action.[99] This is particularly problematic to the extent that public enforcers choose to apply competition law to further broader social objectives outside the realms of antitrust as such, for example market liberalisation. Indeed, liberalisation presents an interesting dilemma in this context: whilst related to wider themes within competition policy, it is not mandated by competition law orthodoxy, and, furthermore, faces vigorous criticism from many quarters. The pursuit of liberalisation through competition enforcement thus ignores the vitally important political dimension to this social choice.

This links to further risk, identified by Larouche, that the regulatory use of competition law creates scope, and a concomitant danger, that it might be 'instrumentalised' – that is, deployed to further objectives lying outside the purview of competition law, such as market liberalisation.[100] Such instrumentalisation may lead an undesirable 'feedback effect', namely unprincipled expansion of existing competition rules to serve regulatory purposes.[101] The instrumental use of competition law is challenged on the basis that it violates the principle of legal certainty because it leads to alteration of established standards for intervention (a proportionality problem),[102] and that the manipulation of competition law to serve regulatory objectives may crystallise into bad law going forward (a coherence problem).[103] Where application of these expanded principles is confined only to the market concerned, this damages the internal consistency of competition law. Conversely, if these principles become standard competition rules, this may result in inefficient outcomes when applied outside the original market context,[104] an issue considered

[97] Monti (2008:141); Larouche (2000:124). [98] Larouche (2000:124).
[99] Geradin & O'Donoghue (2005:395).
[100] Larouche (2000:353–6); see also Ibáñez Colomo (2010:277); Veljanovski (2008).
[101] Auf'mkolk (2012:150). [102] Ibáñez Colomo (2010:277–9).
[103] Larouche (2000:353–6). [104] Auf'mkolk (2012:153–4).

further in the next part. Ultimately, it had been argued persuasively that the almost-clandestine use of competition law indirectly to achieve regulatory objectives risks undermining public confidence in the fairness and utility of the competition law enterprise as a whole.[105]

c. Error costs and bad bargains

Regulatory competition law risks resulting not merely in bad law; it might also lead to inefficient and thus counterproductive market outcomes.[106] The first concern that emerges from the commentary relates to error costs, and a fear that more expansive doctrines of competition liability unnecessarily restrict the parameters of the area of acceptable conduct. In doing so – in effect, by requiring allocative efficiency – the development of regulatory competition law may destroy dynamic efficiency by inhibiting innovation and investment.[107] Given the complex nature of regulatory decision-making, Type I errors (false positives) are viewed as more likely and more dangerous; this inherent structural deficiency within the decision-making process indicates the need for restraint. Certain commentators take particular issue with the suggestion that competition law might secure equality of opportunity for all competitors in a market, an inherent assumption of the refusal-to-deal doctrine.[108] As Devlin argued, in perhaps overly emphatic terms:

> If one adopts the increasingly prevalent view that antitrust must facilitate unfettered access to markets, thus spurring free entry and expansion by incumbent rivals . . . [competition law] goes from being a prophylactic device aimed at protecting consumers against welfare-reducing acts to being a misguided regulatory tool that potentially sacrifices both consumer welfare and efficiency in a misguided pursuit of more of both.[109]

The danger of false-positive outcomes in antitrust enforcement and the concomitant suspicion that this risk might be overstated are core debates within competition law more broadly, which will be considered further in Chapter 4. Such concerns are not, accordingly, limited to the quasi-regulatory context, but rather sound an overarching cautionary note about the potential pitfalls of any departure from the classic *laissez-faire* model of antitrust. The more directly and intensively that competition enforcers – or even antitrust doctrine – are involved in the functioning of a market, the greater the possibility that a mistake might be made in

[105] Larouche (2000:319). [106] See, generally, Ginsburg & Wright (2013).
[107] Devlin (2012:850–2). [108] Ibáñez Colomo (2010:283). [109] Devlin (2012:830).

assessing the presumed optimal market outcome. Such concerns must be balanced against the need to secure the effectiveness of antitrust supervision, and, ultimately, the protection of consumer welfare.

A second economic concern relates more specifically to negotiated settlement processes. Absent robust scrutiny of any concluded settlement procedure, there is a risk that defendant firms will commit to sub-optimal market arrangements, particularly when effects on third parties are taken into account.[110] The extent to which negotiated settlements can influence future competition enforcement is controversial. Although settlements are essentially private agreements,[111] under the regulatory approach to competition law such administrative practice serves to guide future competition cases. Yet compromise is inherent within negotiated settlements, so that concessions accepted by one firm may prove to be sub-optimal if applied in future cases. This links back to the legitimacy objection that negotiated settlements are rarely subject to robust scrutiny at trial or on appeal, meaning that unduly burdensome competition theories and inefficient remedies might, inadvertently, enter the general competition framework. This suggests that, to the extent that negotiated settlements are private agreements that reflect individual compromises, these should not simultaneously be treated as authoritative statements of competition law's scope or requirements. Although competition law might legitimately be enforced, in individual cases, in a manner that reflects such private preferences, provided that it succeeds in its task of prohibiting anticompetitive conduct to protect general consumer welfare, the law itself ought not to be established or advanced in such a manner.

The final concern under this heading is one that affects regulation more generally: the argument that regulatory remedies can be unduly static in nature, which makes them vulnerable to changes in market conditions that render regulatory solutions less effective or even a source of inefficiency.[112] The relative weakness of regulatory remedies is thrown into sharper relief, moreover, when contrasted with the (assumed) competition-enabling nature of one-shot antitrust remedies. Regulatory competition law might therefore fail to respect the basic tenet of antitrust that competition should be preferred where possible. The decision to regulate is, moreover, one with its own cost/benefit calculations and safeguards, and is generally the province of officials with special expertise in the sector. Within regulatory policy-making, for example, the 'better

[110] Melamed (1995:14). [111] Easterbrook (1987:25). [112] De Bow (1987).

regulation' movement has sought to address some of the conventional criticisms of inefficiency or ineffectiveness within the regulatory enterprise. Regulation by antitrust thus brings some of the risks of regulation without necessarily incorporating the safeguards that protect its quality standards. The soundness of this concern (alongside the validity of objections to the regulatory enterprise to more generally) is not one that can be assessed in the abstract, however, and instead depends on, amongst other things, the particular regulatory mechanisms utilised and the nature of the market problems to be addressed.

d. Politicisation

The final objection is the most pragmatic: that is, a fear that the movement from legalistic competition law to competition law-as-regulation renders the law itself more vulnerable to political pressures and influence.[113] If antitrust becomes regulation and not strictly law – 'once the veneer of law enforcement is stripped away'[114] – then it becomes more susceptible to the typical criticisms of regulation. Accordingly, competition authorities may become more prone to regulatory capture; competition enforcement may be suppressed if it conflicts with the economic policies of the government in power; or the substance of the competition rules could be distorted or instrumentalised to secure other policy objectives. Thus, the move towards regulatory competition law is described as a Faustian bargain:[115] by gaining the advantages of the regulatory enterprise, competition law surrenders the protections of the legal one. Under this view, in order to protect the force of law behind competition law it is necessary to preserve its wholly legal character, rather than allow it to become a bureaucratic tool of market regulation.

Again, this fear is perhaps most potent in the US context, where senior officials of both federal antitrust agencies are political appointees, and the tenor of public enforcement has tended to vary with changes in government.[116] The mélange of functions granted to the European Commission under the EU treaties and secondary legislation suggests, by contrast, that the separation-of-powers model employed in the EU is less rigid, so the fact that the Commission might 'regulate' through application of its competition powers is neither entirely unanticipated nor unwelcome.

113 First (1995:11–12); Weber Waller (1998:1448).
114 Weber Waller (1998:1448).
115 Weber Waller (1998:1448).
116 See, e.g., the differing approaches taken by the DOJ under the Clinton and Bush administrations in the long-running *Microsoft* case, discussed by Melamed (2007).

The structure of the EU institutions also renders the Commission further removed from the intense political pressures of national government. As a result, it is arguably less vulnerable to pushback or interference from other branches of EU government than it would be within a more sharply delineated system. Nonetheless, political pressure – and the attendant compromise that this can necessitate – is not unknown within the context of EU competition enforcement,[117] or its market regulatory activities more generally.[118] Often, these pressures reflect less of a jostling for power and positioning within the 'domestic' EU system, and instead reflect more global power struggles between the EU and other international actors. Although relatively rare, such examples expose vulnerability within EU law regarding political influence and pressures, whether internal or external. Thus, the argument that a more politically charged deployment of EU competition law renders the Commission more exposed to political interference, while a perhaps remote possibility, remains a valid concern.

e. Assessing the pros and cons of regulatory competition law

Assessing the desirability and acceptability of regulatory competition law requires a balancing exercise of sorts. The potential benefits relate, primarily, to the short-range effectiveness of competition supervision, by increasing the scope for antitrust to correct and deter socially harmful market arrangements. These must be weighed against potential pitfalls, which challenge both the legitimacy and, potentially, the longer-term effectiveness of antitrust as it moves into the regulatory sphere. Rejecting regulatory competition law outright would confine antitrust to a narrow and relatively legalistic scope of application, which adheres closely to the *sui generis* crime-tort model envisaged by the Sherman Act. Permitting more regulatory conceptions of competition law at a procedural and/or doctrinal level creates a more powerful, and arguably more effective, tool for market supervision. We thus suggested that not only

[117] See e.g. the pressure exerted on the Commission by the US Senate to approve the merger of two US-based technology firms: Case COMP/M.5529 – *OracSun M/Sun Microsystems* (OJ C 91/7, 9.4.2010).

[118] See, e.g., the Commission's decision to 'stop the clock' on application of the EU Emissions Trading System Directive 2009/29/EC (OJ L 140/63, 05.06.2009) to flights that originate or land outside the EU, in response to serious and coordinated international opposition: *see* European Commission MEMO/12/854, 'Stopping the clock of ETS and aviation emissions following last week's International Civil Aviation Organisation (ICAO) Council', published 12 November 2012.

the inevitability but also the considerable practical utility of regulatory competition law marks this doctrinal shift as a positive development in many ways.

Yet regulation itself has been, frequently, a much-critiqued enterprise. Conventional regulation moreover incorporates various safeguards, and a degree of political accountability for wealth distributive choices, that are arguably absent in the case of competition law-as-regulation. The question is not, therefore, merely whether competition law can, in a particular scenario, depart from its narrow standard model; it must also be considered whether it is socially beneficial, on balance and all things considered, to do so. We therefore turn to consider further several concrete examples of this purported regulatory shift, namely the use of negotiated settlements in public enforcement, and the substantive doctrines of excessive prices and essential facilities. In so doing, our aims are to illustrate how this shift towards regulation arises in practice, to probe its rationale, and to assess the validity of the criticisms of regulatory competition law that have been considered in this part.

III. Procedural regulatory competition law: negotiated settlements

The archetype of public antitrust enforcement involves a formal finding of breach by one or more natural or legal persons, where penalties such as fines or imprisonment are imposed. Negotiated settlements, by contrast, typically involve a consensual process that results in agreement to modify a firm's behaviour or structure prospectively, but without any formal finding of antitrust violation or admission of liability. Within US antitrust, negotiated settlements called 'consent decrees' have been used to conclude public antitrust enforcement for over a century, with almost all such cases now concluded in this manner. A broadly equivalent procedure, the 'commitment decision', was introduced into EU law in 2004. As the preceding discussion indicated, negotiated settlements are considered to play a central role in the movement towards competition law-as-regulation, facilitating, *inter alia*, application of quasi-regulatory antitrust doctrines, implementation of quasi-regulatory remedies, the shift towards more consensual bureaucratic enforcement mechanisms, and, potentially, the realisation of non-antitrust goals. We consider, first, consent decrees as regulatory antitrust in the US context, in respect to which a well-developed jurisprudence and rich academic commentary exists. The newer EU procedure will then be explored in light of the US experience, considering in particular the use of commitment decisions within the EU energy sector. Our aim is to explore how and why negotiated settlements are 'regulatory' in character, and to give some consideration to the appropriateness of such usage of competition law.

(i) The American experience: consent decrees in US antitrust

Consent decrees are used by the federal antitrust authorities, the DOJ and FTC, to conclude civil antitrust actions on a consensual basis. As noted, the bulk of US antitrust enforcement occurs as private damages actions, which do not result in consent decrees; instead, private plaintiffs 'take their triple damage awards and run'.[119] The DOJ (but not the FTC) may also pursue antitrust investigations as criminal actions, and, again, consent decrees are unavailable in such cases. Civil enforcement by the DOJ involves suits in equity brought in federal court,[120] whereas the FTC pursues 'cease-and-desist' orders, equivalent to prospective equitable relief, under its administrative procedures.[121] Consent decrees, accordingly, enable (non-cartel) defendants to settle litigation through concessions agreed with the government agency.

Consent decrees as utilised by the DOJ are judicial orders, which must be approved by a federal court; whereas FTC decrees can be approved by the FTC Commissioners without additional judicial involvement. Under the Tunney Act,[122] DOJ decrees are subject to a public consultation procedure that is intended to prevent mere 'judicial rubber-stamping' of settlements;[123] following this, the court determines whether approval is in the public interest. This process has been praised as providing a mechanism by which to identify and deter abuse of process, increase public transparency, facilitate third-party input, and enable courts to

[119] Epstein (2007:6).

[120] The objective is to 'effectively pry open to competition a market that has been closed by defendants' illegal restraints': *International Salt Co.* v. *United States* 332 US 392 (1947), 401.

[121] Areeda & Hovenkamp (2006:¶325a, p. 3).

[122] Now 15 USC §16.

[123] *United States* v. *Microsoft Corporation* 56 F.3d 1448 (1995), 1458; see also Frankel (2008:553). There was concern, prior to enactment of the Tunney Act, that the DOJ was bowing to pressure from powerful private interests and agreeing to decrees that were inadequate to address the competition problems at issue; effectively, 'giving away the store': Easterbrook (1987:29).

eliminate ambiguous or unenforceable provisions *ex ante*.[124] Yet the extent to which federal judges review the substance of proposed decrees is disputed,[125] and, indeed, the appropriate scope of this judicial discretion is a contentious question.[126] In *Microsoft I*, the DC Court of Appeals held that courts should, generally, accept proposed relief if the resulting settlement is 'within the reaches of the public interest', which is distinct from the solution 'that will best serve society'.[127] The Court thus acknowledged the inherent tension within the Tunney Act process: rejection of a decree on the basis that greater concessions are available would force the competition agency either to drop the complaint entirely, leaving anti-competitive practices unremedied, or to pursue a case theory or seek remedies that it had deemed unnecessary or unwise.[128] Review under the Tunney Act remains a precondition for acceptance of any consent decree, but in reality presents a low hurdle where the government and defendant reach agreement on acceptable terms.[129] While FTC decrees are not subject to Tunney Act scrutiny,[130] the agency engages in a similar process of consultation and public-interest analysis prior to accepting any settlement.[131] FTC decrees routinely contain a standard clause waiving all rights to seek judicial review, however, meaning that petitions for review are virtually impossible.[132]

Why would a defendant – or, indeed, a government agency – opt against fighting a case, but instead choose to settle by consent decree? Settlement can provide considerable benefits for both enforcement agencies and firms under investigation. A key advantage is the procedural economy gains of settlement, in terms of both monetary and institutional resource savings: it is quicker and cheaper for both prosecutors and

124 Frankel (2008:550–1). 125 Elhauge (2008:28).

126 Given that, usually, consent decrees involve no finding of illegality, to permit a judge too much leverage in changing the terms of a decree would enable her to act without effective standards of legality: Areeda & Hovenkamp (2006:¶327e, p. 37).

127 *United States* v. *Microsoft Corporation*, 1460.

128 *United States* v. *Microsoft Corporation*, 1456.

129 Amendments to the Tunney Act in 2004 sought to reinforce the role of judicial oversight within the consent decree process, although, according to the DC District Court in *United States* v. *SBC Communications, Inc. and AT & T Corp*. 489 F.Supp.2d 1 (DDC, 2007), the 2004 amendments do not change the standard of review simply but make the procedure more prescriptive by, e.g., listing more factors for consideration.

130 The absence of a requirement for judicial consent may reflect the historical status of the FTC as an expert body, established specifically to determine appropriate remedies for unfair or deceptive trade practices: see Rosch (2011).

131 See FTC (2010a:6.11–.15). 132 16 CFR §2.32; see also Rosch (2011).

defendants to settle than to litigate fully. Enforcement agencies see benefit because the underlying market problems can be remedied more quickly than where a case is pursued to full trial. Assuming that the public interest is equally well served by correcting market failures rather than punishing antitrust transgressors, it may be sensible to prioritise the former under a consent decree over the latter in a drawn-out liability procedure. The DOJ expressly seeks relief that will 'stop the illegal practices alleged in the complaint, prevent their renewal, and restore competition to the state that would have existed had the violation not occurred',[133] and thus prioritises prospective improvements in competition over retrospective punishment of breach. The FTC, too, has an explicit preference for settlement: it aims 'to secure an effective order – by consent if feasible, or by litigation if necessary'.[134] Consent decrees are also easier to enforce if there is reoccurrence of prohibited behaviour, as the government can simply initiate clarification or contempt proceedings in federal district court, rather than filing – and proving – a fresh complaint.[135] A finding of contempt on this basis establishes only that the defendant breached the terms of the decree, however, saying nothing about the compatibility of its behaviour with substantive antitrust.[136]

For defendants, settlement provides a mechanism for managing risk. Settling an antitrust investigation avoids the risk of an adverse holding, while the defendant gains significant control over the remedies imposed. Crucially, the defendant also avoids collateral estoppel in follow-on actions for the same violation. Whereas a final antitrust judgment becomes *prima facie* evidence of guilt in subsequent private antitrust litigation, the antitrust rules expressly prohibit collateral estoppel for consent decrees,[137] and most consent decrees state explicitly that settlement is not an admission of guilt.[138] A defendant that chooses to pursue a public-enforcement action to trial thus does so in the knowledge that an adverse finding would facilitate follow-on actions by private plaintiffs. This, of course, makes settlement more attractive. A finding of breach by public enforcers in one jurisdiction may also encourage enforcement

[133] DOJ (2014:IV-50). [134] FTC (2010a:6.2).

[135] Areeda & Hovenkamp (2006:¶327, p. 25); (Broder (2010:189).

[136] *United States* v. *Armour & Co. et al.* 402 US 673 (1971), 674.

[137] 15 USC §16(a). See also *In re Microsoft Corp.* 355 F.3d. 322 (4th Cir. 2004), 328, and Hovenkamp (2011:645).

[138] Areeda & Hovenkamp (2006:¶327c, p. 29).

activity by authorities in other jurisdictions,[139] which further increases the value of settlement for risk-averse firms.

Consent decrees are settlements, nonetheless, which mean compromise.[140] Although the bargain struck is unlikely to represent the best deal that either side could potentially have achieved had the case gone to a final determination on the merits, the language of compromise suggests that such concessions are mutually beneficial.[141] The government agency furthers the public interest by restoring competition, while the firm avoids a unilateral finding of breach and the undesirable consequences that follow. A more critical approach would, however, portray compromise as a failure to protect rights: that is, the right of society to have antitrust violations punished, and the right of firms in compliance with antitrust to act independently. In this sense, settlement is 'avoidance' because '[t]o settle for something means to accept less than some ideal' in terms of justice.[142] The government might settle a case on excessively lenient terms because it is captured or coerced; or it may oppress a weaker defendant to extract disproportionate concessions or to resolve a dubious case.[143] In the antitrust context, the settlement compromise may present an inefficient outcome, involving either insufficient control of the victorious firm or unnecessary restraint of the losing one. Another pertinent criticism of settlement is that such arrangements do not produce concrete rules of law, but merely involve private bargains. Settlements therefore fail to develop the parameters of law or enrich its content. This problem may be particularly acute in the antitrust context, where prohibitions are broadly drawn, and where firms need a sufficiently clear prospective understanding of the law in order to avoid *ex post* prosecution. Easterbrook suggested that, where increased use of settlements leads to 'too few precedents', the resulting uncertainty encourages greater litigation, so that new precedents are created and settlement levels increase

139 Melamed (2007:301). 140 Easterbrook (1987:21).

141 The US Supreme Court expressly recognised the give-and-take nature of the process:

> The parties waive their right to litigate the issues involved in the case and thus save themselves the time, expense, and inevitable risk of litigation. Naturally, the agreement reached normally embodies a compromise; in exchange for the saving of cost and elimination of risk, the parties each give up something they might have won had they proceeded with the litigation.
>
> *United States* v. *Armour et al.*, 681.

142 Fiss (1984:1086). 143 See, generally, Yeung (2012:327–30).

again.[144] In the antitrust context, however, uncertainty might have the opposite effect. Antitrust rules are broadly drawn, standards of illegality have varied over time, and extra-legal policy considerations apply to a greater extent than in other legal areas. Uncertainty might therefore encourage defendants to settle, not because their conduct fits within recognised categories of wrongdoing, but because of a fear that existing legal standards are so malleable and indistinct as to allow *ex post* extension of those broad prohibitions to catch almost any conduct deemed undesirable by competition adjudicators.

a. The nature of consent decrees: accommodating bargains, novelty and regulation

Antitrust consent decrees have been divided, broadly, into three categories: decrees that apply established legal standards, decrees that develop more novel theories of antitrust harm, and decrees that predominantly regulate firm behaviour or the operation of markets.[145] Taking these categories in turn, we consider the extent to which consent decrees might be conceived as a form of regulatory antitrust, and whether such a designation might be problematic.

Given that consent decrees contain no findings of liability and thus, formally, establish no rules of law, such decrees do not contain authoritative statements of antitrust in the same manner as litigated judgments.[146] While a decree may say much about the permissible conduct of a particular market actor in the future, it establishes little about the parameters of antitrust more generally. Instead, consent decrees are, effectively, contractual bargains between enforcement agencies and defendants. It is generally accepted, nonetheless, that '[s]ettlements in the shadow of the law reflect the content of the law'.[147] Accordingly, the Supreme Court has sought to develop an approach to consent decrees that encapsulates this duality: part contract, part judicial decree. The Court rejects the view that consent decrees are merely contracts, instead emphasising a continuing quasi-judicial function resulting from their inherently judicial nature.[148] Yet, the origins of the decree in the contractual bargain between enforcement agency and firm must be acknowledged, alongside the importance of deferring to the substance

[144] Easterbrook (1987:26). [145] Weiner (1995). [146] Mengler (1988:327).
[147] Easterbrook (1987:25).
[148] *United States* v. *Swift & Co. et al.* 286 US 106 (1932), 115.

of that bargain in exercising its judicial scrutiny role.[149] While a consent decree is not wholly a private law instrument, in dealing with the substance of a decree courts are prepared to defer to the 'private' bargain embodied in its terms rather than to the substance of antitrust.[150] Moreover, because the content of consent decrees is not determined by antitrust alone, such instruments can potentially be used to address anticompetitive behaviour falling outside the established categories of antitrust infringement. Insofar as consent decrees are private bargains, the principle of freedom of contract mandates that the parties should be free to structure these arrangements however each deems most advantageous, provided that there are no public-policy concerns against judicial acceptance of an 'unconscionable' bargain. As consent decrees are not formal antitrust rules, furthermore, any novel case theory that underpins a consent decree does not gain acceptance as an established antitrust rule simply by virtue of its oblique inclusion in the decree. Even if the novel theory of liability is problematic, it is confined to a particular bargain rather than having broader effects. On this view, novelty does not prevent parties from adopting individualised private solutions to market problems, which may include distinctly quasi-regulatory, as opposed to purely antitrust-oriented, arrangements.

Using antitrust consent decrees to address behaviour that is not clearly incompatible with competition law raises difficult questions. The hybrid nature of consent decrees – part contract, part judicial order – places the novel theory encapsulated in the decree in legal limbo. Although not established as a rule of law, its inclusion confers greater weight than a merely speculative argument advanced in private litigation. It represents the considered view of the enforcement agency that such conduct violates antitrust and merits enforcement action, and, although the underlying antitrust claim does not receive judicial endorsement, the decree provisions that incorporate the novel case theory require court approval. This ambiguity creates uncertainty, which means that prudent firms

[149] In *United States* v. *Armour et al.*, 681–2, the Supreme Court held that 'the decree itself cannot be said to have a purpose; rather the parties have purposes, generally opposed to each other, and the resultant decree embodies as much of those opposing purposes as the respective parties have the bargaining power and skill to achieve'. In *US* v. *ITT Continental Baking Co.*, 420 US 223 (1975), 236–7, the Supreme Court went so far as to assert that, 'a consent decree or order is to be construed for enforcement purposes basically as a contract'.

[150] Although the private bargain is not binding on third parties, the decree becomes 'a fact of economic and legal life in this industry', which may impact upon, *inter alia*, subsequent private antitrust actions: *BMI* v. *CBS* 441 US 1 (1979), 13.

might be advised to respect the parameters established obliquely by the consent decree and not merely the limits of the recognised rules. Consequently, although the novel theory is not antitrust law as such, its inclusion within a consent decree may confer upon it the effect of restricting the commercial freedom of other firms, without any substantive legal basis for this result. A related criticism is that, where novel cases are resolved by consent decree, the underlying theory largely escapes judicial scrutiny and challenge. Absent robust review and critique, legally unsound or economically unreasonable theories might slip though the antitrust net, providing ostensibly valid grounds for future enforcement and gaining soft law status as established law. Without the check provided by a substantive adjudicative process, antitrust may develop in a manner inconsistent with sensible competition policy. The difficulty of creating effective and appropriate remedies for novel breaches is a connected problem.[151]

The issue of novelty within consent decrees thus remains controversial. A policy against settlement by decree, unless the alleged conduct would fairly certainly be illegal,[152] arguably best protects the integrity of public enforcement and substantive antitrust law. The simplicity of this approach, however, belies the difficult choices that it requires. Given that consent decrees are the principal means of case disposition for non-criminal public enforcement, an antitrust agency that identifies anticompetitive behaviour just beyond the established parameters of antitrust would face a significant dilemma. Either the agency would have to commit, *ex ante*, to litigate the case to final judgment even if the defendant would settle on terms that remedy the competition problem, or it must abandon the investigation leaving the competition problems unresolved. This unyielding choice not only interferes with the enforcement agency's discretion to determine the best use of its limited resources; the unavailability of the settlement procedure is moreover unfair to defendants prepared to settle, who are denied access to a settlement tool available where the infringement is more clear-cut. The wider social benefits of generating precedents to clarify the law would therefore come at the expense of parties that wish to minimise costs by settling, yet which are forced to litigate.[153]

What does this mean in terms of the use of consent decrees as a form of quasi-regulation? As discussed, consent decrees are considered to have

[151] Epstein (2007:15). [152] Melamed (1995:15). [153] Easterbrook (1987:28).

a central role in the perceived movement from an historical law-based model to the current regulation-based model within US antitrust.[154] Undoubtedly, the hybridised law-contract status of consent decrees, and the fact that decrees are largely disconnected from the constraints of conventional antitrust doctrine, contributes to a perception of antitrust settlements as a flexible tool for bureaucratic market governance, which is distinguishable from the legalistic model of antitrust enforcement. The content of consent decree remedies can differ markedly from typical litigated antitrust remedies, which tends to bring such instruments within the sphere of regulation. Remedies not infrequently go beyond the scope of what could be required under antitrust law: often the objective is not to address discrete instances of anticompetitive behaviour, but rather to improve the functioning of the market more generally. Decree provisions may place defendants under affirmative duties that require on-going monitoring to ensure compliance, and so many decrees also establish on-going judicial or governmental supervision mechanisms. The sometimes-static nature of settlement terms is another source of criticism. Although markets evolve constantly in dynamic waves of creative destruction, the decreed optimal behaviour of a firm as encapsulated in a consent decree with behavioural remedies is tied to particular market circumstances frozen at a particular point in time.[155] Recognising this genuine problem, the DOJ, in particular, has sought to limit the temporal impact of consent decrees, by incorporating 'sunset clauses' into all decrees concluded after 1979,[156] and to introduce a degree of flexibility, by progressively streamlining procedures for modification and termination of existing decrees.[157] Additionally, the process by which

[154] See e.g. First (1995:9–10); Melamed (1995:13–5); Weber Waller (1998:1409–17); Ginsburg & Wright (2013).

[155] As Epstein (2007:52) argued, provocatively, '[u]nder competition, the best party wins. Under an antitrust decree, the heavy hand of the law can destroy a wholly viable competitor'.

[156] DOJ (2014:III-146). This approach has been adopted by the FTC since 1994. The default position of the DOJ is that decrees should last for ten years, although alternative durations may be appropriate in special circumstances: DOJ (2014:IV-56). DOJ attorneys assigned to monitor compliance with existing decrees are, additionally, required to review the desirability of maintaining these in force, or whether modification or termination is preferable: DOJ (2014:III-146).

[157] Because DOJ consent decrees constitute court orders, modification or termination requires approval of the relevant court. A streamlined procedure for modification or termination, where appropriate, was introduced by the DOJ in 1999, and updated in 2014 to include a presumption in favour of vacating or modifying perpetual decrees absent evidence to the contrary: DOJ (2014:III-146–53).

decrees are agreed upon is primarily administrative rather than judicial or adversarial. While the argument is not (yet) that antitrust has become a purely regulatory exercise, current enforcement practice thus leans in this direction and away from a law enforcement model.[158] Regulatory consent decrees are not pure regulation, as such – but nor are these instruments antitrust in the traditional black-letter sense, either.

The on-going use of consent decrees to supervise, closely, the activities of the two largest collecting societies in the USA – the American Society of Composers, Authors and Publishers (ASCAP) and Broadcast Music, Inc. (BMI) – illustrates the potential for such instruments to be applied in a decidedly quasi-regulatory fashion. Collecting societies administer the collection of licensing fees for public performances of copyrighted works on behalf of copyright owners. Although such agencies can minimise transaction costs for artists and those who use their work, their activities have nonetheless been subject to antitrust scrutiny in numerous jurisdictions on the basis that collecting societies facilitate collusion over price-setting by apparent competitors. In 1941, the DOJ entered into consent decrees with ASCAP[159] and BMI,[160] placing limitations on the licensing provisions that each could apply. Remarkably, although each decree has undergone significant court-approved modification in the intervening period, both remain in force as the primary means of regulating the activities of these organisations almost three-quarters of a century later. The decree provisions include, since 1950 for ASCAP[161] and 1994 for BMI,[162] the appointment of rate-setting courts to determine licence fees, which has often involved close and on-going judicial involvement in the process of setting fees.[163] The complexity of the finely balanced competition issues persuades even those more sceptical commentators that regulation of some sort is necessary to secure effective performance,[164] and the enduring nature of the ASCAP and BMI decrees suggests that these instruments provide a workable, even if imperfect, solution. Nonetheless, as a mechanism of regulation, the decrees have faced criticisms. Given that each reflects, in essence, a private bargain, the weight of the regulatory burden imposed on each entity has not always been equal,

[158] Melamed (1995:13); Crane (2011:93–107).

[159] *United States* v. *ASCAP*, 1940–43 Trade Cases ¶56,104 (S.D.N.Y. 1941).

[160] *United States* v. *BMI*, 1940–43 Trade Cases ¶56,096 (E.D. Wis. 1941)

[161] *United States* v. *ASCAP*, 1950–51 Trade Cases ¶62,595 (S.D.N.Y. 1950)

[162] *United States* v. *BMI*, 1996–1 Trade Cases ¶71,378 (S.D.N.Y. 1994)

[163] Lunney (2010).

[164] See, e.g., Epstein (2007:32–4); Einhorn (2001).

a fact which, Epstein argued, directly benefitted the market performance of BMI, the less heavily regulated entity.[165] The limitations of what can be achieved by consent decrees – for instance, bargaining between the DOJ and defendant firms cannot result in the creation of a new administrative agency to oversee compliance – have also meant that administration of the decree provisions must occur through relatively inefficient judicial procedures.[166] This has been a serious drawback, given that the collecting societies have tended to act like typical regulated entities and thus resist efficient innovation unless forced to do so through judicial amendment of the relevant decrees.[167]

Intriguingly, US courts have effectively accepted this quasi-regulatory role for consent decrees. In *US* v. *BMI*, for example, the Second Circuit Court of Appeals, adjudicating on a rate-setting dispute arising from the BMI decree, recognised that the organisation was 'regulated by court-approved consent decrees', because of 'the inherently anticompetitive conditions under which [they] operate'.[168] Moreover, to date, in exercising the Tunney Act duty to review settlements in the public interest, no court has rejected a decree as being excessively regulatory in nature. The *AT&T* consent decree, considered in the preceding chapter, has been described as 'the ultimate regulatory decree in modern times',[169] yet it was approved with only minor modification.[170] The essentially regulatory nature of the monitoring process under the *AT&T* decree involved a federal district court judge, the DOJ and the FCC in a complex supervisory procedure, which meant that initial judicial approval was 'only the first chapter of a looming chain novel'[171] of supervision that continued until the Telecommunications Act in 1996. Nonetheless, the complexity in practice of administering the AT&T decree did not dissuade public enforcers from embracing regulatory schemes within later consent decrees, or courts from approving such arrangements. For better or worse, consent decrees facilitate the application of antitrust in a strategic manner to pursue market objectives, and in particular to achieve market structures, that would appear to sit, more comfortably, within the regulatory paradigm.

165 Epstein (2007:34). 166 Epstein (2007:36). 167 Lunney (2010:370).
168 *United States* v. *Broadcast Music, Inc.* 426 F.3d 91 (2nd Cir. 2005), 93.
169 Weber Waller (1998:1414).
170 *United States* v. *American Telephone & Telegraph Company et al.* 552 F.Supp. 131 (DDC, 1982).
171 Epstein (2007:67).

(ii) Commitment decisions within EU competition law

Next, we examine commitment decisions, the broadly equivalent negotiated settlement procedure within EU competition law introduced by Regulation 1/2003. Commitment decisions permit the Commission to conclude investigations into alleged breaches of Articles 101 or 102 TFEU without finding breach, based on binding commitments from the undertaking(s) concerned to modify market behaviour or make structural changes to address competition concerns. Although, previously, there was an informal Commission practice of accepting commitments in lieu of infringement decisions,[172] Regulation 1/2003 created a legal basis for this practice alongside a formal enforcement framework.[173] Much like consent decrees in the US context, introduction of the commitment procedure has been justified principally on grounds of procedural economy: the 'primary purpose of the commitment decision is to preserve effective competition and to obtain faster changes in the market for the future'.[174] Commitment decision similarly involve compromise by all parties: while there is no formal finding of breach in respect of apparent antitrust infringements, defendants are required to make often substantial behavioural or structural changes in return.[175] The same pragmatic considerations that motivate consent decrees nonetheless prompt settlement: namely, resource savings, a faster resolution of market problems,

[172] See, e.g., Commission Decision of 17 September 2001 in Case COMP/34.493 – *DSD* (OJ L 319/1, 4.12.2001), in which an agreement was cleared under Article 81(3) EC on the basis of undertakings by the firms involved, which were market tested before approval.

[173] The informal practice of accepting commitments was governed only by general principles of EU law: Wils (2006:347).

[174] Commission Staff Working Paper accompanying the Communication from the Commission to the European Parliament and Council, *Report on the functioning of Regulation 1/2003* (COM(2009)206 final), published 29 April 2009, p. 31.

[175] See the CJEU in Case C-441/07 P *Commission* v. *Alrosa Company Ltd* EU:C:2010:377. para. 48:

> Undertakings which offer commitments on the basis of Article 9 of Regulation No 1/2003 consciously accept that the concessions they make may go beyond what the Commission could itself impose on them in a decision adopted under Article 7 of the regulation after a thorough examination. On the other hand, the closure of the infringement proceedings brought against those undertakings allows them to avoid a finding of an infringement of competition law and a possible fine.

and, for defendants, the avoidance of fines, adverse publicity and follow-on actions.[176]

Article 9(1) of Regulation 1/2003 empowers the Commission to accept undertakings in lieu of a finding of breach, where 'the undertakings concerned offer commitments to meet the [competition] concerns expressed to them by the Commission'. Commitment decisions are unavailable in cartel cases, which can be concluded only through infringement decisions under Article 7 of Regulation 1/2003,[177] although a cartel-specific settlement procedure exists that provides a discounted fine for co-operation.[178] Before a commitment decision is taken, there must be *prima facie* evidence of breach of Article 101 or 102 TFEU.[179] Commitments offered can be behavioural or structural; they must address the competition concerns identified and be 'unambiguous and self-executing'.[180] Under Article 27(4) of Regulation 1/2003, proposed commitments are subject to a 'market-testing' process that has parallels to public consultations under the Tunney Act. With some regularity, market tests conducted to date have caused defendants to modify their proposed commitments in order to address further concerns identified by respondents. Market-testing might even indicate that the commitments offered are wholly unsuitable, with the result that defendants must provide a radically revised proposal to avoid infringement proceedings.[181] Unlike the Tunney Act procedure, however, the Commission does not require approval from the CJEU to conclude commitment decisions. Any commitments made binding must comply with the principle of proportionality, although, following the judgment in *Alrosa*, this requires only that commitments are suitable to address competition concerns and that no less onerous alternative commitments offered by the firm would also be suitable to achieve that objective.[182]

[176] Cook (2006:210–13); Cengiz (2011:135); Wagner-von Papp (2012:958–9).

[177] Recital 13 of the Preamble to Regulation 1/2003 states that '[c]ommitment decisions are not appropriate in cases where the Commission intends to impose a fine', which the Commission interprets to mean that this instrument should not be used in the cartel context: see also European Commission, *Notice on best practices for the conduct of proceedings concerning Articles 101 and 102 TFEU* (OJ C308/6, 20.10.2011) ('*Best Practices*'), para. 116.

[178] See Commission Regulation 622/2008 of 30 June 2008 amending Regulation 773/2004, as regards the conduct of settlement procedures in cartel cases (OJ L 171/3, 1.7.2008).

[179] *Best Practices*, para. 121.

[180] *Best Practices*, para. 127–8.

[181] As occurred during the procedures leading to Commission Decision in Case COMP/B-2/38.381 – *De Beers* (OJ L205/24, 27.7.2006).

[182] C-441/07 P *Commission* v. *Alrosa Company Ltd*, para. 41.

This deferential approach allows a generous margin of discretion to the Commission, and, as we shall see, enhances the potential for the Article 9 procedure to be used as a quasi-regulatory tool. By contrast, under Article 7, remedies imposed in infringement decisions cannot exceed what is necessary and suitable to address the competition problems. Finally, although commitment decisions involve a determination that there are no longer grounds for action,[183] the Commission is expressly precluded from reaching any conclusion as to 'whether or not there has been or still is an infringement'.[184]

As suggested, significant parallels exist between consent decrees and commitment decisions, meaning that it is instructive to consider the latter in light of the jurisprudence and commentary discussed in the preceding section. Commitment decisions, like consent decrees, occupy an uncertain place between formal statements of antitrust and private contracts.[185] Self-evidently, such decisions contain no formal findings of breach, and cannot provide any authoritative statements regarding the requirements or limits of competition law. The Commission has suggested, nevertheless, that its decisional practice under Article 9 should be treated, in subsequent national enforcement, as a reliable source of 'guidance' or 'orientation' as to the law's scope and requirements.[186] Use of the commitment procedure is not restricted to case theories that are clearly established under existing law, however, nor to remedies that can be imposed in infringement decisions. Substantive novelty is no bar to an Article 9 decision.[187] In *Rambus*, for example, the Commission premised its underlying Article 102 TFEU case on the concept of 'patent ambush', a wholly novel theory that avoided judicial scrutiny through inclusion in the negotiated settlement.[188] Similarly, more contentious theories of harm such as the rule against excessive prices or the essential facilities doctrine, which are typically disfavoured by public enforcers and difficult to prosecute successfully under the infringement procedure, have formed the basis for a surprising number of commitment decisions.[189] At the

[183] Article 9(1), Regulation 1/2003. [184] Recital 13, Regulation 1/2003.

[185] Wagner-von Papp (2012:933). [186] Commission *Staff Working Paper*, para. 109.

[187] Wagner-von Papp (2012:962–4).

[188] Commission Decision of 9 December 2009 in Case COMP/38.636 – *Rambus* (OJ C30/17, 6.2.2010).

[189] Excessive prices: Commission Decision of 15 November 2011 in Case COMP 39.592 – *Standard & Poor's* (OJ C31/8, 4.2.2012). Essential facilities: Commission Decision of 4 May 2010 in Case COMP/39.317 – *E.ON Gas* (OJ C278/9, 15.10.2010); Commission

level of remedies, the majority of decisions to date involved significant concessions from the undertakings concerned, including divestment of business units,[190] commitment to additional investment,[191] quasi-regulated pricing,[192] commitments regarding cooperation with competitors,[193] and alteration of standard contracting practices.[194] These remedies, in many instances, go considerably beyond the penalties or remedial action that could be imposed under Article 7 on equivalent facts. Although this divergence between commitment decision practice and established competition law has been criticised by commentators principally on rule-of-law grounds,[195] the substantial margin of discretion allowed to the Commission under the deferential standard of review adopted in *Alrosa* confirms that this expansive approach complies with EU law.

This flexibility, and particularly the capacity to diverge from conventional competition law and practice, accordingly creates scope for application of the commitment decision procedure in a quasi-regulatory manner. Combined with the Commission's practice of applying competition law to support liberalisation in certain sectors, negotiated settlements therefore take EU competition law into the realms of regulatory policy-making. This approach raises significant separation-of-powers issues, given the potential divergence between the legislative activity of the Council and Parliament, on the one hand, and the Commission's quasi-regulatory enforcement activity, on the other. A particularly clear, and perhaps problematic, example is seen in the strategic deployment of commitment decisions in the EU energy sector.

Decision of 18 March 2009 in Case COMP/39.402 – *RWE Gas Foreclosure* (OJ C133/10, 10.12.2009); Commission Decision of 29 September 2010 in Case COMP/39.315 – *ENI* (OJ C352/8, 23.12.2010).

190 *ENI*; *RWE Gas Foreclosure*; Commission Decision of 26 November 2008 in Case COMP/39.388 – *Germany Electricity Wholesale Market* and Case COMP/39.389 – *German Electricity Balancing Market* (OJ C36/8, 13.2.2009).

191 Commission Decision of 14 April 2010 in Case 39.351 – *Swedish Interconnectors* (OJ C142/28, 1.6.2010).

192 *Rambus*; *Standard & Poor's*; *Visa MIF*.

193 *E.ON Gas*; Commission Decision of 14 July 2010 in Case COMP/39/596 – *BA/AA/IB* (OJ C278/14, 15.10.2010).

194 Commission Decision of 11 October 2007 in Case COMP/B-1/37966 – *Distrigaz* (OJ C9/8, 15.1.2008); Commission Decision in Case COMP/39.386 – *Long-term contracts France* (OJ C133/5, 22.5.2010).

195 Temple Lang (2003:356); Wils (2006:351–2); Cengiz (2011:151–2); Wagner-von Papp (2012:937).

a. Commitment decisions and policymaking in the EU energy sector

European electricity and gas markets were, historically, characterised by high degrees of vertical integration, with a single, usually State-owned, entity performing all functions. While certain segments comprise natural monopolies (e.g., transportation, distribution), other activities (e.g., generation, retailing) are potentially competitive, provided that entrants can secure effective access to natural monopoly portions of the incumbent's infrastructure. Liberalisation to date has focused upon opening up these potentially competitive segments, with vertical separation as the central pillar. Initial EU-wide requirements were introduced via directives on electricity in 1996[196] and gas in 1998,[197] which aimed to create competition through third-party access to transmission and distribution systems. Within the electricity sector, Member States were required to establish a transmission system operator (TSO), with responsibility for operation, maintenance and development of transmission systems, and a distribution system operator (DSO) with equivalent responsibilities for distribution systems. Two further directives on electricity[198] and gas[199] in 2003 streamlined and strengthened the approach, by requiring legally unbundled TSOs and DSOs for both electricity and gas networks. Member States were also required to establish transparent, objective and non-discriminatory access procedures, administered by an independent national regulator.

Despite these efforts, the Commission's Energy Sector Inquiry in 2007 revealed significant difficulties with the process of liberalisation. Although some meaningful benefits had been realised, notably wider consumer choice and more cost-reflective prices, significant problems remained, including high wholesale market concentration, vertical foreclosure, a lack of integration and transparency, ineffective price

196 Directive 96/92/EC of the European Parliament and of the Council of 19 December 1996 concerning common rules for the internal market in electricity (OJ L 27/20, 30.1.1997).

197 Directive 98/30/EC of the European Parliament and of the Council of 22 June 1998 concerning common rules for the internal market in natural gas (OJ L 204/1, 21.07.1998).

198 Directive 2003/54/EC of the European Parliament and of the Council of 26 June 2003 concerning common rules for the internal market in electricity and repealing Directive 96/92/EC (OJ L176/37, 15.07.2003).

199 Directive 2003/55/EC of the European Parliament and of the Council of 26 June 2003 concerning common rules for the internal market in natural gas and repealing Directive 98/30/EC (OJ L176/57, 15.07.2003).

formation mechanisms including artificially low regulated tariffs, limited retail competition and uncompetitive balancing markets. In response, the Commission outlined a two-pronged strategy that utilised both antitrust and regulatory remedies.[200] It reasoned that key issues regarding market structure could be addressed successfully only through regulation, and, in this regard, it recommended mandatory ownership unbundling of vertically integrated infrastructure. This proposal was unpopular with certain Member States, however, and proved to be politically untenable. The Third Directives on liberalisation of the electricity[201] and gas[202] sectors, subsequently passed under circumstances of great political compromise,[203] therefore allow three options for unbundling: full ownership unbundling, an ownership-unbundled independent system operator, or a legally (but *not* ownership) unbundled system operator.

Although the Commission thus failed to achieve its goal of fully unbundled energy markets at the regulatory level, it has instead secured considerable concessions on ownership unbundling directly from incumbents energy firms through strategic antitrust enforcement under Article 9, thereby bypassing entirely the politically charged regulatory process. From 2007 onwards, the Commission pursued an active enforcement policy against alleged breaches of Article 102 TFEU by energy firms.[204] Examining the energy commitment decisions concluded to date, common themes emerge. Almost all addressed market problems that had arisen, directly or indirectly, from the vertically integrated nature of the dominant firm.[205] Several decisions involved long-term contracts with large customers[206]

[200] European Commission, *DG Competition Report on Energy Sector Inquiry* (SEC(2006) 1724), published 10 January 2007.

[201] Directive 2009/72/EC of the European Parliament and of the Council of 13 July 2009 concerning common rules for the internal market in electricity and repealing Directive 2003/54/EC (OJ L221/55, 14.08.2009).

[202] Directive 2009/73/EC of the European Parliament and of the Council of 13 July 2009 concerning common rules for the internal market in natural gas and repealing Directive 2003/55/EC (OJ L221/94, 14.08.2009).

[203] Boscheck (2009); Manoussakis (2009).

[204] *Distrigaz*; *E.ON Gas*; *ENI*; *RWE Gas Foreclosure*; *Long-term contracts France*; *Swedish Interconnectors*; *German Electricity Markets*; Commission Decision of 3 December 2009 in Case COMP/39.316 – *Gaz de France* (OJ C57/13, 9.3.2010), Commission Decision of 10 April 2013 in Case AT.39727 – *CEZ* (OJ C251/4, 31.8.2013).

[205] The principal outlier, *Swedish Interconnectors*, involved the State-owned operator of the Swedish electricity transmission network, where the largest electricity company is also State-owned. The alleged anticompetitive practices were designed to keep domestic electricity prices artificially low rather than exclude competition.

[206] *Distrigas*, *EDF*.

or supply contracts where the incumbent was a monopsony purchaser,[207] which allegedly prevented new entrants from gaining a foothold and thus foreclosed the market. Other cases alleged a *de facto* refusal to supply access to the incumbent's monopoly infrastructure despite existing regulatory access obligations. These purported refusals can be categorised, broadly, into two groups: those premised on a disproportionate allotment of transport capacity to the incumbent's subsidiaries,[208] and those premised on inadequate development or improper management of capacity resulting in artificial shortages.[209] This latter theory of harm – strategic underinvestment – is noteworthy, given that it goes far beyond the recognised parameters of the already contentious 'essential facilities' doctrine, discussed later, which itself occupies an unsettled position within EU competition jurisprudence.[210] The energy decisions demonstrate, additionally, a distinct preference for structural remedies. The Commission has, in certain cases, received commitments to divest full ownership of energy infrastructure, encompassing both generating capacity[211] and transport facilities.[212] It has thereby achieved, individually, a much greater degree of vertical separation than it proved possible to require, market-wide, by regulation. Other decisions have involved commitments that effectively strengthen the undertaking's regulatory sharing obligations, by, for example, freeing up additional capacity for rivals within the incumbent's infrastructure.

The energy decisions provide a remarkable example of the strategic use of competition law, and in particular the negotiated settlement procedure provided by Article 9 of Regulation 1/2003, to achieve market outcomes that are – as this example makes clear – more usually achieved through sector-specific regulation. Competition law was deployed, in this instance, to supplement or fill gaps in energy regulation, whether these had arisen due to inadequate implementation of regulation at the Member State level or political compromise at the EU level. It is difficult, moreover, to avoid the conclusion that competition law has been deployed in these instances to achieve a policy objective that lies outside

207 *German Electricity Markets.*

208 *E.On Gas; Gas de France; ENI.* In *CEZ*, the incumbent was alleged to have made disproportionate pre-emptive reservations in the independently owned electricity transmission system, thereby preventing potential competitors from accessing this facility.

209 *Gaz de France; ENI; RWE Gas Foreclosure; Swedish Interconnectors; German Electricity Markets.*

210 Case C-7/97 *Oscar Bronner GmbH* v. *Mediaprint Zeitungs* EU:C:1998:569, para. 41.

211 *Germany Electricity Markets, CEZ.*

212 *German Electricity Markets, RWE Gas Foreclosure; ENI.*

the immediate purview of antitrust, namely the furtherance of energy sector liberalisation. This almost overt use of competition law in a regulatory fashion raises several problematic questions. First, beyond the fact that full ownership unbundling within energy markets is not mandated by competition law as such, the merits of the project more generally remain disputed.[213] Given that the decisions involved are of a political and not merely a legal nature, therefore, the choice of the Commission to address these issues through enforcement might be questioned. Second, the dubious merits of some of the underlying antitrust cases at issue have been noted, and thus there is a non-negligible risk that illegitimate concessions might be extracted from defendants. These issues are considered further in the next section.

Finally, it is perhaps interesting to compare the strategic deployment of commitment decisions in energy markets with the similarly recurrent use of Article 9 in the technology sector, including decisions involving Microsoft,[214] IBM,[215] Apple,[216] the curious Rambus case,[217] and a long-standing investigation of Google that has been pursued, firmly, with a view to settlement.[218] If the Commission uses the commitment procedure against energy firms in order to compensate for apparent shortcomings of liberalisation, its use in technology markets is perhaps in recognition of the inappropriateness of either conventional regulation or conventional competition enforcement for these highly dynamic markets. The Commission indeed reasoned that commitment decisions may be particularly suited to the digital economy, suggesting that, '[i]n a nascent and fast-moving market . . . it is vital that we nip in the bud any competitive restrictions', in order to ensure that 'the business environment remains open and dynamic'.[219] Technology markets are marked by high levels of innovation, network effects and 'winner-takes-all' competition, which often creates (at least temporary) dominance for

[213] Compare, e.g., Pollitt (2008); Joskow (2008); Lafontaine & Slade (2007).

[214] Commission Decision of 16 December 2009 in Case COMP/C-3/39.530 – *Microsoft (tying)* (OJ C 36/7, 13.2.2010).

[215] Commission Decision of 13 December 2011 in Case COMP/C-3/39692 – *IBM Maintenance* Services (OJ C 18/6, 21.01.2012).

[216] Commission Decision of 12 December 2012 in Case COMP/39.847 – *E-BOOKS* (OJ C 73/17, 13.03.2013), and Commission Decision of 25 July 2012 in Case COMP/39.847 – *E-BOOKS (Penguin)* (OJ C 378/25, 24.12.2013).

[217] See p. 110, fn. 188.

[218] See, e.g., European Commission, *Statement on the Google Investigation by Vice President Joaquín Almunia*, SPEECH/14/93, delivered on 5 February 2014.

[219] See Almunia (2012:6)

successful firms.[220] Although the technology sector is not immune from competition problems, a consensus is lacking regarding the suitability of sector-specific regulation within such fast-moving environments. Conventional competition enforcement also focuses primarily on the prohibition of discrete forms of anticompetitive behaviour, rather than a more general emphasis on maintaining openness within a market. The use of commitment decisions might therefore be viewed as part of a more cooperative, 'responsive' form of regulation for digital markets.[221] Nonetheless, it is important to reemphasise that commitment decisions must be grounded in *prima facie* antitrust violations. Absent this crucial threshold requirement, Article 9 should not be used as a means by which to achieve the 'best' market solution.

(iii) Negotiated settlements as regulation: a critical assessment

Negotiated settlements are compromises, which involve neither a formal finding of antitrust infringement nor acquittal. Settlements are located on the boundary between (public) competition rules and (private) contract, which, arguably, lends such instruments to application in a regulatory fashion. Within both the US and EU systems, a quasi-regulatory deployment of negotiated settlement procedures can be discerned. On the one hand, the quasi-regulatory use of settlement mechanisms may reflect a disjoint between the archetypal crime-tort model of competition law, with its preference for one-shot solutions, and the types of market problems that competition law might encounter, which often require a degree of on-going regulatory input to keep the market working well. On the other hand, as the EU technology market example demonstrates, antitrust settlements can provide a more nuanced and flexible tool for regulation, or, as in the EU energy sector example, function as an informal regulatory mechanism where political agreement regarding a more formal scheme proves impossible.

In a sense, regulation through negotiated settlements empowers firms by providing them with a central role within the regulatory process. This can result in more effective remedies for market problems and also more acceptable burdens for firms. In the EU context, the regulatory use of commitment decisions, in particular in furtherance of liberalisation objectives, might potentially be defended by reference to competition

[220] OECD (2012). [221] See Ayres & Braithwaite (1992).

law's supplementary role in creating and protecting the internal market.[222] In the USA, as we have seen, the DOJ has progressively adapted its consent decree practices to counter concerns about the static nature of regulatory consent decree requirements.[223] It is relevant, moreover, that consent decrees are utilised in civil rather than criminal enforcement, the former being widely recognised as an increasingly technical and economics-focused enterprise,[224] an observation that applies with equal force to the administrative decision-making procedures of the European Commission. Regulatory antitrust settlements might therefore be defended in similar terms to sector-specific regulation more generally: that is, as a detailed, expert response to a specific market problem where the remedy is tailored to solve the market problem, and not simply to punish defendants for breach.

Many of the general objections advanced against regulatory competition law find specific application in the negotiated settlements context, however. There is, first, a general lack of accountability within the negotiation process when compared with either litigated competition cases or the normal processes of regulation. By their nature, negotiated settlements are appealed infrequently.[225] Consequently, neither the underlying case theory nor the settlement bargain is subject to judicial scrutiny, which increases the risk that erroneous theories might gain indirect approval or that inefficient or unfair deals are struck. Although the use of negotiated settlements can be an effective and efficient means by which to conclude antitrust investigations and remedy market problems, it may come at a cost in terms of the status and integrity of the underlying competition rules. While regulatory settlements can have spill-over effects, third parties have limited scope to participate in the process of regulation or to appeal against concluded settlements. Public consultation, as required by the Tunney Act and Article 27(4) of Regulation 1/2003, may facilitate limited third-party involvement, but it provides a weak substitute for the lobbying efforts and public

[222] This still leads to a number of conceptual and legal difficulties, however, which are explored further in Chapter 4.

[223] See p. 105. [224] Crane (2011:120).

[225] It is unclear whether undertakings that offer commitments can challenge Commission decisions to make binding those commitments. Arguably, the correct approach is that advanced by the General Court in Case T-170/06 *Alrosa Company Ltd* v. *Commission* [2006] ECR II-2601, and endorsed by Schweitzer (2008:23), namely that settling undertakings should have the same rights of appeal as undertakings that have agreed to merger commitments. The factual context is likely to heighten the scrutiny of review.

accountability that characterises the regulatory process,[226] while *ex post* appeal against finalised settlement by third parties is generally impossible.[227] Accordingly, third parties can neither influence significantly the shape of the resulting regulation – because, in theory, this is the outcome of a judicial procedure – nor can they challenge the regulatory measures encapsulated within the private bargain.

The risks of politicisation and the instrumental use of competition law are also recurrent concerns. The wide margin of discretion permitted to enforcement agencies creates a risk that investigations will be pursued to further goals lying beyond the objectives of competition law, leading to 'cheap decrees'[228] or settlements that degrade antitrust in order to achieve other political aims. The problematic EU energy example is obviously relevant here. Conversely, an enforcer's discretion might be used to compromise viable competition cases that are politically unpopular. The *Microsoft* consent decree provides an example of this risk: following an administration change at the political level, the DOJ agreed to considerably more lenient remedial measures than it had initially sought.[229] Here, politics rather explicitly invaded law through the conduit of private bargaining involved in the negotiated settlement. A related more formalistic argument is that regulation through negotiated settlements may permit competition authorities or antitrust courts, effectively, to legislate, which risks usurping the prerogatives of the legislature and/or executive. Again, this is a risk that has arguably been realised in our EU energy sector example.

The still on-going chronicle of regulating collecting societies by consent decree in the USA illustrates many of the advantages but also the drawbacks of using antitrust settlement as a primary means of market supervision. The consent decree procedure, in this instance, has proved to a fairly flexible yet enduring tool of market regulation; one that avoids the potential dangers of political stalemate and has been able to adapt,

[226] In *Swedish Interconnectors*, for example, market testing indicated that the proposed commitments were likely to have significant negative (albeit indirect) impact on existing electricity supply contracts. While the Commission acknowledged the objection, it rejected it as merely an inherent risk faced by market participants.

[227] In the EU, a third-party defendant must satisfy the restrictive test for standing for non-privileged applicants under Article 263 TFEU, typically impossible in all but the most unusual of cases (cf. *Alrosa*), or seek indirect review of the commitment decision through national courts under Article 267 TFEU, again difficult in practice.

[228] Rosch (2011).

[229] *US* v. *Microsoft Corp.*, 231 F. Supp. 2d 144 (DDC, 2002); see Melamed (2007:294).

sooner or later, with markets change. At a technical level, however, consent decrees have proved far from perfect as an instrument of regulation, with difficulties that include regulatory time lags, inequality and ineffectiveness, while the compatibility of the underlying conduct with antitrust remains murky at best.[230] In this instance, regulatory competition law provides an adequate but hardly optimal solution to a genuine market problem; the question is, perhaps, whether we should commend a glass half full, or strive, possibly in vain, to improve a glass half empty.

IV. Doctrinal regulatory competition law: excessive prices and essential facilities

We turn now to consider another aspect of the movement towards regulatory competition law, but this time at the doctrinal level. Whereas negotiated settlements provide a procedural mechanism to resolve antitrust cases that, perhaps inadvertently, introduces certain regulatory elements to public enforcement, the doctrines to be examined here – namely, the rule against excessive prices and the so-called 'essential facilities' theory – relate, more directly, to the substance of competition law. Such doctrines are of plenary application, therefore, and may potentially be invoked in both public and private enforcement. As hinted at in the EU energy example explored earlier, there is, nonetheless, considerable overlap between the use of negotiated settlements and such quasi-regulatory doctrines, insofar as the flexibility and largely consensual nature of the former may facilitate application of the latter. Both doctrines concern negative market outcomes that may result where a single firm holds significant market power: the rule against excessive prices concerns, essentially, the extraction of monopoly rents, whereas the essential facilities theory concerns market foreclosure by a monopolist that refuses to cooperate with rivals. In this sense, both doctrines would appear to fall squarely within the general aim of antitrust to prevent the abusive exercise of market power. Nonetheless, the purportedly regulatory nature of these doctrines stems from the considerable overlap in practice between the coverage and operation of competition rules governing excessive prices and essential facilities, on the one hand, and the classic regulatory instruments of, respectively, rate-making and mandatory access obligations, on the other. Both doctrines have thus faced

[230] See the somewhat equivocal approach of the Supreme Court in *BMI* v. *CBS* 441 US 1 (1979).

considerable criticism and resistance as rules of *antitrust*, due in large part to the nature of the decision-making, at both technical and policy levels, that each entails.

(i) *Excessive prices under competition law*

We consider first the treatment of excessive prices under competition law. Exploitative abuses – broadly, extracting unacceptable profits from consumers – are 'textbook' examples of undesirable monopoly behaviour.[231] As discussed in the preceding chapter, neoclassical economic theory tells us that the exercise of monopoly power causes allocative inefficiency, meaning a departure of prices from marginal cost. This harms consumers, as wealth is transferred to producers, and also society more generally, as monopoly pricing results in deadweight loss.[232] These costs arise independently of the manner in which market power was acquired, so that an innocently obtained and maintained monopoly can and is likely to engage in monopoly pricing.[233] In some circumstances, particularly where the market concerned has natural monopoly elements or network effects that are likely to strengthen dominance, the appropriate (or unavoidable) policy response to any perceived problem of excessive returns is direct regulation of prices – i.e., rate-making – by the State or, more usually, a designated sector regulator.[234] Given that the conventional antitrust prohibitions on exclusionary abuses aim, essentially, to prevent acquisition or entrenchment of monopoly in order to avoid future exploitation, the charging of excessive prices on the strength of a seller's market power might, therefore, be considered a paradigmatic antitrust violation.

Surprisingly, perhaps, this is not the case. Competition enforcement against high prices *per se* tends to be strongly disfavoured, and indeed is impossible in certain jurisdictions, most notably the US. While many commentators agree that, in theory, avoidance of monopoly pricing would benefit consumers,[235] the conventional viewpoint is that a rule against excessive prices can be unworkable and unhelpful in practice. The overriding considerations here are a dynamic understanding of markets, which emphasises the importance of entry, innovation,

[231] Lyons (2007:66); O'Donoghue & Padilla (2013:734).
[232] Gellhorn (1975:34–5). See also p. 15. [233] Gal (2004:344).
[234] See, e.g., Viscusi et al. (2005:429–52).
[235] O'Donoghue & Padilla (2013:735–6); Evans & Padilla (2005:99).

and the capacity of markets to self-correct, with a parallel scepticism about the ability of States to implement efficient outcomes.[236] A well-developed series of reasons against antitrust supervision of excessive prices has been advanced, which encompass both justiciability and policy concerns. Taken together, these arguments underpin a consensus that, on balance, excessive prices are an inappropriate area for antitrust enforcement.[237] The alternatives are all or nothing: refrain from intervention and wait for market self-correction, or, if the market structure makes this impossible, implement regulatory controls that surpass the market entirely and dictate an optimal outcome.

The first category of objections focuses on the justicability of a rule against excessive prices, the concern being that it is impossible to devise a sufficiently precise rule, to apply it with certainty, and to have effective remedies available in cases of breach. First, it has been claimed that, conceptually, it is difficult to devise an acceptable criterion of 'excessiveness', in either legal or economic terms.[238] Particularly once dynamic considerations are factored in, it becomes problematic to formulate an assessment standard that is both efficient and objective.[239] Whatever the definition of excessiveness adopted, moreover, there are practical difficulties in applying the various economic tests available to assess whether prices are excessive.[240] Measuring the profitability of a firm, considered to be the most accurate way to assess the acceptability of price and profit levels, is hard to quantify accurately.[241] Other metrics for excessiveness – sales margins, for example, or a comparison of the price under scrutiny and real or hypothetical competing products – are less accurate, and not without their own difficulties of application.[242] Finally, the typical remedy in excessive-price cases is, effectively, a form of price regulation. This is claimed to be an inappropriate antitrust remedy, both because competition authorities have insufficient sector-specific knowledge to regulate properly and because regulatory remedies require regular monitoring and enforcement of compliance, which is viewed as an improper task for competition agencies.[243]

[236] Gal (2004:344). [237] See, e.g., Motta (2004:69); Whish & Bailey (2012:720).
[238] O'Donoghue & Padilla (2013:757); Motta (2004:69).
[239] Evans & Padilla (2005:110–13). [240] Motta & de Streel (2007:33–7).
[241] Grout & Zalewska (2008).
[242] Williams (2007); O'Donoghue & Padilla (2013:748–57).
[243] O'Donoghue & Padilla (2013:763–4); Whish & Bailey (2012:719–20).

A second set of objections focuses on the optimal tenor of antitrust policy, and exhibit a distinct preference for dynamic over static theories of markets.[244] The concern here is that antitrust intervention may therefore do more harm than good within already weakened markets. First, it is claimed that high prices encourage investment and innovation, a crucial aspect of dynamic competition. Although competition may temporarily sow the seeds of its own ruin – through 'creative destruction' – it results in new improved products. High profits reward successful innovation, and the pursuit of potential monopoly profits thus drives research and development. Prohibiting such profits, this theory posits, harms welfare because firm have diminished incentives to invest and innovate. In sectors with high sunk and/or fixed costs, additionally, high profits may be necessary to recover initial outlay; prohibiting recovery impacts negatively on dynamic efficiency.[245] The second strand of this objection emphasises that excessive prices encourage entry as the prospect of monopoly profits attracts new entrants, which consequently increases levels of market competition. Entry brings two benefits: new entrants compete down the high prices; and, given the prospect of entry, monopolists may charge lower, and thus less tempting, prices initially.[246] Underlying both the investment and entry arguments is the fear that antitrust is an imprecise and unreliable tool against excessive prices. As discussed, enforcement generates risks of both Type I and Type II errors; the fear is that, while the harm from Type II errors in such cases is low, the potential injury to dynamic efficiency from Type I errors is high. Although effective enforcement against excessive prices would bring benefits, in practice error costs may outweigh gains.[247] The issue of 'political legitimacy' is another concern: regulatory-type market interventions, such as price-setting, necessitate political choices, which, it has been argued, should be taken by a body with greater political accountability, and a clearer policy mandate, than courts or competition authorities.[248]

Taken together, these objections provide a compelling argument against excessive prices as a competition abuse for many commentators – and enforcers. The argument that high prices should be *per se* legal is not uncommon amongst academics,[249] and represents US law. Whilst influential, however, the criticisms advanced against excessive-price cases

[244] Evans & Padilla (2005:118). [245] O'Donoghue & Padilla (2013:738–41).
[246] Ezrachi & Gilo (2009:254). [247] O'Donoghue & Padilla (2013:762).
[248] Motta & de Streel (2007:19). [249] Evans & Padilla (2005:118); Motta (2004:69).

have engendered certain scepticism. Ezrachi and Gilo, in particular, have argued forcefully that, individually, these assumptions fail to provide an *a priori* argument against intervention, and their work has challenged both justiciability and policy concerns.[250] They have argued, for example, that potential entrants generally consider the post-entry rather than the inflated pre-entry price when contemplating entry. They therefore dismissed the signalling benefits of high prices as restrictive and uncertain, and, conversely, as equally applicable where excessive prices are prohibited. Where a potential entrant is unsure about its costs and the incumbent's, high prices might deter entry by suggesting that operating costs are high.[251] In response to criticism that enforcement chills investment, they emphasised the default antitrust assumption that competition spurs innovation, questioning why dominant firms are entitled to supra-competitive profits in this context.[252] Similarly, they noted that complexity of application creates difficulties for many antitrust theories, including predation, price discrimination and margin squeeze, and so is not unique.[253] The remedies objection has also been challenged on the basis that price regulation is not inevitable in excessive-price cases.[254] Motta and de Streel, for example, argued that price regulation is a remedy of last resort, with removal of barriers to entry or modification of consumer conduct preferable where possible.[255]

a. Antitrust approaches to excessive prices: the apparent US/EU dichotomy

We consider next the treatment of excessive prices under competition law within our two core jurisdictions, the US and EU. At first glance, another transatlantic dichotomy apparently exists: excessive prices can constitute a monopoly abuse in EU law but not US law. In reality, however, enforcement against excessive prices is strongly disfavoured in both jurisdictions: while, formally, excessive prices are prohibited under Article 102 TFEU, the EU enforcement record is almost as sparse as the US's.

It is firmly established that US antitrust does not prohibit monopoly pricing as a stand-alone abuse.[256] The possession of monopoly power is not prohibited, but only its anticompetitive acquisition or maintenance; the corollary being that the ordinary exercise of such power (namely, charging high prices) is not prohibited either. Thus, 'more than

250 Ezrachi & Gilo (2009); Ezrachi & Gilo (2010). 251 Ezrachi & Gilo (2009:255–66).
252 Ezrachi & Gilo (2010:895). 253 Ezrachi & Gilo (2010:893).
254 Lyons (2007:77–9). 255 Motta & de Streel (2007:40–1). 256 Gal (2004:346–58).

monopoly power is necessary to make the charging of a non-competitive price unlawful. . .A pristine monopolist. . .may charge as high a rate as the market will bear'.[257] In *Trinko*, the Supreme Court characterised the charging of monopoly prices as a 'concomitant' aspect of a monopoly market position. Indeed, the Court viewed that ability as an 'important element' of the free-market system, as it rewards businesses for, and thus incentivises, innovation.[258] This deferential approach is premised upon two related beliefs: that monopoly prices are inherently self-correcting because competition erodes monopoly over time; and that, even where markets are uncompetitive and cannot self-correct, the costs of regulation outweigh its benefits in addressing the harms of monopoly.[259] These two strands fit neatly with the policy and justiciability objections outlined. This approach can also be reconciled with the letter of US antitrust, insofar as Sherman Act, §2, covers only 'monopolisation' – anticompetitive acquisition or maintenance of dominance – but not exploitation of monopoly.

By contrast, Article 102(a) TFEU expressly cites, as an example of abusive conduct, 'directly or indirectly imposing unfair purchase or selling prices'. The CJEU has thus confirmed that this prohibition applies where dominant firms charge disproportionate prices or one that bears no reasonable relationship to the economic value of the goods or service.[260] A two-part test to identify excessive prices was established in *United Brands*: first, the difference between the costs incurred and the price charged must be excessive; and second, the price charged must be unfair in itself or when compared to competing products.[261] These criteria are cumulative.[262] Although the Court in *United Brands*

[257] *Berkey Photo, Inc.* v. *Eastman Kodak Co.*, 603 F.2d 263 (2d Cir. 1979), 297.

[258] *Trinko*, 407. The principle that Sherman Act, §2, prohibits only *anticompetitive* monopoly conduct was established in *Standard Oil Co. of NJ* v. *United States*, 221 US 1 (1911); restated in *United States* v. *Aluminium Co. of America*, 148 F. 2d 416 (1945), particularly 429–30.

[259] Gal (2004:358).

[260] Case 26/75 *General Motors Continental NV* v. *Commission* EU:C:1975:150, para. 12; Case 27/76 *United Brands Company and United Brands Continentaal BV* v. *Commission* EU:C:1978:22, para. 250; reaffirmed in Case C-52/07 *Kanal 5 Ltd, TV 4 AB* v. *Föreningen Svenska Tonsättares Internationella Musikbyrå (STIM) upa.* EU:C:2008:703, and Case C-385/07 P *Der Grüne Punkt – Duales System Deutschland GmbH* v. *Commission* EU:C:2009:456.

[261] *United Brands*, 252.

[262] Advocate General Trstenjak summarised this test as requiring 'analysis of the economic value of the benefit conferred, the consideration rendered and the relation between

presented this formulation as merely an example of how excessiveness might be determined,[263] subsequent practice treats the test as definitive.[264] In practice, however, the Commission has rarely pursued excessive-price cases unless the price charged is clearly exorbitant.[265] In a review of unilateral conduct enforcement in 2005, its own economic experts advised against antitrust intervention in excessive-price cases.[266] Similarly, the Commission's guidance on enforcement priorities for Article 102 TFEU notes the possibility of intervention against exploitative abuses, but the guidance itself covers only exclusionary conduct,[267] from which it might be inferred that exploitative abuses are a low priority if not entirely discounted. The 2004 decision to reject an excessive-price complaint against a Swedish port is instructive: although the prices charged were high, the Commission found that the services provided were particularly valuable to passengers and ferry operators, and so it could not be established that price bore no reasonable relationship to cost.[268] Although, as noted, the CJEU accepts the possibility of an excessive-price claim under Article 102, it has never condemned a pricing practice solely on the ground that it is sufficiently excessive to constitute an abuse.[269] Ezrachi and Gilo attributed this dearth of enforcement, directly, to a deliberate policy of restraint premised on the conventional justiciability and policy-based objections.[270]

Two qualifications must be added. First, the general reluctance at EU level to find prices excessive does not prevent the possibility of a divergence at national competition authority level, or in private enforcement actions.[271] This possibility is tempered somewhat by the broad consensus regarding the exceptional nature of competition enforcement against excessive prices, and the restrictive conditions

benefit and consideration', and noted the difficulty of this exercise. See Opinion delivered on 11 September 2008 in C-52/07 *Kanal 5*, para. 39.

263 *United Brands*, 251–3.

264 See, e.g., Order of the Court in Case Case C-159/08 P *Isabella Scippacercola and Ioannis Terezakis* v. *Commission* EU:C:2009:188.

265 Gal (2004:376); see also Hellwig (2009:214).

266 Report by the EAGCP, *An economic approach to Article 82*, published July 2005, p. 11.

267 European Commission, *Guidance on the Commission's enforcement priorities in applying Article 82 of the EC Treaty to abusive exclusionary conduct by dominant undertakings* (OJ C 45/7, 24.2.2009) (hereafter '*Enforcement Priorities for Article 102*'), para. 7.

268 Rejection Decision of 23 July 2004 in Case COMP/A.36.568/D3 – *Scandlines Sverige AB* v. *Port of Helsingborg*.

269 Wahl (2007:62). 270 Ezrachi & Gilo (2009:253–4).

271 O'Donoghue & Padilla (2013:766).

outlined in *United Brands*. Second, and linking closely to our previous discussion on negotiated settlements, excessive-price issues have arisen, directly or obliquely, in a number of Commission investigations that were resolved subsequently by commitment decision. Obviously, such decisions contain no formal findings of breach, but, arguably, lend greater credence to the underlying antitrust doctrines. Most notably, the *Standard & Poor's* decision was based expressly on the premise that the defendant charged prices that were excessive – or, as the Commission put it, 'unfair' – within the meaning of the *United Brands* test.[272] Other Article 9 decisions involved claims of excessively high prices as an element of abuse of dominance. In *IBM*, the Commission alleged that very high prices charged for certain spare parts, when compared with prices for similar products, amounted to a *de facto* refusal to supply.[273] In *Rambus* the prices charged for access to standard-essential patents were claimed to be excessive, given the historical context of an alleged patent ambush that led to incorporation of proprietary technology within an industry-wide standard. One of the claimed abuses in the *German Electricity Markets* case, furthermore, involved the short-term withdrawal of generation capacity in order to drive up prices for consumers, perhaps the archetypal example of an exercise of monopoly market power. Additionally, because commitment decisions do not constitute formal statements of competition law, the Commission need not satisfy the exacting standards for liability required by the case law. The *Standard & Poor's* decision, for example, set out the legal test for excessive prices, and noted the Commission's view that these requirements are fulfilled. Given the commitment decision context, however, the Commission was not obliged to demonstrate that this exacting standard for liability was satisfied on the facts, and the decision patently neglects to do so.[274] The recurrent use of excessive-price theories in the context of negotiated settlements, to mutually reinforcing effect, suggests that the availability of a quasi-regulatory procedure for case disposition renders this substantive competition doctrine, which also has significant regulatory overtones, both more palatable and more practicable from an enforcement perspective.

[272] *Standard & Poor's*, particularly paras. 28–30.

[273] Commission Decision of 13 December 2011 in Case COMP/C-3/39692 – *IBM Maintenance Services* (OJ C18/6, 21.2.2012)

[274] *Standard & Poor's*, paras. 26–38.

b. Excessive prices, regulation and the role of competition authorities

At first glance, the US and EU competition rules adopt dichotomous approaches to the treatment of excessive prices. A common assertion is that US law is 'non-interventionist', whereas EU law is 'interventionist' in this regard.[275] Gal, for example, argued that US law is process- rather than outcome-oriented, whereas EU law places more emphasis on distributional justice and equity of outcomes. While both jurisdictions justify their approaches on fairness grounds, under US law this is fairness to producers, whereas in EU law this is fairness to consumers.[276] As we have seen, however, excessive-price cases can be as difficult to pursue under EU competition law as under US antitrust. US law excludes the possibility of such claims expressly, by rejecting this doctrine within the jurisprudence of the Sherman Act. EU law cannot escape the text of Article 102 TFEU, which refers explicitly to exploitative abuses, and therefore retains the prospect of finding an abuse of dominance through excessive prices. Nonetheless, the possibility of bringing a successful case is unlikely unless it is pursued under the quasi-regulatory commitment procedure provided by Article 9 of Regulation 1/2003, which dispenses with most of the negative legal consequences (e.g., fines, a formal finding of breach) that would, conversely, accompany the infringement procedure under Article 7.

The question is why these justiciability and policy arguments have made such an impact: why condemn exclusionary abuses, yet disregard exploitative abuses? This division is surprising, given that the latter represent crystallisation of the monopoly power that exclusionary conduct rules endeavour to prevent being accrued. This scepticism extends to EU competition law, which has usually been less receptive to blanket policy-based restrictions. Even within jurisdictions where excessive prices fall within competition law, enforcers often limit investigated cases by applying various 'screens' designed to restrict antitrust intervention to only the most egregious cases where the market can neither self-correct nor be corrected by other regulatory means.[277] Inherently,

[275] Ezrachi & Gilo (2009:252); Hou (2011:48). [276] Gal (2004:382).

[277] Commonly cited screens include high non-transitory barriers to entry; super-dominance approaching monopoly; where super-dominance originated in special rights held by the firm or unprosecuted past exclusionary abuses; the risk that excessive prices may prevent the emergence of new goods and services; and the absence (or inaction) of a sector-specific regulator: see Evans & Padilla (2005:119); Motta & de Streel (2007:22–9).

there is a paradox within the conventional approach to excessive prices: exclusionary abuses are condemned, *inter alia*, because they might lead ultimately to consumer exploitation, yet antitrust cannot address exploitation directly in the guise of high prices.[278]

At its most basic, the explanation may be that competition authorities do not wish to act as price regulators. Competition enforcers generally prefer to focus on opening markets to competition and allowing the market mechanism to determine the optimal outcome, rather than intervening directly. The European Commission, for example, has stated categorically that it 'is not and does not wish to act as a price regulator'.[279] The objection to price regulation in competition cases encompasses both justiciability and policy concerns: price regulation is seen as inherently difficult to get right, and competition adjudicators are, moreover, the wrong body to perform such quasi-regulatory functions.

There remains a question as to how high prices should be combated if not directly under antitrust. In circumstances where a dominant position has been acquired through investment, innovation and competition on the merits, some would argue that such prices should not be challenged, because a legitimate monopolist is entitled to monopoly rewards even if this causes consumer loss.[280] For excessive-price sceptics, above-cost pricing is generally efficient insofar as it encourages innovation and invites entry. High prices may, however, provide evidence that other abusive behaviour is occurring.[281] Where dominance is attributable to a past antitrust violation, such as predation for instance, the more appropriate response might be to pursue competition enforcement against the earlier breach.[282] Where dominance is entrenched because of high, durable barriers to entry and the market cannot self-correct, sector-specific regulation may be necessary. *Ex ante* regulation is seen as a more appropriate mechanism to address monopoly pricing, in particular with respect to technical expertise and monitoring.[283] There is some irony, however, in that the preferred solution to potentially inefficient competition intervention is to overreach the market mechanism entirely via regulation – an approach, as we shall see, which has also come under sustained attack from more conservative scholars. In practice, moreover, competition authorities already address many pricing issues, albeit

[278] Lyons (2007:65).
[279] European Commission (1997) *XXVIIth Report on Competition Policy*, 77.
[280] Motta (2004:69). [281] Grout & Zalewska (2008:173); Motta (2004:70).
[282] Motta (2004:69). [283] Motta (2004:69); Evans & Padilla (2005:122).

indirectly, when assessing other competition offences, including fidelity rebates, margin squeeze, predation, constructive refusals to deal and price discrimination.

Despite this apparent inconsistency, it remains the case that excessive-price claims tend to fall either outside the enforcement jurisdiction or the enforcement priorities of most competition authorities. One potential explanation is that such cases shift the emphasis of enquiry from private behaviour to the functioning of the market more generally, and in particular, to a counterfactual analysis of the assumed competitive outcome. Excessive prices are a matter of market dynamics, or lack thereof: if a firm charges high prices, it acts not necessarily with anticompetitive intent, but rather because an absence of countervailing competitive pressures permits it to charge what the market can bear. The problem might therefore lay with the market itself, which either self-corrects (making antitrust intervention redundant) or which can never self-correct (rendering intervention ineffective, because the market mechanism is inherently defective). In neither case, under this approach, is competition enforcement likely to provide an effective longer-term solution. An alternative, rather more cynical explanation is that excessive-price cases have simply developed a bad reputation amongst competition enforcers, as presenting difficult and perhaps dubious cases for enforcement that, on balance, do not merit expenditure of limited agency resources. The quasi-regulatory nature of the antitrust determinations involved in excessive-price cases would appear to be a decisive factor against a more enthusiastic embrace of such theories by antitrust adjudicators. Whatever the rationale, excessive-price cases establish a clear frontier of competition enforcement for many agencies, beyond which lies the 'all-or-nothing' alternatives of sector-specific regulation or simple deference to the (ostensible) self-correcting power of markets.

(ii) The essential facilities doctrine

The 'essential facilities' doctrine provides further illustration of a contentious, quasi-regulatory competition theory, this time derived from the case law on anticompetitive refusals to deal. As a general rule, all firms, including dominant or monopoly firms, are free to determine their trading partners.[284] This fundamental precept stems from the principles

[284] 'In the absence of any purpose to create or maintain a monopoly, the [Sherman] act does not restrict the long recognized right of trader or manufacturer engaged in an entirely

of freedom of contract and respect for property rights that underpin market economies.[285] In limited circumstances, however, where the refusal to transact harms consumer welfare, derogation from this non-interventionist precept may be mandated by competition law, an exception that has been recognised within both the US and EU competition systems.[286] The essential facilities doctrine is perhaps the most notable expression of the refusal-to-deal theory, and also its most notorious application.[287] Broadly speaking, the concept of an essential facility relates to physical or intangible infrastructure that cannot be duplicated easily, yet where access is required for market participation.[288] In such circumstances, the State may choose to enact public-utility regulation that imposes, *inter alia*, mandatory sharing requirements on the owner of the facility. Absent such regulation – or, more controversially, where regulation exists but is ineffective, as we will consider further in Chapter 4 – the question arises as to whether competition law can be employed to force a facility owner to open its infrastructure and share access with other market participants, thus enabling otherwise unfeasible competition. The essential facilities doctrine accordingly balances diminutions in individual property rights and commercial freedom

private business, freely to exercise his own independent discretion as to parties with whom he will deal': *United States* v. *Colgate & Co., 250 US 300 (1919), 307.* '[A]ny undertaking, whether dominant or not, should have the right to choose its trading partners and to dispose freely of its property': *Enforcement Priorities for Article 102*, para. 75. See also Hay (2005:530–3).

285 O'Donoghue & Padilla (2013:509); Vickers (2010:376).

286 See, under US law, *United States* v. *Terminal Railroad Assn. of St. Louis*, 224 US 383 (1912) (concerted refusal to deal) and *Aspen Skiing Co.* v. *Aspen Highlands Skiing Corp.*, 472 US 585 (1985) (unilateral refusal to deal); under EU law, Case 73/74 *Groupement des fabricants de papiers peints de Belgique and others* v. *Commission* EU:C:1975:160 (group boycott) and Joined Cases 6 & 7/73 *Istituto Chemioterapico Italiano S.p.A. and Commercial Solvents Corporation* v. *Commission* EU:C:1974:18 (unilateral refusal to deal).

287 A recurrent threshold objection to the essential facilities doctrine is its claimed superfluity, insofar as such cases can be accommodated within general refusal to deal principles rather than requiring discrete categorisation; see, most famously, Areeda (1990); also Hay (2005:536); Hovenkamp (2011:336). The doctrine is nonetheless a resilient feature of debates regarding the appropriate scope of unilateral conduct rules.

288 Alternative formulations include, 'a facility or infrastructure which is essential for reaching customers and/or enabling competitors to carry on their business, and which cannot be replicated by any reasonable means': Commission Notice on the application of the Competition Rules to access agreements in the telecommunications sector (OJ C265/02, 22.8.98), para. 68, and '[a]ny input which is deemed necessary for all industry participants to operate in a given industry and which is not easily duplicated': Motta (2004:66).

against general consumer welfare gains that follow from the introduction of competition.[289] Essential facilities cases typically arise in network or natural monopoly markets, where the presence of indispensable infrastructure creates a bottleneck to competition.[290] It is generally accepted, moreover, that genuine essential facilities cases must involve a degree of vertical integration.[291] The principal competition concern, in such circumstances, is that the infrastructure owner will leverage its dominance from the bottlenecked market into a vertically related sector.

The essential facilities doctrine has the dubious distinction of featuring in almost every antitrust textbook yet remaining formally unrecognised by either the US Supreme Court or the CJEU. The origins of the doctrine are traced to a handful of US cases[292] in which the phrase 'essential facility' found no mention, but where, effectively, access to certain infrastructure or services was deemed indispensable to competition, and so mandatory sharing obligations were imposed.[293] While in the US Supreme Court's more recently applicable decision in *Trinko*, Scalia J. maintained that the Court has never formally recognised the doctrine and declined to recognise (or repudiate) it in that instance,[294] an express essential facilities doctrine has been articulated and adopted widely at lower court level.[295] The legal test advanced by the Seventh Circuit Court of Appeals in *MCI* v. *AT&T* represents the orthodoxy of the doctrine as an example of unlawful monopolisation contrary to Sherman Act, §2. It identifies:

> 'four elements necessary to establish liability under the essential facilities doctrine: (1) control of the essential facility by a monopolist; (2) a competitor's inability practically or reasonably to duplicate the essential facility; (3) the denial of the use of the facility to a competitor; and (4) the feasibility of providing the facility'.[296]

289 O'Donoghue & Padilla (2013:511–13); Pitofsky et al. (2002:460).

290 Viscusi et al. (2005:324); Ibáñez Colomo (2010:270–6).

291 Areeda & Hovenkamp (2006:¶771a, p. 192); Spulber & Yoo (2007:1834); O'Donoghue & Padila (2013:541); *contra* Pitofsky et al. (2002:460).

292 *United States* v. *Terminal Railroad Assn. of St. Louis*, 224 US 383 (1912); *Associated Press* v. *United States*, 326 US 1 (1945); *Lorain Journal Co.* v. *United States* 342 US 143 (1951); and *Otter Tail Power Co.* v. *United States*, 410 US 366 (1973).

293 Areeda (1990:843–4); Pitofsky et al. (2002:446–7); Spulber & Yoo (2007:1829–33).

294 *Trinko*, 411. Scalia J. took the view that, even if the doctrine existed, it was unavailable on the facts due to the presence of a regulator with ability to compel access.

295 Pitofsky et al. (2002:447–8); Rubin (2005:733–4).

296 *MCI Communications* v. *AT&T Corp.* 708 F.2d 1081 (7th Cir. 1983), 1132–3.

Within EU law, the CJEU established in *Commercial Solvents* that refusal to supply could constitute an abuse of dominance under Article 102 TFEU.[297] Developing this approach, the Commission subsequently imposed mandatory sharing obligations for a broad range of infrastructure, service networks and intangible property,[298] going so far as to recognise expressly the essential facilities doctrine in its *Sealink/B&I – Holyhead* decision.[299] In *Oscar Bronner*, however, the CJEU stopped short of approving explicitly a distinct essential facilities doctrine within EU law, not unlike the US Supreme Court's approach in *Trinko* several years later. Instead, the Court articulated a restrictive three-part test to assess claims for mandatory access, requiring that the refusal to supply be likely to eliminate all competition in the affected market on the part of the person requesting access, that the refusal be incapable of objective justification, and that the requested access be indispensable to carrying on that person's business, inasmuch as there are no actual or potential substitutes in existence for the required infrastructure.[300] This restrained approach has been reiterated in the Commission's statement of enforcement priorities for Article 102 TFEU, where it confirmed the exceptional nature of any mandatory duty to deal, emphasised the need to consider potential impact on innovation, and added likelihood of consumer harm to the *Oscar Bronner* test.[301]

Again, we must ask why there is general judicial reluctance to embrace unequivocally a clear statement regarding the existence and parameters of the essential facilities doctrine. The primary advantage of mandatory access through antitrust enforcement is clear: namely, increased competition, and the benefits it brings. Yet, as with rules against excessive prices, this doctrine has been subject to the strongest academic criticisms, which find reflection in contemporary enforcement practice. Critics of the essential facilities doctrine challenge, in essence, its overtly regulatory leanings, which require competition adjudicators to make determinations and impose and monitor obligations that are more typically within the purview of sector-specific regulators. Broadly speaking, three strands

[297] This principle was subsequently applied, *inter alia*, in Case 27/76 *United Brands* v. *Commission* EU:C:1978:22, Case 311/84 *CBEM* v. *SA CLT and IPB ('Telemarketing')* EU:C:1985:394 and Case 238/87 *Volvo* v. *Veng* EU:C:1988:477.

[298] See Whish & Bailey (2012:703–6) for a wide-ranging list.

[299] [1992] 5 CMLR 255; an essential facility was defined as 'a facility or infrastructure without access to which competitors cannot provide services to their customers' (para. 41).

[300] *Oscar Bronner*, para. 41.

[301] *Enforcement Priorities for Article 102*, paras. 75 & 81.

of objection can be identified – excessive intrusion into commercial freedom, harm to investment incentives, and administrability concerns – which we shall consider briefly.

First, the refusal-to-deal case law in general, and the essential facilities doctrine in particular, is considered to require significant derogation from the ordinary propositions that even dominant firms remain at liberty to choose their trading partners, and that competition law does not impose positive obligations.[302] The obligation to share infrastructure – whether it comprises a physical facility, a tangible manufacturing input, or even intellectual property – compromises the property rights of infrastructure owners, even where the mandatory access obligations provide fair compensation. The owner loses its right to determine with whom it does business, while, instead, competition law requires it to transact with parties standing in a relationship of necessity to its essential facility. In many cases the infrastructure owner is indeed required to transact with, and effectively assist the business of, its direct competitors. Accordingly, the essential facilities doctrine risks violating the accepted principle that competition law is intended merely to safeguard the competitive process, and not to protect competitors as such. While property rights are not absolutely inviolable, it might be argued, quite convincingly, that the wealth redistributive preferences encapsulated in any decision to compromise of private property rights through mandatory access obligations involves political, and not merely legal, decision-making. In such circumstances, conventional regulation rather than quasi-regulation competition enforcement may provide the appropriate instrument.

Second, mandatory sharing can have negative impacts on investment and innovation, reducing incentives for either the facility owner or would-be competitors to develop additional infrastructure.[303] This objection turns the 'protect competition not competitors' axiom on its head: by assisting competitors to enter the market, the essential facilities doctrine may hamper dynamic competition. From the perspective of investors, a risk of *ex post* expropriation of their investment through obligations to deal imposed under competition law may diminish *ex ante* incentives for development. Once a facility has been created, consumer welfare may be increased in the immediate term by opening the infrastructure to competition; future welfare can be harmed, however, by a

302 Motta (2004:68); O'Donoghue & Padilla (2013:514–15).
303 Hausman & Sidak (1999:470–1).

longer-term diminution in investment and innovation.[304] By allowing competitors to 'free ride' on the investment and infrastructure of the original developer, this may also inhibit beneficial innovation by new entrants.[305] Given the greater benefits of facilities competition over mere price competition in the longer term, mandatory sharing obligations may further sacrifice dynamic efficiency for short-run static efficiency.

Third, when a court or competition authority finds an essential facility and consequent duty to deal, this is merely the beginning of the remedial process. An abstract right of access is of limited use. Instead, at least in theory, the competition adjudicator must then determine the price and conditions for access, and subsequently monitor on-going compliance with access requirements. On this basis, the essential facilities doctrine has been criticised for the administrative complexity of the remedies required, the high rate and cost of error, and in particular, the fact that it obliges competition adjudicators to perform functions more akin to those of a sector-specific regulator.[306] Because there are no suitable 'one-shot' competition remedies available in such cases, it has been argued, the essential facilities doctrine is inappropriate for inclusion within the corpus of competition law. In practice, competition authorities or courts tend to avoid these issues by delegating implementation of remedies to any sector-specific regulator already in place, although this perhaps raises the question as to why the impugned conduct was addressed by competition law rather than through regulatory mechanisms initially.[307]

In sum, the essential facilities doctrine distinguishes itself from more conventional competition rules by requiring dominant firms positively to improve competition (at least in the short term) rather than merely to refrain from anticompetitive behaviour. This vision of market governance, it may be argued, takes the doctrine towards the realms of economic regulation, in terms of the policy calculations and trade-offs required, as well as the practical implications of implementing such legal obligations. As a paradigmatic example of regulatory competition

[304] Areeda (1990:851); Motta (2004:68); O'Donoghue & Padilla (2013:515–16); Whish & Bailey (2012:697); Spulber & Yoo (2007:1843–5).

[305] Hovenkamp (2011:340); O'Donoghue & Padilla (2013:516); Spulber & Yoo (2007:1845). Where competitive entry is unfeasible – e.g., where there is a true natural monopoly – the usual solution is sector-specific regulation: Spulber & Yoo (2007:1845).

[306] Areeda (1990:853); Hay (2005:543); Hovenkamp (2011:339–40); O'Donoghue & Padilla (2013:517); Hausman & Sidak (1999:470).

[307] Areeda & Hovenkamp (2006:¶773a, p. 238); Hellwig (2009:212).

law, the doctrine encapsulates neatly the dilemma of this more expansive conception of competition law's mission: as antitrust becomes more proactive in facilitating certain dimensions of competition, simultaneously its broader impact may become more unpredictable and erratic.

It is useful, finally, to consider the relationship between the essential facilities doctrine under competition law and sector-specific regulation's imposition of mandatory access requirements. Concurrent competition enforcement in regulated markets will be examined in detail in Chapter 4. Nonetheless, the similarities and synergies between these legal regimes necessitate some preliminary consideration at this juncture. As noted, claims of essential facilities arise most frequently in network or natural monopoly markets: that is, markets that also present the most likely candidates for regulation. In unregulated markets, successful invocation of the doctrine may point to natural monopoly elements that would benefit from regulation. In this manner the doctrine performs a gap-filling function, similar to that identified in the earlier part of this chapter, by identifying a need while providing a substitute for sector-specific regulation.[308] Where a regulatory duty to deal has already been imposed, the added value of the essential facilities doctrine is more questionable. Under US law, the *Trinko* antitrust preclusion approach appears to remove most of the scope for concurrent application of the essential facilities doctrine where mandatory access requirements are imposed by sector-specific regulation.[309] Brennan noted a contradictory similarity between the approach in *Trinko* and the essential facilities doctrine itself: each would locate both antitrust and regulatory functions within a single agency, the former within the sector-specific regulator and the latter within the competition authority.[310] The European Commission, however, has chosen to treat the presence of sector-specific regulation as a justification for lowering standards for intervention under the essential facilities doctrine, taking the cynical view that investment incentives are already affected by regulation within such markets.[311] In recent years, the Commission has increasingly deployed refusal-to-deal principles to justify access to infrastructure in competition cases that arise in markets undergoing liberalisation, without systematic application, it might be

[308] A role defended by Whish & Bailey (2012:706); see generally Monti (2007:240).
[309] Hay (2005); Brennan (2008); cf. Rubin (2005). [310] Brennan (2008:143).
[311] *Enforcement Priorities for Article 102*, para. 82.

noted, of the three-part test from *Oscar Bronner*.[312] The application of this doctrine to quasi-regulatory effect in EU energy markets, in particular, was considered earlier in this chapter. Larouche's criticisms of the instrumental use of competition law to further – legitimate, but non-antitrust – regulatory objectives[313] are, moreover, clearly of relevance here.

Once again, we may conclude that quasi-regulatory elements at a doctrinal level within competition law may enhance the ability of antitrust to address, at least in the short term, the sort of problems that tend to arise in markets with enduring monopoly components. Yet the objections raised to the essential facilities doctrine are not dissimilar to those advanced against the control of excessive prices under competition law: effectively, that competition adjudicators are ill-placed, both in terms of technical knowledge and democratic accountability, to make and also monitor compliance with the type of decisions that these doctrines entail. These concerns are most acute if and when such doctrines are deployed by wholly self-interested private plaintiffs in damages litigation. There has, conversely, been greater willingness by the European Commission, in particular, to apply these doctrines in the context of the commitment procedure under Article 9 of Regulation 1/2003, which, as we have seen, has its own quasi-regulatory quirks. This asymmetry reflects, indirectly, the potential breadth and power of these antitrust doctrines to both make and constrain markets, thus going beyond the perceived realm and role of competition law. As we shall see in the next chapter, often this is where economic regulation is called upon to take up the slack. Yet the insistent critiques of much regulation suggest that, sometimes, it may be more sensible to come full circle and return to an – interventionist, but episodic – regulatory antitrust approach.

V. Conclusions

The concept of regulatory competition law, explored in this chapter, denotes a movement from the archetypal or core conception of competition law towards a model that more closely resembles the paradigm of regulation. On the one hand, this movement may reflect the progressive

[312] See, e.g., Commission decision of 22 June 2011 in COMP/39.525 – *Telekomunikacja Polska* (OJ C324/7, 9.11.2011); *RWE Gas Foreclosure*; *E.ON Gas*. See also Monti (2007:231–2), describing earlier aggressive enforcement within liberalising sectors.

[313] Monti (2007:243).

development of competition law in order more effectively to address certain types of market failures. The use of negotiated settlements, for example, can facilitate the more timely and amicable conclusion of public-enforcement activity, and, indeed, can result in market outcomes that are more nuanced and effectively tailored to address the competition problems at issue. Although contentious, more far-reaching competition theories such as the rule against excessive prices and the essential facilities doctrine can provide at least a temporary respite from market defects that cause immediate diminution of consumer welfare. Whilst, ideally, effective and expeditiously enacted sector-specific regulation might provide a more appropriate solution, in the imperfect real world, antitrust enforcement may provide a much-needed 'second-best' stopgap.

On the other hand, however, regulatory competition law can compromise the protections built into the conventional antitrust model, and might negate the efficiency of the entire competition law enterprise once dynamic considerations are taken into account. Thus, regulatory competition law could be used strategically, for example, to subvert the democratic process; the non-adversarial and largely non-reviewable nature of negotiated settlement procedures might be abused to extract unfair concessions from defendants or to hide dubious case theories; and, where the application of potentially expansive quasi-regulatory substantive theories such as the essential facilities doctrine are placed in the hands of self-interested private plaintiffs, the ultimate outcome may be counterproductive. By extending competition law's reach and increasing its flexibility, the purported shift towards regulatory competition law makes antitrust a more valuable and powerful legal tool, but concomitantly, a more volatile one as well.

Weber Waller has identified two competing jurisprudential theories to explain this move towards competition law-as-regulation. From a legal process perspective, administrative agencies are more suited than courts to the task of balancing competing values, in order to answer the polycentric questions posed by competition law, a move that should, moreover, be encouraged by courts.[314] From a public-choice perspective, by contrast, the deepening powers of a competition agency match its increasingly entrenched and respected position within the economy.[315]

314 Weber Waller (1998:1418–25).

315 Weber Waller (1998:1426–30). Public-choice theories are considered at pp. 145–9.

Both explanations reflect a positive aspect of the regulatory turn: the competition authority's central role in identifying, remedying and preventing market problems. Yet, Weber Waller cautioned that politicisation is a less desirable side effect,[316] insofar as regulation is inherently more politicised, and thus more impermanent, than law.

Within competition law, the extent of the regulatory influence differs depending on the mode of enforcement and the particular competition rules involved, and between different jurisdictions. It is clear that contemporary competition law and enforcement incorporates – unavoidably, but not necessarily unfortunately – certain regulatory elements. This state of affairs brings certain advantages for defendant firms and enforcement agencies, including more effective and efficient enforcement mechanisms, and a greater substantive reach to address market problems that harm consumer welfare. To the extent that use of regulatory competition law instruments or case theories begins to have a detrimental impact upon the integrity of a competition system, or appreciably harms dynamic competition, one might question whether divergence from the conventional conservative-but-safeguarded model of competition law has gone too far. The line delimiting the acceptable scope for regulatory elements within competition law remains, however, an elusive one.

316 Weber Waller (1998:1448).

3

Regulation, deregulation and the space for competition law

Regulation occupies a somewhat uneasy position within modern microeconomic thinking, and indeed society more generally. As Chapter 1 acknowledged, economic regulation in its various guises continues to be an integral – vital, even – component of all developed economies, and, usually to an even greater extent, of developing markets. We have seen that market forces alone cannot solve certain market problems, even when augmented by competition law, something that is explored further in this chapter. Profound and enduring criticisms, which come from two directions, have been levelled at what might be called the 'regulatory enterprise', however.[1] Some critics have argued that, even at a conceptual level, regulation is an inherently flawed enterprise. Given the impossibility of second-guessing or besting the unencumbered market outcome, they contend that States should refrain from counterproductive intervention. Alternatively, while other commentators would accept the theoretical benefits that regulation can bring, it has been argued that the actual results of regulation tend to be highly imperfect in practice, and that bad regulation is more harmful to consumer welfare than none at all. The considerable difficulties of designing and successfully implementing a regulatory framework thus support regulatory restraint. This chapter explores the paradox of regulation: though viewed by many as unwelcome, it is also practically unavoidable.

Decisions to regulate, or to deregulate, are policy choices that reflect the results of a process of political mobilisation.[2] Regulation has been a recurring feature of Western market economies for centuries, long before

[1] Stewart (1988:128) suggested that advocates of deregulation have either 'a profound faith in the virtues of competitive market allocations or a deep scepticism about government's ability to deal with market failures'.

[2] Hovenkamp (2005:228); Clarke (2000:3–4).

enactment of the earliest antitrust statutes.[3] Regulatory practice has historically been cyclical, indicating greater or lesser confidence in the robustness of free markets (or governments).[4] The past fifty years or so have witnessed tumultuous developments with respect to regulation in many economies: from a high point of regulatory activity in the 1960s, through emphatic and sustained calls for deregulation in the 1980s, to a more ambivalent modern attitude encompassing knowledge of both regulatory *and* deregulatory failures, including renewed recognition of the necessity of certain regulation following the Global Financial Crisis (GFC) at the end of the last decade. Clarke described as a paradox of capitalism's success that 'it owes its very survival to regulatory and state intervention and yet it continues to rail at it as an unjustified burden and interference in the sacred freedom of the market'.[5] On the one hand, sector-specific regulation offers, in theory, a promising mechanism to address market defects, allowing regulators to craft tailored remedies that address market problems directly and facilitating on-going and context-sensitive market oversight. On the other, sector-specific regulation is frequently less successful in practice than this archetype supposes: information asymmetries may make it difficult for regulators to design effective remedies; regulators may be captured by industry or political interests, compromising their commitment to the public interest; and the strong market-intervention power of (many) regulators means that, if they get it wrong, the negative consequences can be significant.[6] It is generally accepted that competition is preferred over regulation, where possible, in most instances.[7] In practice, however, both economic and social regulation remain as constant aspects of modern economies.

Various strands of this regulatory puzzle will be examined in this chapter. These include the shift towards deregulation of historically regulated sectors in the latter half of the twentieth century, and, sometimes, back again through reregulation; the strategic use of 'regulation for competition' through liberalisation; the parallel 'better regulation' movement, which seeks to rationalise and improve the effectiveness of regulation; and the inescapable core functions of regulation, which remains necessary to ensure the effective operation of markets in certain

[3] Hovenkamp (2005:227); Sunstein (1990:12–18); Clarke (2000:12–17); Baldwin et al. (2011:4); Ogus (1994:6–7); Hantke-Domas (2003).

[4] Hovenkamp (2005:227); Dempsey (1989:2–3).

[5] Clarke (2000:26).

[6] Hellwig (2009:216–27); see, generally, Breyer (1982); Sunstein (1990).

[7] Crampton & Facey (2002:25–6); Laguna de Paz (2012:77).

circumstances, such as natural monopoly or oligopoly. This chapter functions as a counterpart to Chapter 2 on regulatory competition law, insofar as it examines the internal forces *within* the field of regulation that have caused a departure from the conventional (and expansive) model of regulation, towards a more restrictive, markets-focused approach. A reduced regulatory footprint does not necessitate a concomitant increased role for competition law; however, deregulation, liberalisation or regulatory rationalisation tends to increase the potential application of antitrust by opening up greater portions of the market to competitive forces. Yet there are limits to the possible scope for effective deregulation, and these too will be explored. The preceding chapter considered, for example, the limited utility of competition law in addressing excessive prices or refusals to deal; this is often when regulation becomes indispensable. This chapter thus aims to demonstrate how changes within regulatory thinking have altered the shape and scope of much contemporary regulation, the limits to the deregulatory enterprise, and concurrently, the potential impact of these developments within the competition law arena.

I. Regulation absent competition law

Although our focus is, primarily, the relationship *between* competition law and economic regulation, we begin by considering the possibility that, as in the preceding chapter, market supervision might occur solely through one of these instruments; in this instance, we focus on regulation. Market governance through sector-specific regulation alone implies one of two scenarios: either that no applicable competition law has been enacted, or that the market segment is exempted from application of the competition rules. Given the growing coverage of competition law worldwide, the former situation is possible but increasingly unlikely. Conversely, within many legal systems where competition law is in place, certain sectors that are subject to specific *ex ante* regulatory regimes have been removed from the purview of competition law. Exemptions or immunities of this nature can be implied or express. Detailed consideration will be given in Chapter 4 to the notion of implied exemption from competition law arising from the prior presence of regulation within a market. In the absence of any express antitrust exemption (or savings clause), the extent to which *ex ante* regulation impliedly precludes subsequent application of competition law within the regulated market differs between jurisdictions, and, to an extent, between different types of regulation.

Express exemptions, by contrast, can be contained in the competition law itself, whereby the scope of application of the rules in certain sectors is restricted or excluded entirely, or alternatively, within the particular sector-specific regulatory framework, which might subsequently limit the application of competition law within the regulated market. US antitrust contains full or partial statutory exemptions for, amongst other sectors, export associations,[8] insurance,[9] agricultural cooperatives[10] and fishing.[11] The application of EU competition law is limited in markets relating to nuclear energy,[12] military equipment[13] and agriculture;[14] historically, separate competition law regimes also existed with respect to coal, steel[15] and transport.[16] Potential explanations for exemption include the pervasiveness of any existing regulatory framework; a determination that market dynamics or social policy concerns would render application of ordinary competition law ineffective or possibly counterproductive in this sector; or, less benignly, a response to lobbying efforts that aim to insulate market actors from antitrust scrutiny. To the extent that a

[8] Webb-Pomerene Act of 1918, now 15 U.S.C. §§61–5. Strengthened by the Export Trading Company Act of 1982, now 15 U.S.C. §§4001–3.

[9] McCarran-Ferguson Act of 1945, now 15 U.S.C. §§1011–15.

[10] Contained in the Clayton Act, §6, now 15 U.S.C. §17. Extended by the Capper-Volstead Act of 1922, now 7 U.S.C. §§291–2.

[11] Fishermen's Collective Marketing Act, now 15 U.S.C. §§521–2.

[12] Under the Treaty Establishing the European Atomic Energy Community ('Euratom') of 1957.

[13] Article 346 TFEU.

[14] Article 42 TFEU; see also Council Regulation 1184/2006 of 24 July 2006 applying certain rules of competition to the production of, and trade in, agricultural products (OJ L214/7, 4.8.2006) and Council Regulation 1234/2007 of 22 October 2007 establishing a common organisation of agricultural markets and on specific provisions for certain agricultural products (OJ L299/1, 16.11.2007).

[15] Subject to sector-specific competition rules under the Treaty Establishing the European Coal and Steel Community of 1951.

[16] Although subject to the general competition provisions, separate procedural frameworks existed for enforcement of competition law in transport sectors: see Council Regulation 1017/68 of 19 July 1968 applying rules of competition to transport by rail, road and inland waterway (OJ L175/1, 23.7.1968); Council Regulation 4056/86 of 22 December 1986 laying down detailed rules for the application of Articles 85 and 86 of the Treaty to maritime transport (OJ L378/4, 31.12.1986); and Council Regulation 3975/87 of 14 December 1987 laying down the procedure for the application of the rules on competition to undertakings in the air transport sector (OJ L374/1, 31/12/1987). Regulation 1/2003 brought the transport sector within the general framework of EU competition law.

sector is immunised from application of competition law through express exemption, any ostensibly anticompetitive conduct occurring within that market cannot be addressed through antitrust, although alternative regulatory tools will typically be available to address any resulting market failures.

II. Critiques of regulation – the public-choice movement

In the introductory chapter we explored, broadly, the concept of regulation, settling on, for the purposes of this work, a definition of economic regulation as State-imposed, positive, coercive alteration of or derogation from the operation of the free market in a sector, typically undertaken in order to correct market defects of an economic rather than social nature. Chapter 1 also gave brief consideration to the justifications for or goals of regulation; that is, it considered the sort of market problems – whether efficiency or equity-focused – that such regulation might be enacted to address, as well as the technical mechanisms utilised to tackle such difficulties. From a functional perspective, we might therefore conceive of economic regulation, very generally, as a category of means by which to achieve a variety of socially desired ends. Yet Chapter 1 also hinted at an alternative, 'interest theory' approach to regulation, which probes the causes or political motivations behind regulation, rather than its ostensible goals or technical application.[17] Interest theories tend to be more sceptical of the reasons for, and value of, much regulation. The 'public-choice' movement, in particular, has been highly influential in advocating more minimalist, *laissez-faire* approaches to market supervision. In this section and the next, we examine the closely associated phenomenon of deregulation, that is, the removal of sector-specific regulatory controls from regulated markets. We ask, in particular, why deregulation proponents are so strongly and positively opposed to regulation, and whether such staunch criticism is justified.

Two qualifications must be added. The first is the considered view of this author that, although public-choice scholarship provided a thought-provoking and challenging critique of conventional public-interest-oriented conceptions of regulation, it is much too emphatic and single-minded in

[17] Morgan & Yeung (2007:16) defined theories of regulation, in this sense, as 'a set of propositions or hypotheses about why regulation emerges, *which* actors contribute to that emergence and *typical patterns of interaction between* regulatory actors' (original emphasis), a definition that highlights the political concerns at issue.

its opposition to the regulatory enterprise. Though public interest may be a rather nebulous concept, it is not an empty or insignificant one, and, as has already been argued, regulation remains indispensible, even if it is fairly imperfect, in order to pursue many socially desirable objectives. The lasting influence of the public-choice movement, however, and in particular the wide-scale and robust scepticism of regulation that it engendered, means that it remains an important aspect of the evolution of regulation role's within society, and must be discussed. Second, many of the theories to be considered were developed in the context of a definition of regulation broader than that adopted by this work, encompassing both economic *and* social regulation. Such theories nonetheless apply with equal force to the narrower subsection of regulatory activity under scrutiny here, and have indeed been instrumental in prompting or informing the paring back of economic regulatory controls in many sectors, particularly transport. Perhaps unexpectedly, relatively little scholarship has applied the ideas of public choice to advocate a more comprehensive abandonment of antitrust controls,[18] although, as we shall see, the heyday of the deregulation movement in the USA coincided with the ascendency of minimalist Chicago School thinking in antitrust enforcement.

On the one hand, *public-interest* theories posit regulation as a means to protect social welfare, and thus as a beneficial or at least benign activity undertaken to further the public good.[19] Known alternatively as the Pigovian welfare theory, named for the work of Arthur Pigou,[20] this approach is premised upon two assumptions: first, that markets fail frequently due to monopolies or externalities, and second, that governments are neutral and capable of correcting these failures through regulation.[21] Accordingly, regulators act to achieve collective goals that cannot be realised by unregulated markets alone. Although public-interest theories do not automatically assume a beneficial outcome, as Morgan and Yeung noted, such theories 'are often underpinned by an implicit optimism about the capacity of regulation to promote some form of public interest'.[22] Public-interest theories have faced considerable

[18] A notable exception is McChesney & Shugart (1995).

[19] Breyer (1982), Sunstein (1990). Discussed by Morgan & Yeung (2007:17–43); Baldwin et al. (2011:40–3).

[20] Pigou (1932); cf. Hantke-Domas (2003), who suggested that formulation of the public-interest theory is largely attributable to public-choice scholars who needed a comparison against which to measure their work.

[21] Schleifer (2005:440). [22] Morgan & Yeung (2007:43).

criticism, however, on the bases that conflicting interests render a universal concept of 'public interest' impossible to identify, that the disinterestedness and expertise of regulators is often in question, and that regulation in practice often fails to maximise public-interest outcomes.[23]

On the other hand, *public-choice* theories (also known as private interest theories) view regulation purely as the product of self-interest: it is sought by and benefits only the regulated, creating an undesirable equilibrium and necessitating deregulation.[24] Building on earlier work,[25] Stigler applied the ideas of public choice directly to State regulation, arguing that the regulatory process involves a relationship of demand and supply between interest groups and regulators. In order to remain in power, politicians provide regulations that benefit interest groups in exchange for votes.[26] Accordingly, public choice posits that private demand rather than general public necessity motivates much regulation, in order to shield firms from the 'inconvenience of competition'.[27] This critique incorporates elements of 'capture theory', which holds that the impact of regulation tends to be pro-industry because regulators work to further the interests of regulated firms, whether due to subversion through lobbying, influence or bribery by interest groups.[28] Indeed, Posner drew provocative parallels between regulation and cartelisation, arguing that the practical effect of each is the same: namely, higher prices.[29] Regulation can also lead to rent-seeking behaviour, that is, expenditure of firm resources in pursuit of advantageous regulation, which ultimately results in deadweight loss for consumers.[30] Unlike public-interest theories, which implicitly assume that regulators act in pursuit of the collective good, public choice emphasises the overall negative impacts of regulation for society. Unsurprisingly, public-choice advocates tend to be highly critical of most regulatory regimes, whereas public-interest advocates stress the social benefits that only regulation can deliver. Public choice has been criticised for its lack of empirical robustness, however, and for its inability to explain whether a *particular*

[23] Baldwin et al. (2011:42–3); cf. Sunstein (1990).

[24] Stigler (1971); Posner (1974); Peltzman (1976). Discussed by Ogus (1994:55–75); Peltzman (1989:4–17); Baldwin et al. (2011:43–9).

[25] Coase (1937); Black (1948); Coase (1960); Buchanan & Tullock (1962).

[26] Stigler (1971), whose work was later formalised by Peltzman (1976).

[27] Demsetz (1968:61).

[28] Jordan (1972); Viscusi et al. (2005:379–80); Ogus (1994:57–8); Dogan & Lemley (2009:698–700).

[29] Posner (1974:344–5).

[30] Krueger (1974); Posner (1975).

instance of regulation (or failure to regulate) is socially harmful or beneficial, as opposed to merely providing a generalised descriptive explanation for bad regulatory decisions.[31]

Beyond the polarised public-interest/choice divide, various alternative theories of regulation have been advanced to explain regulatory developments. Williamson's 'transaction cost efficiency' approach, for example, supports regulation only when it is the most efficient means to structure a market.[32] Institutional theories of regulation emphasise the impact that institutional arrangements, dynamics and social processes play in influencing the enactment and shape of regulation.[33] The public interest versus public choice debate is most relevant for our purposes, however, insofar as it demonstrates the clear divergence between a vision of regulation as a necessary and socially beneficial element of market systems and a vision of regulation as an inefficient and undesirable interference with free markets. This divergence, moreover, finds reflection in contemporary political discourse, alongside the inherent tensions and uncertainty regarding the appropriate role for regulation in society. These opposing viewpoints might therefore explain, and have to a considerable extent informed, modern cycles of regulation and deregulation.[34]

III. Public choice in practice: deregulation and privatisation

We move to the question of regulatory failure, or why bad regulation is considered 'bad' as such. We saw, in Chapter 1, that the so-called normative-justificatory approach to regulation links its existence directly to the market defects to be remedied, which comprise, essentially, the substantive goals of regulation.[35] Regulatory scholarship also identifies a number of administrative goals of a more procedural nature by which to

[31] Hovenkamp (2005:240).

[32] Williamson (1975); Williamson (1981); Richman & Boerner (2006).

[33] Institutionalist theories comprise three broad strands, which focus upon intra-institutional dynamics, inter-institutional dynamics and the impact of networks of regulators, respectively: Baldwin et al. (2011:53–65); Morgan & Yeung (2007:53–74).

[34] Although the earliest origins of the deregulation movement in the USA pre-date the broader acceptance of the public-choice theory (Peltzman (1989:2), many scholars link the emergence of public-choice thinking with the more prominent examples of the Reagan administration's anti-government agenda: e.g., Hovenkamp (2005:238–40); Shughart (2000:276).

[35] See pp. 37–9.

measure the effectiveness of any regulatory scheme, that is, the extent to which it is successful in achieving its substantive goal(s).[36] Yeung, for example, identified three such regulatory yardsticks – efficiency; clarity and predictability; and flexibility, responsiveness and timeliness – by which the success of regulatory intervention should be assessed.[37] Yet regulation in general, even regulation that might be viewed as objectively successful by reference to these metrics, has been subject to numerous criticisms of varying degrees of persuasiveness. Breyer, for example, identified high costs, ineffectiveness and waste, procedural unfairness, complexity and delay, unresponsiveness to democratic control, and the inherent unpredictability of outcomes as common objections to regulation.[38] Sunstein put the point succinctly: regulation is viewed by critics as 'imposing large costs for uncertain or non-existent gains'.[39] Nonetheless, because regulation involves a democratically accountable political choice to impose State control in the market to address identified public-policy concerns, whether efficiency-based or in furtherance of non-economic goals, the notion of regulatory failure must require something beyond mere generalised criticism of the intrinsic nature of regulation.[40] Baldwin et al. suggested that regulators 'fail . . . when they do not produce (at reasonable cost) the outcomes that are stipulated in their mandates or when they do not serve procedural or representative values properly'.[41] Examples of failure might include circumstances where the costs of regulation greatly exceeded its benefits, where there are unanticipated negative side-effects, or where the outcome of regulation is significantly less successful than anticipated.[42] So-called 'paradoxes of regulation' arise where regulation is self-defeating, in the sense that it generates results that are the opposite of those intended.[43] The potential causes of regulatory failure are numerous and may arise at any point in the regulatory process. Regulation may suffer from a misdiagnosis of the underlying policy concerns,[44] poor design or choice of regulatory instrument,[45] inadequate or improper implementation,[46] over-prescriptiveness

[36] Yeung (2004:30). [37] Yeung (2004:30–6). [38] Breyer (1982:4).

[39] Sunstein (1990:74).

[40] See also Breyer (1982:4): 'defenders of particular programs and of regulation in general can respond by pointing to achievements of individual programs or by claiming that in the absence of regulation, matters would be far worse'.

[41] Baldwin et al. (2011:69). [42] Sunstein (1990:74); Ogus (1994:56).

[43] Sunstein (1990:74,106–7). [44] Sunstein (1990:86–9).

[45] Sunstein (1990:89–94); Baldwin et al. (2011:70); Ogus (1994:56).

[46] Sunstein (1990:98–102); Baldwin et al. (2011:70–1); Ogus (1994:56).

that inhibits dynamic efficiency[47] or where inefficiencies arise as the regulatory framework becomes obsolete with market changes.[48] The concept of regulatory failure thus implies a market outcome that falls appreciably short of the 'second-best' result for the circumstances, and might even be worse than the market outcome that would exist absent intervention. Regulation is viewed, furthermore, as a self-perpetuating phenomenon[49] – it can lead to even greater amounts of regulation – which, in turn, may perpetuate regulatory failure.

Critics of regulation are also quick to compare disfavourably the market outcomes under failed regulation with the presumed superior result in a deregulated and unencumbered market. Public-choice theory is allied closely to Chicago School thinking, which, as discussed, emphasises the robustness of the market mechanism and its ability to resolve, eventually, almost any market failure.[50] From this standpoint, regulatory failure, whether actual or presumed, may provide justification for market deregulation, meaning the removal of sector-specific regulatory constraints and obligations such as price controls, entry or exit restrictions or mandatory access requirements.[51] Deregulation may also involve new entry to increase competition, or the disaggregation of functions previously bundled together by a monopoly provider.[52] In its most rudimentary form, deregulation implies a total removal of regulatory controls, although, in practice, deregulation is usually a gradual, incremental process. The concept of liberalisation, more specifically, denotes a transition from monopoly to competitive market conditions.[53] Liberalisation is linked directly to the idea of 'regulation for competition', that is, the use of regulatory controls to restructure monopoly markets to create competitive segments that can, subsequently, be administered through market forces rather than regulatory commands. Particularly in markets that retain natural monopoly or oligopoly elements, initial deregulatory efforts may be partial, with regulatory controls remaining in place at least temporarily for market segments that remain as-yet uncompetitive. The aim of such transitional regulation is generally to move the market

[47] Baldwin et al. (2011:70). [48] Sunstein (1990:94–6); Baldwin et al. (2011:71).
[49] Loevinger (1966:117); Kahn (1990:332); Dempsey (1989:2–26). [50] See p. 57.
[51] An alternative is to improve the quality of existing regulation, considered further later in this chapter.
[52] Cudahy (2001:159).
[53] Armstrong & Sappington (2006:325); Gamble (1989:10). An alternative definition conceives of liberalisation as 'less ambitious reductions in control' than full deregulation (McCrudden (1990:546).

towards circumstances of greater competition and, ultimately, removal of all sector-specific controls.[54] Yet enduring structural obstacles to competition, and/or the need to secure non-market goals within the sector, may require on-going regulatory supervision in the longer term. Partial deregulation might also result in asymmetries and distortions between regulated and unregulated market segments,[55] which can create a need for further regulation in other areas, for example to address emerging bottlenecks. Deregulation of the US airline industry in the 1970s, for instance, gave rise to competition problems at certain airports, necessitating new airports regulation.[56] The transition to *full* competition thus remains an unrealised potentiality in many network or utilities markets.[57]

Deregulation often goes hand-in-hand with privatisation of State-owned enterprises. Indeed, both are elements of the (much-disputed) 'Washington Consensus' regarding economic policy reforms for developing economies.[58] Public ownership functions, in a sense, as a particularly intensive form of market regulation.[59] Yet privatisation may be pursued for policy or political reasons that go beyond the classic justifications for deregulation such as increasing competition and efficiency; additional motivations may include the extension of freedom of choice, the financing the State, the weakening public-sector unions, widening of share ownership in the State, and enlarging the concept of active citizenship and decreasing dependency on the State.[60] Evidence on the desirability of privatisation is rather equivocal, however – as Stigliz summarised succinctly, 'it depends'[61] – insofar as the benefits of moving away from abusive or inefficient State-ownership models must be balanced against significant difficulties that can arise after privatisation, such as wealth inequality, declines in product/service quality or even undermining of the entire market.[62] The marketisation of public-service provision, in particular, generates strong criticisms, and raises challenging political and social questions regarding the appropriate dividing line between the market and the State.[63]

[54] Hellwig (2009:205–6); Crampton & Facey (2002:35–6); Burton (1997:162–3).

[55] Kahn (1990:333–4). [56] Rose-Ackerman (1990:520–2).

[57] Hellwig (2009:207); Dabbah (2011:139–40). [58] Williamson (1990).

[59] Cf. Breyer (1982:181–3), who suggested that nationalisation provides an alternative to classic command-and-control regulation, albeit a disfavoured one.

[60] Gamble (1989:11). [61] Stiglitz (2008:ix). [62] Stiglitz (2008); Roland (2008).

[63] See, generally, Prosser (2004).

By focusing primarily on the efficiency of regulation, the deregulation/privatisation agenda also fails to account for another important aspect of many regulatory regimes: namely, the incorporation of non-efficiency-based values within the regulatory framework, such as the protection of human rights or furtherance of social solidarity.[64] Where the purpose of regulation is to safeguard non-economic values, the claim that market-ordering is inherently superior to government-ordering becomes suspect. Instead, regulation may be required precisely *because* the market outcome is undesirable when viewed from a broader public-policy context, which incorporates, for example, considerations of equity and fairness. The core non-economic functions of regulation are considered further in section V.

The advisability of (even partial) deregulation, and the optimal approach for achieving this, is therefore difficult to determine *a priori*. Writing specifically in the context of liberalisation of monopoly markets, Armstrong and Sappington, in a thorough survey of existing economic literature, observed that:

> even the comparatively simple choice between regulated monopoly and unregulated competition can be intricate and complex in practice. . . . [T]he decision to introduce competition into an industry is only the beginning of a journey down a long and winding road that can present many obstacles and detours. Furthermore, the best route from monopoly to competition can differ substantially in different settings. Therefore, there is no single set of directions that can guide the challenging journey from monopoly to competition in all settings.[65]

Given the wide variety of deregulatory strategies available, and the fact that the merits of these policies vary considerably, they concluded that it is more appropriate to enquire about the advisability of a *specific* deregulation policy than to question whether deregulation *per se* is desirable or undesirable.[66] This viewpoint has, similarly, been echoed in the privatisation context.[67]

As the public interest versus public choice arguments considered here suggest, nonetheless, the deregulation debate towards the end of the twentieth century began to adopt polarised and ideological undertones.[68] This modern deregulation movement is associated with the transatlantic meeting of minds between Ronald Reagan in the USA and Margaret

[64] Baldwin et al. (2011:22–3). [65] Armstrong & Sappington (2006:326).
[66] Armstrong & Sappington (2006:326, 345). [67] Stiglitz (2008:xvii).
[68] Cudahy (2001:171–2); McCrudden (1990:546).

Thatcher in the UK – each a conservative political leader in power during the 1980s, and each sharing a vision of society in general, and the economy in particular, premised on a minimal role for the State. Reagan and Thatcher were influential figures of the New Right, a form of neoliberalism that placed faith in market coordination in preference to political or administrative coordination.[69] In order to understand how deregulation can assume an ideological dimension, and how this might distort regulatory analysis, it is worthwhile considering briefly the trajectory of regulation and deregulation in these countries over the last century.

(i) Deregulation in practice: the US and UK experiences

The first half of the twentieth century witnessed a notable increase in levels of economic and social regulation in both the USA and the UK. Within the US, the Progressive Era (1890–1920 approx.) and New Deal Era (1933–8 approx.) had each seen a significant uptick in regulatory activity, in order, respectively, to address perceived accumulations of power and abusive practices by big businesses, and to counter the negative effects of the Great Depression.[70] The size and scope of the federal bureaucracy was thus increased through creation or expansion of various government agencies with responsibility for discrete policy areas. The 'rights revolution' of the 1960s led to further social regulation, in particular, including anti-discrimination and environmental protection statutes.[71] By the 1970s,[72] however, in the midst of severe economic recession together with high inflation, high unemployment and sharp decreases in US competitiveness internationally, both public and political support for government regulation declined.[73] With the emergence of a 'market-centred discourse',[74] regulatory controls were now viewed as unnecessary and anticompetitive, and were linked, in popular

[69] Gamble (1989:4–5). [70] Hantke-Domas (2003:172–8); Sunstein (1990:18–24).

[71] Sunstein (1990:24–9). Even by the early 1960s, scepticism regarding the extent and impact of *economic* regulation in the USA had been voiced by President Kennedy: Mikva (1990:522).

[72] Although the US deregulation movement is most closely associated with the presidency of Ronald Reagan, many of the key deregulatory efforts occurred prior to Reagan taking office: Kahn (1990:325–6).

[73] Sunstein (1990:30–1); Kahn (1990); Hovenkamp (2005:237–44); Galambos (2004:155); Mikva (1990:522–7); Freyer (2006:135–9).

[74] Freyer (2006:134).

imagination, to the US's economic decline.[75] Perhaps counterintuitively, given that the period marked the ascendency of public-choice thinking,[76] deregulation was also supported by private interests (that is, regulated firms) that were disenchanted with their regulatory bargains.[77] As part of a governmental reform agenda seeking 'deregulation, decentralisation and privatisation',[78] regulatory constraints were attacked through a two-pronged approach. First, the late 1970s and early 1980s saw the removal of economic regulation in various sectors. Transport (airlines, railroad and trucking), where regulatory controls on pricing and entry had long been decried as inefficient and counterproductive, provided the most prominent example, alongside reform of certain financial services and price control of oil.[79] Second, in 1981 the Reagan administration implemented a requirement of cost-benefit analysis of any proposed regulation, an analytical technique that will be considered later in this chapter. This had the result, in particular, of limiting or redirecting much social regulation as well as controls on telecommunications and broadcasting.[80]

A parallel movement began in the UK with the 1979 election of a Conservative government led by Thatcher, which was to focus on privatisation as the means to reduce the role of the State. As in the US, economic and social regulation in the UK had increased considerably over the twentieth century. The post–World War II period, moreover, saw the nationalisation of the UK's major utilities, plus introduction of a comprehensive system of social entitlements (the 'welfare state').[81] The concept of social democracy lay at the heart of this programme, giving the State an enlarged role with respect to markets and society.[82] Again, by the 1970s, however, the UK economy was perceived by many as in decline, with high inflation, industrial unrest and inefficient public industries.[83] As support for the social democratic model – and its heavy dependence on government intervention – fell,[84] the focus of political discourse shifted from collectivism to individualism.[85] Thatcher came to

[75] Sunstein (1990:31). [76] Hovenkamp (2005:239–40). [77] Kahn (1990:330–2).
[78] Rose-Ackerman (1990:519). For a general description of 'Reaganomics', see Jacob (1985).
[79] Peltzman (1989); Kahn (1990); Sunstein (1990:31); Breyer (1982:317–40); Dempsey (1989:28).
[80] Sunstein (1990:31), Mikva (1990); cf. Rose-Ackerman (1990:522), who argued that efficiency-based reforms of social regulation were minimal during this period.
[81] Ogus (1994:9–10); Baldwin et al. (2011:4–5); Gamble (1989:1–2).
[82] Gamble (1989:1–2); Gerber (1998:213). [83] Bolick (1995:529–30).
[84] Gamble (1989:2–3). [85] Loughlin (1989:22).

power promising to re-order social democracy by reducing the role of the State and maximising free markets.[86] Privatisation of formerly nationalised industries became a flagship Tory policy, as telecommunications, gas, coal, electricity, steel, water, airports and later rail were all privatised. Yet Thatcherite privatisation encompassed more than simple de-nationalisation:[87] it also involved the opening of many State activities to private competition, and contracting out, via competitive tendering, of certain public services formerly provided by public bodies.[88] Privatisation was accompanied by deregulation in certain sectors – including, again, financial services and the airline industry[89] – while the Thatcherite 'obsession' with efficiency[90] extended, *inter alia*, to costs of regulatory compliance for businesses and reducing the strength of labour unions.[91]

Thatcherism, like Reaganism, was a fundamentally ideological enterprise.[92] The most enduring result of the New Right deregulation movement has been, perhaps, a shift in political discourse towards a new norm where State market intervention is inherently suspect until otherwise established.[93] The deregulation/privatisation movement, moreover, has encouraged similar developments elsewhere.[94] Coupled with the ascendency of the Chicago School, neoliberal thinking has had a lasting impact on the views of society regarding regulation, resulting in something of a paradigm shift towards a default deregulation standard, at least until the more recent GFC.[95] Like regulation, moreover, deregulation tends to be a progressive self-perpetuating phenomenon,[96] so that the deregulation movement generated significant momentum over time.

Almost equally remarkable, however, is the relative modesty of the results actually achieved by Reagan and Thatcher.[97] Despite trenchant 'small government' rhetoric – Reagan once quipped that the most terrifying words in the English language are, 'I'm from the Government and I'm here to help',[98] while Thatcher declared that there is 'no such thing as

[86] Gamble (1989:6). Loughlin (1989:23) describes Thatcherism as involving 'an atomistic view of individuals and an idealised view of free markets'.
[87] Gamble (1989:4). [88] McCrudden (1990:545).
[89] McCrudden (1990:546); Bolick (1995:541). [90] McCrudden (1990:550).
[91] Bolick (1995); McCrudden (1990).
[92] McCrudden (1990:546); Grenfell (1999:221–2). [93] Gamble (1989:13).
[94] See e.g. Bortolotti & Milella (2008), who assessed privatisation in other Western European countries following Thatcher.
[95] Baldwin et al. (2011:1); Jenny (2012:170). [96] Kahn (1990:332).
[97] Gamble (1989:13); Ogus (1994:11); Rose-Ackerman (1990); cf. Bolick (1995); Peltzman (1989).
[98] Williams (1990:97).

society'[99] – their impact has been rather less-encompassing than this uncompromising language suggests.[100] To an extent, the US deregulation policies of the 1980s represented merely a continuation of reform efforts that were already on-going.[101] Such efforts were largely continued by Reagan's successors from both the right *and* the left,[102] and resulted more in a rationalisation of regulation rather than wholesale deregulation as such. Almost paradoxically, the initial Thatcherite model for privatisation allowed little room for competition. While privatisation reduced the size of the state-owned sector, much existing regulation remained unchanged.[103] Privatisation of utilities as vertically (or horizontally) integrated monopolies was routine,[104] particularly in the initial stages, as liberalisation was viewed as a secondary consideration to the need to secure sufficient investment.[105] This had the parallel effect of creating an abundance of new regulatory regimes and agencies to administer competition in privatised sectors, many of which retained natural monopoly segments.[106] Burton thus memorably described the UK model as an example of 'ordered competition',[107] rather than a truly competitive order as such. Furthermore, although scope for competition has gradually increased in line with a government policy to inject competition progressively into these markets,[108] many of the competition difficulties that have arisen in utilities sectors in recent years have stemmed either from the ineffectual activities of these regulatory agencies,[109] or from the legacy of integrated privatisation.[110]

The mixed results of privatisation under Thatcher, particularly once longer-term impact is considered, indicates that it is important, also, to explore some of the deregulatory failures – in contrast to the notion of regulatory failure, considered earlier – that have followed the New Right

[99] Evans (2004:137). [100] Rose-Ackerman (1990).

[101] Mikva (1990:522–4); Viscusi et al. (2005:24–7). [102] Viscusi et al. (2005:28–9).

[103] McCrudden (1990:553).

[104] See, e.g., the privatisation as vertically integrated entities of British Telecommunications under the Telecommunications Act 1984 and of British Gas under the Gas Act 1986, as well as the privatisation of the British Airports Authority as a horizontally integrated concern under the Airports Act 1986. Increasing disenchantment with the approach of privatising utilities as monopolies, however, resulted in the vertical separation of the Central Electricity Generating Board under the Electricity Act 1989, prior to privatisation in 1990–1: see Newbury (1997:366–7).

[105] Coleman & Grenfell (1999:494).

[106] Baldwin et al. (2011:5); Ogus (1994:10); Burton (1997:164). [107] Burton (1997:174).

[108] Grenfell (1999:222–30); Ogus (1994:10).

[109] Baldwin et al. (2011:4–6); Burton (1997:181–2). [110] See pp. 290–3.

deregulation agenda. The GFC of 2007 onwards provides probably the most compelling example of a severe market failure that was caused, at least partly, by insufficient or unduly lax regulation. Deregulatory failures here included the inability of regulators to counter continuing moral hazards within financial markets, the anticompetitive impact of the oligopoly structure of the sector, and the potential for contagion flowing from network effects.[111] Yet there was precedent for this in the Savings and Loan crises of the late 1980s, which saw the wide-scale failure of small financial institutions in the USA as a result of corruption that, similarly, followed deregulation.[112] California's energy crisis of 2000 provided another prominent example: following partial and ill-conceived deregulation, unregulated wholesale electricity prices soared above regulated retail prices, leading to retailer bankruptcies and supply blackouts.[113] In the UK, rail privatisation and unbundling eventually resulted in bankruptcy of the privatised entity responsible for maintenance of railway infrastructure, after years of alleged mismanagement, underinvestment and light-touch regulation.[114] In each of these examples, governments were subsequently forced to spend vast amounts of public money to remedy the markets failures that followed from failures in deregulation. Much like bad regulation, deregulation when poorly implemented does not merely fail to live up to its free-marketeering promise; it might actually lead to a deterioration of market conditions and overall public welfare. A not-unlikely outcome is some degree of reregulation, or strengthening of existing regulatory controls, within the sector in the future.[115] Moreover, Reaganite and Thatcherite economic policies resulted in large increases in inequality within US and UK societies,[116] thus compromising other important societal values, such as solidarity and fairness, in pursuit of apparent efficiency.

(ii) Deregulation and the role of competition law

Is there a role for competition law within these processes of deregulation, privatisation and potential reregulation? At first glance, by

[111] OECD (2011a). [112] Freyer (2006:142). [113] Cudahy (2001:172–85).

[114] Whitehouse (2003).

[115] See, e.g., repeal of the Glass-Steagall Act of 1933, which prohibited the affiliation of commercial banking and securities activities in the US, by the Gramm-Leach-Bliley Act of 1999, which is considered to have been a significant cause of the GFC; these provisions were reinstated, albeit in watered-down form, by the Dodd-Frank Act of 2010.

[116] Piketty (2014:42).

removing government-imposed restraints and raising greater awareness of the importance of competitive market mechanisms, deregulation et al. would appear to create greater possibilities for the application of competition law.[117] Deregulation usually involves removal of express or implied antitrust immunity; indeed, as we saw in the preceding chapter, initial efforts to liberalise electricity markets in Germany involved only the removal of antitrust immunity for electricity contracts.[118] Deregulation, furthermore, opens at least part of the market to competitive forces. By playing an 'enabling role' for competition through the dismantling of historic monopolies and regulatory controls,[119] and also raising the possibility of independent anti-competitive market behaviour, deregulation can create potential space within which competition law might apply, as well as a concomitant need for such supervision. In the *E.ON/GDF* pipeline cartel, for example, EU competition law became applicable within the relevant markets only after liberalisation: that is, once pre-existing legal and *de facto* monopolies were abolished, these markets became potentially competitive, and, therefore, vulnerable to anticompetitive behaviour.[120] As noted, the process of market liberalisation often involves a degree of 'regulation for competition', which is intended to generate, proactively, new and perhaps slightly artificial competition within previously uncompetitive market sectors. This may involve, in the first instance, mandatory access or interconnections requirements; more progressive regulatory frameworks can include express obligations of non-discrimination, make provision for a sector regulator to administer the access regime, and even require legal or ownership unbundling of certain business units or market segments. The general tenor of much EU-level regulation aimed at liberalising utilities markets – for example, energy,[121] telecommunications,[122] rail[123] and

[117] See also Jenny (2012:172).
[118] See pp. 76–7.
[119] Semeraro (2003:159); see also Speta (2003:113); Smith (2004:61).
[120] Case T-360/09 *E.ON Ruhrgas AG, E.ON AG* v. *Commission*, EU:T:2012:332.
[121] Considered in further detail at pp. 112–3.
[122] Considered in further detail at pp. 169–73.
[123] See Council Directive 91/440/EEC of 29 July 1991 on the development of the Community's railways (OJ C 237/25, 24.8.91), supplemented by the Second Railway Package contained within Directive 2004/49/EC of the European Parliament and of the Council of 29 April 2004 ('Railway Safety Directive') (OJ L 164/44, 30.04.2004), Directive 2004/50/EC of the European Parliament and of the Council of 29 April 2004 ('Interoperability Directive') (OJ L 1644/114, 30.04.2004), and Directive 2004/51/EC of the European Parliament and of the Council of 29 April 2004 amending Council Directive 91/440/EEC on the development of the Community's railways (OJ C 164/164, 30.04.2004).

post[124] – incorporates the dual objectives of strengthening regulatory obligations at the domestic level to develop and protect structural competition in potentially competitive markets, on the one hand, coupled with increased scope for use of *ex ante* competition enforcement to correct competition problems that arise subsequently, on the other. The application of EU competition law to supervise energy market performance was considered in the preceding chapter; its application in telecommunications markets is assessed in the next. It is worth remembering, additionally, that liberalisation in the EU context pursues the additional goal of single market integration, alongside the efficiency-focused benefits of greater market competition as such.

Newly deregulated markets are rarely perfectly competitive, whether due to remaining structural or legal barriers to competition, lingering sluggish market dynamics, or strategic behavioural resistance by the former market incumbent. This may create a *prima facie* case for antitrust intervention. The process of gradually deregulating AT&T, the US telecommunications incumbent, for example, received a considerable boost when the firm agreed to voluntary divestiture of certain business units by antitrust consent decree.[125] Alfred Kahn, an enthusiastic supporter of deregulation who oversaw airline deregulation in the USA, nonetheless recognised the limitations of such policies. He therefore advanced two propositions to guide deregulation and the transition to market competition: first, even imperfect competition is preferable to command-and-control regulation wherever possible; and second, in the event of deregulation, robust government intervention, for example, through antitrust enforcement, is needed to remedy imperfections and market failures that may arise, although such interventions should aim to supplement rather than suppress the emergence of competition.[126] Similarly, it has been argued that competition enforcement may help to bridge the gap between inefficient heavy regulation and insufficient control of anticompetitive conduct within a market.[127] On this view, it may indeed be legitimate to heighten competition law scrutiny in

[124] See Directive 97/67/EC of the European Parliament and of the Council of 15 December 1997 on common rules for development of the internal market of Community postal services and the improvement of quality of service (OJ C 15/14, 21.01.1998), as amended by Directive 2002/39/EC of the European Parliament and of the Council of 10 June 2002 (OJ C 176/21, 05.07.2002) and Directive 2008/6/EC of the European Parliament and of the Council of 20 February 2008 (OJ C 52/3, 27.2.2008).

[125] *United States* v. *AT&T* 552, F.Supp. 131 (DDC 1982), considered at pp. 63–4.

[126] Kahn (1990:340, 353). [127] Shelanski (2012:506).

newly deregulated markets, given the likelihood that competition problems may arise.[128] Krattenmaker identified four ways in which deregulation might increase the need for antitrust scrutiny, namely, to address the legacy of any facilitating practices for anticompetitive coordination that were tolerated or approved by regulators, to scrutinise mergers prompted by deregulation, to address anticompetitive lobbying efforts by deregulated firms that had a historically close relationship to government, or to spearhead the transformation of antitrust doctrine into a legal tool focused principally upon fostering competition.[129] In markets that remain subject to partial regulation, questions arise regarding the potential application of competition law to scrutinise regulated conduct, either where the firm seeks to avoid or exploit the regulatory regime, or where the regulation itself generates inefficient market outcomes. The substantive interaction between competition law and sector-specific regulation when applied concurrently within a sector is the subject matter of the next chapter.

An enhanced role for competition law does not result automatically from the shift to deregulation, however. The deregulation movement of the 1980s was informed greatly by Chicago School thinking, which, of course, disfavours State intervention in the guise of antitrust enforcement in much the same manner that it rejects economic regulation. The movement from market supervision by economic regulation to antitrust enforcement has been described as contradictory insofar as it involves the removal of one set of State controls only to replace these with another.[130] The episodic nature of competition enforcement when compared with a systemic regulatory framework may go some way to answering this criticism. In its most extreme incarnation, however, the embrace of a deregulation agenda may imply an abrogation of most if not all market controls, including the more restrained and discrete guidance of the 'invisible hand' that competition law provides. In parallel with the movement towards deregulation in the USA in 1980s, for example, this period also saw the adoption of a considerably more permissive and restrained attitude to competition enforcement by federal antitrust agencies.[131] These developments have been attributed, primarily, to the *laissez-faire* attitudes of the Reagan administration towards *any* form of market intervention – not merely economic regulation in the classic

[128] Schwartz (1987:1056). [129] Krattenmaker (1984).
[130] Kahn (1987:1059), who nonetheless advocated such an approach.
[131] Shughart (2000); Freyer (2006:139,147–9).

sense, but also intervention through antitrust enforcement. The administration's opposition to antitrust manifested itself, *inter alia*, in efforts to narrow the scope of existing competition laws through adoption of the 'total-welfare' efficiency standard as the primary goal of antitrust, to restrict existing antitrust legislation and extend statutory immunities, the appointment of antitrust-sceptic federal judges, alongside a highly deferential exercise of enforcement discretion.[132] This led to a significant decline in antitrust enforcement during the eight years of the Reagan administration,[133] although critics remain divided, upon largely ideological lines, about whether the Reaganite approach is defensible on balance.[134]

Alternatively, as the UK example demonstrates, rolling back the State through privatisation may require significant quantities of additional regulation to administer newly privatised markets. Here again, competition law may be excluded, simply because of the absence of competitive space within which market forces can operate. Thatcher, unlike Reagan, was not ideologically opposed to antitrust as such. Indeed her government passed the Competition Act 1980, which sought, somewhat unsuccessfully in practice, to supplement the existing UK restrictive practices regime with an effects-based competition system.[135] As noted, however, the Thatcherite approach to market reform frequently involved

[132] Campbell (1985); Kovacic (1991); Litvack (1982); Ponsoldt (1988); Galambos (2004); Dempsey (1989:30). Cf. Eisner & Meier (1990), who attribute these changes in antitrust policy to internal shifts within the bureaucracy of enforcement, in particular the increased influence of academic economists rather than litigation attorneys in determining agency policy. The Supreme Court's jurisprudential shift towards a more economics-focused (and thus narrower) conception of antitrust began in the mid-1970s, with cases like *United States* v. *General Dynamics Corp.*, 415 US 486 (1974) and *Continental Television* v. *GTE Sylvania*, 433 US 36 (1977): see Kovacic (1991:50–1); Campbell (1985:353).

[133] Shughart (2000:282).

[134] Contrast Galambos (2004), who celebrated the improved performance of the US economy that he attributed to deference to concentrations of power via mergers and non-application of the monopolisation provisions, with Ponsoldt (1988), who emphasised the significant income inequality that arose during the period.

[135] Gerber (1998:222–3); Beath (2002:223). The difficulties of the revised competition regime were attributable, primarily, to inadequate implementation, and do not reflect a diminished government commitment to antitrust as such: Gerber (1998:224–5). The UK competition regime was substantially reformed by the Competition Act 1998 and Enterprise Act 2002, enacted by the New Labour government, and has been strengthened further by the Enterprise and Regulatory Reform Act 2013, enacted by the Conservative-Liberal Democrat coalition, thus reflecting the fact that a commitment to competition is not necessarily a partisan issue.

privatisation of integrated monopolies, which created new problems of private market power that could not be controlled effectively by either regulators or antitrust. Caught between the inadequacy of existing regulation and the non-applicability of conventional competition law, recourse was had instead to the hybridised market-investigation powers of what is now the Competition and Markets Authority. In 2005, for example, in lieu of a market investigation reference by the regulator that was likely to result in involuntary ownership separation, the telecommunications incumbent, BT, made a series of legally binding undertakings with respect to supplying competitors, legal separation and investments in new infrastructure.[136] In 2009, following an in-depth market investigation, BAA, the privatised operator of various UK airports, was mandated to sell three such facilities in order to address competition problems in airport markets in Scotland and the South East of England[137] Although the market investigation procedure, which is considered in Chapter 5, provides a novel means by which, effectively, to extend the reach of UK competition law, its use in these instances perhaps says more about the limitations of both antitrust and regulatory controls than the merits of the market inquiry procedure itself.

The choice between regulation and deregulation is, nonetheless, rather less stark than the more incendiary rhetoric would suggest. The sceptics of the public-choice movement clearly go too far in rejecting regulation out of hand without any consideration of its potential impact in practice, or the potentially negative consequences of its absence. A 2013 study by Pelkmans and Luchetta on the results of twenty-five years of network industry liberalisation in the EU illustrates, instead, the complexity of these issues.[138] The authors concluded that relatively similar approaches to liberalisation have met with varying degrees of success across different industries, suggesting that there can be no 'one-size-fits-all' solution to good market performance. Competition has been achieved, to a large extent, in both airline and telecommunications markets, with resulting benefits for consumers and in terms of innovation. Persistent structural obstacles to competition in the electricity and rail sectors, however, mean that liberalisation remains at a relatively early stage of development in

[136] See OFCOM, *Consultation on undertakings offered by British Telecommunications plc in lieu of a reference under Part 4 of the Enterprise Act 2002*, published 30 June 2005; and OFCOM, *Undertakings given to Ofcom by BT pursuant to the Enterprise Act 2002*, published 22 September 2005.

[137] See p. 290. [138] Pelkmans & Luchetta (2013).

those markets. Moreover, both within industries where liberalisation has succeeded and those where it has been less successful, market opening has had certain negative consequences for workers within such sectors, as well as potentially negative impacts on incentives for infrastructure investment. These findings highlight the need to account, within both regulatory *and* deregulatory frameworks, for any potential knock-on consequences that might follow from policy choices about market intervention. This may necessitate modification of the proposed approach, or enactment of supplementary economic or social regulation to avoid undesirable outcomes. The 'better regulation' agenda, considered next, represents, to an extent, efforts at an institutional level to improve the quality of existing and future regulation to avoid adverse side effects. Following that, we consider market circumstances where regulation remains indispensable to achieve either efficiency or non-economic goals, what might be called the unavoidable or substantive core of regulation.

IV. Reforming regulation: 'better regulation'

Whereas the deregulation agenda posits that regulation is inherently unsuccessful as a means of market organisation, and should be reduced or avoided wherever possible, the 'better regulation' (BR) approach is more nuanced and optimistic. The BR debate assumes that one acknowledges the possible necessity for regulation, but differentiates between ineffective and more efficacious regulatory controls, seeking to eliminate the former while developing and fostering the latter. It thus accepts the existence, but not the inevitability, of regulatory failure. At its core, BR aims to improve the quality of regulation, whether *ex ante* in relation to proposed regulation, or through *ex post* review of existing regulation. Much like theories prompting deregulation, BR has been conceived in a broader context that goes beyond economic regulation to also address social regulatory controls, although, again, it remains fully applicable solely in the context of the former. In contrast to pure deregulation, this approach is concerned with identifying and enacting successful regulation, and is not simply a question of lessening or eliminating regulatory controls – at least in theory. There is a significant overlap with liberalisation polices here, which, usually, aim to introduce competition to the fullest extent possible as expeditiously as possible, while retaining in place necessary, and ideally effective, regulatory supervision. BR is relevant for our purposes insofar as improvements in the effectiveness of regulation may diminish pressure for deregulation, and is likely to reduce the need for concurrent application of antitrust in regulated markets. 'Better' regulation may thus provide a more palatable alternative, or 'middle way', for markets where competition enforcement alone offers an incomplete solution, yet which might nonetheless avoid the counterproductive consequences of regulatory failure.

In contrast to the notion of 'failed' regulation, considered earlier, 'good' regulation has been defined as regulation that is both *effective* (it achieves its planned objectives) and *efficient* (at the least cost, both in terms of administrative costs and compliance costs).[139] What constitutes BR, as such, can, however, be difficult to define. Wiener described BR in instrumental terms as, 'a form of structured reasoning to inform sound public policy and bureaucratic governance'.[140] Weatherill suggested that BR programmes typically seek, 'to achieve a more satisfactory balance between the demands of proper protection from market failure and inequity, on the one hand, and commercial freedom and the potential for innovation on the other'.[141] He nonetheless acknowledged that, in practice, this balancing exercise often requires 'complex and controversial' measurements and value judgments.[142] BR typically involves an emphasis on transparency and more elaborate policy articulation.[143] A central tenet, furthermore, is that the quality of regulation can be enhanced through application of a series of regulatory improvement tools.[144] Accordingly, BR programmes generally involve use of regulatory impact assessment, public consultations and other transparency-enhancing measures, efforts to cut 'red tape', recourse to non-traditional regulatory instruments, the issuance of enforcement guidelines, sunset clauses to avoid regulatory obsolescence, and regular policy reviews.[145]

Amongst these various tools, impact assessment is the core element of any BR programme. Impact assessments are conducted to identify the likely real-world impact of regulation, including its associated costs, benefits and likely outcomes, in order to determine, essentially, whether the scheme is worth enacting or maintaining.[146] The technique of cost-benefit analysis (CBA) is the basis of any comprehensive quantitative impact assessment. Based on the Pareto criterion,[147] CBA involves an economic evaluation of proposed regulation that takes account of both its

[139] Kirkpatrick & Parker (2007:2). [140] Wiener (2006:6). [141] Weatherill (2007:4).
[142] Weatherill (2007:4). [143] Weatherill (2007:8). [144] Baldwin (2007:32).
[145] Baldwin (2007:32). [146] See generally OECD (1997).
[147] Mishan & Quah (2007:171); see also p. 7, fn. 22.

anticipated social benefits and opportunity costs.[148] It is therefore an example of evidence-based policy-making, whereby the CBA is intended to identify and then inform decision-makers of the consequences of their policy choices.[149] Contemporary approaches to CBA consider both costs and benefits of any regulatory scheme, reflecting a nuanced recognition that regulation is not problematic *per se*, but instead must be assessed on a case-by-case basis.[150] This explicit identifying and weighing of economic costs and benefits may bring to mind the efficiency analysis that lies at the heart of contemporary antitrust analysis. CBA recommends regulatory action only when it is efficient to do so; likewise, the conventional viewpoint is that antitrust should intervene only when the costs of intervention are less than the expected gains.

As a basis for regulatory policy-making, however, CBA has limitations. It can be costly to conduct,[151] and the analysis is complex and difficult to perform in real-world situations.[152] More fundamentally, CBA is a wholly economics-focused assessment, conducted solely in terms of economic valuation without taking into account distributional effects or other socially relevant, non-economic values.[153] Attempts to render the CBA technique more responsive to non-economic concerns are resisted by economists due to the difficulties of identifying, measuring and allocating non-economic values within an inherently economics-focused exercise.[154] Yet, as discussed, regulatory policy-making frequently promotes non-efficiency-based objectives that cannot be accommodated within conventional CBA. A solely quantitative approach would, therefore, risk reducing regulation's role to a technical matter of correcting market failures.[155] Instead, it is generally acknowledged that the outcome of a cost-benefit calculation cannot claim to be socially decisive, and CBA should not supplant political judgment or governmental policy.[156] While CBA can aid policy-makers, or act as a corrective to political concerns, it remains merely an (important) element of the data necessary for informed collective decision-making.[157] While an impact assessment may take account of qualitative factors such as distributional justice concerns, in addition to quantitative impacts, the relative

[148] Baldwin et al. (2011:315); Mishan & Quah (2007:5).
[149] Kirkpatrick & Parker (2007:2).
[150] Kirkpatrick & Parker (2007:1); Allio (2007:73).
[151] Baldwin et al. (2011:324).
[152] Baldwin et al. (2011:322–3); Mishan & Quah (2007).
[153] Mishan & Quah (2007:12); Baldwin et al. (2011:320).
[154] Mishan & Quah (2007:13–14).
[155] Prosser (2006:372).
[156] Mishan & Quash (2007:12–13); Kirkpatrick & Parker (2007:3); Baldwin (2007:32).
[157] Mishan & Quah (2007:13).

weightings to be apportioned between these elements should be determined by policy-makers rather than economists. Even though it relies upon economic evaluations, therefore, the BR approach to regulatory reform is better suited to protection of non-economic values than a pure deregulatory approach. BR deliberately creates space within which informed political decision-making about economic *and* non-economic values can take place – 'regulation after reflection'[158] – whereas deregulation has a more blinkered efficiency focus that may disregard the importance of non-economic concerns.

Impact assessment, and in particular the technique of CBA, has been used to assist policy-makers since the 1930s.[159] It was in the 1980s, however, in parallel to the deregulation movement, that impact assessment became a mainstream practice within regulatory policy-making. In 1981, President Reagan adopted Executive Order 12291,[160] which required CBA prior to enactment of any federal regulation that would have an annual impact of $100 million or more on the economy. Regulators could proceed only where it was established that the benefits of the regulation outweighed its costs, with formal powers of regulatory oversight granted to the Cabinet-level Office of Management and Budget (OMB). Evidently, a strategy of subjecting prospective regulations to a cost-benefit screening exercise has the potential to achieve indirectly what the deregulation programme aimed at directly: that is, to reduce the overall quantity of regulation. Yet a key advantage of the BR approach encapsulated in Order 12291 over wholesale deregulation is that the former filters out only ineffective or inefficient regulation, with the corollary that beneficial cost-effective regulation is permitted. Although controversial, the policy of requiring CBA prior to enactment of federal regulation was continued by President Clinton in Executive Order 12866,[161] albeit under a more flexible framework that acknowledged considerations of equity and took account of qualitative as well as quantitative factors. Order 12866 recognises, in effect, both the value and the limitations of the CBA exercise; it retains the technique at the core of regulatory oversight, yet supplements it with considerations that reflect the additional non-economic values of regulation. A 2005 review concluded that these Orders have had a significant impact on regulatory

[158] Wiener (2006:63). [159] Mishan & Quah (2007:243–4).
[160] 46 Federal Register 13193 (17 February 1981).
[161] 58 Federal Register 5911 (22 January 1993).

policy-making in practice, although OMB oversight has focused on reform of individual regulations rather than overall regulatory culture.[162]

Clinton's adoption of this strong pillar of Reaganite economic policy, and its continuance through the G.W. Bush[163] and Obama[164] Administrations, indicates the less ideologically charged nature of the BR movement when compared to deregulation. Leaving aside the question of whether regulation is necessary or desirable *per se*, the proposition that good regulation is to be preferred over bad must appeal both to supporters and to opponents of regulation more generally. In the UK, the move towards BR is associated with the New Labour government, which had sought to distance itself from what it perceived as failed Tory economic policies without a wholesale return to 'Old' Labourite central planning.[165] Yet the foundations for the UK's BR agenda had been laid in the mid-1980s,[166] when, in parallel to its programmes of deregulation and privatisation, the Thatcher Government sought to ease what were styled as 'burdens on business' by limiting ('to stem the flow') the quantity of new regulation enacted.[167] To do so, it adopted, essentially, the approach of Order 12291 by requiring use of CBA. Under New Labour, a programme of better quality – as opposed to merely cost-effective – regulation was adopted as central policy, with the establishment of a Better Regulation Task Force to spearhead efforts to develop and implement principles of BR at all levels of government.[168] BR is now administered by the Better Regulation Executive, within the Department for Business, Innovation and Skills.

By contrast, BR was a comparatively late development within the EU.[169] The Protocol on the Application of the Principles of Subsidiarity and Proportionality attached to the Treaty of Amsterdam in 1997 provided the first statement, somewhat oblique and perhaps aspirational, on the scope and procedures for good regulation at EU level.[170] Due to an

[162] Hahn & Litan (2005).

[163] Executive Order 13258, 67 Federal Register 9385 (28 February 2002).

[164] Executive Order 13563, 76 Federal Register 3821 (21 January 2011).

[165] Baldwin (2007:27); Weatherill (2007:1). [166] Andrews (2007:52).

[167] White Paper, *Lifting the Burden*, Cmnd. 9571, *HMSO*, 1985, particularly para. 8.1.

[168] Baldwin (2007:28–9).

[169] Wiener (2006:4–12) argued that BR was 'a conscious exercise of legal borrowing' from Member States, US law, and other EU integration mechanisms and policies for good governance and competitiveness.

[170] Article 4 of the Protocol calls for use of qualitative and quantitative indicators to substantiate compliance with the principle of subsidiarity. Article 6 states that '[t]he form of Community action shall be as simple as possible, consistent with satisfactory achievement of the objective of the measure and the need for effective enforcement'.

increasing realisation of the links between improved regulatory structures and economic competitiveness,[171] and following the Mandelkern Report that proposed the adoption of a comprehensive BR agenda,[172] the Commission subsequently adopted a programme that comprised six key objectives for reform of EU-level regulation: simplification, consolidation, codification, review of the organisation and presentation of regulation, transparency, and effective monitoring.[173] Periodic reviews suggest that implementation has been an on-going yet positive process.[174] Impact assessment, in the EU context, applies to a very broad range of legislative activity – from occupational health and safety to data protection, intellectual property, border controls and even public procurement – and is, therefore, affected more overtly by political factors, such as social and environmental concerns, than in the US context, where it applies more narrowly and with a clearer efficiency focus.[175] More recently, the Commission has switched its rhetoric from 'better regulation' to 'smart regulation', which it defines as regulation 'of the highest quality possible'.[176] 'Smart regulation' focuses on the most effective combination of different institutions and techniques,[177] and, according to Commission, requires a continuous process of reinvigoration within regulatory policy-making.[178]

171 European Commission, *Better Regulation for Growth and Jobs in the European Union* (COM(2005) 97 final), published 16 March 2005, p. 4; also Wiener (2006:10).

172 *Mandelkern Group on Better Regulation: Final Report*, published 13 November 2001.

173 European Commission, *Updating and Simplifying the Community Acquis* (COM(2003) 71 final), published 2 February 2003; also European Commission, *Action Plan 'Simplifying and Improving the Regulatory Environment'* (COM(2003) 71 final), published 5 June 2003.

174 European Commission, *A Strategic Review of Better Regulation in the European Union* (COM(2006) 689 final), published 14 November 2006; Commission, *Second Strategic Review of Better Regulation in the European Union* (COM(2008) 32 final), published 30 January 2008; and Commission, *Third Strategic Review of Better Regulation in the European Union* (COM(2009) 15 final), published 28 January 2009.

175 See Centre for European Policy Studies, *Assessing the Costs and Benefits of Regulation. Study for the European Commission, Secretariat General*, published 10 December 2013, p. 7.

176 European Commission, *Smart Regulation in the European Union* (COM(2010) 543 final), published 8 October 2010, p. 3. See also European Commission, *Communication from the Commission: Strengthening the foundations of Smart Regulation – improving evaluation* (COM(2013) 686 final), published 2 October 2013.

177 See, e.g., Gunningham & Grabosky (1998).

178 European Commission, *Communication from the Commission: Regulatory Fitness and Performance (REFIT): Results and Next Steps* (COM(2013) 685 final), published 2 October 2012, p. 2.

The increased use of CBA, and its broadened scope to encompass both costs and benefits of regulation, reflects something of a shift from *less* regulation to *improved* regulation at the level of political discourse.[179] Although BR provides considerable advantages over both the extremes of careless regulation *and* careless deregulation, however, it is not an absolute panacea for all of the difficulties of the regulatory enterprise. Accordingly, it is not possible to meet all of the criticisms levelled against regulation simply by invoking the notional benefits that BR might, in theory, generate. There is a gap, first of all, between the rhetoric and reality of BR.[180] Yeung, accordingly, criticised the BR concept itself as unduly simplistic and one-dimensional.[181] Although a heightened focus on effectiveness of regulation is laudable, in practice the task of regulating remains rather blunt and unpredictable. The improvements offered by quantitative tools such as CBA must be balanced against their technical complexity and the risks of error and analytical distortion that may be introduced. There is also considerable variation between jurisdictions in terms of the quality of oversight of the process of regulation that can be offered.[182] Baldwin et al. question whether the ideas regarding what constitutes BR that emerges from the CBA process – which focuses on assessing conventional forms of regulation, and addresses single projects rather than cumulative effects – can be reconciled with the increasingly prominent notion of smart regulation.[183] Moreover, alternative yet overlapping conceptions of what good regulation entails, such as Baldwin and Black's enforcement-focused notion of 'really responsive regulation',[184] emphasise that BR, though influential, is neither definitive nor exhaustive.

A contrasting problem is the risk that, over time, BR may become equated with the 'less-is-more' philosophy of deregulation, thereby shifting the emphasis from effective to retreating regulation.[185] Something of a policy shift of this nature was discernible in the BR policies of the UK's New Labour government, which, from 2005 onwards, began to favour a minimalist approach to regulation that rediscovered the Thatcherite language of regulation as 'burdens'.[186] This trend has, unsurprisingly, continued following the change in Government in 2010.

179 Kirkpatrick & Parker (2007:1). 180 Hardacre (2008:8). 181 Yeung (2012).
182 Hahn & Litan (2005).
183 Baldwin et al. (2011:329–34); see also Baldwin (2007:33–8).
184 Baldwin & Black (2008). 185 Wiener (2006:50).
186 Weatherill (2007:2); Baldwin (2007:29).

The Tory-led coalition thus introduced an express requirement of 'one-in, one-out' for new regulation,[187] which was subsequently ratcheted up to 'one in, *two* out',[188] demonstrating a clear change in emphasis from quality to quantity concerns. Over time, the rhetoric may begin to suggest that regulation must be impeccable or else not exist, when practice indicates that the former is generally impossible to achieve while the latter is, frequently, highly undesirable.

Finally, two further objections to the BR concept – one legalistic, the other political – should be mentioned. Yeung, first, has argued that, by divorcing regulation from its normative origins as law, and by switching the emphasis of supervision from 'hard' command-based tools to a 'softer' bargaining-focused approach, BR may, viewed from a public-law perspective, conflict with rule-of-law principles.[189] This echoes concerns identified in the preceding chapter, and may thus reaffirm the potential risks of a more consensual approach to law enforcement. Baldwin et al., secondly, highlight a noteworthy political question generated by the BR approach that arises given the widely differing conceptions of 'good' regulation that different interest groups may hold, namely: '[b]etter for whom?'[190] This is a question that, often, can be answered only by a political decision regarding competing values, which increases the risks of incorporating inefficiency into the market outcome, whether deliberately to further non-economic goals, or inadvertently due to confusion within the regulatory analysis. It may also bring to mind aspects of the public-choice critique of regulation, discussed though not endorsed earlier.

(i) *Better regulation and the role of competition law*

Assuming a 'second-best' approach to market supervision based on BR – meaning that regulatory controls are improved, not removed – what role, if any, might competition law play? Unlike deregulatory policies, BR is not intended specifically to reduce the quantity of regulation, although it may do so indirectly by preventing enactment, or recommending

[187] See, e.g., HM Government, *One-In, One-Out (OIOO) Methodology*, published July 2011.

[188] Department of Business, Innovation & Skills, *Better Regulation Framework Manual. Practical Guidance for UK Government Officials*, published July 2013, paras. 1.9.1–1.9.49. Any regulatory measure that results in direct net costs to business must be offset by deregulatory measures that provide savings to business of at least double that amount.

[189] Yeung (2012). [190] Baldwin et al. (2011:333).

removal, of inefficient or ineffective regulation. A robust BR analysis might even conclude that sector-specific regulation as such is unnecessary, as antitrust enforcement alone is sufficient to counter potential anticompetitive behaviour. BR therefore may, but does not necessarily, result in greater market opening, which would enhance the potential scope for application of competition law. Conversely, BR is intended to address directly the problem of failed regulation that results in market difficulties that might, alternatively, be addressed through competition enforcement. As the next chapter will argue, competition enforcement provides a clumsy mechanism by which to remedy regulatory failures, and so efforts to address these problems directly via regulatory reforms are to be encouraged. At a more fundamental level, adoption of a BR approach may represent a closer alignment between principles of competition policy and regulatory policy within an economy. BR, in general, demands a more rigorous, thoughtful and economics-based approach to regulating, which is matched in the realms of antitrust by the adoption of more economic approaches to competition assessment. Within both regimes, efficiency thus becomes a core value, to be advanced where possible, and derogation from which requires justification. Of course, regulation often advances non-economic values that may introduce inefficiency, yet the value of the BR approach is that such trade-offs must be identified and deemed worthwhile politically.

A more explicit connection between improved regulation and competition law arises where antitrust concepts are utilised directly within the regulatory framework, generally to provide a disciplining influence that directs the regulatory scheme towards a more efficient, quasi-market-based outcome. The EU framework for telecommunications illustrates such an approach. Beginning in the mid-1980s, telecommunications reforms within the EU have comprised two aspects: harmonisation of rules across the Member States, and progressive liberalisation of potentially competitive markets.[191] Successive waves of regulation have sought to open former monopoly markets to competition,[192] while preserving

[191] Klotz (2009b:57). The foundations for this two-pronged approach were set out in the European Commission's Green Paper on Telecommunications, *Towards a Dynamic European Economy* (COM(87)290 final), published 30 June 1987.

[192] Harmonisation began with Council Directive 90/387/EEC of 28 June 1990 on the establishment of the internal market for telecommunications services though the implementation of open network provision (OJ L192/1, 24.07.1990), while liberalisation began with Commission Directive 90/388/EEC of 28 June 1990 on competition in the markets for telecommunications services (OJ L192/10, 24.07.1990) and Commission Directive 96/19/EC of 13

integral public-interest aspects of telecommunications such as universal service[193] and data protection.[194]

Two central elements of the liberalisation agenda are noteworthy for our purposes. First, certain antitrust concepts have been imported directly into the regulatory framework, which requires national regulatory authorities (NRAs) to use market analytical tools developed in the competition law context in order to determine whether national markets merit sector-specific regulation.[195] Effectively, the EU telecommunications

March 1996 amending Directive 90/388/EEC with regard to the implementation of full competition in telecommunications markets (OJ L74/13, 22.03.1996). This early framework was revised by enactment of Regulation 2887/200 of the European Parliament and of the Council of 18 December 2000 on unbundled access to the local loop (OJ L336/4, 30.12.2000); Directive 2002/19/EC of the European Parliament and of the Council of 7 March 2002 on access to, and interconnection of, electronic communications networks and associated facilities (Access Directive) (OJ L108/7, 24.4.2002); Directive 2002/21/EC of the European Parliament and of the Council of 7 March 2002 on a common framework for electronic communications networks and services (Framework Directive) (OJ C108/33, 24.4.2002); Directive 2002/20/EC of the European Parliament and of the Council of 7 March 2002 on the authorisation of electronic communications networks and services (Authorisation Directive) (OJ L108/21, 24.4.2002); and Commission Directive 2002/77/EC of 16 September 2002 on competition in the markets for electronic communications networks and services (OJ L249/21, 17.9.2002). The existing liberalisation framework has been rationalised further with the Directive 2009/140/EC of the European Parliament and of the Council of 25 November 2009 amending Directives 2002/21/EC on a common regulatory framework for electronic communications networks and services, 2002/19/EC on access to, and interconnection of, electronic communications networks and associated facilities, and 2002/20/EC on the authorisation of electronic communications networks and services (OJ L337/37, 18/12/2009), plus the establishment of an association of Member State telecommunications regulation under Regulation 1211/2009 of the European Parliament and of the Council of 25 November 2009 establishing the Body of European Regulators for Electronic Communications (BEREC) and the Office (OJ L337/1, 18.12.2009).

193 Directive 2002/22/EC of the European Parliament and of the Council of 7 March 2002 on universal service and users' rights relating to electronic communications networks and services (Universal Service Directive) (OJ L108/51, 24.4.2002), modified by Directive 2009/136/EC of the European Parliament and of the Council of 25 November 2009 amending Directive 2002/22/EC on universal service and users' rights relating to electronic communications networks and services, Directive 2002/58/EC concerning the processing of personal data and the protection of privacy in the electronic communications sector and Regulation 2006/2004 on cooperation between national authorities responsible for the enforcement of consumer protection laws (OJ L337/11, 18.12.2009).

194 Directive 2002/58/EC of the European Parliament and of the Council of 12 July 2002 concerning the processing of personal data and the protection of privacy in the electronic communications sector (OJ L201/37, 31.7.2002), modified by Directive 2009/136/EC.

195 Bavasso (2004:88) argued that: '[t]he reform of regulation in electronic communications that is so profoundly inspired by antitrust principles marks a previously unattained level of mutual interaction between regulation and [EU] antitrust law

framework requires the enactment of Member State–level regulation to supervise any market in which a firm (or several firms jointly) is found to hold 'significant market power' (SMP) following a market analysis conducted by the NRA. In determining whether SMP exists, the regulatory framework specifies that the tasks of market definition and assessing dominance must be carried out in a manner equivalent to the case law on these concepts established under the EU competition rules.[196] While the initial regulatory framework utilised a standalone definition of SMP, the 2002 revisions adopt the competition law analytical approach in order 'to suit more complex and dynamic markets',[197] indicating the perceived superiority of antitrust over command-and-control regulation in terms of understanding and harnessing the power of the market mechanism. Accordingly, the regulatory framework adopts what Bavasso called 'a middle-ground approach' that aims to bridge the distance between *ex ante* regulation and general competition law.[198] The coherence of this approach has been questioned, however, particularly regarding the viability of the use of dynamic antitrust concepts within a static regulatory framework, and the difficulties that may arise from using the same terms within separate legal regimes pursuing different objectives.[199] An example of the latter arose in *Telefónica*, where the defendant argued that it was entitled to assume that its behaviour, approved by the NRA, was compliant with Article 102 TFEU given that the regulatory framework was premised on antitrust concepts. The General Court rejected this argument, holding, somewhat dogmatically, that dominant firms have an independent responsibility to

and a new step in the relationship between the internal market and antitrust law in the European legal system'.

[196] Directive 2002/21/EC, recitals (25) & (27) and Articles 14 & 15; also Commission Guidelines on market analysis and the assessment of significant market power under the Community regulatory framework for electronic communications networks and services (C165/6, 11.7.2002); Commission Recommendation of 11 February 2003 on relevant product and service markets within the electronic communications sector susceptible to *ex ante* regulation in accordance with Directive 2002/21/EC of the European Parliament and of the Council on a common regulatory framework for electronic communication networks and services (OJ L114/45, 8.5.2003); and Commission Recommendation of 17 December 2007 on relevant product and service markets within the electronic communications sector susceptible to *ex ante* regulation in accordance with Directive 2002/21/EC of the European Parliament and of the Council on a common regulatory framework for electronic communications networks and services (OJ L244/65, 28.12.2007).

[197] Directive 2002/21/EC, recital (25). [198] Bavasso (2004:106).

[199] Hellwig (2009:228–30); Bavasso (2004:117–18); Oldale & Padilla (2004).

ensure compliance, separately, with competition law.[200] The coherence of the General Court's approach will be explored in the next chapter.

Second, EU telecommunications regulation is expressly premised on the assumption of built-in obsolescence: that is, a core purpose of the regulatory framework is to progress markets towards a situation of sustainable competition so that, over time, sector-specific regulation becomes unnecessary. Telecommunications markets will then be controlled, instead, solely through competition enforcement.[201] Such an approach reflects, on the one hand, the conventional preference for market-ordering over regulation where possible, yet on the other hand, a pragmatic acceptance that unencumbered competition is not yet practicable in some markets.[202] The current framework nonetheless has the capacity to reflect technological advancements and trends towards convergence within this rapidly developing sector. So, for example, whereas the Commission's 2003 Recommendation on market analysis identified eighteen separate product markets that NRAs might analyse and consider for regulation,[203] its 2007 Recommendation whittled that list down to seven markets, although NRAs retain discretion to impose regulation elsewhere if appropriate given national circumstances.[204] Thus, at least in theory, regulation gives way to competition as it emerges, and moreover, well-designed regulation speeds up this process by facilitating market opening and access. It is doubtful whether regulation will ever become entirely dispensable in certain segments of the telecommunications sector, however, even in the longer term.[205] Instead, the Commission is seeking to further integrate, and in some instances strengthen, the

[200] Case T-366/07 *Telefónica SA* et al., EU:T:2012:172, paras. 321–5; essentially confirmed on appeal in C-295/12 P *Telefónica SA* v. *European Commission*, EU:C:2014:2062.

[201] For example: '[t]he aim is progressively to reduce *ex-ante* sector specific riles as competition in the markets develops and, ultimately, for electronic communications to be governed by competition law only. . . .[I]t is essential that *ex-ante* regulatory obligations only be imposed where there is no effective and sustainable competition': Directive 2009/140/EC, recital (5). See also recital (13) of Directive 2002/19/EC: '[t]he aim is to reduce *ex ante* sector specific rules progressively as competition in the market develops'.

[202] Cave & Crowther (2005:487) argued that the telecommunications framework 'seeks at a high level to render to competition policy what is competition policy's (episodic interventions in potentially competitive markets) and to regulation what is regulation's (persistent interventions in markets with established dominance)'.

[203] OJ L114/45, 8.5.2003, Annex.

[204] OJ L344/65, 28.12.2007, recital (17) and Annex.

[205] Oldale & Padilla (2004).

existing regulatory framework for telecommunications in the EU to achieve what it has styled a 'connected continent'.[206]

V. Regulation's substantive core: non-economic values and structural inefficiency

Thus far, this chapter has considered, generally, efforts to reduce or reform regulation, thereby minimising its distortive influences on the market, or – to invoke the incendiary language of neoliberalism – lessening the burden of regulation. The emphasis on the desirability of curtailing the extent and impact of regulation discernible in modern policy discourse thus raises a question as to why it nevertheless retains such prominence even within the most free-market-focused of economies. In short, why does regulation, ostensibly so disfavoured in theory and so dysfunctional in practice, remain so integral to the modern market system?

To understand this apparent anomaly, we must switch our focus from the difficulties and failures encountered by regulation back to an issue considered in Chapter 1, namely, the underlying motivations for enactment of market regulation. The preference of neoclassical economics for market-based ordering is, of course, subject to the proviso that some markets produce socially undesirable or sub-optimal distributions and therefore merit or require State intervention. The public-choice literature suggested that the preference for regulation reflects merely non-welfare-maximising political decisions to abandon free markets in order to advance particular policy interests. Yet public choice considerably overstates its case by discounting the existence and urgency of certain public-interest concerns while, tacitly, overestimating the value and adequacy of the unencumbered market mechanism. Although competition law can augment the functioning of markets by prohibiting anticompetitive behaviour by market actors, even the antitrust-buttressed market mechanism cannot prioritise distributional justice concerns or address inherently structural market failures. Although regulation may, therefore, be a second-best solution

[206] See European Commission, *Proposal for a Regulation of the European Parliament and of the Council laying down measures concerning the European single market for electronic communications and to achieve a Connected Continent, and amending Directives 2002/20/EC, 2002/21/EC and 2002/22/EC and Regulations (EC) No 1211/2009 and (EU) No 531/2012* (COM(2013)627 final), published 11 September 2013.

to market defects, it remains indispensable to obtain a more equitable distribution or a more efficient outcome in certain markets.[207]

These two regulatory concerns – distributional justice and structural inefficiency – therefore comprise the substantive, inescapable core of regulation: that is, in these circumstances regulation is generally unavoidable in order to attain the preferred market or societal outcome. The remainder of this chapter discusses these regulatory concerns, and considers a practical example of such apparently inescapable regulation – the EU's Roaming Regulation – in order to illustrate the limits of competition law and the concomitant residual role for regulation even within market economies.

(i) Distributional justice and other non-economic values

As explained in Chapter 1, the efficiency criterion does not account for distributional concerns. A market that functions well from an economic perspective is not necessarily one that is a fair or equitable when viewed from a broader public-policy perspective. The State may therefore choose to become involved in order to curtail the 'excessive successes' that accrue to some market participants.[208] One simple mechanism by which to rebalance the market distribution after the fact is taxation: that is, to tax the profits of successful corporations and then distribute the proceeds amongst the broader population in the form of social welfare provision. Alternatively, policy-makers may intervene, prospectively and more directly, by limiting the commercial freedom of market participants in order to guide the market towards what is viewed as a fairer outcome. Prosser, for example, argued that 'social solidarity', in contradistinction to the technical task of resolving market failures, provides a central justification for much regulatory activity.[209] Prosser's account is significant because it rejects the contention that regulation must always be viewed as the second-best solution; conversely, sometimes regulation may be preferred to the market allocation in order to 'limit the socially fragmenting role of markets'. Here, regulation is unavoidable, not (necessarily) because the market does not work well, but because, instead, non-market values should be prioritised.[210]

An archetypal example of economic regulation that focuses on concerns of distributional justice over efficiency is found in universal service

[207] Breyer (1987:1007); Laguna de Paz (2012:77). [208] Weatherill (2007:5).
[209] Prosser (2006). [210] Hovenkamp (2005:229–30).

obligations (USOs), such as a requirement that service providers must serve all potential customers and charge geographically uniform retail prices, even where the cost of network provision varies significantly between customers and regions. USOs are, typically, imposed where non-discrimination between customers is viewed as socially desirable, but at the same time, the unencumbered market mechanism alone would not result in service provision in this manner. USOs often require detailed regulation, particularly in markets that are open to (partial) competition, in order to prevent cream-skimming from more profitable segments and to provide cross-subsidies that finance loss-making customers.[211] Other non-economic values that may be pursued through regulation include human rights protection, paternalism and altruistic or community values.[212] Public-interest regulation may lead to some diminution in market efficiency; however, non-efficiency benefits are assumed to outweigh any resulting inefficiencies.[213] On this view, regulation is necessary in order to deliberately depart from the likely market outcome, shifting the emphasis of debate to political justifications for the non-market values to be pursued.

(ii) Structural market inefficiency

Competition law augments the market mechanism by prohibiting and punishing anticompetitive behaviour that might inhibit its free functioning. Conversely, given that competition law is expressly targeted at firm conduct, it tends to be less ineffective at remedying structural market problems that hinder competition. Structural barriers can generate something of a vicious cycle, insofar as the underlying and inherent competition problems mean that, *a priori*, competition does not function adequately and so the market cannot self-correct. Natural monopoly and oligopoly are examples of market structures that result in diminished competition overall. Neither involves, necessarily, anticompetitive firm conduct as such, and so neither is readily amenable to resolution through competition enforcement. Even where discrete instances of enforcement are possible, piecemeal antitrust intervention against anticompetitive behaviour that is linked, inextricably, to structural difficulties fails to provide a systemic market-wide solution to these problems.[214] In such

[211] Baumol (1999); Armstrong (2001).
[212] Ogus (1994:46–54); Prosser (2004:38); Baldwin et al. (2011:22).
[213] Crampton & Facey (2002:39). [214] Hellwig (2009:212).

circumstances, regulation may offer the only effective or comprehensive means by which to introduce competition into a market or to secure a more socially desirable outcome, albeit providing only 'an imperfect substitute for the missing market discipline'.[215]

Natural monopoly arises where it is most efficient for a single firm (or facility) to serve an entire market.[216] Competition in natural monopoly markets can be socially wasteful, involving unnecessary duplication of infrastructure and loss of economies of scale. Natural monopolists are still monopolists, however, and so such markets often suffer from the high prices, diminished innovation and dead-weight losses associated with monopoly market structures. The contemporary movement towards liberalisation of markets that were previously maintained as natural monopolies reflects a shift in economic thinking: natural monopoly markets may support significantly greater amounts of competition than previously understood, meaning that potentially competitive segments should be liberalised where possible.[217] Bottlenecks that hinder the development of competition in competitive segments are, however, a recurrent problem in partially deregulated markets with natural monopoly components.[218] The existence of a monopoly market position means that the activities of natural monopolists generally fall under competition laws governing unilateral conduct. Yet, as Chapter 2 demonstrated, the antitrust theories best suited to controlling the claimed abuses of natural monopolists – the essential facilities doctrine and the rule against excessive prices – are controversial in theory, and complex to apply and administer in practice. Structural remedies are likely to provide the greatest potential for future competition,[219] yet, in order to impose structural remedies under an antitrust rubric, liability must be grounded in identified instances of anticompetitive conduct, while separation usually creates an attendant need for new regulation to police restructured markets.

Instead, proceeding directly via specifically enacted regulation may provide policy-makers with a more comprehensive and effective means by which to remedy on-going market failures than through episodic competition enforcement.[220] Natural monopoly regulation may seek only

[215] Sappington & Weisman (2010:229). [216] See pp.16–7.

[217] Hellwig (2009:204); see generally OECD (2001).

[218] Breyer (1987:1032); Ibáñez Colomo (2010:270–6); Faulhaber (2008:38–9).

[219] Such as ownership separation of competitive and natural monopoly business segments of a dominant vertically integrated firm: OECD (2001).

[220] Geradin & Kerf (2003:8–10); Larouche (2000:322); Laffont & Tirole (2000:279).

to control the monopolist's behaviour, for example by capping prices that may be charged. Alternatively, the regulation may be more ambitious, and aim at deregulation by imposing mandatory access requirements for the monopolist's infrastructure in order to introduce competition into potentially competitive segments.[221] A clear advantage of pursuing market supervision through sector-specific regulation rather than competition law is that it permits the enactment of a comprehensive framework that may impose, *inter alia*, clear regulatory duties, sanctions for non-compliance and a supervisory structure under a designated regulator. As we saw in the preceding chapter, a significant benefit of the use of negotiated settlement procedures in antitrust enforcement is the extent to which such quasi-regulatory instruments allow public enforcers to craft a remedial framework that replicates, to an extent, the more comprehensive provisions available under sector-specific regulation.

Oligopolies, on the other hand, arise in concentrated markets with few competitors.[222] Recognising their substantial interdependence, market participants have greater opportunity for tacit collusion and fewer incentives for vigorous competition, resulting in less efficient market outcomes. Yet, oligopolistic behaviour often escapes scrutiny under competition law because the conduct involved amounts neither to anticompetitive coordination nor to abuse of dominance.[223] EU law, for example, has had limited success in applying the competition provisions to oligopoly conduct. Under Article 101(1) TFEU, mere parallel market conduct by firms provides evidence of anticompetitive coordination only where there is no plausible alternative explanation for the parallelism.[224] Similarly, while Article 102 TFEU has been interpreted to include collective dominance[225] – that is, a dominant position held jointly by

[221] Faulhaber (2008). [222] See pp. 17–8.

[223] The precise coverage of antitrust in respect of oligopoly conduct has long been contentious. Turner (1962) stressed the absence of agreement between oligopolists to argue that oligopoly conduct, as such, should not be prohibited. He drew parallels to the rules on unilateral conduct, arguing that since a mere monopoly market position is not prohibited, then an oligopoly market position should likewise not be illegal. Posner (1969), by contrast, would treat rational profit-maximising oligopolists like cartelists, albeit he acknowledged potential problems of evidence and remedies. In a more recent economics-focused account, Kaplow (2011) argued that game theoretic approaches can be employed to identify oligopoly practices that harm social welfare, although detection remains a problem.

[224] Case C-89/85 etc. *Ahlström OY* v. *Commission*, EU:C:1993:120, para. 71.

[225] First established in Case T-342/99 *Airtours* v. *Commission*, EU:T:2002:146, para. 62, a merger decision; applied in relation to Article 102 TFEU in Case T-193/02 *Laurent Piau* v. *Commission*, EU:T:2005:22.

two or more firms – a demanding legal test is applied to determine whether collective dominance exists, which greatly limits the practical application of this approach.[226] US antitrust is even more permissive towards oligopoly practices:[227] while tacit collusion is the hallmark of oligopoly conduct, under US law an anticompetitive agreement must be demonstrated to establish that the oligopolists have breached either §1[228] or 2§ (through a conspiracy to monopolise)[229] of the Sherman Act. Given the constrained ability of antitrust to control anticompetitive oligopoly practices, and in the absence of countervailing competitive pressures in the relevant market, policy-makers may alternatively, in appropriate circumstances, turn to regulatory mechanisms to address any resulting market inefficiencies or public-policy concerns.

Like the pursuit of non-economic societal values, structural market problems often find no ready solution within the market system. Instead, to the extent that State intervention is considered necessary to resolve the market failure (or, conversely, to advance a non-economic goal), this requires regulatory measures that supersede the market rather than antitrust measures that strengthen the market mechanism. There can also be significant overlaps in practice between the pursuit of distributional justice and efforts to address structural competition problems; for example, price regulation imposed on a utility company that holds a natural monopoly may seek to prevent the extraction of monopoly rents both in order to avoid inefficiency and to prevent the unfair exploitation of consumers that access essential services. The EU's Roaming Regulation, considered next, addresses alleged exploitative pricing practices in an oligopoly market with a significant non-economic dimension. It provides an example of a regulatory measure that was adopted within the broader context of an antitrust enforcement procedure, yet which has been used to solve a competition problem that lies beyond the reach of

226 Members of the oligopoly must be able to (i) monitor compliance and (ii) punish deviations, and (iii) the foreseeable reaction of current and future competitors, and of consumers, must not jeopardise the expected results: *Laurent Piau*, para. 111. Monti (2001), echoing Turner (1962), argued that extension of Article 102 TFEU to cover collective dominance does not prohibit all oligopoly practices, given that it does not prohibit oligopoly but rather *abusive* behaviour by oligopoly firms.

227 See generally Brock (2006:229–32).

228 In *Theatre Enterprises* v. *Paramount Film Distribution Corp.* et al., 346 US 537 (1954), the Supreme Court rejected the contention that conscious parallelism was sufficient to establish conclusive proof of agreement contrary to the Sherman Act; reaffirmed in *Bell Atlantic Corp.* v. *Twombly*, 550 US 544 (2007).

229 ABA (2007:317–18).

antitrust. The measure illustrates, moreover, the potential disjoint that may arise between equity-based societal aims – here, consumer protection – and the fostering of unencumbered competitive markets.

(iii) Regulating in lieu of antitrust: the EU Roaming Regulation

The Roaming Regulation has its origins in a sector inquiry by the European Commission into conditions and pricing of national and international mobile telephone 'roaming' in the EU.[230] Roaming occurs when customers of a mobile telephone provider whose network is located in one Member State travel to and use their phones in other Member States. The home provider must, accordingly, purchase wholesale-level network access from a host provider in order to supply its retail customers with coverage abroad. Rates for wholesale access charged by host network operators were, historically, very high, which were then reflected in equally inflated retail prices for international roaming services.[231] The EU's roaming inquiry aimed to establish the levels of existing competition in mobile roaming markets, to collect data on potential anticompetitive practices and to identify any structural barriers to competition.[232] Initial findings pointed to a high degree of market transparency facilitating oligopolistic practices, with a likelihood of excessive pricing by and collusion between mobile operators.[233] Although these market conditions were analysed within the framework of the competition rules under Articles 101 and 102 TFEU,[234] potential remedial alternatives included the provision of guidance on competition issues, increasing consumer awareness of competition issues in the roaming sector, benchmarking of roaming prices, or even delaying intervention to ascertain whether technological advances might provide an organic solution.[235]

230 European Commission Press Release IP/00/111, 'Commission launches second phase of telecommunications sector inquiry under the competition rules: mobile roaming', published 4 February 2000. The Roaming Inquiry was part of a larger investigation of the telecommunications sector, which also covered access to leased lines and the local loop. Sector inquiries are considered in Chapter 5.

231 IP/00/111.

232 European Commission, *Working Document on the Initial Findings of the Sector Inquiry into Mobile Roaming Charges*, published 13 December 2000, p. 1.

233 *Working Document on Roaming*, p. 20–6.

234 *Working Document on Roaming*, p. 14.

235 *Working Document on Roaming*, p. 28–31.

Dawn raids were subsequently conducted at the premises of various mobile operators as part of the 'follow-up' to the roaming inquiry,[236] indicating a shift from a general market assessment to a more specific investigation of discrete claims of anticompetitive conduct. The investigation culminated in issuance of statements of objections (SOs) to various mobile network operators based in the UK[237] and Germany.[238] Each SO alleged that the undertaking concerned had abused its dominant market position for the provision of international roaming services at wholesale level on its own network by charging excessive prices for access, contrary to (now) Article 102 TFEU.[239] This enforcement action suffered from a number of significant problems, however, rendering successful competition intervention potentially unviable. There was a difficulty, first of all, in establishing dominance to trigger application of Article 102 TFEU. On the facts, collective dominance was difficult to demonstrate, so the investigation employed a notion of single network dominance for each operator, on the basis that mobile users could not choose their roaming services provider. Even if this rather tenuous theory was accepted, it could not be maintained beyond the end of 2003, when it became technically possible for customers to choose their roaming operator for cross-border calls. After that point, any negative decision could only state a past abuse. Moreover, the rigorous legal test for excessive prices applied under EU law[240] meant that it was quite uncertain whether, even if dominance could be established, the pricing policies could be found abusive.[241]

Instead, the Commission chose a regulatory approach to address both the overarching market problems and the specific instances of anticompetitive conduct that had been identified. Initially, it sought to tackle these issues through soft law mechanisms, by requesting mobile operators to reduce roaming tariffs voluntarily and by publishing data on comparative rates.[242] A complementary EU-wide investigation into

[236] European Commission MEMO/01/262, 'Statement on inquiry regarding mobile roaming', published 11 July 2001.

[237] European Commission Press Release IP/04/994, 'Commission challenges UK international roaming rates', published 26 July 2004.

[238] European Commission Press Release IP/05/161, 'Commission challenges international roaming rates for mobile phones in Germany', published 10 February 2005.

[239] IP/04/994 and IP/05/161. [240] See pp. 124–5.

[241] See Klotz (2009a:132–3) for discussion of the case theory against the mobile operators.

[242] Klotz (2009a:133); also European Commission Press Releases IP/05/901, 'Commission warns consumers on cost of using mobile phone abroad and targets lack of price

mobile roaming tariffs was launched by a group of national regulators, with the support of the Commission.[243] When these softer approaches failed to bring about a reduction in wholesale rates,[244] the Commission turned to more concrete market controls. In July 2006, it published a Proposal for a Roaming Regulation that recommended the adoption of a two-part approach to price-setting for roaming services: an EU-wide maximum price limit for wholesale access services, coupled with a limitation on the permissible retail mark-up to 130 per cent of wholesale prices, in order to avoid a price squeeze.[245] This approach sought to address the 'core problem' that 'prices for EU-wide roaming at both wholesale and retail levels stand in no meaningful relationship to the underlying costs',[246] resulting in 'unjustifiably high' charges.[247] This difficulty stemmed, in the first instance, from the oligopolistic nature of mobile telephony markets in the EU, a structural competition problem that, as discussed, tends to be difficult to address through antitrust enforcement. Yet the impetus behind the Roaming Regulation was not, solely, a desire to remedy inefficiencies that arose from the oligopoly market structure, as there were also strong market-integration and non-economic (consumer protection) considerations at issue. On the one hand, by its nature the levying of high additional costs for the use of mobile phones between Member States was seen as a barrier to integration and free movement. Moreover, the inherently cross-border nature of the markets at issue meant that national regulators were unable to address these problems adequately.[248] On the other, there was a strong populist dimension to the Roaming Regulation, as high roaming costs

transparency', published 11 July 2005 and IP/05/1217, 'Commission launches consumer website on the costs of mobile roaming in Europe', published 4 October 2005.

243 European Commission Press Release IP/04/1458, 'Commissioner Reding welcomes EU-wide investigation on cost of using a mobile phone abroad', published 10 December 2004.

244 European Commission Staff Working Paper, *Impact Assessment of Policy Options in Relation to a Commission Proposal for a Regulation of the European Parliament and of the Council on Roaming on Public Mobile Networks within the Community* (COM(2006) 382 final), published 12 July 2006, pp. 12–3.

245 European Commission, *Proposal for a Regulation of the European Parliament and of the Council on roaming on public mobile networks within the Community and amending Directive 2002/21/EC on a common regulatory framework for electronic communications networks and services* (COM(2006)382 final), published 12 July 2006. The price squeeze concept is considered further at pp. 191–3.

246 *Impact Assessment for Roaming Regulation*, p. 17.

247 *Impact Assessment for Roaming Regulation*, p. 22.

248 *Impact Assessment for Roaming Regulation*, pp. 17, 25–6.

were perceived to be exploitative of ordinary non-business travellers in particular.[249] Thus, the Commission called for 'a clear demonstration that Europe can act in the interest of citizens in a case where Member States are not equipped to act'.[250]

Despite fierce opposition from mobile operators,[251] the Roaming Regulation was approved by the Parliament and Council, and entered in force in June 2007.[252] In its *Vodafone* judgment, the CJEU upheld the validity of the Roaming Regulation as being compliant with EU rules regarding proportionality and subsidiarity, plus lawfully enacted under (now) Article 114 TFEU as a measure for internal market harmonisation.[253] Although, initially, the Roaming Regulation covered only roaming services for voice calls, it was subsequently extended to cover text messages[254] and internet data roaming, while costs for calls and texts have been reduced progressively.[255] The Commission now has ambitious plans to abolish roaming surcharges entirely.[256]

As discussed, the default position within EU telecommunications regulation is that normal market forces should govern commercial arrangements where possible.[257] The Roaming Regulation, which amounts to direct rate-making for roaming services through use of a price-ceiling,[258] represented a significant departure from this basic principle. The drafters of the Roaming Regulation took the view, however, that the 'unique characteristics' of the wholesale and retail markets

249 *Impact Assessment for Roaming Regulation*, pp. 19–20.

250 *Impact Assessment for Roaming Regulation*, p. 26.

251 Brandenburger & Janssens (2007:17).

252 Regulation 717/2007 of the European Parliament and of the Council of 27 June 2007 on roaming on public mobile telephone networks within the Community and amending Directive 2002/21/EC (OJ L171/32, 29.6.2007) ('Roaming Regulation').

253 Case C-58/08 *Vodafone Ltd, Telefónica O2 Europe plc, T-Mobile International AG, Orange Personal Communications Services Ltd* v. *Secretary of State for Business, Enterprise and Regulatory Reform* [2010] EU:C:2010:321.

254 Regulation 544/2009 of the European Parliament and of the Council of 18 June 2009 amending Regulation 717/2007 on roaming on public mobile telephone networks within the Community and Directive 2002/21/EC on a common regulatory framework for electronic communications networks and services (OJ L167/12, 29.6.2009).

255 Regulation 531/2012 of the European Parliament and of the Council of 13 June 2012 on roaming on public mobile communications networks within the Union (OJ L172/10, 30.6.2012).

256 See p. 173, fn. 206.

257 Roaming Regulation, recital (12).

258 See Opinion of Advocate General Poiares Maduro, C-58/08 *Vodafone et al.*, EU:C:2009:596, para. 1, arguing that the core question to be addressed was 'whether the Community can regulate prices under [Article 114 TFEU], and if so, to what extend and under which conditions'.

concerned 'justify exceptional measures which go beyond the mechanisms otherwise available'.[259] While the essence of the market failure at issue was exploitative pricing practices by individual firms, discrete instances of antitrust enforcement would not provide a viable alternative to *ex ante* market regulation. Instead, the Commission argued that, 'competition rules and regulatory measures should be seen as complementary rather than as substitutes' in the circumstances.[260] Application of competition law would have enabled the Commission to address the overall market failure only on a piecemeal basis, rather than through a comprehensive measure that caught all market operators. The Commission furthermore alluded to the 'complexity' of antitrust enforcement in these cases, thus supporting the view that such market problems actually fall outside the ambit of competition law.[261] In his Opinion in *Vodafone*, Advocate General Poiares Maduro argued that, '[i]f the Community can prohibit a certain action by a private party it should be competent to simply regulate that action',[262] which suggests a considerable blurring of the line between competition law and regulation. The CJEU, by contrast, limited itself to confirming that the Roaming Regulation fell within the Union's harmonisation power under Article 114 TFEU.[263] Notably, once the Roaming Regulation had been adopted, the Commission closed, without any finding of breach, the on-going antitrust investigations against British and German mobile operators, holding that enactment of the Regulation resolved the problems identified.[264]

While the tenor of EU telecommunications regulation generally has sought to move towards competitive markets wherever possible, the extent to which a measure such as the Roaming Regulation can lead to the development of robust competition is doubtful. Industry participants, although now accepting the inevitability of regulation in this sector, have expressed considerable scepticism about the potential for the Regulation to foster competition in this sector.[265] In theory, the Regulation simply

[259] Roaming Regulation, recital (13).

[260] *Impact Assessment for Roaming Regulation*, p. 38.

[261] *Impact Assessment for Roaming Regulation*, p. 38.

[262] Opinion of Advocate General Poiares Maduro, C-58/08 *Vodafone* et al., para. 22.

[263] C-58/08 *Vodafone* et al., para. 48.

[264] European Commission Press Release IP/07/1113, 'Commission closes proceedings against part roaming tariffs in the UK and Germany', published 18 July 2007.

[265] European Commission, *Report from the Commission to the European Parliament, the Council, the European Economic and Social Committee and the Committee of the Regions on the outcome of the functioning of Regulation 717/2007 of the European Parliament and*

imposes maximum caps for wholesale and retail rates; in practice, however, these have been treated as *de facto* prices, with operators generally not competing below the maximum levels.[266] The Roaming Regulation has therefore achieved its aim of reducing prices for roaming services – hardly a surprise, given that operators have no scope to charge above maximum wholesale or retail rates – but, at the same time, it has done so in a manner that results in a highly regulated, artificial market. In May 2012, the Parliament and Council agreed to extend the Regulation until 2022,[267] confirming the otherwise unsustainable nature of the competition it has generated, and illustrating the essentially self-perpetuating nature of such regulation. As noted, the Commission has, more recently, sought to eliminate roaming charges entirely, thus indicating a more radical approach to market supervision that involves, in essence, the absolute proscription of products or services that, though neither dangerous nor morally suspect, are deemed undesirable on other public-policy grounds.[268]

The Roaming Regulation provides a clear example of use of a regulatory measure to address a market problem that might be more readily conceptualised as an antitrust issue, but where competition enforcement alone would provide an ineffective or incomplete vehicle for market improvement. Ackermann identified both pull and push factors motivating use of regulation in this instance: both the popular support for reducing high prices and the difficulty of antitrust enforcement.[269] Accepting the premise of the EU telecommunications framework that competition should be preferred over regulation where possible, the reliance placed upon prescriptive regulation under the Roaming Regulation may be problematic. Not only does it appear to sacrifice the benefits of competitive markets, the very existence of the Regulation may render the development of competition more difficult to achieve in the longer term insofar as the key external determinant of mobile operators' conduct is now the Regulation rather than competition as such. If, instead, the Commission had pursued discrete competition cases against individual operators, the determining factor would be the efforts of market operators to comply with (or not) the broad proscriptions of competition

of the Council of 27 June 2007 on roaming on public mobile communications networks within the Community, as amended by Regulation 544/2009 (COM(2011) 407 final), published 6 July 2011.

266 *Report on Functioning of Roaming Regulation*, pp. 6–7.

267 See Regulation 531/2012.

268 See p. 173, fn. 206.

269 Ackermann (2010:428).

law, rather than adherence to the prescriptions of a regulatory regime. It remains an open question, however, whether antitrust enforcement was feasible here, and whether such activity would have solved the market failures at issue. Moreover, we should perhaps be wary of viewing this, too emphatically, as a market problem when, instead, a primary motivating factor for this regulation was the pursuit of a largely non-economic value, namely, consumer protection. Accordingly, the policy decision to choose imperfect regulation over imperfect competition reflects both the limited utility of market-based solutions when faced with oligopoly problems and the political need to protect non-economic values – here, distributional justice for consumers – even at the risk of introducing inefficient market distortions.

VI. Conclusions

The tensions at the heart of the regulatory enterprise have been a prominent and recurrent theme throughout this chapter. Regulation, as a concept, finds itself on the defensive in modern society. The rhetoric is damning: regulation breeds inefficiency, fosters corruption and protects only vested interests, or it may be enacted with the best of intentions but is impossible to get right in practice. The neoliberal deregulation movement accordingly advocates a wholesale abandonment of regulatory controls, the liberalisation movement's logic of 'regulation for competition' would use regulatory controls to restructure markets progressively towards competition, whereas the better regulation movement seeks to distil the good from the bad in regulatory practice in a complex effort to discard or avoid the latter. Criticisms of regulation and its limitations, whether deserved or otherwise, have comprised the bulk of contemporary economic and political discourse on the topic.

The practical reality, however, is that regulation has remained largely inescapable in modern economies. Indeed, this is not always a bad thing. Orbach argued that regulation is a by-product of 'imperfect reality and human limitations',[270] an argument that can be expanded to include imperfect markets and their limitations. In well-functioning markets, market-based allocations are generally efficient, and thus, *prima facie* socially desirable. Yet markets do not always work well, and an imperfectly regulated market may nonetheless be preferable to an uncompetitive

[270] Orbach (2012:8).

inefficient free market. Even efficient markets are not always fair ones, moreover, and so regulation may be utilised to protect other non-economic yet socially valued objectives such as distributive justice. While derogation from the market mechanism is typically disfavoured, in many markets this is a precept that is more honoured in breach than in observance.

This is not to suggest that regulatory failures do not occur or that the negative impact of bad regulation should be ignored. As Orbach further observed, the same imperfection and limitations that necessitate regulation guarantee the imperfect nature of regulation itself.[271] The argument here, instead, has been more modest: that regulation is not *a priori* a bad thing, and that effective regulation can significantly improve societal welfare. The difficulties, of course, lie in that proviso: designing, implementing and administering 'effective' regulation are not easy tasks, and the pursuit of numerous, often conflicting goals within a market tends to complicate things further. The strategic combination within liberalisation of regulatory instruments with market forces, alongside efforts to make regulation itself better, smarter or more responsive, demonstrate more nuanced attempts at market regulation going beyond the strident regulation/deregulation dichotomy. As the following chapter demonstrates, however, bad regulation – whether ineffective, unfair or prone to abuse – can still arise in practice; the question to be considered next is what role competition law might play in remedying such regulatory failures.

[271] Orbach (2012:9).

4

Concurrent application of competition law and regulation

Thus far we have considered competition law and regulation individually, addressing interactions that arise indirectly. In this chapter, we explore a more direct, and potentially conflictual, interaction, namely, concurrent application of competition law and regulation. The overlapping scope of application of these mechanisms creates problems of 'transversal coordination',[1] with a possibility of collision. In practice, the question here is, usually, whether competition law is applicable *ex post* in markets already regulated *ex ante*. The optimal extent of concurrent application is a contentious question: a spectrum of approaches is discernible in the case law, and this area is fraught with economic, rule-of-law, institutional and political concerns. In short, this is an issue that arguably cannot, *a priori*, be definitively resolved. The aims of this chapter, instead, are to explain and explore this practical problem, to illuminate the policy considerations that must be addressed in formulating an effective and coherent generalised approach, and to consider the regulatory circumstances in which competition problems may arise and thus the impact of the regulatory context on the threshold question of whether competition law should apply in particular circumstances. In order to avoid potential ambiguity it should be emphasised that concurrency, at this juncture, refers to *substantive* concurrency, concerning the legal effects of applying competition law within markets already subject to regulation. By contrast, we are not concerned with questions of institutional or jurisdictional concurrency, which generally address the allocation of competition law and regulatory enforcement powers between different public agencies. While there can be overlaps in practice, institutional issues are considered in the following chapter.

[1] Larouche (2005:169).

I. Conceptualising concurrency

(i) Concurrent application of competition law in regulated markets: conceptual issues

While competition law and economic regulation are generally distinguishable by their modes of operation, their scopes of application overlap, meaning that some market problems can be addressed either through individual competition enforcement or through implementation of a systematic regulatory framework. The issue of concurrency arises from this potential overlap: instead of choosing between competition law and regulation as mechanisms of market supervision, is it possible to apply both, simultaneously or consecutively, within the same market and even to address the same anticompetitive conduct? To a large extent there is asymmetry here, because the episodic and generally retrospective nature of antitrust intervention means that, typically, it does not cover the same ground as subsequently enacted, forward-facing sector regulation.[2] Prior competition enforcement within a sector should not bar later regulation unless such activity indicates that competition law alone is adequate to ensure well-functioning markets.[3] Essentially, the question to be considered is whether competition law is applicable *ex post* in markets subject to *ex ante* regulation, or, put differently, the extent to which sector-specific regulation ousts antitrust jurisdiction to scrutinise the behaviour of regulated firms or, more generally, economic activity in a sector.

Our starting assumption is that sector-specific regulation has been enacted in the market concerned. The regulatory scheme may be comprehensive or partial, or the sector may be subject to progressive

[2] Cf. Oldale & Padilla (2004:76), arguing that, '*ex ante* intervention necessarily pre-empts *ex post* enforcement'.

[3] As considered in Chapter 2, recurring competition enforcement in a sector may indicate the need for a systemic top-down regulatory approach to market supervision. Difficulties might arise, however, if competition enforcement results in an ongoing positive duty for defendants such as a duty to supply, which is actively administered and enforced by the competition adjudicator. Subsequent enactment of sector-specific regulation applying to the same market behaviour – such as mandatory access and interconnection – subjects the regulated firm to parallel sets of legal obligations to achieve the same objective, resulting in higher costs due to duplication of regulatory efforts, and the risk of regulatory conflicts creating uncertainty and other potential inefficiencies. In practice, subsequent regulation is typically enacted to support and operationalise antitrust obligations (e.g., substantial regulation was enacted to support the structural separation of AT&T in 1984), or is treated as replacing or crystallising general antitrust obligations into a distinct regulatory framework (e.g., the Telecommunications Act of 1996, which replaced judicial supervision of the AT&T decree).

deregulation under a liberalisation programme. For questions of concurrent application of competition law to arise, we must assume that, despite such regulation, *prima facie* antitrust abuses occur. As considered, the objectives of competition law and regulation are often broadly compatible but rarely wholly coextensive. A well-functioning market, from a regulatory perspective, may be different from a well-functioning (efficient) market, from an antitrust perspective. Moreover, not all regulation is effective in practice. A broad spectrum of potential interactions between a regulatory framework and anticompetitive behaviour under scrutiny can be discerned: the conduct may be required or approved by regulation; it may, conversely, constitute a breach of regulation, in letter or in spirit; or the activity may lie entirely outside the regulatory framework, although it arises within the broader regulated market.[4] Regulation may even facilitate distinct forms of anticompetitive conduct, such as discrimination or cross-subsidisation.[5] Our question might therefore be reformulated with two components: (i) whether competition law can *ever* be applied within regulated market, and if so, (ii) to what *extent*.

This is, moreover, a question that links to and builds upon material considered in preceding chapters. As Chapter 3 discussed, deregulation opens previously uncompetitive markets to competition, creating scope for application of competition law insofar as this creates scope for anticompetitive private behaviour. Market liberalisation is typically a gradual process, whereby competitive segments coexist alongside regulated segments, generally because effective competition is not yet possible in those latter markets. As the cases considered in this chapter demonstrate, questions of concurrency almost invariably arise in partially regulated markets, which fall somewhere between full competition and comprehensive regulation. When competition law is applied in regulated markets many features of the claimed shift towards regulatory antitrust, considered in Chapter 2, are evident, particularly a reliance upon demanding and disputed case theories such as the essential facilities doctrine and the corresponding need for regulatory-style remedies. This is unsurprising, given that concurrency issues arise in markets where, by definition, a regulatory solution to perceived market problems has been deemed necessary. The reservations regarding regulatory competition law should nonetheless be borne in mind; when considering the legitimacy of concurrent application of competition law in regulated markets,

[4] Speta (2003:114). [5] Brennan (2005:641–6).

it is appropriate to reflect upon whether competition law provides a suitable remedial instrument in such circumstances.

Accepting that competition law provides a residual supervisory mechanism of general application for (most) markets, one might ask why the presence of regulation makes a difference. In effect, the reluctance to embrace concurrent application of competition law stems from the impact that regulation may have on the market. Conventionally, competition law targets autonomous behaviour of firms that harms competition and/or causes inefficiency. The application of competition law in regulated markets thus encounters two sources of difficulty. First, the impact of the regulation may remove some or all of the firm's scope for independent market conduct. In such circumstances, the anticompetitive outcome results from the firm's behaviour, but responsibility for that behaviour cannot properly be attributed to the firm. Second, the regulation may alter significantly the market dynamics, thus reducing the scope for competitive activity. Consequently, although the firm's actions may fall within the template of antitrust abuses, in reality its conduct may not have (additional) anticompetitive market impact. Thus, there is a genuine risk, in some regulated markets, that *prima facie* competition offences do not satisfy the requirements for substantive liability. This creates a danger that antitrust enforcement in regulated markets violates basic principles of fairness and respect for the rule of law. Related to this risk, various public-policy-based objections to concurrency have also been advanced, such as the risk that unnecessary enforcement chills beneficial market competition and diminishes incentives to invest, or that duplication of enforcement by regulator and competition adjudicator causes wastage of public resources and regulatory uncertainty. Accordingly, opposition to concurrency encompasses both legal and economic objections.

Against this, the primary substantive argument for concurrency is to preserve the effectiveness of competition law within regulated markets, and consequently the economic benefits that result from intervention. Three cumulative strands can be discerned within this argument. First, there is a presumption that competition law operates as an indirect or fall-back mechanism of market control, reflecting an economy-wide commitment to the value of competition as a principle for societal organisation.[6] Second, competition law is generally considered to be more effective than regulation at protecting and advancing competition.

[6] Hovenkamp (2005:10).

Antitrust enforcers have specialised technical knowledge in competition law and economics; they are less likely than regulators to be captured by industry; and (in theory) they are less burdened than regulators by conflicting non-economic goals.[7] Third, it can be argued that the presence of regulation actually increases the need for competition scrutiny, insofar as regulation creates opportunities and incentives for firms to act anticompetitively in order to avoid or exploit the regulatory framework.[8] With the advent of liberalisation and the introduction of partial competition into some markets, the task of regulating has become more complex and regulation may be less effective.[9] Given the pervasiveness of regulation, a broadly drawn rule against concurrency would have the effect of preserving inefficiencies in a range of markets, while simultaneously diminishing the role for competition law within society.

(ii) Competition problems in regulated markets: the example of margin squeeze

In order to understand how questions of concurrency can arise, we consider the case of margin squeeze, which presents an archetypal example of a competition problem that occurs in regulated markets.[10] More specifically, margin squeeze is a consequence of vertical integration, arising in markets where a vertically integrated firm controls a bottleneck or natural monopoly facility (or input) at one level on the production chain. Potential rivals that wish to compete upstream or downstream require access to the bottleneck in order to operate within competitive segments. For margin squeeze to occur, the vertically integrated firm must grant the new entrant access to the facility, but then manipulate the margin between the access price paid by the rival and the market price for the good or service, in order to squeeze the rival's profits and, ultimately, drive it from the market. Margin squeeze harms competition insofar as it excludes as-efficient competitors,

[7] Dogan & Lemley (2009:696–700); Hovenkamp (2011:771). By contrast, sector-specific regulators typically have greater information and technical knowledge regarding their sectors. Controversy, of course, exists regarding possible non-economic goals of competition law; see p. 28.

[8] Dogan & Lemley (2009:687); Brennan (2008:141); Hovenkamp (2011:771).

[9] Shelanski (2011:725).

[10] O'Donoghue & Padilla (2013:415); Faella & Pardolesi (2010:255); Heimler (2010). In the EU, margin squeeze emerged as a distinct antitrust abuse only with liberalisation: Geradin & O'Donoghue (2005:377–8); Auf'mkolk (2012:151).

leading to diminished consumer choice and reduced price and quality pressure on the incumbent.

Two distinct sets of rules can be used to address margin squeezes: *ex ante* sector-specific regulation, which aims to structure the market so as to avoid competition problems before they arise; and *ex post* competition enforcement, to impose retrospective sanctions.[11] Margin squeezes occur in industries with bottleneck components and, as Chapter 3 described, the presence of a natural monopoly provides a compelling reason for partial regulation even where other segments of the sector are liberalised. Regulation of bottlenecks typically involves at least an obligation to provide access, and may also require price regulation at the wholesale and/or retail levels. Avoidance of price squeezes is also regularly factored into regulatory pricing schemes.[12] Within competition law, there is some disagreement about whether maintaining an anticompetitive margin between prices should constitute a stand-alone offence,[13] whether instead its component prices are more appropriately conceptualised as comprising other offences such as predation or refusals to deal,[14] or whether it is a purely regulatory violation.[15] What is interesting, for our purposes, is the question of whether competition law can be applied subsequently to correct a margin squeeze that arises where regulatory duties are already in place – which may extend to regulatory supervision of disputed prices.[16]

Two divergent cases concerning alleged margin squeezes in telecommunications markets demonstrate the still-controversial nature of this question. In *linkLine*, the US Supreme Court held that the presence of a wholesale-level regulatory duty to deal excluded antitrust scrutiny of the defendant's behaviour in that market. Instead, its conduct would breach competition law, if at all, as retail-level predatory pricing.[17] In *Deutsche Telekom*, by contrast, the CJEU upheld a finding of breach of Article 102 TFEU that resulted from an 'inappropriate spread' between wholesale and retail access prices charged by the defendant.[18] Notably, the regulatory scheme at issue in *Deutsche Telekom* was apparently rather more prescriptive than that in *linkLine*, as the defendant was subject to

[11] Geradin & O'Donoghue (2005:360). [12] OECD (2004:98–100).
[13] Heimler (2010); O'Donoghue & Padilla (2013:372).
[14] Faella & Pardolesi (2010:267); Colley & Burnside (2006).
[15] Sidak (2008:307–8); Carlton (2008). [16] See, generally, Bouckaert & Verboven (2004).
[17] *Pacific Bell Telephone Co., d/b/a AT&T California et al.* v. *linkLine Communications, Inc., et al.*, 555 US 438 (2009).
[18] Case C-280/08 P *Deutsche Telekom AG* v. *Commission*, EU:C:2010:603, para. 32.

regulation of access prices at both the wholesale and retail levels in addition to mandatory access obligations relating to its fixed telecommunications infrastructure. The specifics of the US and EU approaches to concurrency are considered in the next section. The key conclusion to take from the margin squeeze example at this juncture is that, when presented with a similar problem, the leading competition jurisdictions worldwide reached opposing conclusions. The question of concurrent application is, clearly, a challenging one.

(iii) Concurrency: conceptual approaches and criteria for application

How are these apparently conflicting approaches to be explained, and even reconciled? At a basic level, it can be argued that this divergence reflects the dichotomous conceptions of competition law and regulation as substitutes or complements, considered in Chapter 1.[19] While these opposing conceptions are extreme positions, the dichotomy is nonetheless useful here given that it effectively frames the most fundamental debate regarding the role of competition law in regulated markets. The vision of competition law and regulation as *substitute* instruments of market control implies a competitive and exclusionary relationship; that is, adoption of one mechanism bars application of the other. Given the asymmetry in terms of prospective impacts of competition law and regulation, in practice this indicates primarily that adoption of a regulatory solution excludes antitrust remedies. Conversely, the contrasting idea of competition law and regulation as *complements* implies a compatible and even mutually reinforcing relationship; it suggests that these instruments are not merely applicable consecutively to the same market behaviour, but, moreover, that a holistic combined approach secures the most effective and successful market outcome. Accordingly, the complementary theory supports the concurrent application of competition law in regulated markets, whereas the substitutionary theory essentially rejects concurrency.

An alternative approach would rely upon the general principle of *lex specialis derogat legi generali*, which establishes that, where two legal rules covering the same subject matter conflict, the more specific rule takes priority. The *lex specialis* principle has complementary and substitutionary aspects: competition law is applicable in regulated markets unless there is a conflict, in which case the more 'specialised' regime applies

[19] See pp. 49–60.

alone. The impact of this principle in delimiting the relationship between competition law and regulation in cases of conflict is difficult to assess, however, insofar as it is not immediately obvious which legal regime is 'specialised' here. In addressing anticompetitive behaviour in a market, the question is whether rules that relate directly to that market, but not necessarily to competition, are more specifically applicable than rules that relate directly to competition but are not unique to that sector. Although, in the abstract, the *lex specialis* principle might balance the effectiveness of competition law against the risks of unnecessary enforcement in regulated markets, in practice it provides little guidance about where to draw this dividing line.[20]

It might be more constructive to search for the 'regulator's intent'; that is, to identify from the regulation the extent to which the regulator anticipated (and therefore took into account within the regulatory framework) the possibility of subsequent antitrust enforcement in the regulated market. The regulator may make this explicit in the *travaux préparatoires* or the enacted regulation. The EU telecommunications framework, for example, foresees a comprehensive interplay between competition law and sector-specific rules, with an underlying current from *ex post* to *ex ante* regulated competition within telecommunications markets.[21] The regulations emphasise that: (i) regulation should be imposed only where competition law alone is inadequate to supervise the market;[22] (ii) competition law remains applicable to address

[20] The *lex specialis* principle was invoked by the Seventh Circuit in *Goldwasser*, in rejecting application of antitrust to conduct regulated by the Telecommunications Act of 1996: '[t]he 1996 Act is, in short, more specific legislation that must take precedence over the general antitrust laws, where the two are covering precisely the same field'. *Goldwasser* v. *Ameritech Corp.* 222 F.3d 390 (7th Cir. 2000), 401.

[21] This approach was clear from the outset of liberalisation: European Commission, *Towards a Dynamic European Economy - Green Paper on the Development of the Common Market for Telecommunications Services and Equipment* (COM(87)290 final), published 30 June 1987, p. 16, foreseeing 'strict continuous review' of telecommunications firms under competition law additionally to regulatory obligations.

[22] Directive 2002/21/EC of the European Parliament and of the Council of 7 March 2002 on a common framework for electronic communications networks and services (Framework Directive) (OJ C108/33, 24.4.2002), recital 27; Directive 2009/140/EC of the European Parliament and of the Council of 25 November 2009 amending Directives 2002/21/EC on a common regulatory framework for electronic communications networks and services, 2002/19/EC on access to, and interconnection of, electronic communications networks and associated facilities, and 2002/20/EC on the authorisation of electronic communications networks and services (OJ L337/37, 18/12/2009), recital 5.

antitrust abuses even in regulated segments;[23] and (iii) the purpose of sector-specific regulation is to generate sustainable competition, so that ultimately the market can be supervised solely by competition enforcement.[24] Yet regulatory policy-makers are rarely so categorical. In circumstances where regulation does not control absolutely the entire market, the question is whether the regulator intended for competition law to be applicable within quasi-competitive segments. Two contrasting views might be advanced, which mirror the complements-or-substitutes debate. On the one hand, it has been suggested that regulators take into account the scope and potential for enforcement of competition law in determining the extent and nature of sector-specific rules,[25] a complementary vision that clearly anticipates concurrent application of competition law in regulated markets. The most robust version of this approach indeed suggests that the decision to regulate may represent a heightened level of concern about competition issues in the sector, insofar as regulation indicates that the behaviour is undesirable not only under antitrust standards but also under other normative standards.[26] On the other hand, it might be argued that a less than fully comprehensive regulatory framework reflects a deliberate policy choice in favour of under-enforcement to avoid over-deterrence.[27] Under this essentially substitutionary approach, the considered view of policy-makers to favour (partially) unencumbered competition should not be undermined through injudicious antitrust enforcement.

There is considerable danger, however, in discussing the concurrency question in too abstract or uniform a manner. Evidently, the desire or need to apply competition law within a regulated market suggests that the presence of regulation has not prevented anticompetitive conduct and/or market inefficiency. The concept of regulation covers a wide spectrum of market controls, however, which vary immensely in terms of comprehensiveness and interaction with the market mechanism.[28] Numerous factors might account for the persistence of market failure in regulated markets – and, as this chapter will argue, the source of the market defect has a significant bearing on the appropriateness of subsequent antitrust enforcement. Regulation may encourage or even compel inefficiency in order to advance non-economic goals such as

[23] European Commission, *Notice on the application of the competition rules to access agreements in the telecommunications sector* (OJ C265/2, 22.8.98), particularly paras. 57–8.

[24] Directive 2009/140/EC, recital 5. [25] Shelanski (2011:729). [26] Elhauge (2008:37).

[27] Weiser (2005:576). [28] Areeda & Hovenkamp (2006:¶240c5, p. 284).

distributional fairness. For example, the regulation may approve cross-subsidies between separate market segments, even if this practice excludes new entrants into the subsidised market. Or the regulatory framework may aim for efficiency but be poorly designed or implemented, and therefore fail to achieve its objectives. The regulator may be captured and consequently favour regulated firms by allowing supra-competitive regulated returns or by excluding rivals from potentially competitive segments, for example, or the legislation may misconceive market dynamics and unnecessarily restrict potentially beneficial competition. The market problem may, alternatively, originate more directly in private behaviour: for example, the regulated firm may seek to subvert the regulation through regulatory gaming, or it may engage in plain-vanilla antitrust abuse (such as price-fixing) in unregulated sectors. The application of competition law to hard-core cartels that happen to occur in regulated markets, for instance, is obviously more appropriate than competition enforcement against prices charged by a regulated monopolist that are set or approved by a regulator. Given the broad array of potential market problems and sources of anticompetitive conduct, the wholesale question of whether concurrency should be permitted or denied presumes the availability of a 'one-size-fits-all' solution, and thus masks the policy choices inherent in any blanket solution.

Instead, it will be argued that the concurrent application of competition law in regulated markets is a substantive question, which hinges primarily on the impact of the regulatory scheme on both the market itself and the prospective defendant's behaviour, and the implications for competition liability that follow. This proposition is fairly uncontroversial: commentators generally agree that the issue of concurrent application cannot be determined *a priori*, and depends on the specific regulatory context and alleged anticompetitive behaviour.[29] More debate has focused on defining acceptable parameters for competition

[29] Areeda & Hovenkamp (2006:¶240c5, p. 284); cf. Epstein (2007:114), who argued more categorically against concurrency:

> [u]se one system of regulation, not two. While there is only one way not to regulate, there are many ways in which to regulate, and these often work at cross-purposes. The wisdom is to keep the lines of regulation as simple and clean as possible, so that one problem has only one regulator. . . . Once a direct form of regulation deals with the monopoly issue, antitrust law is, at best, redundant. If the government agency can fix rates, the danger of monopoly has in most cases been effectively countered . . . Why create opportunities for legal arbitrage? Do it once, and do it right.

enforcement in regulated markets.[30] Several general principles emerge from the literature. Broadly speaking, there is an inverse relationship between the extent, complexity and nature of the duties that a regulatory regime imposes and the scope for subsequent competition enforcement. It is generally accepted that there are some circumstances in which competition law *should* defer to regulation. In particular, if anticompetitive conduct results directly from decisions taken by the regulator, many agree that competition law has only a limited role to play.[31] Conversely, competition enforcement appears most appropriate where an anticompetitive outcome is attributable, exclusively or at least predominantly, to private conduct. This is particularly the case if the regulator itself lacks legal power or suitable remedies to address the market defect.[32] The related issues of regulatory capture and regulatory inaction are more controversial. Even a captured regulator remains a sovereign one, so that anticompetitive regulated conduct may still be attributable in formal terms to regulatory coercion rather than autonomous private conduct.[33] Regulatory inaction may reflect a proactive policy choice to prefer market forces, or indicate regulatory prioritisation of non-economic values, rather than merely a captured or lazy regulator.[34] Yet deference to regulatory decision-making leaves market problems unresolved and consumer welfare diminished, leading some commentators to advocate intervention.[35]

When addressing concurrency, the core question to be asked takes various formulations, each of which focuses to differing degrees on the implications of pre-existing regulation for subsequent competition enforcement. The issue can be construed as one of the *pervasiveness of the regulation*, so that the critical question is the point at which a firm is sufficiently regulated for preclusion of competition enforcement.[36] Alternatively, the assessment may focus on the *scope for independent*

30 Compare e.g., Speta (2003) with Semeraro (2003); see also Nitsche & Wiethaus (2012).
31 O'Donoghue & Padilla (2013:26); Dogan & Lemley (2009:706–7); Speta (2003:144–5); Monti (2008:144); Hovenkamp (2005:230).
32 Dogan & Lemley (2009:708); Hovenkamp (2011:773); O'Donoghue & Padilla (2013:26–7).
33 Dogan & Lemley (2009:707).
34 Monti (2008:144); Weiser (2005:576); Nitsche & Wiethaus (2012:410).
35 O'Donoghue & Padilla (2013:27). Dogan & Lemley (2009:707–8) favour intervention against regulatory inaction but not regulatory capture.
36 Hovenkamp (2011:772); Shelanski (2011:702); Tapia & Mantzari (2012:2); O'Donoghue & Padilla (2013:24).

private conduct, or, conversely, the extent to which the anticompetitive outcome is attributable to regulatory authority.[37] A more policy-oriented formulation considers the *marginal benefit of subsequent competition enforcement*.[38] Under this latter approach, it is possible to have an abstract preference for competition law over regulation, but nonetheless advocate limits on its enforcement in regulated markets because antitrust is less effective or appropriate in such sectors.[39] Each formulation represents an effort to balance the default bias for competition enforcement to correct anticompetitive behaviour with the practical realities of such markets. In sections IV and V, we aim to address the mechanics of this balancing exercise by exploring the range of possible policy considerations and the impact of market circumstances on the weightings of these factors.

II. Concurrency in practice: The US and EU law positions

We now move from the realms of theory to case law, examining and comparing the practice on concurrency within the US and EU systems. This study seeks to demonstrate how prioritisation of a particular policy consideration – such as sovereignty or effectiveness – can determine the permissible parameters of concurrency. Within each jurisdiction, the question of concurrency arises with respect to two sources of regulation: State and federal regulation in the USA, and EU-level and Member State regulation in the EU. We consider first the position on concurrency within US federal antitrust with respect to these two dimensions. The principles determining the relationship are notably different with respect to each: whereas the relationship between antitrust and state regulation focuses on allocation of sovereignty between states and the federal government, the relationship between antitrust and federal regulation hinges upon the substantive interaction of overlapping controls. We subsequently consider the position within EU law, where the effectiveness of competition enforcement is a central concern, an approach that strongly favours concurrent application wherever possible.

37 Hovenkamp (2011:772–3).

38 Shelanski (2011:709); Shelanski (2012:508); Areeda & Hovenkamp (2006:¶243g1, pp. 359–60).

39 Shelanski (2012:509).

(i) US antitrust and state regulation: the significance of sovereignty

Two doctrines govern the relationship between federal antitrust and state regulation: pre-emption and state action, which represent inverse yet reconcilable notions of concurrency. Pre-emption results in disapplication of state law where there is conflict with federal antitrust, whereas state action provides immunity from federal antitrust for activity within the ambit of a state regulatory scheme. Between the spheres carved out by pre-emption and state action there is a middle ground of conduct subject to both state regulation and federal antitrust, where determination of the impact of the state regime on antitrust depends on the substantive requirements of each.

Pre-emption occurs where federal law invalidates a conflicting state statute, pursuant to the Supremacy Clause of the US Constitution.[40] The pre-emption doctrine has a narrow scope,[41] so that the Sherman Act pre-empts state statutes only where there is an irreconcilable conflict between the state scheme and federal antitrust policy.[42] In *Rice*, the Supreme Court held that where a state statute compels a *per se* antitrust violation, the state measure must be pre-empted. Conversely, where the activity concerned is examined under the rule of reason, pre-emption is inappropriate.[43] Accordingly, the doctrine applies only where a hard-core restriction of competition is the inescapable consequence of state law. Mere adverse effects on competition do not trigger pre-emption, on the basis that a robust application of the doctrine would destroy the states' power to engage in economic regulation.[44]

Where the standards for pre-emption are nonetheless satisfied, the measure might still avoid invalidation under the 'state-action' exemption, which provides immunity for certain state regulation. This doctrine was first articulated in *Parker* v. *Brown*,[45] which concerned a California statute that mandated output restrictions and price-fixing. Although it was assumed that the scheme would breach antitrust if implemented by private actors, based on the facts the Supreme Court held that it constituted *state* rather than private action.[46] Taking account of its text and history, the Supreme Court concluded that the Sherman Act prohibits

40 Article VI, Clause 2, Constitution of the United States. 41 Elhauge (1991:669–70).

42 *Rice, Director, Department of Alcoholic Beverage Control of California* v. *Norman Williams Co.*, 458 US 654 (1982), 659.

43 *Rice*, 661. 44 *Exxon Corp.* v. *Governor of Maryland* 437 US 117 (1978), 133.

45 *Parker, Director of Agriculture, et al.* v. *Brown*, 317 US 341 (1943). 46 *Parker*, 350.

only individual action.[47] While states cannot immunise private actors that violate antitrust,[48] conversely the Sherman Act does not apply to conduct that represents a state regulatory programme.[49] Considerations of federalism provide the rationale: '[i]n a dual system of government in which, under the Constitution, the states are sovereign, save only as Congress may constitutionally subtract from their authority, an unexpressed purpose to nullify a state's control over its officers and agents is not lightly to be attributed to Congress'.[50] If state sovereignty is less clear-cut – such as delegated authority – a more restricted and refined version of the doctrine applies. In *Midcal*, the Supreme Court identified a two-pronged test: the challenged restraint must be clearly articulated and affirmatively expressed as state policy, and the policy must be actively supervised by the state.[51] These requirements are distinct but interrelated.[52] The state action doctrine thus applies in circumstances beyond the pre-emption of state legislation, given that it extends to state regulatory policy and activities of private parties falling under the state activity rubric.[53] Where deliberate state action is identified, the motivations for the state's decision to regulate are irrelevant; so, for example, the doctrine applies even if the regulator is captured or bribed.[54] The *Noerr-Pennington* doctrine[55] similarly provides immunity for private actors that lobby government in order to influence the political process; that is, genuine efforts to participate in policy-making do not breach antitrust, even if the parties lobby for changes that have anticompetitive effects or act with anticompetitive motives.[56]

47 *Parker*, 352. 48 *Parker*, 351. 49 *Parker*, 352.

50 *Parker*, 351. The state regulation at issue was compatible with the Commerce Clause despite its impact on interstate trade because, 'upon a consideration of all the relevant facts and circumstances, it appears that the matter is one which may appropriately be regulated in the interest of the safety, health and wellbeing of local communities, and which, because of its local character, and the practical difficulties involved, may never be adequately dealt with by Congress' (362–3).

51 *California Retail Liquor Dealers Assn.* v. *Midcal Aluminum, Inc., et al.*, 445 US 97 (1980), 105.

52 Areeda & Hovenkamp (2006:¶221c–221e1, pp. 50–64).

53 *Southern Motor Carriers Rate Conference, Inc., et al.* v. *United States*, 471 US 48 (1985), 56 & 61–2.

54 Dogan & Lemley (2009:690).

55 Named for the cases that established the doctrine, *Eastern Railroad Presidents Conference* v. *Noerr Motor Freight*, 365 US 127 (1961), and *United Mine Workers* v. *Pennington*, 381 US 657 (1965).

56 Hovenkamp (2011:750–3).

The extent of the state action doctrine's ability to defeat antitrust claims has been debated. Expansive interpretations of the doctrine are criticised on the basis that it facilitates rent-seeking behaviour and inefficiency.[57] The FTC has long been concerned by what it regarded as the acceptance by lower courts of overbroad interpretations of *Parker*, which, it argued, could potentially endanger national competition goals.[58] Consequently, the agency sought actively to strengthen antitrust by constraining the scope of the state action doctrine.[59] In the most recent *Phoebe Putney* decision,[60] the Supreme Court applied a relatively narrow version of the *Parker* exception in the context of merger control. It emphasised, in particular, the need for a 'clear articulation' of anticompetitive purpose within the state statute. Since there was no evidence that the state legislation at issue has envisaged merger to substantially lessen competition, the defence failed. *Phoebe Putney* might therefore be taken to represent a fairly robust restatement of the limits of this doctrine, reaffirming 'the fundamental national values of free enterprise and economic competition that are embodied in the federal antitrust laws'.[61] This decision is nonetheless compatible with the movement from public-interest theories of government, viewing the state as benign and disinterested, to more sceptical public-choice theories.[62] Easterbrook outlined two assumptions underlying the shift towards public choice in state action immunity: that state regulatory laws are anticompetitive dispensations to politically powerful groups that harm consumers and ought to be strictly controlled; and that such control is best achieved by supplying, under antitrust, a set of rules about the kind of regulatory mechanisms a state may employ to dispense special-interest favours.[63] Federal antitrust, while acknowledging the prerogative of sovereign states to engage in anticompetitive regulation where they clearly articulate an intention to do so, thus defers to state regulation only insofar as it adequately replicates the market-supervisory role of antitrust, albeit in pursuit of non-competition objectives.

[57] Muris (2004); see also Crane (2013:424–6).

[58] FTC Office of Policy Planning, *Report of the State Action Task Force*, published September 2003, p. 1. See also Sokol (2012:88).

[59] *State Action Report*, Chapter 5.

[60] *FTC* v. *Phoebe Putney Health System, Inc.* (Docket No.11–1160), judgment of 19 February 2013.

[61] *Phoebe Putney*, Opinion of Sotomayor J, section II.

[62] Delacourt & Zywicki (2005).

[63] Easterbrook (1983:27).

A central concern of both the pre-emption and state action doctrines is the need to accommodate state sovereignty relating to economic regulation with the competition-focused goals of federal antitrust. Whereas antitrust focuses on efficiency, states as economic regulators take into account a broader range of regulatory objectives, and thus do not always arrive at the most efficient outcome. An overbroad pre-emption standard that invalidates all less-than-fully-efficient regulation is incompatible with the aims of federalism, which grants the states a sizeable sphere of legislative jurisdiction. As the Supreme Court argued in *Exxon Corp.*, 'if an adverse effect on competition were, in and of itself, enough to render a state statute invalid, the states' power to engage in economic regulation would be effectively destroyed'.[64] Where states choose to pursue anticompetitive policies, federal antitrust does not invalidate such inherently political choices.[65] Yet, the *Midcal* standard requires that a state derogating from the market model must take responsibility for its actions: it must affirmatively choose to remove competition as the mechanism of control, and establish an adequate substitute framework for market supervision.[66]

The distinction between pre-emption and state action can, however, be complex in practice. In *Midcal*, state regulation was held to conflict irreconcilably with antitrust insofar as it mandated a *per se* violation, and was pre-empted unless saved by the state action exemption, the requirements for which, on the facts, were not satisfied.[67] Hovenkamp suggested that the same fundamental concern underlies both doctrines, namely that states may authorise private conduct that impairs competition, and argued that a more forthright approach would be to merge the doctrines so that state action defines the scope of pre-emption. Under this approach, consideration of whether the statute compels a *per se* violation would be reserved for the merits of an antitrust case, whereas the exemption (or pre-emption) question would focus only on whether the state policy is clearly articulated, and whether private decisions with anticompetitive potential are adequately supervised by the regulating state.[68] An alternative approach might focus on the origin and nature of each doctrine. Pre-emption is a constitutional principle, stemming from the laws that determine the relationship between federal government and the states. State action emerged from the corpus of antitrust

[64] *Exxon Corp.*, 133. [65] Areeda & Hovenkamp (2006:¶230a, p. 235).
[66] Areeda & Hovenkamp (2006:¶221e, p. 63). [67] *Midcal*, 102–3.
[68] Hovenkamp (2011:796).

law and constitutes a substantive part of these rules. Pre-emption might therefore be viewed as a constitutional prohibition on certain forms of state legislative activity that are incompatible with the division-of-powers framework of federalism, while state action represents a substantive limit to the ambit of antitrust, on the basis that the nature of the activity under scrutiny (rather than its effect on competition) falls outside its scope. The rationale for granting precedence to regulation over antitrust is state sovereignty – although the nod to substance within the doctrine brings it closer to the second category of concurrency to be examined, namely, the relationship between antitrust and other federal regulation.

(ii) US antitrust and federal regulation: substance- and policy-focused approaches

Under the Supremacy Clause, antitrust and other federal regulation have equal status, meaning that the pre-emption doctrine cannot apply. Instead, the question of the relationship between these instruments is a substantive one, of 'reconciliation of the antitrust laws with a federal regulatory scheme'.[69] Federal regulation enacted subsequently remains free partially to repeal antitrust by exempting particular industries, either expressly or impliedly.[70] Where exemption is express, the issue is the scope of the immunity granted. Where the issue is one of implied repeal, the question of concurrent application depends upon whether the particularities of the regulation conflict with substantive antitrust. Although, historically, courts were reluctant to find displacement, recent cases suggest a greater readiness to exclude antitrust from markets subject to federal regulation, in contrast to the approach to the state action doctrine.

(a) The conventional approach: a presumption of concurrency

Conventionally, the relationship between federal antitrust and regulation was governed by the precept that, '[w]hen there are two acts upon the same subject, the rule is to give effect to both if possible'.[71] Concurrency was thus the norm. Express exemptions contained in federal statutes were interpreted narrowly, to permit antitrust enforcement in non-exempted segments.[72] In the absence of express statutory exemption, antitrust immunity was not lightly implied, with a presumption of

[69] *Gordon*, 660. [70] Elhauge (2008:36).
[71] *United States* v. *Borden Co. et al.*, 308 US 188 (1939), 198. [72] *Borden*, 196–203.

concurrency unless impossible.[73] In *Philadelphia National Bank*, the Supreme Court established a demanding standard for preclusion absent express immunity, requiring 'plain repugnancy' between antitrust and regulation.[74] The Court in *Silver* added an assumption that antitrust immunity could be implied 'only if necessary to make the [regulation] work, and even then only to the minimum extent necessary'.[75] *Otter Tail*[76] illustrates the (historical) robustness of the presumption against preclusion. Here, a vertically integrated electricity company was alleged to have breached Sherman Act, §2, where it refused to interconnect with and transport power on behalf of customers that wished to self-supply. Under the Federal Power Act, the sector regulator could order interconnection, and the defendant argued that this access regime immunised it from antitrust scrutiny. The Supreme Court denied its immunity arguments, however: the Court saw within the regulation 'an overriding policy of maintaining competition to the maximum extent possible consistent with the public interest',[77] so that the regulation was not intended to displace antitrust.

A consequence of this substance-focused approach to concurrency was that different activities within the same regulatory framework might be subject to or, alternatively, exempt from antitrust, as a trio of cases concerning the Securities and Exchange Commission (SEC) demonstrated. In the earliest, *Silver*, the Supreme Court held a collective boycott was not immunised by a federally mandated duty of self-regulation on securities exchanges, particularly as the regulatory scheme lacked any mechanism by which to control such behaviour.[78] In the later cases of *Gordon*[79] and *NASD*,[80] however, the Court found that exemption was appropriate for other practices under the same regulatory framework. *Gordon* concerned the use of fixed commission rates by exchanges. Since the SEC had clear authority to supervise exchanges,[81] and had conducted a 'thorough review' of rate practices,[82] the standard for implied repeal was satisfied.[83] A key concern in *Gordon* was that the alleged violation (price-fixing) constituted a *per se* antitrust breach,[84] meaning that

[73] *California* v. *FPC*, 369 US 482 (1962), 485.

[74] *United States* v. *Philadelphia National Bank et al.*, 374 US 321 (1963), 350–1.

[75] *Silver, d/b/a Municipal Securities Co. et al.* v. *New York Stock Exchange*, 373 US 341 (1963), 357.

[76] *Otter Tail Power Co.* v. *United States*, 410 US 366 (1973).

[77] *Otter Tail*, 374.

[78] *Silver*, 357–60.

[79] *Gordon* v. *New York Stock Exchange, Inc., et al.* 422 US 659 (1975).

[80] *United States* v. *National Association of Securities Dealers, Inc.*, 422 US 694 (1975).

[81] *Gordon*, 681.

[82] *Gordon*, 682.

[83] *Gordon*, 685.

[84] *Gordon*, 691.

liability was wholly incompatible with the regulatory scheme. Similarly, in *NASD*, concerning alleged illegal vertical practices and a horizontal conspiracy relating to marketing of mutual funds, the Court held that, because antitrust enforcement was inherently incompatible with the approach of the regulatory framework, antitrust had to yield for the latter to work.[85] In both *Gordon* and *NASD*, the majority emphasised the potential unfairness for defendants subject to different (and possibly conflicting) duties under concurrent regulatory and antitrust liability.[86] Thus, while reconcilable with earlier authority on their facts, the *Gordon* and *NASD* decisions may nonetheless prefigure a more general movement towards a default rule of antitrust preclusion in regulated market, a shift reinforced by two more recent Supreme Court decisions: *Trinko*[87] and *Credit Suisse*.[88]

(b) From concurrency towards preclusion: the *Trinko* and *Credit Suisse* decisions

Trinko had its origins in the liberalisation provisions of the Telecommunications Act of 1996.[89] The case involved an antitrust class-action suit brought by customers of the (reconstituted) AT&T against Verizon, another telecommunications provider. The complaint alleged that Verizon had breached Sherman Act, §2, by failing to provide access to its fixed telecommunications network in breach of the 1996 Act. Verizon had previously consented to regulatory penalties in respect of the same conduct,[90] and thus the claim was, effectively, an antitrust follow-on action premised upon breach of regulatory obligations. The issue was whether regulation could comprise the substance of an antitrust violation, or alternatively, might shield the regulated firm from antitrust claims. On its facts, therefore, *Trinko* presented a weak antitrust case.[91] Three Supreme Court Justices would have decided the case on grounds of standing, by holding that only AT&T, and not its customers, could bring suit.[92] The majority opinion, nonetheless, addressed the issue of concurrency in decisive detail.

85 *NASD*, 729–30. 86 *Gordon*, 689; *NASD*, 735.

87 *Verizon Communications, Inc.* v. *Law Office of Curtis V. Trinko*, 540 US 398 (2004).

88 *Credit Suisse Securities (USA), LLC, et al.* v. *Billing et al.*, 127 S.Ct. 2383 (2007).

89 Considered at pp. 64–5.

90 Verizon paid $10 million to AT&T under state regulation and a $3 million fine under FCC regulation: *Trinko*, 403–4.

91 Shelanski (2011:694). 92 *Trinko*, 416–8.

The Court began by noting that breach of regulatory duties does not automatically equate to antitrust violation, even where a firm holds a monopoly position. Generally, in fact, the opposite is true: 'a detailed regulatory scheme. . .ordinarily raises the question whether the regulated entities are not shielded from antitrust scrutiny altogether by the doctrine of implied immunity'.[93] While the 1996 Act was a good candidate for implied immunity, given the 'real possibility' for conflict between the regulatory requirements and antitrust,[94] that result was precluded by the Act itself, which contains an antitrust savings clause.[95] Accordingly, antitrust immunity, as such, could not be conferred. The Court nonetheless considered the impact of the regulation on the established antitrust rules, and concluded that the existence of the sector-specific regime, which created and controlled the access framework, excluded application of antitrust as *itself* a substantive rule of antitrust.[96] In making this determination, the relationship between antitrust and sector-specific regulation was considered at length. The Court started from the proposition that '[a]ntitrust analysis must always be attuned to the particular structure and circumstances of the industry at issue', including the existence of regulation.[97] Where regulation exists specifically to deter and remedy anticompetitive harm, the additional benefits from antitrust enforcement 'tend to be small'.[98] It is thus 'less plausible that the antitrust laws contemplate such additional scrutiny'.[99] The Court construed its decision, not as a restriction on application of antitrust in regulated sectors, but rather as a refusal to extend the contours of existing unilateral conduct rules.[100] This suggests a default position that, where (at least sufficiently pervasive or effective) regulation governs a sector, antitrust is excluded, *unless* the antitrust rules are broadened to cover regulated conduct.

Can *Trinko* be reconciled with earlier approaches to concurrency? A number of policy concerns that informed the Court's restrictive approach can be discerned. First, it emphasised that the regulation at issue created, and not merely added an additional layer of scrutiny to, the market concerned: without the regulatory access obligations, the wholesale-level product would not exist.[101] The 1996 Act is therefore more ambitious than antitrust: whereas the latter seeks only to prevent unlawful monopolisation, the regulatory regime goes further, aiming to

[93] *Trinko*, 406. [94] *Trinko*, 406. [95] *Trinko*, 406. [96] *Trinko*, 411.
[97] *Trinko*, 411. [98] *Trinko*, 412. [99] *Trinko*, 412. [100] *Trinko*, 412.
[101] *Trinko*, 410,

eliminate telecommunications monopolies altogether, and it would be a 'serious mistake to conflate the two goals'.[102] Second, not only did the regulatory framework foresee the breach at issue and make provision for sanctions, but also both federal and state regulators had punished the behaviour in question.[103] Thus, the market defects could be addressed and sanctioned adequately using regulatory instruments, with little need for, or added value from, antitrust enforcement. Third, the Court invoked policy concerns of a more generalised nature, which, it argued, leaned against application of antitrust. These included the risk of false-positive findings of antitrust violation,[104] the difficulties that generalist antitrust courts face if required to determine whether a defendant has breached the technical duties imposed by telecommunications regulation,[105] and the need for quasi-regulatory remedies to address many antitrust problems in regulated markets, which require trial courts to perform a market-supervisory role that is inappropriate for antitrust adjudicators.[106] The implications and validity of these objections are considered in section IV.

Credit Suisse followed the restrictive approach and logic of *Trinko*, although the judgment addressed implied immunity rather than substantive disapplication of antitrust. Here, the context was the potential application of antitrust in securities markets to address allegations of tying, excessive commissions and 'laddering', in breach of Sherman Act, §1.[107] The Supreme Court began from the substance-based orthodoxy of implied antitrust immunity, noting that the determination of whether regulation grants immunity varies between regimes and tends to depend on the relationship of the specific conduct to both antitrust and the regulatory framework.[108] The Court then synthesised the principles emerging from *Gordon* and *NASD* to identify four requirements to find 'sufficient incompatibility to warrant an implication of preclusion'.[109] First, there must be a sector-specific regulator to supervise the activity; in *Credit Suisse*, the SEC had authority to supervise the activities concerned. Second, there must be evidence that the regulator enforced its authority; again, in *Credit Suisse*, the Court found that the SEC had continuously exercised its powers to regulate conduct of the type at issue.

102 *Trinko*, 415. 103 *Trinko*, 413. 104 *Trinko*, 414. 105 *Trinko*, 414.

106 *Trinko*, 414–15.

107 *Credit Suisse*, 2389. 'Laddering' involves an obligation to purchase additional shares after an IPO at increased prices.

108 *Credit Suisse*, 2389. 109 *Credit Suisse*, 2392.

Third, the potential conflict must affect practices within the jurisdiction of the regulator; in *Credit Suisse*, the activities concerned were, the Court held, central to the proper functioning of capital markets.[110] Fourth, there must be a risk of conflict between antitrust and regulation, if applied concurrently. To assess that question, the Court assumed that the SEC had authority over the conduct comprising the substance of the antitrust complaint and that it disapproved,[111] meaning there was no apparent incompatibility between antitrust and securities regulation. Nonetheless, it rejected the application of antitrust in the circumstances. Specifically, the Court emphasised the 'frequently indistinct line' between conduct prohibited and permitted by securities regulation. For antitrust purposes, an appreciable margin of error exists with respect to the permissibility of regulated activities; this is due to the complexity of securities regulation,[112] the potentially ambiguous nature of evidence that might be invoked,[113] and the fact that antitrust claims based on complex securities law would be adjudicated before non-expert judges and juries.[114] Where such uncertainty exists, the benefit of the doubt supports preclusion: a complete reversal of the conventional view that derogations from antitrust are narrowly construed. Moreover, *Credit Suisse* followed *Trinko* in its reliance upon various policy factors that weighed against antitrust liability, such as the risk of false positives, the presence of on-going regulatory supervision and the availability of private redress mechanisms within the regulatory framework.[115]

While *Trinko* was the turning point, the broader rule emerges from *Credit Suisse*; *Trinko* was essentially a 'non-immunity' case whereas *Credit Suisse* was a straightforward implied-immunity decision.[116] Nonetheless, the difference in analysis utilised in each is slight, with similar policy concerns arising in both.[117] Taken together, *Trinko* and *Credit Suisse* represent a significant shift in the Supreme Court's thinking, thus rendering concurrent antitrust enforcement considerably more difficult in regulated sectors. The evidence suggests that, in the future, these decisions will impose significant barriers to antitrust enforcement in the telecommunications and securities sectors. In both *Trinko* and *Credit Suisse*, the Court emphasised the diminished need for antitrust in light of the extensive coverage of the regulatory regimes, and moreover,

[110] *Credit Suisse*, 2392–3. [111] *Credit Suisse*, 2394. [112] *Credit Suisse*, 2394.
[113] *Credit Suisse*, 2395. [114] *Credit Suisse*, 2395–6. [115] *Credit Suisse*, 2392–7.
[116] FTC (2010b:12); Areeda & Hovenkamp (2011:¶243d, p. 43).
[117] Areeda & Hovenkamp (2011:¶243d, pp. 41–4).

the potential mischief that antitrust might create when applied in regulated markets. More concretely, the subsequent decision in *linkLine* treats *Trinko* as creating a 'straightforward' rule that precludes application of antitrust to the access provisions of the 1996 Act.[118] The potential impact of these decisions extends beyond their immediate regulatory contexts,[119] moreover, at least into markets with equivalent regulatory controls. Although the Court's substantive assessments of the regulatory regimes concerned were limited to the particular sectoral circumstances, the more general policy considerations against concurrency have broader application. Breyer J., concurring in *linkLine*, neatly summed up the emerging scepticism: '[w]hen a regulatory structure exists to deter and remedy anticompetitive harm, the costs of antitrust enforcement are likely to be greater than the benefits'.[120]

(c) A holistic approach to concurrency and critiques of the new direction: the decision in *Town of Concord*

A notable aspect of *Trinko*, followed in *linkLine*, is its strong reliance on an earlier decision of Breyer J., written as Chief Judge of the First Circuit, in *Town of Concord*.[121] As in *linkLine*, that earlier case concerned an alleged margin squeeze in a regulated market – electricity – and the lower court similarly concluded that regulation precluded application of antitrust. *Town of Concord* provides additional value, nevertheless, through its sophisticated consideration of the antitrust-regulation relationship, and in particular, how the presence of regulation impacts on the application of antitrust in substantive terms. Breyer J. noted that

> "[R]egulation" and "antitrust" typically aim at similar goals – i.e., low and economically efficient prices, innovation, and efficient production methods – but they seek to achieve these goals in very different ways. Economic regulators seek to achieve them directly by controlling prices through rules and regulations; antitrust seeks to achieve them indirectly by promoting and preserving a process that tends to bring them about. An antitrust rule that seeks to promote competition but nonetheless interferes with regulatory controls could undercut the very objectives the antitrust laws are designed to serve. Thus, where regulatory and antitrust regimes coexist ... antitrust analysis must sensitively recognize and reflect the distinctive economic and legal setting of the regulated industry to which it applies.[122]

[118] *LinkLine*, 1119. [119] Shelanski (2011:705–6). [120] *LinkLine*, 1124.
[121] *Town of Concord, Massachusetts* v. *Boston Edison Co.*, 915 F.2d 17 (1st Cir. 1990).
[122] *Town of Concord*, 22.

Considering the margin squeeze issue, he opined that a fully regulated price squeeze would 'not ordinarily' breach antitrust, not because of any blanket exemption for regulated conduct nor because antitrust applies with lesser force in regulated sectors, but instead because, in light of the requirements and the impact of the regulatory framework, a price squeeze would not ordinarily be exclusionary and so would not violate the Sherman Act.[123] Moreover, the judgment identified numerous policy concerns that were later invoked in *Trinko* and *Credit Suisse*: the likelihood that regulation diminishes the risk of serious antitrust harm, because the regulator controls the market and can avoid such problems; the danger that prohibiting price squeezes could discourage efficiency, as more efficient suppliers are obliged to support the margins of inefficient downstream competitors; the difficulty for antitrust courts in determining a 'reasonable' margin; and the availability to plaintiffs of an alternative remedy, namely, a complaint to the regulator.[124] *Town of Concord* goes beyond the *Trinko* and *Credit Suisse* analyses insofar as it seeks expressly to reconcile these factors with the substance-based approach, demonstrating how these regulatory and market factors render antitrust inapplicable. Where there is a *regulated* margin squeeze, the Court argued, the antitrust considerations are so significantly altered that the legal consequences of the squeeze might also change. What is illegal under antitrust in an unregulated sector may not, accordingly, constitute exclusionary conduct in a regulated sector.[125]

In considering the Supreme Court's treatment of *Town of Concord* shortly after *Trinko*, Weiser identified two differing interpretations of the principles that emerged from the earlier decision. Under the 'categorical' version, the mere presence of sector-specific regulation excludes antitrust. Under the 'discretionary' version, regulation excludes antitrust only where the regulation is reasonably effective at addressing the anticompetitive conduct.[126] Weiser argued that the approach adopted in *Trinko* should be interpreted in line with the nuanced discretionary approach.[127] *Credit Suisse* and *linkLine* suggest, however, that the Court is more persuaded of the generic 'categorical' dangers of antitrust enforcement in regulated markets – and perhaps more generally. Yet not all antitrust scholars are so persuaded, and the *Trinko/Credit Suisse* approach

123 *Town of Concord*, 22: 'regulation makes a critical difference in terms of antitrust harms, benefits, and administrative considerations'.

124 *Town of Concord*, 25–8. 125 *Town of Concord*, 28. 126 Weiser (2005:562).

127 See also Rubin (2005:738–9).

attracted much criticism. Most critiques contend that the Court adopted an unnecessarily 'broad-brushstroke' reform of the existing rules that amounts to a wholesale presumption against concurrency, without giving sufficient consideration either to whether competition problems are likely to occur in regulated markets, or whether antitrust may be beneficial on balance. Thus, it has been argued that this approach fails to distinguish between effective supervision in practice and the existence of a potentially (but unrealised) effective framework for market supervision;[128] that it ignores the existence of competition problems that arise precisely because of (and not merely despite) the regulatory context, such as regulatory gaming;[129] and that the Court disregarded the distinction between public and private plaintiffs, with their very different motivations for antitrust enforcement, in implementing a generalised rule against concurrency.[130]

As a general proposition, the presumption of concurrency appears to have disappeared.[131] US courts are now more suspicious of antitrust enforcement in regulated sectors, and more receptive to the argument that sector-specific regulation adequately resolves market failures. Where the required antitrust remedy is regulatory in nature, the Court now takes the view that antitrust is an inappropriate vehicle to design, and more importantly, implement such measures. From a concurrency perspective, there has therefore been a shift within the established substance-based approach; these assumptions are more abstract and generalised and may represent a movement towards determination of the regulation/antitrust interface question *a priori*, rather than founded on the substantive provisions of the regimes and their interaction. The threshold for incompatibility has reduced; preclusion might now be found where antitrust enforcement is viable in substantive legal terms but disfavoured on policy grounds. Consequently, it has been argued, the legal standard has shifted from the question of whether the substantive provisions of regulation conflict with antitrust to the question of whether, on balance, antitrust enforcement provides added

[128] Shelanski (2011:702); Shelanski (2012:505); Dogan & Lemley (2009:703–6); Blair & Piette (2005); Economides (2005); Jones (2005:709).

[129] Dogan & Lemley (2009); Brennan (2008:141–2).

[130] Shelanski (2011:713–14); FTC (2010b).

[131] This assessment is supported by the weight of commentary – although many disagree with the ultimate outcome. See Shelanski (2011:684–5); Blair & Piette (2005); Dogan & Lemley (2009); Jones (2005:706); Jablon et al. (2005:606–24); Crane (2009); Brennan (2008).

value.[132] Within regulated markets, antitrust has lost its presumption of authority, and now depends largely upon policy-based fiat for its application. As Brennan suggests, the objection to antitrust evinced in *Trinko* and *Credit Suisse* is generic rather than specific: 'that with respect to competition in the presence of regulation, antitrust courts have no business getting involved'.[133]

(iii) Concurrent application under EU law: prioritising effectiveness, compromising legitimacy?

Next, we turn to the concurrent application of EU competition law in regulated markets. EU law strongly favours concurrency, an approach that emphasises the importance of competition law for the effective functioning of competition in EU markets. Moreover, competition law plays a significant role in the process of liberalisation. There is some risk, however, that this vigorous approach ignores the complexity of competition in regulated markets, which may compromise the legitimacy of competition enforcement.

(a) Concurrent application of EU competition law and regulation: general principles

As with US antitrust, two sources or levels of *ex ante* regulation, namely national regulation and EU-level regulation, are relevant when considering the concurrent application of EU competition law in regulated markets. The approach to concurrency under EU law is more straightforward than the US position: the basic rule is that competition law is applicable *ex post* in any regulated market, whether subject to national or EU-level regulation. Moreover, the permissibility of concurrency extends to firm behaviour that has been directed or modified by *ex ante* regulation, provided that the firm retains some, even relatively limited, scope for autonomous market behaviour (and, consequently, anticompetitive market activity.)[134]

Within the EU, the great bulk of sector-specific regulation is enacted at Member State level. There are two reasons for this preponderance of national regulation. First, EU-wide sector-specific regulation is often implemented by directive, which requires subsequent transposition into national law by Member States. Hence, while many regulations originate

[132] Shelanski (2012:508). [133] Brennan (2005:653).
[134] Case C-280/08 P *Deutsche Telekom*, paras. 81–4.

in EU law requirements, ultimately they take their legal form and are applied to undertakings as provisions of domestic law. Second, where a market is not regulated at the EU level or is subject only to partial EU controls, individual Member States remain free to implement domestic regulatory regimes. Yet the precise legal source of regulation has not been an important issue within the jurisprudence on concurrency.[135] In the *Deutsche Telekom* case, for example, the regulatory framework at issue was developed and imposed at the EU level, but was manifested and applied ultimately as domestic regulation. In assessing the implications of the regulation in terms of the application of EU competition law, the Commission and subsequently the EU courts focused almost exclusively on the mere existence and impact of the regulatory obligations on the defendant firm's behaviour, rather than the legal source of those duties.[136]

In practice, the rules regarding concurrency are the same for both national and EU-level regulation. Regardless of its source, the presence of regulation does not displace the jurisdiction of EU competition law as a mechanism for residual *ex post* market supervision. The strong support for concurrency within EU law can be explained, formally, by virtue of the fact that EU competition rules are foundational Treaty provisions, which are hierarchically superior to both domestic and EU-level regulatory regimes and thus take precedence in cases of conflict. While the existence of competition law does not preclude the enactment of economic regulation, the subsequent presence of the latter does not affect the continuing applicability of the former. Explaining the approach to concurrency in *Deutsche Telekom*, Advocate General Mazák used the analogy of two barriers of market supervision: sector-specific regulation, which is within the supervisory jurisdiction of sector regulators, and EU competition law, which lies within the jurisdiction of the Commission (and, under Regulation 1/2003, national competition authorities). Firms must respect the duties and prohibitions imposed by both regimes.[137]

135 Monti (2008:123). See also Case T-398/07 *Spain* v. *Commission*, EU:T:2012:173, para. 55, which held that EU competition law took precedence over national regulation and EU secondary legislation.

136 Commission Decision of 21 May 2003 in Case COMP/C-1/37.451, 37.578, 37.579 – Deutsche Telekom AG (OJ L263/9, 14.10.2003); upheld in Case T-271/03 *Deutsche Telekom AG* v. *Commission*, EU:T:2008:101, and C-280/08 P *Deutsche Telekom.*

137 Opinion of Advocate General Mazák, C-280/08 P *Deutsche Telekom*, EU:C:2010:212, para. 21.

The presence of *ex ante* regulation is not disregarded entirely within the competition analysis, however. In addition to a complete (albeit narrowly construed) defence for State action, *ex ante* regulation is a 'relevant factor' for consideration when applying competition law to the behaviour of regulated undertakings, including for market definition, assessing the abusive nature of market conduct and setting the amount of fines.[138] In practice, however, while regulation has been a significant factor for both market definition[139] and fining,[140] there is a notable absence of case law considering the critical question of the impact of regulation on allegedly anticompetitive market conduct. Recent Commission practice suggests that, to the extent that regulated conduct fails to qualify for exemption under the State action defence, the impact of the regulatory regime on the qualitative assessment of the (abusive or otherwise) nature of firm conduct is negligible.

(b) Concurrency: the EU constitutional dimension

As a matter of EU constitutional law, different principles underlie concurrency with respect to national and EU-level regulation. In terms of national regulation, the principle of primacy[141] establishes that EU law, including competition law, takes precedence over incompatible domestic provisions. The overarching supervisory framework of the competition rules cannot be superseded by enactment of sector-specific regulation at the national level.[142] Consequently, EU competition law must be respected, despite the additional layer of market control that follows from regulation. As a corollary of the principle of primacy, national courts must disapply domestic provisions that conflict with EU law, an obligation that extends to disapplication of domestic regulation that conflicts with competition law.[143] There is also an obligation on Member States to refrain from enacting domestic regulation which conflicts with

[138] C-280/08 P *Deutsche Telekom*, para. 224.

[139] See e.g. Commission Decision of 22 June 2011 in Case COMP/39.525 – *Telekomunikacja Polska* (OJ C324/7, 9.11.2011), para. 625, where the Commission used the market definition principles under telecommunications regulation – which, of course, reflect the competition law approach, see pp. 170–2 – to confirm its antitrust assessment.

[140] Discounting of fines to account for regulation is considered at pp. 249–51.

[141] Primacy as a general principle of EU law was established in Case 6/64 *Costa* v. *ENEL*, EU:C:1964:66; see also Case 14/68 *Walt Wilheim and others* v. *Bundeskartellamt*, EU: C:1969:4, establishing the primacy of EU competition law over inconsistent national law.

[142] C-280/08 P *Deutsche Telekom*, para. 90; see also Hellwig (2009:208).

[143] Case 106/77 *Simmenthal II*, EU:C:1978:49; Case C-198/01 *Consorzio Industrie Fiammiferi (CIF)*, EU:C:2003:430, paras. 48–50.

EU competition law,[144] unless the limited exception for services of general economic interest is satisfied.[145] It might even constitute a breach of the duty of loyal cooperation, contained in Article 4(3) TEU, for Member States to enact or maintain in force measures that render ineffective the competition rules applicable to undertakings.[146]

With respect to EU-level regulation, the EU competition rules are Treaty provisions, and thus top the hierarchy of legal norms. To the extent that provisions of EU secondary legislation, such as directives or regulations, are incompatible with the competition rules, the Treaty provisions take priority and conflicting regulatory measures are invalidated.[147] The CJEU took the view in *Deutsche Telekom* that the relationship between EU-level sector-specific regulation and the competition rules is complementary; so that the latter supplement, through *ex post* review, the market-supervisory framework specified by *ex ante* regulation.[148] When EU sector-specific regulation is enacted, the intention is not to exclude subsequent application of competition law, but rather to introduce additional sector-wide obligations while retaining competition law's general prohibitions.

(c) Concurrency and 'State action' in EU law

Thus, regulated markets – and, consequently, regulated market behaviour – remain subject to concurrent scrutiny under EU competition law.[149] Three principal exceptions to this general rule exist. First, EU competition law does not apply in regulated markets where there is express derogation to that effect,[150] although any national regulatory scheme that expressly derogates from EU competition requirements risks breaching the Member State's duty of loyal cooperation. Second, EU competition law does not apply where the impact of the regulatory

[144] Article 106(1) TFEU: '[i]n the case of public undertakings and undertakings to which Member States grant special or exclusive rights, Member States shall neither enact nor maintain in force any measure contrary to the rules contained in the Treaties, in particular to those rules provided for in Article 18 and Articles 101 to 109'.

[145] Art.106(2) TFEU. [146] *CIF*, para. 45. [147] *Spain* v. *Commission*, para. 55.

[148] C-280/08 P *Deutsche Telekom*, para. 92. In *Spain* v. *Commission*, para. 56, the General Court interpreted this complementary relationship to nonetheless mean that competition law and *ex ante* regulation 'have distinct purposes and objectives'.

[149] Historically, certain markets were removed from the jurisdiction of EU competition law, and subject to sector-specific supervision incorporating competition principles (see p. 142). Increasingly, this approach has been abandoned, with inclusion of these markets within the general scheme of EU competition law.

[150] *Spain* v. *Commission*, para. 50.

framework means that the sector is not open to competition: for example, where it results in legal or *de facto* monopoly.[151] In such markets, given that there is no possibility of competition even absent the ostensibly anticompetitive conduct, the impugned behaviour cannot have a negative impact on competition. Third, the principal general exception to concurrency is the 'State action defence', a distinct EU law concept albeit sharing terminology with the US rule. The key idea is that competition law prohibits only instances of anticompetitive market conduct by undertakings. Where sector-specific regulation removes all scope for autonomous business activity, no independent anticompetitive behaviour of undertakings can arise, and so there is no scope for applying competition law against the firms concerned.

The foundations of this defence can be traced to the *Suiker Unie* judgment,[152] in which the CJEU partially annulled a Commission decision finding a cartel amongst sugar producers. With respect to certain instances of alleged anticompetitive coordination, the Court held that the market structure at issue had resulted, largely, from Italian regulations implementing EU rules on sugar production. To the extent that the national regulatory regime permitted independent market conduct, the scope of such activity was constrained and largely dictated by the underlying regulatory framework. In such circumstances, sugar producers did not have the ability to impede market competition; rather, any impediments to competition were wholly attributable to the regulatory structure, and so did not come within (now) Article 101 TFEU.[153] Conversely, with respect to other aspects of the sugar producers' behaviour, while the regulatory framework had had an impact on their coordination, it allowed sufficient scope for independent market action, and so Article 101 TFEU was applicable. The Court found that the presence of regulation rendered the anticompetitive conduct less severe, however, and so the amount of the fine imposed was reduced to account for the defendants' diminished culpability.[154]

This approach was crystallised into the distinct State action defence in *Ladbroke Racing*,[155] in which the CJEU confirmed the centrality of

[151] Case T-360/09 *E.ON Ruhrgas AG and E.ON AG* v. *Commission*, EU:T:2012:332, paras. 84–6.

[152] Joined Cases 40/73 etc. *Suiker Unie and Others* v. *Commission*, EU:C:2012:23.

[153] *Suiker Unie*, paras. 63–73.

[154] *Suiker Unie*, paras. 612–24; considered further in section IV(iii)b.

[155] Joined Cases C-359/95 & C-379/95 P *Commission* v. *Ladbroke Racing Ltd*, EU:C:1997:531.

independent market behaviour in establishing liability under EU competition law:

> Articles [101 and 102 TFEU] apply only to anticompetitive conduct engaged in by undertakings of their own initiative. ... If anticompetitive conduct is required of undertakings by national legislation or if the latter creates a legal framework which itself eliminates any possibility of competitive activity on their part, Articles [101 and 102 TFEU] do not apply. In such a situation, the restriction of competition is not attributable, as those provisions implicitly require, to the autonomous conduct of the undertakings.[156]

Therefore, where regulatory requirements prevent a firm from acting autonomously in the market, its behaviour falls outside the scope of the competition rules. There may be market failure, but the cause of the problem is structural, stemming from the regulatory framework, rather than behavioural. Advocate General Jacobs, summarising the *Ladbroke Racing* exception, explained the State action defence in the following terms: 'Under that principle, undertakings charged with an infringement of the competition rules in Articles [101 or 102 TFEU] can claim that their conduct falls outside the scope of those rules where it was required by national legislation or where the national legal framework itself eliminated any possibility of competitive activity on their fault'.[157]

O'Donoghue and Padilla conceive of State action as a three-pronged defence under EU law, applying in cases of: (i) State compulsion, (ii) regulatory elimination of competition, and/or (iii) where private actors exercise public-interest functions under State supervision.[158] The crux of the defence in each instance is the indirect restriction of competition by the State, by requiring that private undertakings act in an anticompetitive manner.[159] Formulated initially as a broad principle referring to any form of legal compulsion imposed by national or EU authorities, the *Deutsche Telekom* judgment confirmed that the defence extends to the realm of *ex ante* sector-specific economic regulation, albeit it was not accepted on the facts.[160] Under EU competition law, the State action defence functions, effectively, as an excuse rather than a justification for ostensibly anticompetitive behaviour. The defendant firm does not claim that its behaviour is not anticompetitive, nor that it has

[156] *Ladbroke Racing*, para. 33. [157] Opinion of Advocate General Jacobs, *CIF*, para. 1.
[158] O'Donoghue & Padilla (2013:22–4). [159] O'Donoghue & Padilla (2013:21–2).
[160] C-280/08 P *Deutsche Telekom*, paras. 80–4; see also Case T-336/07 *Telefónica, SA and Telefónica de España, SA* v. *European Commission*, EU:T:2012:172, paras. 293 & 339.

complied with the requirements of competition law. Rather, the firm claims that its admittedly anticompetitive conduct cannot be attributed to it for the purposes of liability, as its actions were dictated instead by regulatory obligations. Rather than claiming the absence of a competition offence, the claim is absence of an offender.

As a practical barrier to competition enforcement, however, the State action defence has been interpreted and applied restrictively. As Advocate General Mazák argued in *Deutsche Telekom*, EU competition law operates from the premise that the objective conduct of an undertaking should normally be attributed to it.[161] Consequently, a regulatory regime must remove *all* scope for autonomous market conduct for the defence to apply. Where regulation allows the possibility of competition between firms, then competition law applies to any anticompetitive market behaviour.[162] The fact that one dimension of competition – such as price competition – is excluded by regulation is insufficient to exclude application of competition law where other forms of competition are possible.[163] Even if anticompetitive behaviour is encouraged, facilitated or approved by regulation, this does not prevent the application of competition law provided that some independent market conduct can be identified.[164] The threshold for autonomous conduct is low; the mere fact that a dominant firm has some 'leeway'[165] or 'scope'[166] to prevent an anticompetitive regulated outcome may suffice for liability. In direct contrast to *Trinko*,[167] the fact that the market was created by regulation has no implications for the applicability of competition law.[168]

In recent years, the Commission has shown itself increasingly willing to apply competition law in heavily regulated sectors, and to market activity that has been affected significantly by regulation. In *Deutsche Telekom*, the national telecommunications regulation at issue involved a mandatory duty to deal; wholesale prices that were (under the Commission's case theory) wholly set by the regulator; and retail prices that were included within a 'basket' of prices subject to a regulated cap, where price changes required regulatory approval. Nonetheless, the incumbent operator was held to have committed an anticompetitive margin squeeze between wholesale and retail prices for network access, contrary to

161 Opinion of Advocate General Mazák, *Deutsche Telekom*, para. 15.
162 C-280/08 P *Deutsche Telekom*, para. 80; T-336/07 *Telefónica*, paras. 328–9.
163 *CIF*, paras. 69–71.
164 C-280/08 P *Deutsche Telekom*, para. 82.
165 *Spain* v. *Commission*, para. 50.
166 C-280/08 P *Deutsche Telekom*, para. 125.
167 *Trinko*, 410; see p. 206, fn. 101.
168 T-336/07 *Telefónica*, para. 289.

Article 102 TFEU. Even within this constrained regulatory environment, the Commission was satisfied that Deutsche Telekom retained sufficient scope for autonomous action to avoid the squeeze, by petitioning the regulator to increase the retail price.[169] Similarly, in *Telefónica*, the Commission found a breach of Article 102 TFEU based on a margin squeeze in the regulated Spanish telecommunications sector, which involved a regulatory duty to deal.[170] Recent years have also seen a significant number of cases involving undertakings in the heavily regulated gas and electricity sectors, concluded through commitment decisions under Article 9 of Regulation 1/2003, which was considered in Chapter 2.[171] A prominent feature of these cases is the recurrent use of the refusal-to-deal doctrine, whereby the Commission had alleged *de facto* refusal to supply access to the incumbent's bottleneck infrastructure, despite existing regulatory obligations to that effect.

With its *Telekomunikacja Polska* decision, the Commission went further in developing a concurrent (or even conglomerate) approach to the relationship between competition law and regulation. The case involved the incumbent telecommunications operator in Poland, which, under domestic regulation implementing the EU telecommunications framework, was subject to a mandatory duty to provide wholesale broadband access, with a residual regulatory power to impose terms and conditions where these could not be agreed through negotiation. The Commission held that the incumbent's repeated failures to comply with its regulatory duties – through delaying tactics, attempts to impose unfavourable contractual terms on competitors, and failure to provide relevant system information – amounted to an anticompetitive refusal to deal, contrary to Article 102 TFEU.[172] Accordingly, failure to comply with regulatory obligations became a competition abuse, in addition to a regulatory offence. The fact that the initial duty to supply arose under sector-specific regulation was barely considered in the Commission's Decision, beyond acknowledgement of the existence of regulation[173] and a statement that full implementation of regulatory measures was essential for effective retail competition.[174] The Commission expressly

[169] C-280/08 P *Deutsche Telekom*, paras. 84–9.

[170] Commission Decision of 4 July 2007 in Case COMP/38.784 – *Wanadoo España* v. *Telefónica* (OJ C83/6, 2.4.2008); confirmed in T-336/07 *Telefónica* and C-295/12 P *Telefónica SA* v. *European Commission*, EU:C:2014:2062.

[171] See pp. 112–6. [172] *Telekomunikacja Polska*, paras. 695–706.

[173] *Telekomunikacja Polska*, paras. 804–11. [174] *Telekomunikacja Polska*, para. 814.

rejected the defendant's contention that the regulatory context excluded the application of competition law, emphasising the established nature of the concurrency principle within EU law.[175] Concurrent application was therefore permissible even where the national regulator had imposed regulatory penalties for the same behaviour, again contrary to the approach in *Trinko*. This decision has, unsurprisingly, been challenged before the General Court.

A notable aspect of the State action defence is the possibility that, even where it is rejected on the basis that the undertaking retains scope for autonomous conduct, the anticompetitive outcome may nonetheless also be attributable, at least partly, to conduct of the national regulator or restraints contained in the regulatory framework.[176] The Commission has a choice about whether to pursue competition enforcement against a defendant firm, or to bring action against the Member State for its failure to implement or ensure adherence to EU-level regulatory obligations or for breach of its duty of loyal cooperation by enacting or maintaining in force national regulation resulting in breach of the competition rules.[177] With respect to the duty of tariff rebalancing in telecommunications, for instance, the Commission chose to pursue an action against Spain for failure to act,[178] yet with respect to the German market, it brought a competition action against the incumbent on the basis of a margin squeeze attributable, largely, to the Member State's failure to rebalance tariffs.[179] The Commission might even bring actions against both a Member State and a firm on the same facts, as such actions are considered to complement rather than replace each other.[180] In determining whether to proceed against the Member State or private firm, the Commission has a large margin of discretion, and the appropriateness of these decisions is not a matter amenable to review.[181] In EU law, therefore, problems of anticompetitive regulated conduct may be conceived, on the one hand, as a competition issue, and on the other, as a constitutional question concerning the relationship between the Union and its Member States.[182]

175 *Telekomunikacja Polska*, para. 126.
176 C-280/08 P *Deutsche Telekom*, para. 91.
177 C-280/08 P *Deutsche Telekom*, paras. 45 & 91.
178 C-500/01 *Commission* v. *Spain*, EU:C:2004:8.
179 C-280/08 P *Deutsche Telekom*.
180 Opinion of Advocate General Mazák, C-280/08 P *Deutsche Telekom*, para. 13.
181 C-280/08 P *Deutsche Telekom*, para. 47.
182 In relation to the latter, one might draw parallels to the pre-emption doctrine, considered earlier.

(d) The EU approach: analysis and critique

The EU approach to concurrency displays a clear preference for competition enforcement and competition-focused outcomes, notwithstanding pre-existing regulation. Nominally premised upon the hierarchical superiority of the competition rules, this strong bias towards concurrency can have significant substantive consequences if competition law is applied in circumstances where a firm's scope for autonomous market conduct is insufficient to merit antitrust liability. In assessing the appropriateness of this apparent trade-off of legitimacy for effectiveness, we consider four relevant aspects: the Commission's use of competition enforcement to supplement liberalisation; its robust preference for competition over other social values; the question of shared responsibility of national regulators or Member States for competition breaches; and the potential problem of private enforcement.

It is widely acknowledged that the Commission uses competition law as a tool to assist market liberalisation.[183] Competition enforcement may trigger liberalisation in some sectors,[184] whereas it supplements this process in others, correcting perceived defects or failures. The energy commitment decisions, for example, illustrate the Commission's strategic use of competition enforcement to achieve a degree of vertical separation considerably beyond the political agreement for energy liberalisation.[185] Although EU efforts often aim at harmonisation in addition to market opening, the broad discretion retained by Member States under liberalisation directives has sometimes resulted in rather heterogeneous developments in terms of the extent and direction of liberalisation in different national markets.[186] The Commission has limited ability within the liberalisation rubric to require Member States to alter their implementation of EU regulation, unless it pursues formal proceedings for breach under Article 258 TFEU.[187] It therefore tends to take full advantage of the continued application of EU competition law in regulated sectors, frequently bringing competition actions against regulated firms in circumstances where a more obvious obstacle is the inadequacy of regulation.

[183] Monti (2007:240); O'Donoghue (2008:16–17); Faella & Pardolesi (2010:267); Auf'mkolk (2012:159).

[184] Such as airports liberalisation, considered at pp. 72–5. [185] See pp. 114–5.

[186] Tapia & Mantzari (2012:8–11).

[187] The margin of discretion for national regulation in liberalised sectors reflects a political decision to retain domestic control in these areas: Monti (2008:130).

Although doubtless a useful instrument for market control, this aggressive approach to competition enforcement in furtherance of liberalisation generates certain difficulties. The first problem was identified in Chapter 2: the risk that competition law is instrumentalised to achieve social goals outside the realms of competition policy. While EU competition law and EU liberalisation efforts have a common ancestry – pursuit of the internal market[188] – these instruments differ significantly in terms of objectives and technical elements. Liberalisation seeks, typically, to open markets and foster competition in newly competitive sectors. To do so, it may impose positive regulatory duties on firms, and engage in 'differential handicapping'[189] or asymmetric regulation, limiting the ability of certain economic actors to compete in order to assist and protect new entrants. The difficulty here, as Chapter 2 considered, is that such goals and duties extend beyond the accepted parameters of competition law. Monti accordingly argued that the claimed necessity of concurrent application of competition law in order to make liberalised markets work effectively does not support the legitimacy of concurrency, but instead reflects a failure of the underlying liberalisation scheme, or its implementation or enforcement at the national level.[190] Given the generous approach to concurrency adopted by EU law, competition law may be applied in markets and to problems where, arguably, the underlying principles and limitations of antitrust make it an ill-suited tool.

Such instrumental use of competition law can have negative effects: the established rules are distorted to achieve regulatory objectives;[191] certainty for regulated firms is diminished, as compliance with national regulation becomes insufficient to secure the acceptability of market activity;[192] and the outcome of competition cases may represent merely substitution of one regulatory decision for the Commission's own regulatory preferences, where its ability to make policy value judgments is largely unfettered by the administrative controls that constrain the powers of national regulators.[193] In their appeals against the *Telefónica* decision, both the defendant firm and the Spanish government argued that the Commission acted *ultra vires* in applying Article 102 TFEU in a manner going beyond the substantive powers granted under that provision.[194] Although Spain's claim was dismissed for vagueness,[195]

[188] Bavasso (2004:111). [189] Kahn (1987:1060). [190] Monti (2008:130).
[191] Larouche (2000). [192] Ibáñez Colomo (2010). [193] Monti (2008:141).
[194] *Spain* v. *Commission*, para. 101; T-336/07 *Telefónica*, 288.
[195] *Spain* v. *Commission*, para. 105.

and Telefónica's was rejected on narrow substantive grounds,[196] these arguments address essentially the point under discussion, namely that the Commission's application of competition law in liberalised markets takes competition law itself into the realm of regulatory (not antitrust) policy.

Two examples from Commission enforcement practice in regulated markets illustrate these difficulties. In *Deutsche Telekom*, the restrictive impact of the relevant national regulation upon the incumbent's scope for independent market action meant that, effectively, its 'abusive' conduct comprised an omission to petition the regulator to alter the latter's determination about the optimal regulatory framework. Counterintuitively, given the assumption that Deutsche Telekom had no authority over wholesale prices, the firm was effectively found to breach Article 102 TFEU through its failure to seek to *raise* retail prices. The underlying case theory therefore went beyond the mere prohibition of inefficient exclusionary conduct, and instead placed positive obligations on the dominant firm to protect and facilitate competition. Furthermore, the Commission invoked the controversial refusal-to-deal/essential facilities theory of liability in recent energy cases and the *Telekomunikacja Polska* decision. As Chapter 2 noted, the Commission's enforcement priorities for Article 102 TFEU take the curious position that the presence of regulation justifies relaxation of the otherwise demanding legal standards for abusive refusals to deal,[197] allowing the instrumental quasi-regulatory use of competition law in these sectors. The implicit assumption that the presence of a regulatory duty to deal is a proxy for satisfying the *Oscar Bronner* conditions has rightly been challenged on the basis that regulatory choices to impose access are not subject to the same rigorous criteria.[198] Moreover, the specific theories of refusal to deal that were invoked in these recent cases arguably push this already-controversial theory over the precipice of antitrust legitimacy. In several of the energy cases, for example, the Commission applied a theory of 'strategic underinvestment' by dominant firms, resulting in reduced capacity that limited opportunities for competition.[199] The power to direct how a firm invests

[196] T-336/07 *Telefónica*, pp. 288–95.

[197] European Commission, *Guidance on the Commission's enforcement priorities in applying Article 82 of the EC Treaty to abusive exclusionary conduct by dominant undertakings* (OJ C45/7, 24.2.2009), para. 82.

[198] Nitsche & Wiethaus (2012:413–4); Auf'mkolk (2012:155);

[199] *Gaz de France* (OJ C57/13, 9.3.2010); *ENI* (OJ C352/8, 23.12.2010); *RWE Gas Foreclosure* (OJ C133/10, 12.6.2009); *Swedish Interconnectors* (OJ C142/28, 1.6.2010); and

in and develops its business is not one granted by competition law, however, but is rather the province of more politically accountable regulators.[200] *Telekomunikacja Polska* involved the almost direct translation of frustrated regulatory obligations into the *actus reus* of a competition abuse. The defendant thus 'refused to supply' services that it was obliged to provide under national (and EU) regulation, a neat sleight of hand that essentially allowed the Commission to police and enforce national regulation using its antitrust powers. EU competition law thus can become a 'regulator's regulator',[201] second-guessing national regulatory regimes.

A second, related objection advanced against the EU approach to concurrency is its assumption that, even within regulated environments, competition should take precedence over other public-interest objectives.[202] In the energy cases, for instance, the Commission's decision to pursue a series of cases against large EU energy companies reflects a clear preference for structural competition, although greater regulatory certainty and vertical integration might provide better investment incentives and promote energy security. O'Donoghue highlighted the paradox inherent in the absolute prioritisation of competition in regulated markets, insofar as the enactment of regulation itself represents a deviation from the model of full competition.[203] Yet the Commission's approach is more blinkered: generally, competition must take precedence.[204]

A third objection to concurrency stems from the triangular relationship that can arise between the Commission, defendant firm(s) and Member States. Most EU enforcement actions in regulated markets originate in the Commission's desire to further liberalisation. Generally, liberalisation occurs through the use of framework directives that require implementation and enforcement by Member States. The mechanisms for enforcing the Member States' duties – the action for failure to act

Germany Electricity Wholesale Market and *German Electricity Balancing Market* (OJ C36/8, 13.2.2009).

[200] Under the ISO/ITO unbundling models of the Third Energy Directives, these investment questions are specifically entrusted to the TSO, freed of influence from the owner of the asset. Moreover, the TSO are required to submit their plans with respect to issues such as transmission capacity, development and investment to the national regulatory authorities: see further Del Guayo & Pielow (2012).

[201] Monti (2007:496). [202] O'Donoghue (2008:12–13); Monti (2008:138).

[203] O'Donoghue (2008:13); Veljanovski (2008).

[204] Monti (2008:127) criticised the EU approach in unambiguous terms, arguing that it amounts to application of competition law 'without any regard to the regulatory framework'.

under Article 258 TFEU, or for breach of the duty of loyal cooperation relying upon Article 106(1) TFEU – are formalistic, slow and relatively ineffective. The strategic decision to pursue competition problems in regulated sectors indirectly through competition enforcement may remedy existing market defects more quickly and effectively. Yet, this approach neglects the fact that the alleged antitrust abuse may originate in Member State action (or inaction), or even in a policy disagreement between the Commission and the Member State regarding the permissible or preferable parameters of national regulation. Where such difficulties are addressed through concurrent application of competition law, Member States typically escape liability for reasons of political compromise, while private defendants may face liability even when fully compliant with domestic regulatory obligations.[205] The fairness and legitimacy of antitrust enforcement in such circumstances must be questioned.[206]

An example of such potential unfairness was seen in *Deutsche Telekom*, where the defendant was held to breach Article 102 TFEU by maintaining an anticompetitive margin between prices for wholesale and retail access to telephone lines. While Deutsche Telekom's own retail business was also loss-making, both it and its competitors subsidised losses resulting from below-cost access charges through higher call charges. This pricing structure resulted from historic pricing policies pursued by Deutsche Telekom, as the national telecommunications provider, on social policy grounds – presumably, to make access affordable, even if usage costs were high – which continued after privatisation.[207] The fact that telecommunications tariffs had not yet been rebalanced to a more cost-reflective structure stemmed from Germany's failure to comply with obligations imposed on national regulators under the EU telecommunications directives.[208] In applying the margin squeeze test, however, the Commission proceeded *as if* tariffs had been rebalanced by refusing to take account of cross-subsidisation effects from profitable service charges used by all market participants.[209] Deutsche Telekom duly failed the test precisely because tariff rebalancing was not

[205] O'Donoghue (2008:1–2). [206] Klotz (2009b:102).

[207] T-271/03 *Deutsche Telekom*, para. 260.

[208] In particular Commission Directive 96/19/EC of 13 March 1996 amending Directive 90/388/EEC with regard to the implementation of full competition in telecommunications markets (OJ L74/13, 22.3.1996); see T-271/03 *Deutsche Telekom*, paras. 196 & 260.

[209] O'Donoghue & Padilla (2013:388–90).

yet in place.[210] The Commission's choice to prosecute the margin squeeze under competition law rather than to pursue Germany for failure to fulfil obligations under Article 258 TFEU thus facilitated, obliquely, the enforcement of EU-level obligations, imposed initially on the Member State, against the private defendant.[211] The case illustrates the dilemma that concurrency may pose for firms facing conflicting obligations under sector-specific regulation and competition law, and, moreover, the potential injustice of enforcing the latter to correct the former.

Thus far, our assessment has considered only competition enforcement by the Commission. Private enforcement is also of growing importance within EU competition law.[212] Private plaintiffs enforce the conventional EU competition rules, as these have developed through decades of almost exclusively public enforcement, in order to seek compensation for losses suffered as a result of antitrust violations. From the perspective of private enforcement, the expansive rules on concurrency and quasi-regulatory theories of competition harm that have been developed in the context of Commission activities to further liberalisation are problematic. It is undisputed here that the Commission acts in the public interest in pursuing enforcement activity in regulated markets,

[210] T-271/03 *Deutsche Telekom*, para. 260. See also Advocate General Mazák's Opinion, C-280/08 P *Deutsche Telekom*, paras. 54–9.

[211] Conventionally, horizontal direct effect of unimplemented or incorrectly implemented directives – that is, between or against individuals – is not permitted: Case 152/84 *Marshall* v. *Southampton and South-West Hampshire Area Health Authority (Teaching)*, EU:C:1986:84. In this instance, arguably a form of quasi-direct effect is seen, which is somewhat analogous to the 'incidental' direct effect permitted in cases like Case C-194/94 *CIA Security International SA* v. *Signalson SA and Securital SPRL*, EU:C:1996:172, whereby an unimplemented directive can have an impact in national litigation. The difference here is that the impact of the directive is felt in EU-level proceedings brought by the Commission against a private firm, although presumably this approach could also be adopted in a private damages action. An alternative means by which to avoid the rule against horizontal direct effect is to adopt a wide conception of the 'State' thus extending the ambit of vertical direct effect in line with the approach in C-188/89 *Foster* v. *British Gas*, EU:C:1990:313. To the extent that regulated utilities are considered to be 'subject to the authority or control of the State or [to have] special powers beyond those which result from the normal rules applicable to relations between individuals' (*Foster*, at para. 18) so that they can be treated as an organ of the State, direct effect is permissible. Exceptions to the rule against horizontal direct effect cannot aggravate criminal liability (Case C-168/95 *Luciano Arcaro*, EU:C:1996:363) but may heighten civil liability (Case C-456/98 *Centrosteel* v. *Adipol*, EU:C:2000:402); on the status of EU competition proceedings, see p. 240, fn. 278.

[212] See p. 25.

albeit it does not always act solely in furtherance of antitrust policy. Private plaintiffs, conversely, act (not unreasonably) with generally selfish motives, sometimes seeking recompense for losses suffered, but at other times, less benignly, seeking to hamstring or punish rivals. The EU rules on concurrency are best suited to a centralised model of enforcement: one where, moreover, realisation of the internal market constitutes a basic and compelling aim. Within such a system, the Commission can be more readily entrusted with the enforcement of competition law to develop the internal market; in effect, competition law becomes a market-making power. EU competition enforcement has become increasingly decentralised, however, and such broad market-making powers are less appropriate in the hands of private plaintiffs, who pursue purely private rather than broader public interests. The EU's enthusiastic approach to concurrency might be compared with the more reluctant and suspicious US approach, which displays a deep scepticism about the benefits of private enforcement, and a concomitant tendency towards diminished antitrust liability generally to curtail private litigation. Considering Larouche's contention that the instrumental use of competition law distorts the law itself,[213] the broad rules on concurrency within EU law may require revision – or at least, limitation to public enforcement – as private enforcement develops in Europe.

(iv) Analysis: differing approaches to concurrent application in practice

The three systems of concurrency considered earlier demonstrate a broad range of approaches to the question of whether and when concurrent application of competition law should be permitted. These examples illustrate the fundamental tension within concurrency debates: that is, whether and why competition law should defer to regulation or *vice versa*. In US law, the approach to concurrency with state regulation emphasises the centrality of sovereignty: the sovereign state can *always* choose to derogate from federal antitrust and its efficiency-maximising approach, but must do so expressly. In effect, the rule is that competition law defers to regulation, but only to the extent that this is desired by the regulatory scheme. Within EU law, the approach to concurrency emphasises the pre-eminence of competition law over incompatible regulation. Although nominally premised upon the constitutional superiority of

[213] See p. 92.

Treaty provisions, in practice the application of this principle demonstrates a robust substantive preference for competition law over regulation, perhaps underestimating the impact that regulation may have on market conditions or firm behaviour. The issue of substantive interaction is, ostensibly, at the forefront of the approach to concurrency between US antitrust and federal regulation. Recent jurisprudential developments suggest, however, that questions of substance are not entirely immune from policy considerations that may, alternatively, favour or disfavour concurrency.

Drawing upon this discussion, two central elements relating to concurrent application of competition law in regulated markets can be identified. First, this is an area in which policy considerations abound, leaning both for and against concurrency. In the next section, we group these concerns into three broad categories – economic and analytical, rule-of-law and institutional issues – and consider generally the relevance and impact of each in determining the desirably of concurrency. Second, the relative weightings given to each policy concern, and the task of balancing conflicting factors, tend to differ between different regulated markets and different sources of anticompetitive behaviour. Section V examines, more particularly, the considerations that arise in different market circumstances, which may inform the appropriate parameters of concurrency. Accordingly, whereas section IV considers generally the range of *potential* policy considerations that may arise with concurrency, Section V addresses the *likelihood* that any factor will arise in a particular instance.

III. The parameters of concurrency: economic, rule-of-law and institutional concerns

The effectiveness of antitrust supervision and the attendant benefits of well-functioning markets are obvious rationales for concurrent application of competition law in regulated markets. The particularities of the regulatory context tend to complicate the antitrust analysis, however, which may generate negative consequences for competition enforcement. We consider first issues that might arise with the application of competition law in regulated markets.

(i) Analytical and economic concerns

We begin by examining analytical and economic considerations. Three distinct-but-related concerns emerge: the possibility that regulation removes scope for autonomous anticompetitive conduct by firms, the implications of false positives and a potentially inefficient duplication of enforcement.

a. Accounting for the impact of regulation on markets and behaviour

Economic regulation tends to alter the functioning of competition within a market, usually by changing the terms on which market participants interact.[214] As we have seen, competition law is concerned, broadly, with private behaviour that impedes market competition and causes inefficiency. The presence of regulation, particularly its extent and effects, is relevant insofar as the regulatory context may prevent antitrust liability from attaching to *prima facie* anticompetitive conduct.[215] First, the presence of regulation may so alter the functioning of the competitive process that a firm's behaviour does not, in reality, have the effect of further restricting competition or diminishing efficiency. Accordingly, behaviour that might harm competition within a competitive market may have a negligible impact within regulated sectors. Second, regulation may constrain the firm's scope for independent conduct, or even control directly its actions, so that responsibility for ostensibly infringing behaviour is more properly attributed to regulation than to the firm. There is a risk, however, that conventional antitrust analysis fails to account for these special characteristics of competition in regulated or partially regulated markets.[216] This concern relates to the problem of second best: what might be efficient and acceptable in an unregulated market is not necessarily constant across regulated sectors.[217] Competition adjudicators may be more predisposed to find liability in regulated markets than competition law itself would sanction if it were applied in a more context-sensitive manner. Viewed from an antitrust theory perspective, the pertinent analytical question is not whether regulation does or should grant immunity from enforcement. The critical issue is whether the regulatory environment means that competition law does not attach liability to private behaviour, either because the firm's conduct does not have actual anticompetitive effects or because, in the circumstances, responsibility for 'its' actions cannot be attributed to the firm. This approach reflects the holistic analysis suggested in *Town of Concord*, which emphasised that antitrust consideration of alleged anticompetitive

214 Shelanski (2011:700). 215 Kovacic (1995:496–8).
216 Breyer (1987:1011); Kovacic (1995:489). 217 See p. 229.

conduct can be significantly different in regulated sectors when compared with assessment of similar behaviour in unregulated markets.[218] The presence of regulation might therefore have implications for antitrust liability.

It is important to note that the *Town of Concord*–style approach is not an absolute bar to concurrent application, nor is it even a concrete argument against concurrency. That case addressed an alleged margin squeeze in a highly regulated sector, including price regulation of both wholesale and retail prices, and the court concluded that, *in those circumstances*, antitrust would not find liability. By implication, antitrust liability might attach to less intensively regulated behaviour. Under this approach, the degree of market autonomy necessary to generate liability, or the strength of the required causal link between the defendant's behaviour and actual competitive harm, are questions of competition law to be determined within its legal rules. Although neither the current US nor EU approaches incorporate a full substantive *Town of Concord* assessment, it is clear that ordinary competition law is sufficiently subtle and adaptable to incorporate the complexities of competition in regulated markets.[219] In practice, however, the use of immunities or presumptions in favour or against concurrency tends to short-circuit this analysis. While this approach can be defended on grounds of legal certainty and sound administration, any competition policy decision to favour concurrency *a priori* must incorporate flexibility to avoid the danger that liability is imposed in circumstances where a more thorough antitrust assessment would reveal that the necessary elements for breach are not satisfied.

More specifically, several recurring technical difficulties for antitrust analysis in regulated markets can be identified. One is the need to establish monopoly power or market dominance to trigger application of unilateral conduct rules. Both the US and EU law concepts of market power imply that defendant firms can act independently and impose their will on the market.[220] The existence of regulatory controls usually reduces a firm's ability to act independently, however, meaning that

[218] *Town of Concord*, 28. [219] See also Semeraro (2003:158–60).

[220] Under Sherman Act, §2, '[m]onopoly power is the power to control prices or exclude competition': *United States* v. *E.I. du Pont de Nemours & Co.*, 351 US 377 (1956), 391–2. Under Article 102 TFEU, dominance requires 'a position of economic strength enjoyed by an undertaking which enables it to prevent effective competition being maintained on the relevant market by giving it the power to behave to an appreciable extent independently of its competitors, customers and ultimately of its consumers': Case 27/76 *United*

although a firm may hold a large or even monopoly market share, it does not fit easily within these established concepts.[221] Hovenkamp suggested that the most accurate measure of market power in regulated markets focuses on the firm's ability to exclude competitors, even within its regulated activities.[222] Even this basic measure of market strength might run into the identified difficulties of antitrust analysis in regulated markets, insofar as it may be difficult to separate the exclusionary ability of firms from the impact of regulation or the market structure more generally (e.g., natural monopoly). Yet, in *Telefónica*, the General Court rejected the argument that the presence of regulation negated dominance, holding that the ability to increase prices is not indispensable.[223] Instead, the Court emphasised the importance of market shares within the dominance assessment,[224] an approach that facilitates findings of dominance in markets with natural monopoly components.

A second difficulty, considered in our analysis of EU practice, is the frequent use of the refusal-to-deal doctrine in regulated sectors.[225] The presence of regulatory restraints might also create insurmountable entry barriers that lead to declaration of an essential facility.[226] The cautions advanced in Chapter 2 against the refusal-to-deal/essential facilities doctrine apply with even greater force in regulated markets, however. Where a regulated access regime is available, it is questionable whether a parallel antitrust duty to deal provides additional value. Regulation offers a more appropriate mechanism to impose mandatory sharing obligations, both in terms of political accountability for the decision to compromise the defendant's property rights, and implementation of the necessary regulatory framework to operationalise the duty to share. Where regulation does not incorporate a duty to deal and yet the market cannot function effectively without access to an indispensable input or bottleneck facility, the better approach is to supplement the incomplete regulatory framework with access obligations. The contours of a regulatory duty to deal are not the same as an antitrust one, however, which should exclude cases like

Brands Company and United Brands Continentaal BV v. *Commission*, EU:C:1978:22 para. 65.

221 Kovacic (1995:490–1); Laguna de Paz (2012:80–1). 222 Hovenkamp (2011:779).

223 T-336/07 *Telefónica*, para. 166. 224 T-336/07 *Telefónica*, paras. 148–50.

225 Hovenkamp (2011:779). 226 Hovenkamp (2011:780).

Telekomunikacja Polska, in which competition enforcement became an expedient mechanism to enforce regulatory duties.[227]

b. Risks of competition enforcement: false positives and inefficient outcomes

The risk that concurrent application results in mistaken findings of liability has implications that extend beyond the question of legality. As Chapter 1 discussed, most contemporary competition laws are closely aligned to the economic concept of efficiency. Competition enforcement in regulated markets is generally premised on the desirability of correcting inefficiencies that persist despite, or even result from, the regulatory framework. Like regulation, however, competition enforcement is vulnerable to error, the costs of which can be as significant as regulatory errors.[228] In particular, Type I errors in competition enforcement – false positives – result in erroneous condemnation of efficient (or, at least, not inefficient) behaviour.

Two categories of inefficiencies might follow from false-positive findings of liability in regulated markets. The immediate effects of the decision may condemn efficient market arrangements, leading to an overall diminution in consumer welfare. Even where the false-positive outcome does not generate inefficiencies, competition enforcement may upset the delicate balance struck between market liberalisation and effective competition, on the one hand, and other legitimate goals, such as securing an adequate rate of return for regulated firms, on the other.[229] This risk is more acute with respect to private rather than public enforcement, insofar as private plaintiffs pursue personal interests.[230] The risk of false positives may also have a chilling effect on market competition more generally, resulting in reduced investment and innovation, 'the very conduct the antitrust laws are designed to protect'.[231] Although fear of false positives is, historically, a preoccupation of the minimalist Chicago School, in the context of regulated markets scepticism regarding the efficacy of antitrust enforcement has been embraced by a more moderate mainstream.[232] In both *Trinko* and *Credit Suisse*, the Supreme Court held that conditions existing in each of the regulated markets concerned

[227] O'Donoghue & Padilla (2013:389), questioning why the existence of regulation drives competition analysis given that the underlying rationale for regulation tends to differ significantly from competition policy.

[228] Kovacic (1995:495).

[229] O'Donoghue (2008:11); Speta (2003:129–32).

[230] Speta (2003:132).

[231] *Trinko*, 414.

[232] Crane (2009:123–7).

created a high likelihood of false-positive findings of antitrust liability, and moreover, that such false positives would have high costs in the circumstances. Specifically, *Credit Suisse* suggested that antitrust liability might inhibit beneficial competition in securities markets for fear of overstepping the indistinct boundary between permissible and impermissible conduct,[233] while *Trinko* expressed a fear that competition enforcement would distort investment.[234]

These claims are disputed as vigorously as they are asserted. The risk of false positives, critics argue, is overstated, both in terms of the likelihood of occurrence and the potential negative impacts. General thresholds for antitrust liability have heightened significantly in recent years, with a corresponding reduction in the likelihood of false positives.[235] In direct contradiction to the *Trinko/Credit Suisse* assumptions, others argue that the presence of regulation makes false positives less likely, provided that antitrust scrutiny is directed solely to the permissibility of private behaviour.[236] As the EU experience demonstrates, however, determining when regulated behaviour is 'private' for antitrust purposes is not straightforward. Carstensen similarly attacked what he views as the Supreme Court's blithe acceptance of the false positive 'myth' in *Trinko*, arguing that this fundamentally contradicts the standpoint that monopolies are disfavoured and should be curtailed.[237] Despite singling out *Trinko*, however, Castensen fails to address the distinct circumstances of regulated markets and the potential implications for antitrust liability considered earlier.[238] Yet, this emphasis on the indispensability of antitrust to remedy monopoly abuses – and the concomitant dangers of false *negatives* – is echoed elsewhere.[239] A recurring theme in defence of concurrency is competition law's preeminent ability to intervene in problematic markets and (supposedly) eliminate inefficiencies. Blair and Piette argued for concurrency on the basis that competition enforcement can deter regulatory misconduct more effectively by making it unprofitable by virtue of the fines or damages incurred for breaches.[240] This approach would

[233] *Credit Suisse*, 2396. [234] *Trinko*, 414.

[235] Dogan & Lemley (2009:700–2); Shelanski (2011:712). While these authors refer to US antitrust, a parallel rationalisation within EU competition law has similarly tightened standards.

[236] Dogan & Lemley (2009:703). [237] Carstensen (2008).

[238] Carstensen (2008:327) accepted that *Trinko* can be distinguished by its regulatory context, but argued that it establishes a general principle denouncing false positives.

[239] See, e.g., Cavanagh (2010:641). [240] Blair & Piette (2005).

legitimise cases like *Telekomunikacja Polska*, and is defended on the basis that desirable behaviour should be induced by making undesirable behaviour unprofitable.[241] But it would also significantly, and arguably inappropriately, obscure the line between regulation and competition law once again, and might therefore compromise the coherence of the latter.

Alternatively, in contrast to the claim that regulation reduces the applicability of antitrust, it has been suggested that regulation itself is less effective in partially competitive markets. This diminution in effectiveness creates a greater need for competition oversight particularly in liberalising markets.[242] The question arises, however, as to whether competition enforcement is an appropriate mechanism to compensate for regulatory failures. A related, and fairly plausible, argument is that the availability of concurrent application encourages deregulation, insofar as the regulator is aware that an antitrust 'safety-net' exists for newly competitive markets.[243] Conversely, and perhaps equally plausibly, it has been argued that the threat of concurrent enforcement of competition law might deter incumbent monopolists from opening markets voluntarily as it creates exposure to competition liability.[244]

c. Duplication of market supervisory functions

Finally, there is a risk that concurrent application of competition law results in duplication of market-supervisory functions: that is, where the same activity is subject to proceedings by both a sector-specific regulator and the competition authority.[245] Duplication is costly and therefore inefficient. Two sources of inefficiency can be identified. There are the *direct* costs of mounting two sets of proceedings, which are incurred by both the public agencies and the defendant(s). Given that enforcement action by one agency ought to be sufficient to remedy the market defects, the costs of the second proceeding are essentially wasted. Moreover, there are *indirect* costs resulting from uncertainty, which may arise if the defendant is subject to conflicting duties under two legal regimes. Such conflict is particularly likely where the sector-specific regulation pursues non-economic values instead of, or additional to, efficiency. Although EU telecommunications regulation embraced enthusiastically the possibility of concurrency, for example, nonetheless it foresaw the risk that concurrent proceedings might involve 'unnecessary duplication

[241] Blair & Piette (2005:685). [242] Shelanski (2011:725). [243] Shelanski (2012:505).
[244] Speta (2003:136). [245] Geradin & O'Donoghue (2005:409).

of investigative efforts',[246] and accordingly made provision to apportion jurisdiction between the Commission and national agencies.[247] By contrast, while the possibility that concurrency might result in a regulated firm being subject simultaneously to two sets of legal duties was anticipated,[248] the telecommunications framework provides no mechanism for resolving potential substantive conflicts, such as arose in *Deutsche Telekom*. In keeping with EU law's generous approach to concurrency, therefore, this regulation addresses potential direct costs yet largely ignores the risk of indirect inefficiencies.

Objections to concurrency premised upon inefficient duplication are roundly rejected by Dogan and Lemley, who argued that the existence of competition problems in regulated markets suggests that the regulator has failed in its job of supervising the functioning of competition; it may lack remedies, be captured, lack competition expertise, or fail to prioritise competition.[249] This argument does not consider the possibility, however, that existing inefficiencies may stem from a regulatory decision to prioritise non-economic values, such as universal service, which may require cross-subsidisation between market segments. As we have emphasised, efficiency is only one of numerous values that a State may, legitimately, choose to advance. At a more pragmatic level, Dogan and Lemley point to existing overlaps within the US antitrust framework – between federal enforcement agencies, and between state and federal enforcement – to question whether duplication is such a pressing problem.[250] This aspect of their argument applies equally to the EU system, where there are overlaps in enforcement between the Commission, national competition authorities and some national regulatory authorities, as well as enforcement of domestic competition rules. Again, however, this approach focuses only on direct costs of dual enforcement, and overlooks potential indirect costs for firms subject to conflicting duties. Duplication issues are also less relevant in the context of private enforcement, insofar as private litigation is undertaken mainly for the purposes of obtaining compensation for specific losses, rather than

[246] European Commission, *Notice on the application of the competition rules to access agreements in the telecommunications sector* (OJ C265/2, 22.8.98), para. 28.

[247] Ibid., paras. 28–33.

[248] European Commission, *Commission guidelines on market analysis and the assessment of significant market power under the Community regulatory framework for electronic communications networks and services* (OJ C165/6, 11.7.2002), para. 31.

[249] Dogan & Lemley (2009:704).

[250] Dogan & Lemley (2009:704–6).

the general public interest in remedying on-going competition breaches and deterring future violations.

(ii) *Rule-of-law concerns*

The second category of policy considerations that may influence the acceptable parameters of concurrency fall broadly under the rubric of the 'rule of law'. The concept of the rule of law, which is the subject of much debate amongst constitutional scholars,[251] is used here in a relatively informal sense to denote concerns regarding the legality of concurrency when judged in accordance with generally accepted legal principles, somewhat analogous to the US-constitutional-law concept of due process.[252] We will consider, more specifically, whether concurrent application of competition law in regulated markets raises rule-of-law—focused concerns that challenge the legitimacy of competition enforcement. In addressing these issues, we seek to identify potentially problematic aspects of concurrency, as distinct from economic or other concerns; this book does not, however, purport to provide a specific account of legality principles as they arise in any legal system. Reference will be made, in particular, to certain rule-of-law concepts as developed within EU law.[253] This is because EU law's generous approach to concurrency when compared with US antitrust means that these issues are simply more likely to arise in the EU context, and, moreover, because these principles are not only particularly well-developed, but also linked to the wider corpus of international human rights law through the Charter of Fundamental Rights (Charter)[254] and its relationship to the European Convention on Human Rights (ECHR).[255] Although this discussion refers primarily to enforcement by the European Commission, these general principles are also binding on the CJEU and national courts

[251] Theoretical accounts of the rule of law identify two contrasting conceptions: a formal version that addresses the propriety of enactment of law, and a substantive version that covers the qualitative question of the nature of the law and its respect for principles such as justice and equality: see Craig (1997) for discussion.

[252] See generally Chapman & McConnell (2012).

[253] Within EU law, these principles are derived expressly by the CJEU from the rule of law. The concept of the rule of law here is a distinctive one, analogous to the German notion of *Rechtsstaat*, meaning that the exercise of public power is subject to substantive and procedural limitations: Tridimas (2006:4).

[254] Charter of Fundamental Rights of the European Union (OJ C364/1, 18.12.2000).

[255] Article 6 of the revised Treaty on European Union grants full Treaty status to the Charter and enshrines fundamental rights as protected by the ECHR as general principles.

when enforcing EU law, including the right of private action.[256] We furthermore focus on legality concerns that arise exclusively or predominantly in the context of concurrent application of competition law in regulated markets, rather than concerns that relate to competition enforcement by the European Commission more generally.[257] As this discussion demonstrates, the generous approach to concurrency within EU law is supported by relatively deferential interpretations of general legal principles adopted by the CJEU, which impose weak constraints upon the Commission's enforcement discretion.

Our starting point is the overarching normative principle of legitimacy in law.[258] Although promotion of efficiency is broadly accepted as a central objective of competition law, antitrust is not simply a mechanism for improving market performance; moreover, it comprises a set of legal restrictions on private behaviour, and must be enforced as well as enacted in a manner that respects the rule of law. Accordingly, any application of competition law should both be efficient *and* sound from a legitimacy perspective. Yet the potential breadth of competition law under both the Sherman Act and the Treaty on the Functioning of the European Union renders it vulnerable to abusive as well as inefficient implementation. By analogy with Weatherill's assumptions regarding the principle of competence within EU law,[259] it might be argued that the legitimacy of competition enforcement, from a substantive perspective, dictates that competition law should be applied only to conduct falling within both the letter and spirit of its prohibitions.[260] First, the competition rules prohibit anticompetitive *private* behaviour, and should not be applied against firms if the resulting market defect had its origins, solely or predominantly, in either State action, such as restrictive regulation, or non-competitive market structures. Second, competition law addresses *anticompetitive* behaviour, that is, conduct by firms harming competition or diminishing efficiency, which involves legal condemnation of firms whose behaviour violates its prohibitions. Competition law therefore

[256] Case C-199/11 *Europese Gemeenschap* v. *Otis NV*, EU:C:2012:2390, para. 45–77.

[257] See generally Forrester (2009); Wils (2011).

[258] See Dyzenhaus (2001) considering the relationship between the rule-of-law concept and legitimacy of law.

[259] Weatherill (2009:17) posited as uncontroversial that, 'the legitimacy of the European Union is damaged if it trespasses beyond the sphere of competences attributed to it by its founding treaties'.

[260] Albeit retaining scope for progressive development to reflect technological changes where necessary.

cannot be legitimately deployed to achieve other policy goals, such as liberalisation, without unduly compromising the rights of defendants, even though it may be legitimate for society to pursue such goals by alternative means. Two further principles were also emphasised by the General Court in *Telefónica*: the presumption of innocence, now contained in Article 47 of the Charter;[261] and the related rule that, where doubt exists regarding breach, the benefit of such doubt should exonerate defendants.[262]

Where application of competition law conflicts with pre-existing regulation, two concerns arise. First, the defendant is subject to two opposing sets of legal duties, and must comply with both. By definition, simultaneous compliance is impossible, which places the firm in a position of unavoidable conflict.[263] Although commercial uncertainty is an inherent part of any competitive business environment,[264] this is qualitatively different from, and less objectionable than, legal uncertainty. Potential unfairness to defendants subject to conflicting duties under antitrust and regulation was invoked by the Supreme Court in *Gordon*[265] and *NASD*,[266] for example, to support its findings of antitrust preclusion. Within EU law, such conflict might trigger application of the principle of protection for legitimate expectations, a specific expression of the principle of legal certainty.[267] Protecting legitimate expectations requires the EU and national institutions 'to exercise their powers over a period of time in such a way that situations and relationships lawfully created under [EU] law are not affected in a manner which could not have been foreseen by a diligent person'.[268] An interpretation of EU competition law that allows breach to be found where the defendant's behaviour is lawfully compliant with regulatory requirements would, in theory, risk

261 T-336/07 *Telefónica*, para. 73. 262 T-336/07 *Telefónica*, para. 72.

263 Geradin & O'Donoghue (2005:409); Hellwig (2009:208). 264 Semeraro (2003:160).

265 *Gordon*, 689. 266 *NASD*, 735.

267 'The principle of legal certainty expresses the fundamental premise that those subject to the law must know what the law is so as to be able to plan their actions accordingly': Tridimas (2006:242). Protection of legitimate expectations differs from legal certainty by virtue of its temporal dimension; legal certainty concerns the clarity of law at a given time, whereas protection of legitimate expectations is an ongoing obligation; see Opinion of Advocate General Cosmas, Case C-63/93 *Duff and Others* v. *Minister for Agriculture and Food, Ireland, and the Attorney General*, EU:C:1995:170, para. 25, and Tridimas (2006:252).

268 Opinion of Advocate General Cosmas, C-63/93 *Duff and Others*, para. 25, emphasis omitted. See also Case 120/86 *Mulder* v. *Minister van Lendbouw en Visserij*, EU: C:1988:213, paras. 26–7.

violating the principle of legitimate expectations. In practice, however, the principle of legitimate expectations has been interpreted in a manner giving it little potency within the area of concurrency. The fact that practices have been scrutinised and deemed acceptable by a national regulator, for example, does not provide the firm with any legitimate expectation of immunity from subsequent competition enforcement against those practices by the Commission.[269] This is the case even where the national authority has purported to apply Article 101 or 102 TFEU,[270] or where the Commission has declined to take action against the regulator for breach of EU law.[271] In *Telefónica*, the General Court rejected legal certainty arguments premised upon *ex post* alteration of the EU telecommunications framework through competition enforcement against regulated conduct, taking the uncompromising position that the latter did not impede application of antitrust.[272] Instead, the CJEU has held that legal certainty is protected by use of 'as-efficient competitor' analysis in assessing compliance with Article 102 TFEU, on the basis that, since a firm knows its own costs and revenues, it can be expected to analyse these to ensure that its commercial practices comply with competition law.[273] This approach may be somewhat disingenuous, however, insofar as it ignores the potential impact of regulation in determining those costs and revenues.

Second, use of competition enforcement to remedy, indirectly, market problems resulting from a regulatory framework that cannot be challenged directly also raises concerns, particularly from fairness and legality perspectives. It is undisputed that competition enforcement can make valuable contributions to the functioning of competition in regulated markets when directed at anticompetitive private conduct. Weatherill indeed defended a role for the EU, more generally, as 'problem-solver and as a means to "tame" the corruptive excesses of nationally-biased political processes'.[274] Strategic deployment of competition law to compensate for badly designed or inadequately implemented regulation can be problematic, however, insofar as it may make a scapegoat of

[269] T-271/03 *Deutsche Telekom*, paras. 267–9. The question of legitimate expectations was ruled inadmissible on appeal: C-280/08 P *Deutsche Telekom*, paras. 105–10. See also the restrictive approach in C-681/11 *Schenker & Co. AG*, EU:C:2013:404, paras. 40–3, where explicit approval by a national competition authority under domestic law was insufficient to preclude application of EU competition law.

[270] T-271/03 *Deutsche Telekom*, para. 120.

[271] T-336/07 *Telefónica*, para. 344–6.

[272] *Spain* v. *Commission*, paras. 106–16.

[273] C-280/08 P *Deutsche Telekom*, para. 202.

[274] Weatherill (2009:26).

defendants in order to remedy what are, effectively, political problems. Given that only private parties and not Member States can be held liable under Articles 101 and 102 TFEU,[275] a 'perverse' asymmetry in liability between regulator and regulated firms arises.[276] At a normative level, the objection is fairness-based: it is unjust and unfair to punish defendants simply because they are economic actors in inefficient markets.[277] At a legal level, the objection is that, in such circumstances, the anticompetitive effects are attributable to regulatory rather than private choices, and antitrust liability does not attach to the former. One might even argue that Article 49(1) of the Charter, which provides that '[n]o one shall be held guilty of any criminal offence on account of any act or omission which did not constitute a criminal offence under national law or international law at the time when it was committed',[278] should, by analogy, preclude competition enforcement as merely a strategic tool for market regulation rather than its proper role within law enforcement. As cases like *Deutsche Telekom* and *Telefónica* demonstrate, however, the CJEU refuses to assess the validity of Commission choices to pursue antitrust enforcement rather than enforcement against Member States.

Consider, next, the rule against double jeopardy, also known as the principle of *ne bis in idem*, which precludes a defendant 'being found liable or proceedings being brought against it afresh on the grounds of anticompetitive conduct for which it has been penalised or declared not liable by an earlier decision that can no longer be challenged'.[279] Although predominantly a legal rule preventing abuse of process and promoting finality of judicial proceedings,[280] Wils argued that it also generates economic benefits when applied within the antitrust context.[281] Double jeopardy is prohibited, *inter alia*, by US[282] and EU

[275] Confirmed in T-271/03 *Deutsche Telekom*, para. 271, and T-336/07 *Telefónica*, para. 307.

[276] Veljanovski (2008). [277] O'Donoghue (2008:1–2).

[278] Article 23(5) of Regulation 1/2003 holds that Commission decisions imposing fines 'shall not be of a criminal law nature'. In her Opinion in Case C-272/09 P *KME Germany AG, KME France SAS and KME Italy SpA* v. *European Commission*, EU:C:2011:63, para. 64, however, Advocate General Sharpston argued that fining decisions relating to cartels should be treated as 'criminal' forms of misconduct under the ECHR.

[279] Case C-17/10 *Toshiba Corporation and Others* v. *Úřad pro ochranu hospodářské soutěže*, EU:C:2012:72, para. 94.

[280] Sims (1979:1402). [281] Wils (2003:136–9).

[282] '[W]here the same act or transaction constitutes a violation of two distinct statutory provisions, the test to be applied to determine whether there are two offenses or only one, is whether each provision requires proof of a fact which the other does not': *Blockburger* v. *United States* 284 US 299 (1932), 304.

law[283] for offences that are penal in character. Considerable academic and, within the EU, judicial consideration has been given to the double jeopardy principle with respect to concurrent application of competition law by different competition authorities to the same behaviour.[284] The double jeopardy principle also raises the possibility of conflict with respect to concurrent application of competition law in regulated markets, to the extent that both regimes are punitive in nature. Veljanovski, for example, argued that cases like *Deutsche Telekom*, in which the incumbent was required to ensure that regulated prices comply with competition law over and above its duty to comply with regulatory pricing constraints, amount to a form of double jeopardy.[285]

Within EU law, the CJEU in *Aalborg Portland* established that the double-jeopardy principle requires satisfaction of a 'threefold condition of identity of the facts, unity of offender and unity of the legal interest protected. Under that principle, therefore, the same person cannot be sanctioned more than once for a single unlawful course of conduct designed to protect the same legal asset'.[286] In *Telekomunikacja Polska*, the defendant argued that, because fines had already been imposed by the national regulator for failure to comply with access obligations, it constituted double jeopardy to sanction the same behaviour under competition law. Invoking the *Aalborg Portland* test, the Commission rejected this argument, holding that at least one of the three cumulative conditions was missing, namely the unity of legal interest protected. Given the different objectives pursued by telecommunications regulation and competition law, and because the national regulation did not incorporate application of Article 102 TFEU into the regulatory framework, it held that the regulatory and competition proceedings did not protect the same

283 Article 50 of the Charter provides,'[n]o one shall be liable to be tried or punished again in criminal proceedings for an offence for which he or she has already been finally acquitted or convicted within the Union in accordance with the law'. An equivalent protection is provided in Article 4 of Protocol 7 to the ECHR.

284 Sims (1979); Wils (2003); Louis & Accardo (2011). See also Case 14/68 *Walt Wilhelm*, which held that the rule against double jeopardy does not bar subsequent Commission enforcement against behaviour already punished by a national competition authority; reaffirmed in Case C-550/07 P *Nobel Chemicals and Akros Chemicals* v. *Commission*, EU:C:2012:512, para. 103. In Case C-17/10 *Toshiba*, paras. 93–103, the Court of Justice held that the principle does not preclude enforcement by a national competition authority where the requirements of Regulation 1/2003 are respected.

285 Veljanovski (2008).

286 Case C-204/00 P etc. *Aalborg Portland A/S et al.* v. *Commission*, EU:C:2004:6, para. 338; reaffirmed in *Toshiba*, para. 97.

legal asset.[287] The Commission nonetheless deducted the amount of the regulatory fines from the fine imposed for the competition violation premised on the same non-compliance.[288] This approach can be criticised on the basis that the legal duty underpinning both the regulatory and competition proceedings was the same, namely the regulatory obligation to provide access, while the phenomena of regulatory antitrust and liberalising regulation, discussed in Chapters 2 and 3, has seen a significant convergence in terms of the 'legal interest' pursed by each. This highly technical and restrictive view of double jeopardy nonetheless appears to limit application of the principle in concurrency circumstances, and consequently, its ability to prevent abusive enforcement.

Notably, in *Franz Fischer* the European Court of Human Rights held that the double jeopardy principle could be infringed, not merely by successive prosecutions for the same offence, but also by successive prosecutions for distinct offences with 'the same essential elements'.[289] Arguably, this presents a more expansive interpretation than the *Aalborg Portland* formulation, insofar as the notion of 'essential elements' is less prescriptive than the cumulative requirements of 'identity' between offences. Accordingly, *Franz Fischer* may prohibit decisions like *Telekomunikacja Polska* where the same behaviour – deliberate non-compliance with regulatory obligations – comprises the *actus reus* of both regulatory and antitrust offences. The Court in *Franz Fischer* also held that simply deducting one penalty from the other – the approach adopted in *Telekomunikacja Polska* – was insufficient to resolve double jeopardy concern.[290] Following the entry into force of the Lisbon Treaty, the Strasbourg Court's interpretation of the double jeopardy principle should be treated as controlling.[291]

Finally, two further rule of law–focused objections to concurrency can be identified, relating primarily to the potential effects of competition enforcement in regulated markets. First, given that regulated markets are often highly complicated and technical in their operation, there may be an increased risk of inconsistent decision-making relating to the same market activities between different competition adjudicators.[292] This risk

[287] *Telekomunikacja Polska*, paras. 138–41. [288] *Telekomunikacja Polska*, para. 142.

[289] *Franz Fischer* v. *Austria*, judgment of 29 May 2011, Application No.3795/97, para. 25.

[290] *Franz Fischer*, para. 30.

[291] Louis & Accardo (2011:106); see, generally, Douglas-Scott (2011:655–8).

[292] In *Credit Suisse*, 2395, the Supreme Court expressed the fear that, if numerous civil courts were asked to address antitrust violations in regulated markets, the outcomes of these proceedings would be inconsistent.

is insufficiently related to the regulatory context to support a specific rule against concurrency, however, and it would also be lessened by faithful application of the principle that benefit of the doubt should accrue to defendants. Second, where competition law is applied in a manner that effectively co-opts regulatory duties as antitrust obligations, this permits, indirectly, the expansion of competition law, given that regulatory duties are typically more demanding than antitrust prohibitions.[293] Although this risk is specific to the regulated markets context, again it is best addressed, not by denying concurrency outright, but rather through a more sceptical and doctrinally rigorous application of competition law where market activities are also controlled by regulation.

(iii) Institutional concerns

Finally, we consider two sets of institutional considerations that can impact upon the appropriate scope of concurrency: the divide between public and private competition enforcement; and the availability of suitable antitrust remedies to address problems in regulated markets.[294]

a. Private enforcement

The European Commission's antitrust enforcement activities in regulated markets demonstrate a distinct 'market-making' potential if deployed within a regulatory setting. The use of competition law to correct ineffective or inefficient regulation permits competition authorities to oversee sector-specific regulation, while quasi-regulatory case theories enable *de facto* extension of regulation to markets or remedial powers beyond those contemplated by the original regulatory framework. Whether this effective extension of public powers is considered legitimate may depend upon one's views regarding the permissible role for the State within the market; what is clear, however, is that this market-making vision of competition enforcement fits more readily within a public-enforcement framework than the private-enforcement model. As a general proposition, public enforcement is undertaken in the public interest, whereas private interests motivate private

[293] Monti (2007:243–4).

[294] The relevance of institutional factors to the concurrency determination was recognised by Roberts C.J. in *linkLine*, 1121, who held that '[i]nstitutional concerns also counsel against recognition of such claims'. Vickers (2010:382) attributed the apparent US/EU divide on concurrency, largely, to institutional differences.

enforcers.[295] Public enforcers also have greater technical knowledge, including in respect of potential adverse consequences for regulated markets, and are more likely to coordinate enforcement with sector-specific regulators.[296] The risk of false positives, inefficient outcomes and interference with regulation is, accordingly, much lower in the public context.[297] Moreover, these distinctions persist even though public enforcement can have an indirect impact on private interests, and vice versa.[298] A rule permitting concurrency is therefore more defensible if subsequent antitrust enforcement is undertaken by public agencies rather than private plaintiffs.

Substantive competition law comprises a generic body of law, however, which involves standards that are equally applicable for both public and private enforcement. This includes rules governing concurrency where this is perceived as a substantive competition rule.[299] To the extent that concurrency is permitted it may, equally, be applied by private plaintiffs seeking damages. Where concurrency is prohibited, this inhibits, *inter alia*, public enforcement in regulated markets undertaken presumptively in the public interest to remedy market failures. A universally applicable rule governing concurrency, which covers both public and private enforcement, may therefore risk over- or under-inclusiveness.

Scepticism of private enforcement is a central element of Chicago School antitrust,[300] and such scepticism is reflected in *Trinko* and *Credit Suisse*. US private enforcement has certain unique characteristics that make it particularly attractive for plaintiffs, yet also vulnerable to inefficiencies and abuse.[301] The apparent *volte-face* regarding concurrency discernible in recent US jurisprudence has been attributed, largely, to concerns that arise directly (and perhaps exclusively) from private enforcement.[302] In *Credit Suisse*, the Supreme Court opined that, if generalist courts are required to decide private actions premised on antitrust violations in highly technical regulated markets, there is an increased risk of false positives.[303] Moreover,

[295] Foer (2001) and Wils (2009:6–9); cf. Tollison (1985), who argued that the public-interest motivations of public enforcers must be proven rather than presumed, and, more generally, McChesney & Shugart (1995).

[296] Shelanski (2011:713–4). [297] Shelanski (2011:714).

[298] See, e.g., Case C-360/09 *Pfleiderer AG* v. *Bundeskartellamt*, EU:C:2011:389, on the interplay between public and private interests in competition enforcement.

[299] Shelanski (2011:713). [300] Easterbrook (1984); Crane (2012:51–2).

[301] Crane (2009:125); Cavanagh (2010:640). [302] See p. 211.

[303] *Credit Suisse*, 2395. See also *Trinko*, 414, holding that claimed breaches of regulatory duties were ‘difficult for antitrust courts to evaluate, not only because they are highly

it identified the risk that private plaintiffs might use antitrust to avoid heightened procedural requirements imposed to eliminate unmeritorious securities lawsuits, holding that '[t]o permit an antitrust lawsuit risks circumventing these requirements by permitting plaintiffs to dress what is essentially a securities complaint in antitrust clothing'.[304] In order to avoid the presumed inefficiencies and abuses of private enforcement,[305] the Court restricted general liability norms, therefore barring concurrency in both public and private cases.[306] This *de facto* deference to regulatory supervision is also reconcilable with public-choice scepticism regarding the limited benefits of regulation: it merely reflects an even greater scepticism regarding the utility of private antitrust litigation.[307]

Of course, restricting standard liability norms is not the only possible response to problems of private enforcement. Alternatively, more closely tailored reforms of private antitrust litigation generally could be introduced. As noted, three Justices concurring in *Trinko* would have resolved the issue at the standing stage, by holding that customers of disadvantaged competitors of the monopolist have no right to claim damages for harms suffered by their provider.[308] In *Twombly*, another antitrust case on the Telecommunications Act of 1996 (albeit one in which concurrency was not addressed specifically), the Court raised pleading requirements for private litigation, making such cases more difficult to initiate.[309] Another approach is to apply the *Trinko/Credit Suisse* principles asymmetrically, to prohibit concurrency in private but not public antitrust actions, although, as US law currently stands, this would require legislative intervention or judicial clarification.[310] Nonetheless, even public enforcement in regulated markets should not be unbounded; as

technical, but also because they are likely to be extremely numerous, given the incessant, complex, and constantly changing interaction [between market participants involved]', so that antitrust scrutiny would merely 'lead to a new layer of interminable litigation'.

304 *Credit Suisse*, 2396.

305 US-style private enforcement is not without its defenders, e.g., Lande (2010); Connor (2010); Cavanagh (2010).

306 Crane (2009:127).

307 Hovenkamp (2011:775); Crane (2009:125) construed the issue as one of 'comparative institutional competence', whereby imperfect regulators are preferred over even more imperfect antitrust juries.

308 *Trinko*, 416–18.

309 *Bell Atlantic Corp.* v. *Twombly*, 550 US 544 (2007).

310 See FTC (2010b), advocating Congressional action to confirm or restore the availability of concurrent public enforcement, and Crane (2009:131–2), arguing that the antitrust agencies must make a similar case before the courts. Posner (2001:276) suggested that a 'public monopoly' on enforcement might avoid unmeritorious private actions.

the discussion in sections IV(i)–(ii) illustrates, the presence of regulation may negate any finding of substantive antitrust liability. In view of this qualification and the US experience more generally, an interesting unresolved issue is whether the anticipated emergence of private enforcement within the EU may impact upon its strongly permissive rules governing concurrency, as considered earlier.

b. Remedies

The question of remedies can impact upon the concurrency determination in three ways. First, in regulated markets, defects might potentially be, or have already been, remedied alternatively by a regulator exercising sector-specific powers. Second, where competition law is applied in regulated markets, and particularly when applied to problems that might more readily find regulatory solutions, there is a question of the availability of suitable antitrust remedies if liability is imposed. Finally, where competition law is applied to anticompetitive behaviour that is attributable, in part, to the impact of regulation, the issue is whether and how the diminished culpability of the defendant might be reflected in the penalty or remedy imposed. All three scenarios are worthy of consideration.

First, the regulatory framework itself may incorporate remedial powers that enable the regulator to address the market problems. In determining whether an additional layer of antitrust scrutiny is necessary or desirable, the pre-existence of regulatory remedies is thus relevant. This relates to questions of duplication and double jeopardy: where a regulator has authority to intervene directly to correct the problem, is it unnecessarily duplicative, or unfair to defendants, to allow additional or alternative antitrust intervention? On the one hand, redress through sector-specific regulatory remedies may be quicker and more appropriate for the market and its specific defects. On the other, regulators can be captured, or may choose less effective 'light-touch' solutions, or inefficiencies may be tolerated to further non-economic goals. A range of options for displacement of antitrust jurisdiction by virtue of regulatory remedies is discernible. The mere existence of potentially exercisable regulatory controls may exclude antitrust; the regulator may need to take actual remedial action for displacement; such action may have to be considered effective to remedy the market problem; or regulatory remedies may be discounted entirely.

Predictably, different approaches to the existence of parallel regulatory remedies exist within US and EU competition law. In *Trinko*, the Supreme Court held that the regulatory regime, which was actively enforced by the FCC and state regulator, provided 'an effective steward of the antitrust function'.[311] This contrasted with antitrust, which, the Court opined, was 'unlikely to be an effective day-to-day enforcer of these detailed sharing obligations'.[312] In *Credit Suisse*, follow-on antitrust actions were precluded even where the regulator disapproved of the disputed behaviour, because, in the circumstances, only the SEC could decide with confidence whether the regulatory duties underlying the antitrust claims had been infringed.[313] Although the regulatory regimes in *Trinko* and *Credit Suisse* were in fact enforced by the relevant regulators, concern has been expressed that, in reality, the Court is more interested in the existence of a regulatory supervision framework than its effective implementation.[314] This suggests a more automatic approach to displacement where potential regulatory remedies exist. In the EU, by contrast, cases like *Deutsche Telekom*, *Telefónica* and *Telekomunikacja Polska* demonstrate that the existence of even proactively enforced parallel regulatory controls does not prevent subsequent application of competition law to the same behaviour. In each of these cases the national regulator supervised the pricing and/or access policies of the incumbent, yet competition law remained applicable, regardless of whether the regulator endorsed or reprimanded the firm's conduct. In one sense, the EU approach reflects the hierarchical superiority of Treaty provisions over national legislation; as a matter of substantive competition law, however, this approach indicates that neither potential nor actual regulatory remedies displaces antitrust review.

Second, there are questions regarding the availability of effective and administrable antitrust remedies to address competition problems in regulated markets. Again, this is a concern that has arisen chiefly in the US context, and comprises two elements: the potential need for quasi-regulatory remedies, and the availability of treble damages. The objection to regulatory-type remedies in the antitrust context, as considered in Chapter 2, is that remedies should not require a competition adjudicator

[311] *Trinko*, 413. See similar sentiments in *Gordon*, 682; *NASD*, 731–4. [312] *Trinko*, 415.

[313] *Credit Suisse*, 2394–5.

[314] In the context of the Telecommunications Act 1996, see FTC (2010b:10), noting *Trinko*'s suggestion (at 412) that concurrency might be appropriate if there was nothing within the regulation that 'performs the antitrust function', and arguing that '[b]etween "nothing" and the actively enforced duties to deal under the 1996 Act there is a lot of room'; see also Weiser (2005:566–7). Speta (2003:105) described FCC enforcement action against local monopolists that fail to provide access as little more than a 'slap on the wrist'.

to set prices or other contracting terms, nor engage in on-going market supervision. Instead, it has been argued, antitrust remedies should be restricted merely to prohibiting defined anticompetitive restraints. A clear reluctance to impose antitrust liability where this requires adjudicators to act as 'central planner',[315] or to engage in on-going policing of contractual terms,[316] is evinced in the *Trinko* and *linkLine* decisions. Both judgments quote Areeda to the effect that '[t]he problem should be deemed irremediable by antitrust law when compulsory access requires the court to assume the day-to-day controls characteristic of a regulatory agency'.[317] Although this difficulty relates to use of quasi-regulatory case theories generally and not merely in regulated sectors, it is particularly pressing in the regulatory context, given that the existence of structural-competition problems justifying regulation may create parallel demands for quasi-regulatory enforcement.[318] Like the risk of false positives, this concern provides a generalised objection to concurrency, because such problems are more likely to result from antitrust enforcement in regulated markets.

Another concern relates to treble or other punitive or exemplary damages, already a much-criticised aspect of US private enforcement.[319] Areeda and Hovenkamp suggested that punitive damages are inappropriate where otherwise innocent defendants rely upon or are largely compelled to breach antitrust by a regulatory agency. Instead, they argued, the 'fairest and most orderly way' to remedy antitrust problems in such circumstances is through a prospective order mandating behavioural remedies.[320] In the US context this proposal ties with the viewpoint that concurrency should be limited to public enforcement, insofar as civil enforcement by federal antitrust agencies utilises prospective equitable relief or the FTC's similar cease-and-desist order.[321] In the EU context, however, high fines are an almost unavoidable outcome of enforcement by the European Commission unless the proceedings are settled by commitment decision, while efforts to foster private enforcement increase the likelihood of additional compensatory damages liability.

Third, there is a problem of apportioning liability between defendants and the regulatory framework where the market problem is partly attributable to the latter, and, in particular, how diminished culpability is

[315] *Trinko*, 408; cited in *linkLine*, 1121. [316] *LinkLine*, 1121.
[317] *Trinko*, 415; *linkLine*, 1121, quoting Areeda (1990:853). [318] Speta (2003:101).
[319] Cavanagh (2010:636–9). [320] Areeda & Hovenkamp (2006:¶240c5, p. 285).
[321] Areeda & Hovenkamp (2006:¶325, p. 3).

reflected in any penalty imposed. Accounting for regulation, where this impacts on liability, is a substantive rather than procedural matter. The effects of regulation may strike at the heart of the alleged antitrust breach, where the regulation effectively aids, abets or approves the anti-competitive conduct, or reduces the possibility for effective competition from the outset. When this is the case, the regulatory regime must take some responsibility for the legal violation that has occurred – with the corollary that the defendant firm should not be liable or punished to the extent that the breach is attributable to regulatory requirements. In this regard, it is instructive to consider the European Commission's approach of discounting competition fines to account for regulation, which seeks, yet arguably fails, to address this substantive problem.

EU law's generous approach to concurrency creates the possibility that such shared responsibility may arise. Commission practice is to discount fines to reflect the impact of *ex ante* regulation, and consequently, the firm's reduced culpability.[322] The permissibility of this practice has been recognised within EU competition law since *Suiker Unie*, where the Court of Justice permitted application of competition law to regulated conduct, but held on the facts, that, due to the regulatory framework, 'the behaviour of the parties concerned cannot be regarded with the usual severity'.[323] This discounting approach is incorporated in the Commission's current fining guidelines, which list as a potential mitigating circumstance the fact that 'anti-competitive conduct of the undertaking has been authorized or encouraged by public authorities or by legislation'.[324] Discounting for regulation received renewed judicial approval in *Deutsche Telekom*, where a 10 per cent discount was considered appropriate to reflect the significant impact of regulation on the margin squeezing behaviour. Regulatory discounts were also applied in several recent Article 101 TFEU cartels cases: *Airfreight*[325] and the remarkable *Bananas* decision.[326] In the latter, fines were reduced by 60 per cent

[322] Under Article 23(2) of Regulation 1/2003, fines can be imposed only where culpability is demonstrated, meaning that the breach must be committed 'intentionally or negligently'. See also Laguna de Paz (2012:81).

[323] *Suiker Unie*, para. 620.

[324] Guidelines on the method of setting fines imposed pursuant to Article 23(2)(a) of Regulation 1/2003 (OJ C210/2, 01.09.2006), para. 29 ('*Fining Guidelines*').

[325] Commission Decision of 9 November 2010 in Case COMP/39258 – *Airfreight*, no public version available.

[326] Commission Decision of 15 October 2008 in Case COMP/39188 – *Bananas* (OJ C189/12, 12.8.2009).

to account for the impact of the 'very specific regulatory regime',[327] which imposed quotas and licensing requirements for importation of bananas.[328] A discount for regulation was, conversely, refused in *Telekomunikacja Polska*, on the sensible basis that the defendant chose not to comply with its regulatory obligations, so that the adverse market outcomes were attributable to its non-cooperation rather than regulatory actions.[329]

Yet the Commission's approach fails to account, substantively, for the impact of regulation on firm culpability, meaning that it becomes tokenistic in practice. Two particular difficulties arise. The first is a technical issue. Discounts in mitigation are calculated as a percentage of the amount of the fine that would otherwise be imposed, which is applied *after* the basic amount of the fine – calculated by reference to value of sales affected, duration and *gravity* of breach[330] – is determined. Accordingly, the seriousness of breach is already reflected within the basic amount of the fine before any discount accounting for the impact of regulation is applied. Instead, the effects of regulation are treated merely as a mitigating factor, which may reduce the defendant's liability for fine, but which does not reduce its culpability nor the severity of the offence. In this regard, the Commission's current practice conflicts with the approach in *Suiker Unie*, which suggested that sector-specific regulation can reduce the *gravity* of breach when viewed in terms of the defendant's culpability.

Additionally, discounting in mitigation is an incomplete way to address the substantive impact of regulation. In addition to the immediate fine, four punitive or detrimental effects of a finding of competition law violation for defendants can be identified, all of which are insufficiently addressed by the current approach. First, there is the legal determination that the firm has broken the law, a formal statement regarding the illegality of the firm's conduct that has a moral condemnatory effect.[331] Second, there is a possibility of criminal prosecutions against

[327] *Bananas*, para. 467.

[328] Approved in Case T587/08 *Fresh Del Monte Produce, Inc.*, EU:T:2013:129, which expressly accepted that the 60 per cent discount was imposed 'on account of mitigating circumstances' (para. 744). See also Case T-588/08 *Dole Foods and Dole Germany* v. *Commission*, EU:T:2013:130.

[329] *Telekomunikacja Polska*, paras. 286–90, 915.

[330] *Fining Guidelines*, para. 19.

[331] See Opinion of Advocate General Sharpston, Case C-272/09 P *KME Germany*, para. 64, who argued in the context of an Article 101 TFEU cartel decision, that: 'the offence involves engaging in conduct which is generally regarded as underhand, to the detriment

officers of the defendant firm taken under domestic criminal law, premised upon breach of EU competition law or parallel national provisions.[332] Third, there is a possibility of follow-on damages actions taken by private parties premised on the Commission's infringement decision.[333] Fourth, a finding of breach in one Commission investigation can be invoked as an aggravating factor in subsequent enforcement action against the firm for the same type of antitrust offence, leading to increased fines in the later case.[334] Accordingly, while discounting in mitigation represents an attempt to reflect diminished or shared responsibility for anticompetitive market outcomes that arise in a regulatory environment, it does so at a formalistic level, which fails to address fully the substantive question of the true extent of the defendant's liability.

IV. Market circumstances where concurrency arises: policy implications

From the earlier discussion, a broad range of policy considerations emerges, which impact upon the appropriate parameters of the concurrent application of competition law within regulated markets. Depending on the circumstances, these factors may either support or disfavour concurrency; they may apply with different intensity in different markets and in addressing different sources of market difficulty; and, moreover,

of the public at large, a feature which it shares with criminal offences in general and which entails a *clear stigma*' (emphasis added).

[332] *Airfreight* provides a good example of such conflict. Finding breach of Article 101 TFEU, the Commission applied a 15 per cent discount to account for the regulatory environment: European Commission Press Release IP/10/1487 'Antitrust: Commission fines 11 air cargo carriers €799 million in price fixing cartel', published 9 November 2010. At the domestic enforcement level, the UK's OFT commenced criminal enforcement proceedings against several UK-based airline executives under section 188 of the Enterprise Act 2002, although the prosecution subsequently collapsed due to procedural irregularities. The case came before the Court of Appeal (Criminal Division) on a point of law in *R* v. *George* [2010] EWCA Crim 1148. Successful criminal prosecutions have, nonetheless, been brought by the US's DOJ in the airfreight cartel.

[333] Article 16(1) of Regulation 1/2003 makes prior Commission decisions regarding Articles 101 and 102 TFEU binding on national courts, meaning that such decisions can, effectively, be relied upon by private plaintiffs to establish the existence of a breach in follow-on actions. The *Bananas* cartel case illustrates the inadequacy of the current approach for addressing this prospect: although the Commission subsequently applied a 60 per cent discount to account for regulation, the decision contains a formal finding of breach of Article 101 TFEU and states that price-fixing is, inherently, a hard-core restriction: *Bananas*, para. 455.

[334] *Fining Guidelines*, para. 28.

they may interact, meaning that the presence of one factor, such as private enforcement, may affect the relevance of others. In this section we identify four broad categories of regulated market circumstances where the question of concurrent application of competition law might potentially arise, and consider how policy factors identified in section III might affect these differing factual scenarios.

(i) Unrelated competition abuse arising in regulated markets

We consider first anticompetitive private behaviour occurring in a market that is partially regulated, but where the suspect conduct falls entirely outside the regulatory framework. That is, the defendant's anticompetitive conduct is neither directed nor controlled, wholly or partly, by regulation; the regulator does not have any potentially applicable regulatory powers over the activities; and to the extent that the conduct has an impact upon regulated market segments, the regulatory context is merely incidental. In these circumstances the application of competition law to *prima facie* competition abuses is generally legitimate. Indeed, it can be argued that this is not an instance of concurrency at all, insofar as the regulatory regime has no particular impact upon the competition enforcement action, and vice versa. Denying the application of competition law here would essentially abrogate its socially beneficial market-supervisory function without any alternative sector-specific supervisory mechanism in place. Thus, even those sceptical of applying antitrust directly to regulated conduct would probably accept that application of competition law does not interfere with the regulator's functions or the regulatory balance.[335]

One proviso must be added to this general proposition. That is the possibility – remote though it may be – that the presence of regulation in the broader market context may alter significantly the dynamics of the entire market, thus rendering *prima facie* anticompetitive conduct benign from a competition law perspective. Consequently, although concurrent application of competition law would not be prohibited as such, there would be no antitrust violation on the facts.

The *E.ON/GDF Suez* pipeline cartel illustrates both this general rule and its proviso in practice, albeit in a perhaps counterintuitive manner.[336]

[335] Speta (2003:142).

[336] Commission Decision of 8 July 2009 in Case COMP/39.401 – *E.ON/GDF* (OJ C248/5, 16.10.2009); partially confirmed and partially annulled by the General Court in Case T-360/09 *E.ON Ruhrgas AG, E.ON AG* v. *Commission*.

The case originated in an agreement, concluded between the State-owned French natural gas incumbent and a privately owned German gas company, to construct jointly a pipeline for gas transportation through Germany into France. In parallel, the companies agreed not to sell gas transported by the pipeline into each other's home markets – what would amount, ordinarily, to a hard-core market-sharing agreement contrary to Article 101 TFEU. Prior to liberalisation of French and German gas markets under the first Gas Directive,[337] however, the existence of monopolies in both national markets meant that neither was open even to potential competition.[338] Accordingly, regulatory choices at the national level redeemed such ostensibly anticompetitive conduct from an antitrust perspective, even though the regulatory framework was unrelated to the alleged offence. By contrast, when French and German markets were opened to competition, the continuing market-sharing agreement attracted liability under Article 101 TFEU.[339] This was so even though the firms were now subject to regulatory sharing obligations within the newly liberalised gas markets; these regulatory duties, by contrast with the previous market controls, did not affect antitrust liability. It is instructive to contrast this case with the Commission's approach in the *Bananas* cartel, where the impact of the EU regulatory framework governing the import and sale of bananas was insufficient to exclude antitrust liability,[340] but justified a 60 per cent reduction in fines.[341] In *Bananas*, the relationship between the regulatory regime and the claimed offences was more complex and ambiguous than the unequivocal findings in *E.ON/GDF Suez*.[342]

The earlier discussion provides a reminder of EU law's generous, but not unlimited, approach to concurrency. An interesting question is whether, after *Trinko* and *Credit Suisse*, US antitrust allows concurrency in regulated markets where the anticompetitive conduct falls outside the regulatory regime. In *Trinko*, the Supreme Court did not envisage an absolute exclusion of antitrust enforcement from regulated

[337] Directive 98/30/EC of the European Parliament and of the Council of 22 June 1998 concerning common rules for the internal market in natural gas (OJ C204/1, 21.7.1998). EU energy liberalisation was considered at pp. 112–13.

[338] A legal monopoly existed in France, while in Germany, exemption of gas supply agreements from competition law meant that *de facto* monopolies arose: T-360/09 *E.ON*, paras. 84–116.

[339] T-360/09 *E.ON*, paras. 90 & 121–25.

[340] *Bananas*, paras. 129–37 & 456.

[341] *Bananas*, para. 467.

[342] See, e.g., Case T-588/08 *Dole Foods and Dole Germany* v. *Commission*, paras. 297–312.

markets.[343] Yet the margin within which potentially illegal conduct is shielded from antitrust scrutiny was drawn broadly by the Court in *Credit Suisse*: while noting that hard-core cartel activities would fall far outside the core regulated business, the Court did not deny the possibility that immunity might extend to such conduct.[344] This stance can be contrasted with its earlier approach in *Pan Am*, where the Court took the view that, despite the broad regulatory powers involved, criminal antitrust powers were unaffected.[345]

(ii) *Regulation in pursuit of non-economic goals*

Each of the remaining concurrency scenarios examines a more complex relationship between the regulatory framework and the purported antitrust violation. In these situations the question is whether competition law applies to conduct that is under the supervisory jurisdiction of a regulator, or conduct that has been influenced significantly by regulation, or conduct that seeks itself to influence or exploit the regulatory context. The first category of circumstances where this may arise is when the regulatory framework incorporates and prioritises non-economic values, resulting in what look like market inefficiencies when viewed from an antitrust perspective. For instance, if an energy regulator grants a 'regulatory holiday' – such as a temporary break from mandatory access requirements for new infrastructure development in order to stimulate investment and protect energy security – could the regulated firm still be liable under competition law for refusal to supply access, even though the regulator expressly opted against imposing such a duty?[346] A practical illustration of this problem is seen in *Deutsche Telekom*. When Germany chose to delay tariff rebalancing, this perpetuated a market structure premised upon cross-subsidisation of telephone lines with call costs, a strategy adopted by all market participants including the incumbent. From an antitrust perspective, however, viewed in isolation and assuming successful rebalancing, the prices charged by Deutsche Telekom for line access failed the 'as-efficient-competitor' test, and amounted to an

[343] *Trinko*, 412: 'Where, by contrast, there is nothing built into the regulatory scheme which performs the antitrust function...the benefits of antitrust are worth its sometimes considerable disadvantages.'

[344] *Credit Suisse*, 2397.

[345] *Pan American World Airways, Inc.* v. *United States*, 410 US 366 (1973), 305.

[346] Monti (2008:135).

abusive margin squeeze. Here, arguably, the regulator prioritised a non-economic value (universal service), the competition enforcer prioritised efficiency, while the defendant firm was caught in the middle.

There are strong arguments against applying competition law to correct inefficiencies that result from purposely – or at least incidentally – inefficient regulation. There are, first, fundamental issues of fairness to defendants and protection of their legitimate expectations. Additionally, there is a 'second-best' question as to whether the antitrust solution is effective, given that the source of the inefficiencies – the regulatory policy favouring non-economic objectives – is unaffected by the competition remedies. Separation-of-powers issues arise that question the authority of competition enforcers to challenge policy decisions by sector-specific regulators in the public interest. A related question is whether, and why, competition and market efficiency must always be prioritised, regardless of other socially valuable goals to which competition may be unhelpful or even anathema. If regulation is condemned too readily on efficiency grounds, this may undermine alternative and equally valuable goals of regulation.[347] Competition law itself is recognised as an ineffective tool by which to pursue non-efficiency objectives.[348] As we have seen, competition ought sometimes to yield to other social concerns, and the rules on concurrency should reflect this possibility.

To the extent that a firm pursues inefficient market practices while acting in accordance with sector-specific regulation that grants precedence to valuable non-economic social goals, it should not be liable under competition law for any anticompetitive outcomes that result from compliance with regulatory obligations. Moreover, liability should not attach to its conduct even if it has ostensible 'leeway' to avoid the *prima facie* competition abuse, unless anticompetitive behaviour independent of the firm's regulatory duties can be discerned. Where the regulatory framework is viewed as unreasonable or unlawful from an antitrust perspective, the proper response is to seek modification of that framework at the political or inter-agency level, an approach that is considered later. Within the EU, the Commission should pursue Member States directly for anticompetitive national legislation or failure to implement or enforce regulatory regimes stemming from EU legislation, rather than indirectly through competition enforcement. Particularly where non-economic values are at issue, it must be borne in mind that competition

347 Hovenkamp (2011:747).

348 Crampton & Facey (2002:30–1); Hovenkamp (2005:45).

is not an absolute priority for society, and moreover, is not itself a 'value' as such. Accordingly, competition and efficiency should be pursued only to the extent that these are compatible with broader social structures. Moreover, the rights of individuals should be respected throughout the enforcement process.

(iii) Broken regulation: design inefficiency or regulatory capture

Next, we consider the situation where regulation of economic behaviour results, inadvertently, in inefficiency. In contrast to the situation just considered, although the regulation does not sanction inefficiency in pursuit of non-economic goals, in practice the regulatory regime incorporates inefficiencies into the market outcome. The risk that this may occur is tied to broader critiques of regulation considered in Chapter 3. Two principal sources of inadvertent inefficiency can be identified: either the regulation may be poorly designed, with a mismatch between the underlying market problem, the regulatory tools utilised and the optimal market outcome; or the regime may suffer from regulatory capture, so that the regulation is implemented in a manner that favours vested interests rather than enhancing general welfare. The problem of regulation that is essentially 'broken', and consequently inefficient, is more complex than the question of what is effectively 'non-economic' economic regulation. Whereas the latter reflects a policy choice to tolerate inefficiencies to further other socially desirable objectives, broken regulation represents regulatory failure, rendering it difficult to maintain that deference to existing regulatory choices is appropriate. The best response to broken regulation is, of course, to fix extant problems within the regulatory framework itself.[349] For our purposes, the question is whether competition enforcement also provides a proper response.

Considerations differ depending upon whether the difficulties originate in faulty design or regulatory capture. Where, by design, regulation is unsuited to remedy the market problems that it was implemented to address, regulatory failure is intrinsic to the formal framework and unrelated to the behaviour of regulatory actors. In essence, the regulation is inherently unfit to realise its public-interest purpose. In cases of regulatory capture, the underlying regulation may be sound but it is implemented in a manner that disregards its public-welfare goals.

[349] Lopatka (1984:639); Cave & Crowther (2005:490); Monti (2008:131).

Regulatory capture is inefficient because the benefits accruing to favoured groups are less than the costs to society.[350] Cases of regulatory capture arguably demonstrate more of an individual 'fault' element than design failure cases, as capture may imply that the regulated firm has sought to subvert administrative processes and that the regulator has abrogated its public-interest responsibilities. The line between design inefficiency and regulatory capture may be unclear in practice, however. Lobbying efforts by vested interests at the legislative stage may succeed in incorporating inefficiencies into regulation subsequently enacted, while regulated firms might take advantage of the laxity or incompleteness of regulation, thereby exacerbating existing inefficiencies. In *United States* v. *AT&T*,[351] for example – the competition case that resulted in break-up of the US telecommunications incumbent, considered in Chapter 1 – a comprehensive regulatory regime was, ostensibly, in place. In practice, however, this regulation was wholly ineffective at controlling the behaviour of AT&T, which had a long history of poor compliance with weak regulatory controls.[352] In essence, the core issue is the same regardless of the reasons for inefficiency: whether the presence of regulation excludes application of competition law even though the regulation itself has failed to achieve its underlying objectives.

On the one hand, competition enforcement, though a second-best solution compared with addressing the broken regulation, has the potential to realise positive improvements for market conditions.[353] Competition enforcement is generally compatible with the underlying rationale for the regulation, even though competition law principles may deviate from the regulatory scheme in practice. This is particularly the case in circumstances where regulatory inefficiency is attributable to capture, meaning that the defendant cannot plausibly claim good-faith compliance and therefore legitimate expectations arising from its regulatory obligations. On the other hand, the root cause of market inefficiencies remains the coercion, or at least the persuasion, of the regulatory framework rather than fully independent anticompetitive behaviour. Competition enforcement to correct for broken regulation thus encounters a basic analytical problem: an absence of autonomous conduct to which competition law can be applied. Attempting to 'pierce the veil' of

[350] Hovenkamp (2011:748–9). [351] 552 F.Supp. 131 (DDC 1982).
[352] Weiser (2005:564).
[353] Geradin & Kerf (2003:316); Cave & Crowther (2005:490); O'Donoghue & Padilla (2013:27).

the regulatory structure to determine what *would* have been required of firms, had regulation been more effectively designed or implemented, is an inherently uncertain task, and one which, moreover, effectively requires the competition adjudicator to substitute its own political judgment for that of the legislator or regulator. Although, in appropriate circumstances, competition law might play a socially valuable role in correcting market problems that arise from broken regulation, it remains difficult to formulate principles for intervention that also respect the rights of defendants. In particular it would be unjust to hold a firm individually liable for a legal violation where the underlying cause is political failure, either in legislating or administering a regulatory framework.[354] Accordingly, competition enforcement undertaken to address broken regulation might compromise the rights of individual defendants, even if pursued by public enforcers in furtherance of public-interest goals.

(iv) Regulatory gaming

Finally, we consider the issue of regulatory gaming, which can be defined as 'private behaviour that harnesses procompetitive or neutral regulations and uses them for exclusionary purposes'.[355] Regulatory gaming is an umbrella term used to describe a variety of purported competition offences that occur in regulated markets, where firms take advantage of the regulatory context for anticompetitive ends. The concept of regulatory gaming implies a closer relationship between the alleged abuse and the regulatory framework than was evident in category (i), yet – unlike categories (ii) and (iii) – the regulation does not direct or control the anticompetitive conduct. Instead, it arises, essentially, from the regulated firm's efforts to subvert the regulation – that is, 'playing the system'.[356]

Allegations of regulatory gaming can be divided, roughly, into two categories: situations where the regulated firm seeks to gain unfair or illegitimate advantage through abuse or manipulation of regulation, and situations where the firm is subject to *ex ante* regulatory duties and attempts to minimise or escape its obligations. The first category is

[354] 'The democratic process contains many flaws, but curing them is not antitrust's assignment': Hovenkamp (2011:747).
[355] Dogan & Lemley (2009:687). [356] McBarnet & Whelan (1999:69).

typified by the EU case of *AstraZeneca*,[357] in which the Commission held that a pharmaceutical company breached Article 102 TFEU through manipulation of regulatory frameworks for patents and medical product authorisation. AstraZeneca was found to have made misrepresentations to various Member State patent offices, and to have sought strategic deregistration of marketing authorisation for certain forms of its most popular drug in order to combat market entry by generic suppliers. Within US antitrust, the *Walker Process* doctrine[358] holds that it may breach Sherman Act, §2, to enforce a patent obtained through fraud on the patent office.[359] Another regulatory gaming strategy was seen in *Unocal*,[360] which involved allegations of fraud in a government standard-setting process. Unocal participated in an environmental rule-making procedure without disclosing that it had patents pending relating to the very standards it advocated, which were subsequently adopted.[361] The case was settled by consent decree, whereby Unocal waived all rights to royalties.[362] The first category of regulatory gaming abuses is, accordingly, premised on the assumption that it may violate competition law for a firm to take advantage of a regulatory framework – essentially, by not playing fair in the circumstances – even where there is no violation, formally, of the regulatory framework itself.

The second category of regulatory gaming abuses arise where a firm is subject to *ex ante* regulatory obligations that it wishes to avoid, the archetypal examples being mandatory sharing of infrastructure or interconnection obligations. The objection, in this instance, is that the

357 Commission Decision of 15 June 2005 in Case COMP/A.37.507/F3 – *AstraZeneca*) (OJ L332/24, 30.11.2006). Essentially upheld by the General Court in Case T-321/05 *AstraZeneca AB and AstraZeneca plc.* v. *Commission*, EU:T:2010:266, and the Court of Justice in Case C-457/10 P *AstraZeneca AB, AstraZeneca plc.* v. *European Commission*, EU:C:2014:28.

358 Named for the case in which the principle was established, *Walker Process Equipment, Inc.* v. *Food Machinery & Chemical Corp.*, 382 US 172 (1965).

359 This 'enforcement' requirement makes *Walker Process* more restrictive than the *AstraZeneca* approach: Leslie (2007); Gallasch (2011).

360 *In the Matter of Union Oil Company of California*, 138 FTC 1 (2004).

361 Parallels can be drawn to the *Rambus* investigations pursued by US and EU enforcers, which alleged breaches of Sherman Act, §2, and Article 102 TFEU, respectively, through 'patent-ambush' resulting from non-disclosure in an industry rather than government standard-setting process: *Rambus, Inc.* v. *FTC*, 522 F.3d 456 (D.C. Cir. 2008) and Commission Decision of 9 December 2009 in Case COMP/38.636 – *Rambus* (OJ C30/17, 6.2.2010).

362 The decree also approved acquisition of Unocal by another energy firm: *In the Matter of Union Oil Company of California*, FTC No.9305, Decision and Order of 27 July 2005.

regulated firm fails to comply with the letter (or spirit) of the regulatory framework, which, furthermore, amounts to an antitrust violation. The EU cases of *Deutsche Telekom* and *Telekomunikacja Polska* fall within this category. In the former, the defendant was criticised for its failure to seek proactively modification of regulated pricing structures maintained by the national regulator. In the latter, the incumbent's persistent failures to comply with regulatory duties were reconceived as an abusive refusal to supply. The US antitrust case that ultimately resulted in the break-up of AT&T was also premised upon persistent failures to fulfil regulatory obligations.[363] Yet, *Trinko*, which cautioned that regulatory duties should not be conflated with antitrust obligations,[364] suggests that such case theories are no longer viable within US antitrust, insofar as the existence of regulatory duties abrogates the need for parallel antitrust obligations. Regulatory gaming theories more generally may stand in opposition to the antitrust preclusion approach associated with *Trinko* and *Credit Suisse*: while the latter views the presence of regulation as justification for excluding application of competition law, regulatory gaming theories treat strategic firm behaviour in the presence of regulation coupled with anticompetitive outcomes as justification for applying competition law, often in unconventional ways, to resolve market failures.

Significant support exists within the literature for regulatory gaming as a theory of competition liability, at least to the extent that the alleged abuse comprises independent anticompetitive behaviour intended to subvert the regulatory process.[365] In such circumstances, the primary objection advanced against using competition enforcement to remedy inefficient regulation – that it makes a scapegoat of the defendant – more or less falls away. Generally it is not unreasonable that the regulatory framework failed to anticipate and avoid such intentionally disruptive conduct unless the risk was obvious. Much like in unregulated markets, competition enforcement against regulatory gaming can perform an important market-policing function that protects competition against discrete instances of anticompetitive behaviour. Regulatory gaming theories become problematic, however, to the extent that they assume equivalence between ordinary regulatory obligations and the requirements of competition law. Certain regulatory gaming theories,

363 Shelanski (2011:715). 364 *Trinko*, 415.

365 Brennan (2008:141); Hovenkamp (2011:746); Dogan & Lemley (2009:688); Lopatka (1984:630).

particularly in the second category, make antitrust compliance conditional on full compliance, in letter and spirit, with sector-specific regulation. This approach is flawed for a number of reasons. The objectives of sector-specific regulation are unlikely to be wholly co-extensive with the goals of competition law, and so it cannot be assumed that competition law covers the same ground.[366] The regulatory framework itself typically incorporates sanctions for non-compliance, and to the extent that these are absent or ineffective, this is a question of broken regulation. Finally, such theories assume that anything less than full and genuine compliance with regulatory duties is suspect under competition law – an almost *moralistic* standpoint that may take antitrust from the realms of law enforcement into the realms of corporate regulation.

For instance, although concurrency is expressly authorised by EU telecommunications regulation, and the framework utilises competition concepts for developing regulation, the regulatory scheme notes that a finding that a market merits sector-specific regulation 'has no bearing on whether that undertaking has committed an abuse of a dominant position'.[367] The Commission has indicated, however, that when enforcing competition law in regulated telecommunications market, it aims 'to build as far as possible' on regulatory principles.[368] This approach is clearly discernible in cases such as *Deutsche Telekom* and *Telekomunikacja Polska*. The overlapping objectives between EU competition law and the telecommunications framework may render any tensions less acute in this particular context. Regulation nonetheless changes the rules of the antitrust enterprise: while the decision to regulate does not itself indicate a competition violation, going forward the regulated firm must comply with its regulatory obligations in order to comply with its antitrust ones. Regulatory gaming theories might therefore demand too much from regulated firms in a competition law context.

V. Conclusions

This chapter sought to explore a vexed question, namely the scope for concurrent application of competition law in regulated markets. Rather than any attempt to provide a definitive answer to this challenging issue,

366 Nitsche & Wiethaus (2012:413–14).

367 European Commission, *Guidelines on market analysis*, (OJ C165/6, 11.7.2002), para. 30.

368 European Commission, *Notice on the application of the competition rules to access agreements in the telecommunications sector*, (OJ C265/2, 22.8.98), para. 58.

this chapter aimed instead to demonstrate that the question of concurrency is more nuanced than it is dogmatic. In practice, it requires the balancing of numerous policy considerations that can weigh in favour of or against concurrent application, and which vary in intensity and relevance depending upon the regulatory context and the source of the competition problem. Moreover, this balancing exercise can itself be influenced by policy or even political considerations, such as the desire to ensure the superiority of competition law as a mechanism to scrutinise national markets and domestic regulatory controls in the EU context, or the risk that competition enforcement in regulated sectors might be wastefully exploited by private litigants, as emerges from recent US jurisprudence.

From this discussion, it can be concluded, quite reasonably, that the mere presence of regulation within a market should not exclude the application of competition law, *a priori*, to anticompetitive firm conduct arising within that sector. Equally, it must be acknowledged that certain competition problems that occur in regulated markets are wholly attributable to the regulatory framework rather than private behaviour, so that antitrust liability should be entirely precluded. In order to provide more substantive guidance for situations falling between these broad rules of liability, the chapter scrutinised three sources of potential concern in cases of concurrent application. The economic objection is that competition enforcement in regulated markets can actually be inefficient, thereby scoring something of an antitrust 'own goal'. The rule-of-law objection is the risk that competition enforcement in regulated markets might override individual rights, particularly in circumstances where regulation itself is inefficient. The institutional or enforcement objections emphasise practical considerations such as the availability of suitable remedies and the identity of the antitrust plaintiff. None of these concerns reject concurrent application definitively, yet together they help to explain the resistance towards competition enforcement that can exist in regulated markets. In certain regulatory settings, moreover, such fears may be sufficiently compelling to merit a complete denial of antitrust liability. Competition law has its limits, and in a sense regulated markets represent another such limitation.

5

Institutional issues at the interface of competition law and regulation

The preceding chapters considered substantive aspects of the interface between competition law and economic regulation that can arise, exploring how the requirements and mode of operation of these mechanisms might influence, and indeed be influenced by, the other. As explained in Chapter 1, the relationships between competition law and regulation at procedural or institutional levels lie, largely, beyond the scope of this work. The notion of 'institutions' is used here in a relatively narrow sense to connote agencies at the public-enforcement level; it concerns, for example, the question of the formal allocation of powers between competition authorities and sector-specific regulators. As the title of this work indicates, our overarching concern is, primarily, the interactions between competition *law* and economic *regulation*, rather than between, for instance, competition *enforcers* and economic *regulators*. The precedence afforded to substantive over procedural concerns reflects the fact that the latter tend to reside, more squarely, in the realms of administrative law, concerning, for example, the structure and powers of government agencies, 'checks and balances' on their operation, judicial review of decision-making and any public-law rules that condition inter-agency interactions.[1] The difficulty of identifying any institutional approach that might comprehensively eliminate potential inconsistencies and overlapping proceedings at a substantive level has also been recognised.[2] As the preceding chapters have nonetheless acknowledged, however, overlaps between ostensible 'substantive' and 'institutional' issues can arise in practice. While most acute with respect to the concurrent application of antitrust in regulated markets, certain institutional questions resound across this broader subject area, and thus have significant implications even at a substantive level. To this extent, consideration of such issues is necessary.

[1] For a work that adopts an explicit 'public law approach', see Yeung (2004).
[2] Petit (2005:202).

In this chapter, we explore three sets of recurrent institutional concerns that tend to overlap significantly with the substantive application of competition law and economic regulation. First, we look at options for the allocation of antitrust and economic regulatory powers between competition authorities and sector regulators, to the extent that this may influence the circumstances and manner in which these legal instruments are deployed. Second, we examine the increasing use of market studies to identify and diagnose market problems, which may then, subsequently, be addressed through antitrust enforcement, sector-specific regulation or via distinct remedial powers provided within the market study procedure. Third, and related to this latter point, we analyse the potential development of a 'hybridised' category of legal powers that lies on the boundary between competition law and economic regulation, merging substantive elements of each within a single legal instrument. The unifying theme that links all of these institutional issues is the extent to which each represents a further blurring of the conventional distinction between competition law and economic regulation, even at a substantive level. In this sense, this chapter aims to demonstrate how, sometimes, form can have a significant influence upon substance, adding further complexity to the already multilayered relationship between competition law and economic regulation.

I. Allocation and sharing of powers between public-enforcement agencies

As the discussion thus far has illustrated, it is not uncommon that a market defect may be remediable through either competition law or economic regulation, which can be applied alternatively or cumulatively. We have considered already why one or other instrument might be preferred to tackle particular market issues, and even whether both *ex ante* regulation and *ex post* antitrust enforcement might be desirable. Here, we address a rather different question that can nonetheless have significant practical impact on any choice made between antitrust and regulatory approaches: namely, the allocation of enforcement powers under an antitrust or regulatory rubric between competition enforcers and sector-specific regulators. The most straightforward approach here, and indeed what has been most common in practice to date, is a 'division of labour'[3] that allots to each their

[3] Jenny (2012:169).

own, meaning that antitrust powers lie with the competition agency and economic regulatory powers lie with the sector regulator.[4] This result is not compelled, inexorably, by the nature of the legal powers at issue, however,[5] so that certain jurisdictions grant antitrust powers to regulators, or vice versa. Indeed, there is some evidence of a recent movement towards greater convergence between the exercise of antitrust and regulatory functions at an institutional level globally.[6] By analysing the long-established, but equally unusual, approaches to the allocation of antitrust and regulatory enforcement powers adopted in the UK and Australia, we consider the potential enforcement benefits, but also any drawbacks, of departure from the conventional model.

Given our focus on substantive aspects of the interaction between competition law and regulation, why do these institutional questions matter? The phenomenon of competition between agencies with overlapping supervisory jurisdiction is well recognised,[7] and, indeed, it has been suggested that the existence of multiple regulatory institutions indicates that such competition was intended.[8] In such circumstances, a public enforcer facing competition from other agencies may experience a degree of pressure to 'legitimate' its existence, funding and powers, and to reinforce the value of its work.[9] Such pressures, whether tacit or explicit,[10] are likely to affect the manner in which an enforcer deploys its market-control powers, perhaps more strategically, in the future. Although this critique echoes certain observations of public-choice theory, it is more equivocal in its assessment of the motivations and overall value of regulators; of greater importance for our purposes is the recognition that institutional factors influence legal choices. Although Chapters 2 and 3 illustrated a degree of convergence between competition law and economic regulation as mechanisms for market supervisions, the enduring distinguishing characteristics that remain – particularly in terms of

[4] By contrast, it is more common to find consumer protection and competition law functions within a single agency: Kovacic & Hyman (2012:533).

[5] Jenny (2012:169).

[6] As documented by the Worldwide Competition Database maintained by the Competition Law Center at the George Washington University, Washington DC, available online at www.gwclc.com/World-competition-database.html (accessed August 2014). See also Delgado & Mariscal (2014), for discussion of recent reforms in Mexico and Spain.

[7] See, e.g., Engel (1995); Haines & Gurney (2003).

[8] Engel (1995:97).

[9] Haines & Gurney (2003:372).

[10] Consider the position of a regulator facing the trenchant critiques of regulation discussed in Chapter 3.

standards for intervention, the objectives that can be pursued, and the remedial or punitive options available – mean that, in some circumstances, one or other approach may, clearly, be more appropriate to remedy the market defect at issue while respecting the rule of law. It would be unfortunate if the ultimate choice of market-intervention instrument was determined, not by the nature of the particular market defect but, instead, as the outcome of jostling for power between public agencies.

Empowering a single public enforcer to perform both antitrust and regulation functions might eliminate this risk by reducing external pressures to deploy its powers to strategic effect. Why else might a jurisdiction choose to depart from the conventional division of labour? Allowing antitrust enforcement by regulators, or regulatory enforcement by antitrust agencies, enhances, according to Decker and Gray, the 'functional substitutability' of these legal instruments as market-supervisory tools.[11] In both the UK and Australian examples, discussed next, the accumulation of expertise and specific market knowledge within a single agency with multiple functions, which would lead both to higher quality and more efficient (i.e., lower cost) decision-making, were touted as key advantages. In both jurisdictions, moreover, there was a presumption that market liberalisation would lead to convergence between antitrust and economic regulation sooner rather than later, and thus render the latter irrelevant. As we shall see, however, the effectiveness and efficiency arguments are tenuous at best, while convergence has failed to materialise for reasons already discussed in Chapter 3. The mixed experiences in both jurisdictions, particularly the UK, suggest a degree of caution, or at least careful planning, prior to adopting more novel arrangements. Moreover, the blurring of the lines between antitrust and regulation at an institutional level may increase opportunities for capture, and thus diminish the independence and objectivity of decision-making, particularly in the competition law context.

Even within jurisdictions that adopt a more orthodox division of labour between competition authorities and regulators, challenging questions can arise regarding the appropriate boundaries between the respective supervisory activities of each agency. The potential for divergence and even conflict between antitrust and regulatory approaches in such circumstances is highlighted by cases such as *Deutsche Telekom*,

[11] Decker & Gray (2011:8).

considered in the preceding chapter, where a firm acting in compliance with domestic regulatory obligations nonetheless was subject to *ex post* antitrust enforcement against the same (regulated) conduct. We therefore consider, additionally, the factors that may condition relationships between antitrust enforcers and regulators, in particular the sharing of enforcement jurisdiction even under a more conventional split of powers. This discussion, it must be emphasised, is without prejudice to potential enforcement of the competition rules by private litigants; we are concerned here, instead, with interactions between public-enforcement agencies.

Although wholesale departure from the conventional division of labour is unusual, lesser overlaps in terms of the enforcement of antitrust and regulatory powers are more common. This might involve the exercise of certain antitrust functions by a sector-specific regulator, such as the role of the US's Federal Communications Commission in merger reviews that involve the transfer of assets or corporate control by telecommunications carriers. Alternatively, it may enable competition agencies to perform certain ostensibly regulatory functions, such the role of the UK's competition and consumer agency, the Competition and Markets Authority, in conducting appeals against regulatory determinations. Explanations for a limited transference or sharing of jurisdiction can range from a desire to utilise distinct market or technical knowledge, or to introduce a different perspective (e.g., efficiency, or non-economic goals), to the need for a degree of neutrality or greater objectivity in decision-making, to potentially merely being a historical hangover stemming from a different allocation of powers.

(i) *The UK model: concurrent competition enforcement by regulators*

We begin with the UK's unusual system of full competition concurrency in regulated sectors, which creates parallel jurisdiction for enforcement of competition law by regulators within their respective spheres of control. Section 54 of the Competition Act 1998 – which also modernised the UK's competition system by bringing its proscriptions in line with those contained in Articles 102 and 102 TFEU – provides that these prohibitions can be 'exercised concurrently' by designated sector regulators.[12]

[12] The Office of Communications, the Water Services Regulation Authority, the Office of Rail Regulation, the Gas and Electricity Markets Authority, the Northern Ireland Authority for Utility Regulation, the Civil Aviation Authority, and Monitor.

For the purposes of Regulation 1/2003, these regulators are also 'national competition authorities' for application of EU competition law within UK markets. Thus, the regulators are, formally, empowered to apply *either* sector-specific regulation *or* UK (or EU) competition law to correct market problems that arise within their respective market sectors. A second dimension of concurrency is the continuing jurisdiction of the UK's competition authority, the Competition and Markets Authority (CMA), additionally, to apply the competition rules in regulated markets. Potential conflict stemming from shared jurisdiction was avoided historically, however, through a set of Concurrency Regulations that established a formal but primarily consensual procedure to determine the appropriate agency to exercise jurisdiction in a given case.[13] A Concurrency Working Party grouping, the membership of which comprised the competition agency and regulators with concurrent powers, provided a forum for multilateral discussions and coordination;[14] informal bilateral interactions also occurred.[15]

The origins of this arrangement are found in the aftereffects of the Thatcherite privatisation policies, considered in Chapter 3. As noted, a counterintuitive outcome was the concomitant need for a variety of new regulatory regimes and agencies to administer competition in privatised markets. The influential Littlechild Report, from 1983, contended, somewhat over-ambitiously, that economic regulation would be a temporary phenomenon, 'holding the fort' until effective competition developed, and to be phased out as competition steadily increased.[16] Consequently, utilities regulators were given a primary duty to promote competition within their respective sectors,[17] and, alongside their regulatory powers, the ability to enforce the then existing UK competition rules 'concurrently with the Director General of Fair Trading', in these markets.[18] Notably, however, the competition provisions that existed

[13] The Competition Act 1998 (Concurrency) Regulations 2004, S.I.No.1077 of 2004.

[14] Office of Fair Trading, *Concurrency Application to Regulated Industries* (December 2004), para. 3.9.

[15] Ibid., para. 3.3.

[16] Department of Industry, *Regulation of British Telecommunications' Profitability: Report to the Secretary of State*, published February 1983 ('Littlechild Report').

[17] See Telecommunications Act 1984, s.3(2)(b); Gas Act 1986, s.4AA; Electricity Act 1989, s.3A; Water Industry Act 1991, s.2; Railways Act 1993, s.4; Transport Act 2000, s.2(4); and Energy (Northern Ireland) Order 2003, S.I. No.419 (N.I. 6), ss.12(1) and 14(5); cf. Health and Social Care Act 2012, s.62(3).

[18] See, e.g., Telecommunications Act 1984, s.50; Gas Act 1986, s.36A; Electricity Act 1989, s.43; Water Industry Act 1991, s.31; and Railways Act 1993, s.67.

prior to the 1998 Act were much more restrictive in terms of the enforcement powers granted to either regulators or the competition agency than the current rules, and were arguably closer to an antitrust-regulatory hybrid than a more conventional prohibition-focused antitrust archetype.[19] The decision to retain concurrency under the 1998 Act, though presented as continuation of the 'status quo',[20] in fact reflected an implicit determination that extension of those new, considerably stronger competition powers, which included a significant adjudicatory role, ought to be extended to sector regulators; a determination that, arguably, lacks an overarching policy rationale.[21]

In theory, the concurrency arrangements envisaged a sharing of jurisdiction between the competition authority and regulators; in practice, however, the precursor to the CMA, the Office of Fair Trading (OFT), tended to defer to regulators within their respective spheres of control. Multiple government reviews of the concurrency arrangements furthermore concluded, essentially, that regulators heavily favoured use of regulatory powers rather than their concurrently exercisable antitrust powers to resolve market problems that came within the ambit of both.[22] Where regulators did attempt to flex their antitrust muscles, overwhelmingly the end result was a finding of non-violation or a consensual settlement to resolve the market problem without a finding of breach. In the decade from 2000 to 2010, the regulators together took thirty-four non-infringement decisions and only two infringement decisions; these figures compare starkly with the OFT's record of twenty-four infringement decisions and nineteen non-infringement decisions during the same period.[23] Regulators similarly failed to make an appreciable number

19 Prior to the 1998 Act, the UK competition framework consisted of a complex series of provisions that empowered the Monopolies and Mergers Commission – precursor to the CMA – to conduct investigations into coordinated and unilateral trade practices against the public interest, pursuant to the Fair Trading Act 1973 and the Competition Act 1980: see also Gerber (1998:215–22).

20 See comments of Lord Borrie, HL Deb vol 583 col 911, 11 November 1997.

21 Dunne (2014).

22 See Department of Trade and Industry, *Concurrent Competition Powers in Sectoral Regulation. A Report by the Department of Trade and Industry and HM Treasury*, published May 2006, URN 06/1244; House of Lords Select Committee on Regulators, 1st Report of Session 2006–07, *UK Economic Regulators*, Volume I: Report, published 13 November 2007, HL Paper 189-I, Chapter 6; and National Audit Office, *Review of the UK's Competition Landscape: Review by the Comptroller and Auditor General*, published 22 March 2010, in particular pp. 12–19.

23 *NAO Competition Review*, para. 2.11.

of 'market investigation references' – a market study procedure considered later in this chapter – apparently preferring instead to conduct such reviews in-house. A variety of reasons have been advanced to account for the regulatory preference for sector-specific powers. From the perspective of regulators, these included a perception that regulated markets lacked the necessary competitive structure to support effective competition enforcement; the fact that regulatory powers were more clearly applicable within, and specifically tailored to, regulated sectors; the greater speed at which regulatory interventions could be conducted in comparison to more drawn-out competition investigations; the greater demands on limited agency resources that were associated with competition enforcement activity; and a presumption of greater certainty for regulated firms already familiar with regulatory interventions. Potential problems of cognitive dissonance and over-familiarity were also identified, whereby regulators were too closely enmeshed and intimately involved in the application of sector-specific regulation to appreciate the likely benefits of competition enforcement as an alternative. Together, these explanations pointed towards a distortion of incentives for regulators, insofar as regulatory interventions were perceived as quicker, easier, more effective in the short term and, not least, less threatening to a regulator's own interests than competition enforcement. The end result was a perceived under-enforcement of competition law within regulated markets.

Unsurprisingly, this empirical evidence of the relative ineffectiveness of the existing arrangements compelled the government to revisit concurrency in its recent restructuring of UK competition law under the Enterprise and Regulatory Reform Act 2013 (ERRA). Perhaps more unexpectedly, however, the reforms enacted both seek to reinforce the primacy of competition enforcement in regulated markets, while, simultaneously, to introduce a range of essentially disciplinary provisions that will serve to expose, rebuke and, potentially, even remove concurrent enforcement jurisdiction from those regulators that continue to shirk their antitrust concurrent responsibilities.[24] The dogged retention of concurrency as the default for regulated markets seems difficult to justify, particularly in view of the implicit acknowledgement within the revisions that, sometimes, either in individual cases or on a more systemic basis,

[24] See ss. 51–3, and Schedules 4 and 14, ERRA, and the Competition Act 1998 (Concurrency) Regulations 2014, S.I. No. 536 of 2014.

antitrust enforcement by the CMA alone in regulated markets is more appropriate.[25] We consider briefly why this approach may be ill advised.

First, the claimed 'added value' that regulators bring to the competition enforcement enterprise, which hinges on their detailed sectoral knowledge, is at least offset by the inconvenience of losing the specific antitrust expertise of a dedicated competition agency. While sharing of resources – in particular, specialist staff – between the CMA and the various regulators has been posited as a means by which to address this deficit of technical antitrust expertise, the reverse would also hold true, as we shall see with the Australian example. The argument that concurrent competition powers are necessary to foster and secure the development of greater competition in regulated markets is also problematic. On the one hand, the fact that such markets retain a significant degree of regulation reflects the reality that, despite efforts towards the progressive liberalisation of utilities markets, these sectors retain inescapable natural monopoly components. Whilst economic regulation may be a second-best mechanism of market control, it remains largely unavoidable in many such markets, while, conversely, competition law tends to be less effective, or less readily applicable, against many of the market difficulties concerned. On the other hand, to the extent that competition has developed sufficiently within a market to support antitrust enforcement, it makes little sense as a matter of regulatory principle to continue to segregate this sector from the market-wide framework of competition supervision administrated by the CMA. Such a 'separate-but-equal' approach would actually appear to conflict with the overarching vision, sketched in the Littlechild Report, of a supervisory framework in which regulation cedes to competition. The 2013 Act also failed to tackle the difficulty of distorted incentives for regulators; that is, a regulatory agency that successfully introduces sustainable competition into a formerly regulated market, thus removing the need for economic regulation beyond competition law, has effectively regulated itself out of business.

The impact of these reforms in practice remains largely to be seen. The UK example nonetheless provides a succinct illustration of the

[25] See, s. 51(1) ERRA, which enables the Secretary of State to prescribe circumstances in which the CMA may decide that, in a particular case, it alone will apply the competition rules in a regulated sector, and, more radically, the procedure envisaged by ss. 52 and 53 ERRA, which allows for a blanket removal of concurrent jurisdiction from a given regulator by statutory instrument.

principal reasons why competition enforcement powers may be entrusted to regulators – to take advantage of significant sectoral expertise, while simultaneously encouraging more competition-focused thinking within regulation – but also why this approach may fail in reality. While regulation rarely ousts antitrust jurisdiction entirely, in theory the movement towards competition leads, almost inexorably, to the dismantlement of the economic regulatory regime, though not necessarily any technical or social aspects of regulation. In this sense, effective regulation to competition becomes self-defeating for the self-interested regulator. More practically, the persistence of natural monopoly in certain segments of utilities markets means that it is difficult for even the most selfless of regulators to dispense entirely with the need for regulation. Accordingly, the limited success of the UK approach perhaps reflects both difficulties within the institutional framework and, as we discussed in the preceding chapter, the diminished utility of antitrust enforcement in regulated markets with structural competition problems.

(ii) The Australian model: an antitrust 'super-regulator'

Australia, by contrast, has implemented a concurrency framework that affords primacy to the federal competition agency, the Australian Competition and Consumer Commission (ACCC), not merely with respect to antitrust enforcement but also by granting it significant economic regulatory powers. Whereas the UK model originated in piecemeal efforts to introduce competition progressively into privatised markets, meaning that the grant of concurrent powers to regulators reflected the somewhat heroic assumptions that these agencies could and would opt to 'regulate' primarily through competition enforcement, the Australian model reflects a planned top-down approach to competition law and policy that places the pursuit of efficiency at the centre of the economy.[26] The influential Hilmer Report,[27] released in 1993, recommended a series of regulatory policy revisions to facilitate microeconomic reform, and precipitated the adoption of an all-encompassing 'national competition policy' in Australia. At the time, economic supervision of utilities comprised a mélange of control mechanisms including public ownership and state-level (as opposed to federal) regulation. The Hilmer Report

[26] Yeung (2004:24).

[27] Independent Committee of Inquiry into Competition Policy, *National Competition Policy*, Canberra: Australian Government Printing Service, 1993 ('Hilmer Report').

advocated, instead, amalgamation of economic regulatory functions across multiple sectors within a single federal agency, which became the ACCC. The rationale for a 'super-regulator'[28] included the desirability of an economy-wide perspective on economic regulation, the need to avoid 'capture' of regulators with close industry links, and the perceived cost-savings that would follow from combining numerous administrative functions within a single agency.[29] This report, with its accompanying focus on competition policy, is widely acknowledged to be the driving factor behind the economic reforms that followed.[30] The economic regulatory functions of the ACCC now extend to telecommunications, energy, transport and postal services. We will examine its role in the telecommunications and energy sectors.

The ACCC itself was established in 1995 through merger of the former Trade Practices Commission and the Prices Surveillance Authority. The Trade Practices Amendment (Telecommunications) Act 1997, which introduced an open access regime alongside partial privatisation of the telecommunications incumbent (Telstra), also empowered the ACCC as both antitrust enforcer and economic (but not technical) regulator for telecommunications,[31] thus decoupling economic and technical regulatory functions.[32] In the ACCC's guise as competition agency, telecommunications firms remain fully subject to the ordinary competition rules now contained in Part IV of the Competition and Consumer Act 2010 (CCA), including prohibitions on anticompetitive coordinated and unilateral monopoly conduct.[33] The 1997 Act recognised, however, that antitrust alone would be insufficient to address competition problems, and so certain telecommunications-specific regulatory provisions were added to the general body of competition law, which aimed at increasing the ability of the ACCC to counter anticompetitive behaviour.[34] The 1997 Act thus established a specific regime for access

[28] Harley & Armstrong (2002:4). [29] Hilmer Report, p. 327.

[30] Harley & Armstrong (2002:4–9); International Competition Network (ICN), *Antitrust Enforcement in Regulated Sectors Working Group. Subgroup 3: interrelations between antitrust and regulatory authorities – Report to the Third ICN Annual Conference*, Seoul, April 2004, 21–22 ('ICN (2004)').

[31] Liberalisation had begun in earnest with the Telecommunications Act 1991.

[32] Technical regulation is performed by the Australian Communications and Media Authority.

[33] See Explanatory Memorandum, Trade Practices Amendment (Telecommunications) Bill 1996, Item 6.

[34] Ibid.

to telecommunications infrastructure,[35] as a corollary of the Part IIIA access regime considered later in this chapter, and provided the ACCC with various industry-specific powers that augment its antitrust powers but reside in the less powerful reaches of regulation.[36] The Explanatory Memorandum to the 1997 Act nonetheless expressed the hope that telecommunications regulation would progressively align with general antitrust,[37] thus echoing both the Littlechild Report and the attitude of EU telecommunications liberalisation, considered in Chapter 3.[38]

Economic regulation of energy markets also falls within the purview of the ACCC, albeit in a manner more removed from its antitrust functions. The 1990s onwards saw concerted efforts towards federal rather than state-level governance of energy markets including greater integration,[39] plus liberalisation and increased privatisation.[40] Three federal agencies now share the task of economic regulation. The Australian Energy Market Commission functions as economic rule-maker; the Australian Energy Regulator (AER), an independent statutory body located within the ACCC, enforces these rules; and the Australian Energy Markets Operator amalgamates the management and planning functions of a number of former energy operators. The relationship between the AER and ACCC is somewhat unusual. Unlike the ACCC's activities within telecommunications regulation, which fall within the broader rubric of the agency's functions, the AER is a legally separate entity; yet it is, nonetheless, a constituent division of the overall ACCC. A desire to facilitate independence in decision-making, while maintaining consistency between competition law and energy regulation, motivated this unconventional arrangement. The AER is empowered to take regulatory decisions independently of the ACCC, but the two agencies share a single body of staff for energy matters, thus, at least in theory, generating a body of specialist skills and knowledge while avoiding duplication of processes.[41] Outside the context of sector-specific regulation, the ACCC retains antitrust, merger control and access to infrastructure functions in

[35] CCA, Part XIC.

[36] Under s. 151AJ, CCA, the ACCC can issue 'competition notices' to firms that breach the antitrust prohibition on monopoly conduct, or where a service provider with significant market power takes advantage of that power with the (likely) effect of substantially lessening competition.

[37] See Explanatory Memorandum, Trade Practices Amendment (Telecommunications) Bill 1996, Item 6.

[38] See pp. 172–3.

[39] See IEA (2005:100–17).

[40] See IEA (2005:97–101, 147–50); and IEA (2012:127–30).

[41] ACCC (2004:1–2).

relation to energy markets. This arrangement enables the ACCC to maintain within it the functions of antitrust, consumer and regulatory protections for the energy sector, while generating a certain distance between its regulatory and other functions.[42]

Does the Australian model recommend itself for export to other jurisdictions? Australia has been feted by the OECD for its 'well-conceived and well-implemented' competition policies that generate 'clear economic performance benefits',[43] although it is difficult to assess whether, and to what extent, its economic regulatory structures contributed to this success. The ACCC itself rationalises its dual antitrust and economic regulatory functions by reference to the significant functional overlaps between these roles and the goals that might be pursued by each mechanism.[44] In many ways, the ACCC acts, more or less, like any conventional regulator; see, for example, the AER's adoption of 'better regulation' policies to improve the quality of its regulatory policy-making.[45] Yet it is far from clear that this example establishes the superiority of antitrust enforcers as economic regulators. Following privatisation of Telstra as a vertically and horizontally integrated concern, the ACCC has struggled, much like its regulatory counterparts in the UK, to control the activities of this de facto private monopolist.[46] Policy-makers have also questioned its future role in the economic regulation of broadband provision in Australia. Given that the convergence between competition law and regulation envisaged at the enactment of the 1997 Act did not occur, and is unlikely to do so at least in the medium term, the appropriateness of the existing 'unusual' allocation of enforcement powers has thus been queried.[47]

(iii) Resolving conflicts within the conventional division of labour

Finally, we address what has been, conventionally, the most typical scenario: namely, where antitrust powers are exercisable at the public-enforcement level primarily by the competition agency, and where economic regulatory powers are exercisable by the relevant sector

[42] See also ACCC (2004:2). [43] OECD (2010:57). [44] ICN (2004:22–3).

[45] See e.g. Australian Energy Regulator, *Overview of the Better Regulation reform package*, published April 2014.

[46] See, e.g., OECD (2012:68–71).

[47] See Department of Communications, *Panel conducting a Cost-benefit Analysis and Review of Regulatory Arrangements for the National Broadband Network. Public Consultation – Regulatory Issues Framing Paper*, published February 2014, p. 7.

regulator. Suppose that a market problem that might be addressed by each arises; for example, the refusal by a utilities monopolist to supply access to its essential infrastructure to a downstream rival. Earlier chapters considered the potential pros and cons, in substantive terms, of proceeding via the 'essential facilities' antitrust doctrine, or enacting sector-specific regulation to impose mandatory access obligations. Here, we consider the potential institutional constraints that may mandate or restrict, in procedural terms, adoption of one or other approach. Although the concerns outlined in Chapter 4 regarding the appropriateness of competition enforcement as a means to correct ineffective regulation should be borne in mind, we are concerned primarily with the institutional principles and procedures that might condition the choice between antitrust and regulatory intervention.

The relevant jurisdiction may provide formal legal mechanisms for resolving conflicts, either as matter of public law or of antitrust or regulatory doctrine, or it may specify, in law, a priority for either the antitrust enforcer or sector regulator. Such 'hard' legal approaches to allocating jurisdiction tend to reflect either administrative law principles or competition policy. Certainty and clarity are, of course, the benefits of such an approach; excessive rigidity and potentially unfair or ineffective outcomes may be the possible downsides.

In the UK, for example, a formal set of rules imposed by statutory instrument exists for the allocation of jurisdiction between enforcers with concurrent powers.[48] Utilising a consensual procedure in the first instance, the Concurrency Regulations previously included a residual role for the Secretary of State to adjudicate if consensus proved impossible,[49] although the recent reforms essentially cede jurisdiction in cases of dispute to the CMA.[50] Although, formally, these Regulations were intended to allocate overlapping antitrust jurisdiction between enforcers, the reluctance of regulators to exercise their concurrent powers has meant that this mechanism often functioned as a dividing line between antitrust and sector regulation in practice.

As we have seen, by contrast, the general principle of primacy within the EU means that national regulators, competition agencies or courts cannot take decisions that run counter to EU law, whether contained in the Treaties or secondary legislation or established by the Court of

[48] See p. 268, fns. 13 & 14.

[49] The Competition Act 1998 (Concurrency) Regulations 2004, s. 5.

[50] The Competition Act 1998 (Concurrency) Regulations 2014, s. 5.

Justice.[51] Regulation 1/2003 affords such binding effect to Commission decisions applying Articles 101 and 102 TFEU, extending to national courts and 'competition authorities',[52] which, as the UK example illustrates, includes sector regulators in some Member States.[53] More specifically, as discussed in the preceding chapter, the EU telecommunications framework makes express provision to apportion jurisdiction between national regulators and antitrust enforcers in appropriate circumstances.[54]

Finally, in the US, the administrative law doctrine of 'primary jurisdiction' has been applied to address procedural priority between sector regulators and courts seized of antitrust suits: where it applies, an antitrust action can proceed only after a regulatory proceeding has concluded. The leading case is *Ricci*,[55] in which the Supreme Court held that antitrust proceedings should be stayed pending the outcome of an investigation by the sector regulator where the regulator had both adjudicative and remedial jurisdiction to determine and punish breach.[56] On the facts, to the extent that the defendant's actions were valid under the regulatory framework, the Court suggested pointedly that those actions would be insulated from antitrust attack. To the extent that the actions breached the regulations, the antitrust action might continue.[57] The primary jurisdiction doctrine does not constitute a permanent impediment to concurrent application of antitrust; where the doctrine applies, '[c]ourt jurisdiction is not thereby ousted, but only postponed'.[58] In *Gordon*, one of the prescient 'implied immunity' cases considered in Chapter 4, the Supreme Court distinguished *Ricci* on the basis that the case merely involved deference to a regulator in determining whether regulatory obligations had been breached, rather than any decision regarding antitrust immunity.[59] Nowadays, however, the existence of a parallel regulatory framework is increasingly likely to establish a substantive bar to concurrency.

Instead, or additionally, public enforcers may utilise more informal cooperation and coordination mechanisms in order to avoid problems of conflicting exercises of jurisdiction, or to resolve such issues should these arise. Most straightforwardly, this can take the form of, for example, relatively informal information exchanges, inter-agency staff

[51] See pp. 214–15. [52] Article 16, Regulation 1/2003. [53] See p. 268.
[54] See pp. 194–5. [55] *Ricci* v. *Chicago Mercantile Exchange* et al., 409 US 289 (1973).
[56] *Ricci*, 299, 304. [57] *Ricci*, 303–4.
[58] *United States* v. *Philadelphia National Bank*, 374 US 321 (1963), 353.
[59] *Gordon* v. *NYSE, Inc.*, 422 US 659 (1975), 688.

secondments and bilateral or multilateral interactions between competition enforcers and regulators. Alternatively, such arrangements might be formalised under a memorandum of understanding between enforcers. The potential to generate more precise and effective solutions to disputes over jurisdiction, and avoidance of inter-agency tensions, are likely benefits. The disadvantage, of course, is that the absence of formality may limit the options available to resolve difficult or recurrent disputes.

The seven guiding principles developed by the Canadian Competition Bureau to structure and inform its relationships with sector regulators may be helpful in this regard. These norms both illustrate potential areas of conflict between public enforcers and suggest how, at least from the perspective of antitrust enforcers, such tensions might optimally be resolved. Inter-agency cooperation and coordination, of both an informal and more structured nature, is, unsurprisingly, posited as a key element.[60] Beyond this, the Bureau supports an explicit role for economic regulators in promoting competition,[61] and it advocates effective mechanisms to remove regulation when its costs begin to outweigh its burdens.[62] Although this principle foresees a central role for regulators in removing regulation, their skewed incentives in this regard, discernible in the UK example, suggests that the Bureau might have greater success by proceeding under another guiding principle, namely its competition advocacy role in promoting pro-competitive reforms in regulated markets.[63] In two scenarios, the Bureau expressly prefers regulatory over antitrust intervention, namely in the control of access to essential facilities[64] and over excessive prices due to incumbent market power,[65] thus echoing the general scepticism of these doctrines as antitrust rules discussed in Chapter 2. Conversely, with respect to most anticompetitive business practices it argues that competition enforcement should take priority unless regulation would be 'demonstrably better'.[66] While it is natural that an agency should defend its own jurisdiction in this regard, this approach again raises the spectre of the sort of antitrust cases discussed in the preceding chapter, where, it was argued, competition intervention is not always appropriate.

Ultimately, when there are no formal institutional rules that dictate or supervise the allocation or exercise of enforcement jurisdiction between antitrust agencies and economic regulators, the configuration of market-supervisory activity is likely to be determined by (ideally informed,

[60] ICN (2004:47–8). [61] ICN (2004:43–4). [62] ICN (2004:46–7).
[63] ICN (2004:41–3). [64] ICN (2004:45). [65] ICN (2004:44). [66] ICN (2004:45–6).

but not necessarily disinterested) agency judgments regarding the advisability or necessity of intervention, on the one hand, and any substantive antitrust or regulatory rules that control the interaction between these mechanisms, on the other.

II. Institutional gateways to competition law and regulation (I): market studies

Having explored how and why enforcement powers may be allocated at an inter-agency level, we now consider an increasingly prominent institutional tool used in the threshold determination of when and why antitrust or regulatory powers should be deployed to address specific competition problems, namely market investigation procedures. The growing importance of market studies in terms of informing enforcement and advocacy efforts by competition agencies, in particular, is widely recognised.[67] Such procedures merit attention at this juncture given the argument that use of market studies 'breaks some of the traditional lines between *ex post* and *ex ante* regulation and broadens the [competition agency's] powers significantly to include "market engineering"'.[68] Market studies, typically, enable competition agencies (or possibly regulators) to conduct broad surveys of markets conditions in order to identify, first, any potential competition problems and, second, the optimal remedial approach(es) to address identified concerns. Notably, the ability to conduct market studies, unlike conventional antitrust investigations, does not depend upon reasonable suspicion that an infringement of competition law has occurred; market studies tend to involve, instead, a more broad-based examination of market dynamics that encompasses sources of market failure that go beyond the parameters of the circumscribed antitrust proscriptions. The former OFT, for example, described its market studies power in the following terms:

> Typically, market studies are examinations into the causes of why particular markets are not working well for consumers, leading to proposals as to how they might be made to work better. They take an overview of regulatory and other economic drivers in a market and patterns of consumer and business behaviour.[69]

[67] Indig & Gal (2013); OECD (2008); see also International Competition Network (ICN), *Draft Market Studies Good Practice Handbook*, presented at the 9th Annual Conference of the ICN, Istanbul, April 2010.

[68] Indig & Gal (2013:9).

[69] See Office of Fair Trading, *Market Studies. Guidance on the OFT Approach* (2010), para. 2.2.

In this regard, the report of the OECD Roundtable on Market Studies explicitly recognised the dual objectives of such procedures: namely, to act as a 'prelude or precursor to [antitrust] litigation', on the one hand, and as a 'spearhead or foundation for competition advocacy', including possible proposals for regulatory reinforcement, revision or retrenchment, on the other.[70] By enabling a more holistic and comprehensive examination of the causes and consequences of market failures, market studies can, in theory, identify and facilitate the most appropriate means to resolve such problems.

At a technical level, the parameters and extent of any market investigative procedure vary, quite naturally, between jurisdictions.[71] Perhaps the most interesting distinction, for our purposes, comes at the end of any market study, and concerns the outcomes that may follow in soft or hard law terms. Indig and Gal identified a primary distinction between procedures that culminate in a purely *advisory* role, whereby the results of market studies are simply presented to government alongside non-binding policy recommendations, and procedures that involve a *supervisory* role, whereby enforcement agencies are empowered to take further legal steps to implement recommendations as an integral aspect of the study process.[72] We will consider two examples of market study procedures – sector inquiries conducted by the European Commission, and market investigations by the UK's CMA – that fall, broadly, within these advisory and supervisory categories, respectively. While both the EU and UK procedures can, as we shall see, lead to significant market changes, the key distinguishing feature is the extent to which remedial powers are integrated within, or conversely, decoupled from, the market study process. As these examples demonstrate, market studies can be a powerful instrument for market reform, and even to facilitate law enforcement. Nonetheless, the substantive overlap between antitrust and regulatory powers contained within market investigation procedures may raise certain procedural or rule-of-law concerns, explored further later.

(i) Sector inquiries in the European Union

EU law contains what is, at first glance, a relatively straightforward example of a market study procedure that adopts an advisory approach to the deployment of antitrust and regulatory remedies to address

[70] OECD (2008:7). [71] See, generally, Indig & Gal (2013); OECD (2008).
[72] Indig & Gal (2013:5–6).

identified competition problems. Specifically, Article 17(1) of Regulation 1/2003 provides that, '[w]here the trend of trade between Member States, the rigidity of prices or other circumstances suggest that competition may be restricted or distorted within the Common Market, the Commission may conduct its inquiry into a particular sector of the economy or into a particular type of agreements across various sectors'. The inquiry process, typically, results in the publication of a report by the Commission of its findings, which provides the basis for further remedial action to address identified concerns. The wide-ranging powers of the Commission, which includes the right of legislative initiative for new regulation in addition to antitrust enforcement, mean that it is more effective in terms of subsequent implementation of inquiry findings than the average national competition authority with a purely advisory role. It remains the case, nonetheless, that the inquiry process establishes only the existence of market problems and cannot, itself, implement suitable remedies to address these issues in the first instance.

Broadly speaking, sector inquiries fall within the purview of the Commission's competition powers. Inquiries are conducted by the Commission's competition division, DG Competition, legal authority is contained in the secondary legislation that implements the competition rules, Regulation 1/2003, and the full range of antitrust investigatory powers is available.[73] Nonetheless, whereas competition investigations are triggered by and address the behaviour of individual firms, sector inquiries examine the functioning of markets more generally. Sector inquiries are not generally initiated to investigate suspected breaches of Articles 101 or 102 TFEU, but rather are conducted where market circumstances suggest that competition is restricted or distorted as a result of *any* market feature, whether behavioural or structural, and whether originating in private practices or the existing regulatory framework.[74] In this manner, the inquiry process brings the tools of competition enforcement beyond the parameters of EU competition law to take account of broader market considerations.

Sector inquiries do not incorporate remedial powers as an element of the investigation process. Instead, any market problems identified can be corrected only through subsequent action undertaken by the

[73] Article 17(2) of Regulation 1/2003, extending the investigative powers in Articles 18–24 to sector inquiries.

[74] European Commission, *A Pro-Active Competition Policy for a Competitive Europe* (COM (2004) 293 final), published 20 April 2004, pp. 16–17.

Commission: that is, antitrust enforcement against firms suspected to have breached competition law, and/or modification of the regulatory framework.[75] The Commission has argued that both competition law and regulation lie within the broader category of 'competition-policy' instruments, and so, depending on the circumstances, either or both might be used to address the identified problem(s).[76] We saw in Chapter 3, for example, that, following its inquiry into mobile roaming charges, the Commission attempted, first, to address the identified market defects through antitrust enforcement, and then, subsequently, through EU-level sector regulation.[77] Where extensive use of both is deemed necessary, the Commission may develop a 'package' of remedial measures that combines competition law and regulatory tools. The components of a package are viewed as not merely compatible but complementary and mutually reinforcing elements of an overall design for the optimal open and competitive internal market.[78] In this manner, the most effective combination of market intervention mechanisms is selected.

Sector inquiries have increased importance following the modernisation and decentralisation of competition enforcement under Regulation 1/2003. While an express power to conduct sector inquiries was provided under the earlier Regulation 17, it was used sparingly.[79] Regulation 1/2003 removed the notification procedure for restrictive agreements, thus releasing greater agency resources to conduct sector inquiries, and conversely, eliminating a significant source of market information for the Commission. Accordingly, sector inquiries are now more frequent and more important as quasi-'Phase I' – i.e., preliminary stage – investigations for competition enforcement.[80] Yet, because the investigative scope of sector inquiries extends beyond breaches of competition law, findings may spill over into certain market problems that are best (or only) addressed through regulatory amendment rather than antitrust enforcement. Sector inquiries thus allow the Commission to analyse the broader market picture alongside the role of individual participants, increasing the effectiveness as well as the ambit of its market-supervisory efforts.

The nature of the inquiry process, particularly use of a competition investigation framework outside the context of a formal enforcement case, has, however, attracted criticisms that relate, broadly, to issues of

[75] Ibid., pp. 16–17. [76] Ibid., p. 17. [77] See pp. 179–85.
[78] Soriano García (2010:175). [79] Olsen & Roy (2007:82).
[80] Ibáñez Colomo (2010:266–7); Olsen & Roy (2007); see also Commission, *Pro-Active Competition Policy*, pp. 16–17.

fairness and legitimacy. Such concerns can be attributed, principally, to the decoupled approach to remedies: while sector inquiries begin as generalised investigations into competition, the process may lead ultimately to the imposition of individual sanctions against specific firms under an antitrust rubric.

First, given the potential for inquiries to transform into formal enforcement proceedings against specific companies, concerns have been expressed regarding protection of the rights of defence. The Commission's full information-gathering powers are available, including the ability to make compulsory demands for information, to conduct dawn raids and to impose fines for failure to comply or provision of incorrect or misleading information.[81] Some commentators advise that firms under review should treat any sector inquiry as equivalent to the initial stages of a competition investigation, since an inquiry acquires this categorisation retrospectively if the Commission decides to pursue competition enforcement against the firm.[82] Yet the safeguards for the rights of defence applicable in antitrust cases, set out in Article 27 of Regulation 1/2003 – such as access to the Commission's case file, and the right to an *inter partes* hearing – are not formally available during sector inquiries.[83] Individual firms are not the subjects of market investigations as such; rather, they are objects within the broader assessment of the functioning of the market. At the same time, sector inquiries are now a significant component of the competition enforcement framework. Again, this raises difficult questions regarding when rights of defence should become a live issue for firms that are ultimately required to defend their actions against allegations of antitrust infringement.[84] This concern is particularly pressing given that competition enforcement by the Commission may, ultimately, result in a finding of breach of EU law by the relevant firm, which can involve a significant fine, and potentially lead to considerable follow-on litigation.

Second, concerns have been raised regarding the potential politicisation of inquiries, whereby the review process is deployed as a tool to achieve political aims rather than merely as an information-gathering exercise. Olsen and Roy, for example, argued that a key purpose of sector inquiries, in reality, is to focus attention on specific Commission

[81] Article 17(2), Regulation 1/2003. [82] Wood & Baverez (2005:5).

[83] Olsen & Roy (2007:86). See also *Commission notice on best practices for the conduct of proceedings concerning Articles 101 and 102 TFEU*, 2011 OJ (C 308) 6.

[84] See also Tamar & Gal (2013).

objectives within the sector reviewed. To the extent that the process becomes politicised – for example, where an inquiry is conducted principally to secure the Commission's policy goals, or to pressurise stakeholders – the integrity of the process is undermined, and questions might be raised regarding the validity or objectivity of inquiry findings.[85] This persuasive concern is particularly acute to the extent that sector inquiries function as 'Phase I' investigations for competition enforcement, which may subsequently result in a formal finding of breach against the firm. Compliance with the rule-of-law demands that competition enforcement ought not be politically motivated. In particular, firms should not be punished under individual theories of liability, or subject to quasi-penal sanctions, where the underlying objective of public enforcement is to improve or restructure the workings of the market more generally.[86] Such utilitarian considerations should be confined instead to sector-specific regulation, which can address issues of fairness as opposed to legality, and is thus better suited to accommodate political decisions regarding wealth redistribution.

To an extent, evidence of both of these dangers can be discerned in the Commission's Energy Sector Inquiry,[87] discussed in Chapter 2.[88] The underlying motivation for that Inquiry was largely policy-driven: to support the liberalisation process. As noted, the Inquiry identified a series of on-going problems within energy markets, but, given the remedial limitations of the sector-inquiry process, it could not, in itself, implement appropriate solutions. Instead, the findings prescribed a two-pronged strategy for remedial action, involving both regulation and competition enforcement. Regulatory efforts culminated in the passage of the Third Electricity and Gas Directives, albeit, as we have seen, on more permissive terms than the Commission recommended. Furthermore, antitrust enforcement activity was pursued against energy incumbents under Article 102 TFEU, demonstrating a clear usage of the sector-inquiry process as a precursor to enforcement.[89] The recurrent use of the commitment procedure in these cases also added a further quasi-regulatory dimension to the inquiry process.

[85] Olsen & Roy (2007:83–6).

[86] See also Larouche (2000:253–6) regarding the 'instrumentalisation' of antitrust to achieve regulatory goals.

[87] See European Commission, *DG Competition Report on Energy Sector Inquiry* (SEC(2006) 1724), published 10 January 2007.

[88] See pp. 112–13. [89] See pp. 113–15.

Another prominent example is the Pharmaceutical Inquiry, concluded in 2009, which sought to investigate the reasons for delayed market entry by generic drug manufacturers into EU markets. Notably, the pharmaceutical sector, like the energy sector, is already subject to substantial EU-level regulation that addresses multiple market aspects. The immediate recommendations of the Pharmaceutical Inquiry were essentially policy-oriented, including a reaffirming of the desirability of a distinct EU patent and the necessity of full implementation of existing harmonisation Directives.[90] Unlike the Energy Inquiry, the Pharmaceutical Inquiry did not identify any immediate need for competition enforcement. It prompted the Commission, instead, to engage in a soft law monitoring exercise for settlements between drug originator companies and potential generic competitors to gather further information on competition within the sector.[91] Based on the evidence that came to light, the Commission subsequently initiated enforcement proceedings against various pharmaceutical companies, fining a number for participation in anticompetitive 'pay-to-delay' agreements in breach of Article 101 TFEU.[92]

(ii) Market investigation references by the UK's Competition and Markets Authority

By contrast, market studies – or 'market investigation references' (MIRs) – as conducted by the UK's competition agency, the Competition and Markets Authority (CMA), incorporate a remedial power that enables the agency to devise and implement remedies as an integral element, in line with the supervisory role identified by Indig and Gal. The remedial options available include the ability to impose significant behavioural or structural remedies on firms within the relevant market, which can take on a strong quasi-regulatory flavour, although the CMA itself can only recommend rather than mandate top-down regulatory

[90] European Commission, *Pharmaceutical Sector Inquiry Final Report*, published 8 July 2009, pp. 525–31.

[91] Ibid., p. 524. See also European Commission, *Third Report on the Monitoring of Patent Settlements (January-December 2011)*, published 25 July 2012.

[92] See European Commission Press Releases IP/13/563 'Antitrust: Commission fines Lundbeck and other pharma companies for delaying market entry of generic medicines', published 19 June 2013, and IP/13/1233 'Antitrust: Commission fines Johnson & Johnson and Novartis €16 million for delaying market entry of general pain-killer fentanyl', published 10 December 2013.

reforms by central government or sector regulators. The inclusion of remedial powers within the MIR procedure, which, moreover, are targeted primarily against the anticompetitive impacts of firms' market activities or structures, thus creates a potential overlap between that procedure and the CMA's competition enforcement role. Whereas the use of the sector-inquiry procedure as a non-contentious precursor to antitrust enforcement raised certain rule-of-law concerns at a procedural level, the overlap between competition law and the MIR procedure creates a particular risk that the latter might be used to avoid or subvert the limits of antitrust, an issue considered later in the context of the BAA investigation. In this manner, market studies may further blur the already indistinct line between antitrust and economic regulation.

The power to conduct market investigations is highly formalised and firmly entrenched within UK law, an artefact of the decidedly quasi-regulatory nature of the competition framework prior to 1998.[93] Although the Competition Act 1998 modernised UK competition law, it nonetheless retained the powers of market review that were available within the older system,[94] which were subsequently reformulated and refined under the Enterprise Act (EA) 2002 and again under the ERRA 2013. Previously, a MIR would have its origins in the work of the UK's generalist competition authority, the OFT, which had responsibility for day-to-day antitrust enforcement and thus gained knowledge of markets experiencing difficulties. Section 131 of the EA 2002 enabled the OFT, plus sector regulators with concurrent competition powers, to make MIRs to the Competition Commission (CC) if there were reasonable grounds for suspecting that market features limited competition. The CC functioned as the UK's expert competition body, exercising distinct antitrust functions (e.g., in-depth analysis of proposed mergers) and regulatory functions (e.g., regulatory inquiries on behalf of sector regulators) in addition to its market investigation powers.[95] Following enactment of ERRA 2013, these functions pass to the CMA; references are made by the CMA (or sector regulators) to 'the chair of the CMA for the constitution of a group' composed of relevant experts.[96] ERRA 2013 also makes provision for 'cross-market references' that cover two or more markets in the UK.[97]

[93] See p. 159, fn. 135.

[94] See Department of Trade and Industry, *A Prohibition Approach to Anti-competitive Agreements and Abuse of Dominant Position: Draft Bill*, published August 1997.

[95] See Geroski (2005).

[96] See Schedule 4, part 3, and Schedule 5, s. 164, to ERRA 2013.

[97] S. 33, EA 2002.

Section 134(1) of EA 2002 requires the CMA to decide whether 'any feature, or combination of features, of each relevant market prevents, restricts or distorts competition in connection with the supply or acquisition of any goods or services'. Where such features exist, there is, according to section 134(2), an 'adverse effect on competition' (AEC). If one or more AECs exist, then, under section 134(4), the CMA must determine whether to take remedial action and/or recommend action be taken by others, such as government or regulators. Under section 161, a broad range of remedies can be imposed by the CMA, which include the power to enforce structural remedies, to proscribe a wide variety of business practices, and even to impose duties to deal or price regulation.[98] The Competition Appeal Tribunal (CAT) has noted the breadth and potential implications of these expansive powers, holding that the (now) CMA:

> has at its disposal enormous powers in the context of a market investigation, and it is obviously of considerable importance that those affected and the wider public should have confidence that those powers are exercised, and the decisions underlying their exercise are reached, in a manner which reflects the highest standards of impartiality and fairness.[99]

The market investigation power, not unlike the sector-inquiry procedure just discussed, shares some characteristics of the generally applicable competition rules against anticompetitive coordinated and unilateral conduct. It is exercisable by an independent competition authority: generalist in the sense that it has jurisdiction across all sectors, yet specialist insofar as it has a specific competition focus and expertise. The focus of any investigation is market competition, and specifically upon factors that prevent competition from functioning freely. Section 134(1) utilises the same formulation – targeting any market feature that 'prevents, restricts or distorts competition' – as the prohibition on anticompetitive agreements under Article 101 TFEU. Any remedies to be implemented are, generally, imposed *ex post*, meaning that the identified competition problems already exist. The remedies imposed address only the AEC identified, and must be proportionate to these problems. Unlike sector-specific regulation, non-competition objectives such as universal service, media plurality or environmental protection play no

[98] The range of potential remedies is specified in Schedule 8, EA 2002.

[99] *BAA Limited* v. *Competition Commission* [2009] CAT 35, para. 117. See also Whish & Bailey (2012:466–86), for discussion of the MIR procedure and cases to date.

role under the MIR procedure. The emphasis, instead, is upon creating opportunities for competition to develop, rather than predetermining any particular 'competitive' outcome.[100] Although sector regulators can also make MIRs, the CMA's powers in this regard are distinguishable from both the focused powers of regulators to supervise their own markets and the specific functions of the CMA within various regulatory frameworks.[101]

Nonetheless, the principal difference between market investigations and antitrust enforcement is that, whereas the latter is directed against individual *firm* conduct, market investigations are directed towards *markets* that do not work well. The threshold for investigation is thus rather different than for competition cases: it is necessary to identify a lack or distortion of competition, rather than specific instances of *prima facie* anticompetitive private behaviour. While a successful competition case results in a finding of breach against individual firm(s), in market investigations there are no findings against firms as such, but instead a finding of diminished competition generally. While structural or behavioural remedies imposed under section 134 can be more onerous than those available under competition law, there is no possibility of fines, nor criminal prosecution, nor private follow-on actions. The procedure is non-adversarial, reflecting the fact that the case is not against individuals, but, rather, focuses on market issues.[102] Whereas competition law imposes individual liability for individual breaches, market investigations take a broader approach to market failures, imposing top-down solutions in a manner akin to industrial policy.

Whish and Bailey present the market investigation procedure as an acknowledgement of the limits of antitrust, which 'recognises that not every market failure can be cured through the application of the "conventional" tools of competition law'.[103] In order to assess the appropriateness of MIRs, the OFT developed a four-stage test, requiring it to be demonstrated that: (i) it is not more appropriate to apply ordinary competition law, (ii) it is not more appropriate to accept binding undertakings from the firm(s) regarding modification of the market or their behaviour, (iii) the scale of the suspected problem merits a reference, and (iv) there is a reasonable chance that appropriate remedies are

100 Competition Commission, *BAA airports market investigation: A report on the supply of airport services by BAA in the UK*, published 19 March 2009 ('*BAA Report*'), para. 5.19.
101 See Rab (2009:507–9), for discussion of the CMA's regulatory roles.
102 Geroski (2005). 103 Whish & Bailey (2012:467).

available.[104] Part (i) necessarily implies that market investigations are distinct from competition law. The OFT Guidance distinguished between specific instances of anticompetitive conduct, which are prohibited by antitrust, and situations where the process of market competition as a whole does not work; in the latter, market investigations are appropriate.[105] Specifically, market investigations can address circumstances where the market does not function properly but where the source of the problems is difficult to locate within any theory of antitrust violation, such as oligopoly markets or widespread use of vertical restrictions.[106] Competition enforcement is preferred wherever appropriate and possible, meaning that MIRs are made only if the problem lies outside the coverage of antitrust, or if enforcement cannot remedy the issue.[107] Insofar as MIRs are made only where application of competition law is inadequate, this brings the power closer to ideas of regulation – overstepping rather than reinforcing the market mechanism – but within the guise of a general power wielded by a competition enforcer in discrete markets, rather than by a specialist regulator setting the parameters of competition in specified markets. Olsen and Roy distinguished market investigations from EU sector inquiries on this basis, arguing that while the latter exists primarily to facilitate future antitrust enforcement, the market investigation model provides a standalone means of remedying dysfunctional markets.[108]

To future explore this idea we consider a recent investigation, the BAA airports inquiry, pursued, unusually, against a single firm. This investigation demonstrates the potential for market investigations to overlap with, and possibly usurp, competition enforcement. The OFT Guidance stated that, generally, market references should not be made in respect of anticompetitive firm conduct, which should instead be addressed by competition enforcement.[109] Three qualifications were, nonetheless, added: (i) where anticompetitive unilateral conduct relates to structural market features, (ii) where existing antitrust jurisprudence renders it inadequate to address the conduct and (iii) where structural remedies are required.[110] The BAA case, concerning the anticompetitive impact of

[104] OFT, *Market Investigation Reference: Guidance about the making of references under Part 4 of the Enterprise Act*, OFT511, published March 2006, para. 2.1.

[105] Ibid., para. 2.2. [106] Ibid., paras. 2.4–.6. [107] Ibid., para. 2.3.

[108] Olsen & Roy (2007:83); also Geroski (2005).

[109] OFT, *Market Investigation Reference Guidance*, para. 2.7.

[110] Ibid., para. 2.8. Note the advent of possible structural remedies under Regulation 1/2003.

airport ownership, arguably falls within each of these exceptions. Our assessment will consider, however, the extent to which a market investigation addressed solely at single firm behaviour, and where no antitrust violation is identified, accords with the rule of law.

a. The BAA airports inquiry

The British Airports Authority was a State company that owned and managed various UK airports. In 1986, in line with Thatcherite ideology, it was privatised as a horizontally integrated entity, BAA,[111] with provision made for economic regulation of individual airports by the Civil Aviation Authority (CAA) where appropriate. In 2006, BAA was subject to a hostile takeover; in May that year, after the merger received clearance[112] but prior to completion, the OFT announced a study of airport markets to determine whether the existing structure worked effectively.[113] The announcement was timed strategically to place the acquiring company on notice of a potential future MIR,[114] and the OFT subsequently referred the 'markets for airport services in the United Kingdom as exist in connection with the supply of airport services by BAA'[115] for investigation. The CC's report, published in March 2009, identified a series of market features with an AEC, the most important of which was joint ownership of the London airports and the Scottish airports by BAA.[116] To remedy these problems, the CC mandated divestiture of Stansted and Gatwick, and either Glasgow or Edinburgh airport, and also made numerous recommendations to government regarding the tenor of aviation policy and the framework of regulation. Gatwick was sold in 2009; in 2011, having determined that there were no material changes in circumstances the CC confirmed the obligation to further divest Stansted and a Scottish airport.[117]

[111] Airports Act 1986.

[112] Non-opposition to a notified concentration in Case COMP/M.4164 – *Ferrovial/Quebec/GIC/BAA*, 2006 OJ (C 182) 12.

[113] OFT Press Release 91/06, 'OFT to look at UK airports market', published 25 May 2006.

[114] Ibid. [115] OFT, *BAA: Terms of Reference*, dated 29 March 2007.

[116] Overturned in *BAA Ltd* v. *Competition Commission* [2009] CAT 35, but reinstated by the Court of Appeal in *Competition Commission* v. *BAA Ltd* [2010] EWCA Civ 1097.

[117] Competition Commission, *BAA Market Investigation: Consideration of Possible Material Changes of Circumstances*, published 19 July 2011; upheld in *BAA Limited* v. *Competition Commission and Ryanair Limited* [2012] CAT 3; and in *BAA Limited* v. *Competition Commission and Ryanair Limited* [2012] EWCA Civ 1077.

The BAA case featured the first use of the MIR power against a single firm, and highlights the substantial risk that the procedure might be used to circumvent limitations within competition law in such circumstances. The principal competition problems attributable to BAA's conduct related to a lack of airport capacity, and poor service quality for airlines and passengers. Such market issues are difficult to fit within conventional abuse of dominance theories, particularly since service prices were capped and BAA did not exclude competing airport operators. By contrast, the MIR procedure can address competition problems that harm consumers but fall outside 'ordinary' antitrust; it is arguably closer to industrial policy in this sense. Given the apparent absence of blameworthy conduct under an antitrust assessment, perhaps the most notable aspect of the BAA investigation is the far-reaching remedies imposed.[118] Indeed, had the OFT pursued competition enforcement against BAA and succeeded in establishing anticompetitive conduct, it would have struggled to impose such substantial penalties. These were considered necessary, nonetheless, to solve 'long-standing problems, which go to the heart of the structure of this market and therefore require a structural remedy'.[119]

In this manner, the CC, as authorised by EA 2002, took a utilitarian approach, viewing the benefits of increased competition as sufficient to outweigh detriment to BAA resulting from the forced sale plus interference with property rights and market freedom. Moreover, such negative consequences were acceptable even though BAA was not 'guilty' of illegal conduct as such. The inquiry procedure itself is non-adversarial and so parties under investigation do not have the full rights of defence that are available in antitrust investigations, although transparency is emphasised in order to achieve fairness.[120] While the UK government has tacitly acknowledged that the MIR process is subject to the fair-trial rights contained in Article 6 of the ECHR, protection of these right is considered to be satisfied through appeal to the CAT.[121] As in the context of sector inquiries, this likewise raises the question of the point at which full rights of defence ought to take effect. The point here is not to argue against divestiture in the BAA case, but rather to stress the strong

[118] The CC acknowledged that the remedy imposed 'constitutes a major intervention in this market and will have a significant impact on BAA's business': *BAA Report*, para. 10.117.

[119] Ibid. [120] Geroski (2005).

[121] See Department for Business Innovation & Skills, *A Competition Regime for Growth: A Consultation on Options for Reform*, published March 2011, para. 3.6.

regulatory flavour of the MIR power. Yet the procedure is distinct from conventional regulation, both in terms of the targeted nature of the solutions offered and the (arguably) less politically accountable nature of the decision to regulate.

The BAA investigation also raised interesting questions about the role of government in creating market situations that effect competition adversely. Alongside joint ownership, negative competition consequences resulted, *inter alia*, from government policy regarding airport development, and the system of economic regulation of airports. In relation to the former, the CC identified certain 'excessively detailed' policy statements, contained in the then government's aviation policy,[122] as having the potential to constrain airports' ability to respond to market changes, and thereby constituting an AEC.[123] The CC argued that this set of quasi-directions 'blurs the boundaries of responsibility between the Government and the airport operator', suggesting that an airport owner/operator is not wholly responsible for development of its facility.[124] In market investigations, which focus on competition more generally, the role of government does not preclude a finding that market features (including government policy) have an AEC. Had BAA been pursued under competition law, however, it remains an open question as to whether governmental influence was sufficient to preclude a finding of autonomous anticompetitive conduct.

Criticisms advanced in relation to the existing framework for economic regulation are also noteworthy, insofar as the complaint of poor service quality is a factor that might, alternatively, have been corrected by regulation. The CC held, however, that both the existing regulatory framework,[125] and the manner in which the CAA administered its regulatory duties[126] were inadequate. Additionally, there were overlaps between regulation and government aviation policy, which suggest that, when so much of an economic operator's market behaviour is attributable to State action rather than individual self-maximising decision-making, it may be bad competition policy to pursue the symptoms (firm conduct) rather than the causes of market failure (government policy choices, at privatisation and subsequently through regulation). In response, the Civil Aviation Act 2012 was enacted to modernise

[122] Contained in a 2003 White Paper: see Department for Transport, *The Future of Air Transport*, published December 2003.

[123] 2003 White Paper, para. 4.78. [124] 2003 White Paper, para. 4.76.

[125] *BAA Report*, para. 6.12. [126] *BAA Report*, para. 6.46.

and improve airport regulation. Arguably, this produces a more sensible, durable solution, yet one the CC had power only to recommend rather than require.

It is important to emphasise, finally, that MIRs permit consideration only of market elements that impact adversely on competition; there is no scope to balance non-economic factors against competition goals. This was a real limitation during the BAA inquiry, given that environmental objections are the principal barrier to capacity development around London.[127] Although constrained capacity manifested itself as a structural market feature amounting to an AEC, it originated in response to a different market defect, namely the negative externality of pollution. During the BAA investigation, however, the CC could not assess whether limited runway capacity brings benefits of reduced pollution, or conversely, whether alleviating the problem of constrained capacity would create externalities such as increased pollution. This is not to suggest that the CC should have acted *ultra vires* and taken account of environmental concerns in its competition assessment. Yet logically, when it comes to the design and implementation of remedies in market investigations, it is arguable that non-economic considerations ought to play a role, particularly where these are a primary market determinant in practice.

(iii) *Market studies: analysis and concluding remarks*

From this brief sample of market study procedures, taken from amongst the many dozens of such processes that have now been enacted, we can see both the potential strengths as well as some of the possible dangers of such approaches. Market studies can, *inter alia*, provide a more thoughtful forum for the detection and assessment of market problems; facilitate adoption of optimal remedies, whether regulatory or antitrust-oriented; and, even where immediate intervention is not warranted, provide public enforcers with a much deeper understanding of the operation of markets, which may prompt or assist enforcement action in the future. By enabling more nuanced 'big-picture' thinking that seeks, subsequently, to match appropriate solutions to identified market defects, markets studies might also help to avoid prosecutorial bias and the distortion of incentives that can, inadvertently, have a negative impact on decision-making by even the most scrupulous of public enforcers.

[127] Including noise and air pollution, road congestion and greenhouse gas emissions: 2003 White Paper, Chapter 3.

Given our focus on the relationship between competition law and economic regulation, market studies are of particular interest. On the one hand, such procedures can assist in a more sophisticated determination of whether antitrust or regulatory (or both) approaches might be appropriate to resolve particular market defects. On the other, as the UK's MIR procedure illustrated, market studies that incorporate a remedial or 'supervisory' component may go some way towards further clouding the dividing line between these mechanisms. The power to conduct investigations provides the CMA with a powerful integrated mechanism to address existing competition problems that goes beyond conventional approaches of either competition enforcement or sector-specific regulation. As the BAA case demonstrates, such controls can grant the enforcer or adjudicator significant power to shape markets and direct private behaviour. Moreover, the CMA's powers are largely liberated from both the limitations of the discrete antitrust prohibitions and the need for political support inherent in regulation. This combination of factors results in a complex and unique legal instrument for market control. For this reason, however, there is a danger that prioritisation of effectiveness may weaken the legitimacy or rule-of-law compliance of State intervention, insofar as the basis for action reflects neither individual bad conduct nor any democratically accountable decision to further general welfare over private property interests.

The absence of an amalgamated remedial power within the EU's sector-inquiry process, by contrast, results in a market-supervisory instrument that is perhaps more complicated, protracted and more uncertain in its application than the comprehensive UK approach. Reliance upon conventional instruments to remedy identified market difficulties also creates certain tensions between the goals of effectiveness and protection of individual rights, which may prove difficult to resolve in practice. Nonetheless, sector inquiries now play a central role in informing and shaping the European Commission's activities in furtherance of both market integration and competition within the EU, whether under an antitrust or regulatory rubric, or both.

III. Institutional gateways to competition law and regulation (II): 'hybridisation'

Finally, we explore an idea hinted at in the preceding section, namely, the concept of legal powers that exhibit a 'hybridised' quality between competition law and economic regulation, combining elements of each mechanism within a single instrument. The central issue to be considered here is the extent to which a single institution might be empowered to perform antitrust and regulatory functions not merely concurrently, but, rather, simultaneously through a distinct legal tool that incorporates aspects of each. Examples of market regulatory approaches that exhibit such a hybridised quality, to a greater or lesser extent, can be found within many legal systems. Such instruments are generally intended, like other legal developments considered in this work, to address limitations that exist within the conventional schema of competition law and economic regulation, that is, in effect, to bridge the gap between these separate mechanisms. Yet hybridisation represents a deeper form of interaction than any considered thus far, namely a consolidation of the conventional formal and substance-based elements of both within a single legal power.

The idea of hybridisation, in its complete form, would thus go beyond a mere blurring of the line between competition law and regulation by rejecting the initial dichotomous choice between these legal instruments as such. Instead, in form and substance, hybridised powers incorporate elements of each, creating distinct instruments of market control pitched between the (supposed) generalist *laissez-faire* antitrust approach of strengthening the market and the sector-specific interventionist regulatory approach of overreaching it. The precise distribution between competition law and regulatory elements in an individual case is not determined by designation as a hybridised power, but, rather, varies depending on the legislative choices in constructing the instrument. We will consider, in particular, two such approaches: the codification of general antitrust principles into concrete legislative provisions, typified by the access to infrastructure provisions contained in Australian competition law; and the grant to public enforcers of expansive powers to supervise the efficient functioning of markets that go beyond the conventional antitrust proscriptions, illustrated by §5 of the Federal Trade Commission Act. In many ways, market investigations by the CMA, just considered, also provide an archetypal example of a hybridised approach to market supervision, combining elements from antitrust and regulation at both the analytical and remedial stages.

The rationale for adopting hybridised approaches to market control can be explained by reference to two, by now familiar, truisms of the market regulatory enterprise: that market-based mechanisms are preferred where possible, yet that regulation remains indispensable or highly beneficial in certain circumstances. Hybridised powers reflect the desire to maximise market efficiency to the greatest extent possible, while recognising that the market itself is not a curative for every possible market defect that might arise. Viewed from a competition law perspective, hybridisation provides a means by which to extend the ambit of the established antitrust rules beyond their conventional parameters to address a greater variety of market problems, while ideally avoiding the contortions of similar, more organic developments considered in Chapter 2. In this sense, hybridised powers might be conceived of as 'competition law *plus*'. Alternatively, viewed from a regulatory perspective, hybridised powers involve the streamlining, generalisation and economic rationalisation of regulatory controls, in essence providing a means by which to discipline the process of regulation. This perspective also favours the reduced need for political choices under the hybridised-powers approach: regulation is triggered by the perceived need to correct competition problems, rather than any political decision to regulate (or not). Enforcement agencies and courts have often been reluctant to embrace the full regulatory potential of hybridised rules, however, which has been the case for both the Australian and US examples discussed later in this chapter. Indeed, although the justification for hybridisation in terms of effectiveness can be compelling, there are also strong policy arguments in favour of retaining a more rigid distinction between competition law and regulation in some instances. The rule-of-law concerns expressed earlier in the context of the MIR procedure reflect one such strand; besides legality, the case studies that follow also illustrate potential economic objections to this approach. These studies therefore aim to illustrate the potential uses of hybridisation – and range of forms that it may take – and to consider the enforcement benefits that such powers might bring, but also to highlight limitations or potential disadvantages within the conception of hybridisation itself.

(i) Concretising competition principles: access to infrastructure regulation

We consider, first, the use of distinct statutory provisions to supply a formalised legal framework for application of discrete competition principles. Antitrust rules that prohibit anticompetitive concerted and unilateral conduct are, typically, formulated at a generalised and abstract level, prohibiting, for example, 'abuse of dominance' or 'restrictive agreements'. Although the relative abstractness of such provisions brings benefits in terms of flexibility and ease of reinterpretation to reflect evolving understandings in economics, it introduces an inherent uncertainty into the task of identifying concrete proscriptions and corresponding entitlements, as well as enforcing these rules. Within many systems, consequently, the legislatures have chosen to enact formal legal rules that codify or crystallise certain individual competition law principles – developed initially from these general antitrust prohibitions – into distinct elaborated restrictions.

The hybridised character of such elaborated rules derives from their frequent use to reinforce more controversial or ambiguous antitrust prohibitions. Certain ostensibly anticompetitive or simply unfair types of market behaviour – such as refusal to supply, price discrimination, or charging very high prices – are often permitted under conventional antitrust frameworks. These limitations to competition law's reach have numerous potential justifications: that the conduct is efficient, or the firm is entitled to a fair reward for innovation, or that regulatory rather than antitrust remedies are required. Nonetheless, in such circumstances the legislature may choose to supplement the ordinary antitrust framework by enacting specific provisions that expressly prohibit such behaviour. Legal rules of this variety can be seen as hybridised powers to the extent that they involve an expansion of competition law towards the spheres of market-planning and regulation. In particular, such rules often expand the purview of antitrust analysis beyond a strict efficiency standard. In contrast to the ostensibly expansive scope of §5 of the FTCA, considered later, however, such legal rules typically address specific examples of defined undesirable market behaviour, thus effectively operationalizing one element of the abstract antitrust prohibitions, whether recognised or not within established competition law.

A prominent illustration is contained in the Robinson-Patman Act, introduced into US law in 1936, which explicitly prohibits price discrimination.[128] The statute was intended to prevent chain-store retailers from benefitting from bulk-purchasing discounts; or, put another way, to protect small retailers from the harsh forces of competition, potentially at the expense of consumers.[129] Framed as an antitrust rule – formally it amends the Clayton Act – in practice the Robinson-Patman Act takes antitrust jurisprudence far beyond the contemporary scope of the Sherman Act. In effect, the Robinson-Patman Act represents a wealth-redistributive industrial policy choice in the guise of an elaborated

[128] Now 15 U.S.C. § 13. [129] Hovenkamp (2000:129–30); Giocoli (2009:754).

antitrust rule, thus fitting within the hybridised-powers rubric.[130] The Act has been the target of strong criticism on the grounds that it is actually *anti*competitive and anti-consumer in practice,[131] while the US Supreme Court has sought to arrest its potentially anticompetitive impact by imposing a requirement of injury to competition.[132] It remains an established part of US antitrust, however, mainly as a result of strong support from the small- and medium-sized business lobby.[133] Notably, unlike many hybridised rules, the 1936 Act is enforceable by private litigants in civil damages actions, and it is this use (or *ab*use) that generates the greatest controversy. These criticisms thus suggest that hybridised instruments are most readily accommodated within a public-enforcement context.

Similarly, price-control laws can be construed as antitrust/regulatory hybrids thereby surmounting the almost paradoxical difficulties encountered when addressing monopoly rents through competition law.[134] An example is found within German law, which relates specifically to excessive prices within the energy sector. In theory, anticompetitive excessive prices could amount to an abuse of dominance under ordinary German competition rules governing unilateral conduct. Nonetheless, in response to a perceived issue of anticompetitive pricing in the energy sector, an additional sector-specific prohibition applicable to dominant electricity and gas firms – namely, demanding fees that 'unreasonably exceed the costs' – was introduced into German competition legislation in 2007. In addition to the explicit proscription of excessive prices, the provision partially reverses the burden of proof, thereby facilitating enforcement.[135]

Another particularly clear illustration of this approach is contained in the Australian regime for access to infrastructure under Part IIIA of the CCA. An adaptation of the disputed 'essential facilities' antitrust doctrine, this legislative scheme creates a formalised framework enabling firms to access the infrastructure of their competitors, including mandatory access requirements where necessary. Yet recent years have

[130] See, e.g., Posner (1970:369), who argued that the Robinson-Patman Act is '…*a price-control rather than an antitrust statute…*'

[131] Loughlin (1970); Calvani (1979); and Hovenkamp (2000).

[132] *Brooke Group Ltd* v. *Brown & Williamson Tobacco Corp.*, 509 US 209 (1993).

[133] Sullivan & Hovenkamp (2003:931). Paradoxically, the Robinson-Patman Act has often been employed to the detriment of small retailers to prevent them from acquiring bulk discounts through trade associations, ibid.

[134] See pp. 120–6. [135] OECD (2011b:39–40).

witnessed a retrenchment from the full hybridised potential of Part IIIA, perhaps reflecting concerns regarding the double-edged sword that expansion beyond the conventional competition rules can represent.

Like Australia's unusual approach to economic regulation, the access to infrastructure regime has its origins in the Hilmer Report, which concluded that access to so-called essential facilities was central to the development of effective competition within natural monopoly markets if structural separation was unavailable.[136] It therefore recommended establishment of a legal framework under which third parties could gain access to essential infrastructure in the public interest.[137] The proposed access regime departed both from antitrust and regulatory approaches. While the general competition provisions governing unilateral conduct were considered to be potentially applicable if facility owners held a substantial degree of monopoly power, a distinct essential facilities doctrine was unrecognised within Australian competition law.[138] Possible justiciability issues, such as determination of terms and conditions of supply, were similarly raised.[139] Yet, following the logic of its approach to economic regulation, the Hilmer Report rejected the idea that access regimes should be legislated and administered on a sector-specific basis. Although different industries have peculiar characteristics, the report contended that there are important cross-sector similarities in access issues. The development of a common framework for access offered the benefits of promoting consistent approaches across the wider market and allowing expertise to be shared across sectors with analogous access issues.[140] While the proposals acknowledged the potential incursion into individual commercial freedom and property rights that mandatory access would entail, these concerns were outweighed by the public benefits that would follow.[141] These recommendations were enacted, in spirit if not wholly in letter,[142] as Part IIIA of the (now) CCA. The codified access framework was pitched between – yet distinct from – what were perceived to be the differing international approaches at the time:[143] that of New Zealand, which relied upon ordinary competition law to regulate utilities;[144] the US, which was considered to incorporate a

[136] Hilmer Report, pp. 239–41. [137] Hilmer Report, p. 239.
[138] Hilmer Report, p. 243. The essential facilities doctrine was rejected in *Queensland Wire Industries Pty* v. *BHP* (1988) ATPR ¶40–841.
[139] Hilmer Report, p. 247. [140] Hilmer Report, pp. 248–9.
[141] Hilmer Report, p. 248. [142] Marshall & Mulheron (2003b:233–4).
[143] Hilmer Report, pp. 244–47; Maddock & Marshall (1997). [144] See p. 77.

distinct essential facilities doctrine within its antitrust rules;[145] and the UK, which relied heavily on sector-specific regulation.[146] The Australian regime is thus codified but generic, applying to essential infrastructure across the entire economy: playing a 'backstop role' for infrastructure sectors that are otherwise unregulated.[147]

Under Part IIIA, there are three distinct (and alternative) avenues available for obtaining access to essential infrastructure 'services'. The infrastructure owner can provide access voluntarily by making formal undertakings to the ACCC. Such undertakings are accepted if deemed appropriate taking into account, *inter alia*, the interests of infrastructure service users and the service provider, and the public interest.[148] Alternatively, if a State or Territory implements a regional access regime, this might be declared as an 'effective access regime' for federal purposes.[149] Finally, the government or private individuals may apply to the National Competition Council (NCC), a public agency tasked with improving domestic competition policy, seeking a recommendation that a service be 'declared', thereby creating a right of access.[150] The NCC recommends declaration where four cumulative criteria are satisfied: (a) access would promote competition in another market; (b) it is uneconomical to duplicate the facility; (c) the facility is of national significance; and (d) there is no effective State, Territory or voluntary access regime in place.[151] The final determination is made by a government minister, who, in acting on this recommendation, must also be satisfied about an additional (e) public-interest requirement.[152] In contrast to access undertakings,[153] declaration does not establish a comprehensive access framework. Rather, declaration merely provides a right to access, which forms the basis for individual commercial negotiation. Where the parties fail to reach agreement on terms and conditions, Part IIIA provides for compulsory arbitration through the ACCC.[154]

In many ways – at least formally – access regulation under Part IIIA presents another paradigmatic example of hybridisation. The access framework derives explicitly from an antitrust concept, the essential facilities doctrine; arguably, Part IIIA merely codifies or operationalises

[145] Current US law is, of course, more equivocal: see p. 131. [146] See p. 154.
[147] See Productivity Commission, *National Access Regime. Productivity Commission Inquiry Report*, No. 66, 25 October 2013 (hereafter 'Productivity Commission Report'), pp. 11& 46.
[148] S. 44ZZA, CCA. [149] S. 44M, CCA. [150] Ss. 44F–44L, CCA.
[151] S. 44G(2), CCA. [152] S. 44H(4), CCA. [153] Reid & Burrows (1997:217).
[154] Ss. 44U–44ZUA, CCA.

this concept, already an element of the legal system by virtue of the prohibition on anticompetitive unilateral conduct in Section 46, CCA. The legislative decision to enact a specific, elaborated regulatory framework for applying this doctrine is nonetheless significant, given its relatively uncertain and contentious position within competition law. The enactment of a stand-alone access regime is, therefore, an acknowledgment of the difficulties of pursuing competition enforcement successfully under the doctrine. A central question is whether Part IIIA represents merely a partial codification, or instead an extension, of ordinary competition law. While, formally, the regime applies *concurrently* with the prohibitions in Section 46, CCA,[155] the weight of academic commentary suggests that Section 46 now functions as a 'fall-back mechanism' or residual power, applying only in situations outside the access regime.[156] As the Hilmer Report acknowledged, access claims are unlikely to succeed under Section 46 in any event. The regulatory nature of Part IIIA is further amplified by *ex ante* usage, as declaration is determined on the basis of the market character of a facility rather than past anticompetitive conduct. Accordingly, the access framework is consistent with Gal's theory of partial regulation-by-declaration: namely, where the existence of monopoly creates a risk of anticompetitive abuse, an *ex ante* declaration of monopoly status heightens scrutiny and facilitates enforcement.[157]

Hybridised elements are also visible in the demarcation of decision-making. Enforcement requires the participation of the ACCC, NCC and government ministers. The central role assigned to the executive, as ultimate decision-maker, is controversial insofar as it suggests a politicisation of the declaration process. It originates in the Hilmer Report, which emphasised the need for political accountability given that decisions to mandate access involve important public-interest considerations.[158] On this view, the participation of government is necessary to legitimise the wealth-redistributive consequences that may result. Ministerial decision-making has been criticised nonetheless as inefficient; incompatible with the rule of law; a source of uncertainty, inconsistency and delay; and weakened by inherent conflicts of

155 S. 44ZZNA, CCA.

156 Marshall (2003:15–18); see also Korah (2000:242). Cf. Pengilley (1998:538), arguing that the legislation leaves the relationship between the access framework and antitrust unresolved.

157 Gal (2006), particularly fn. 16.

158 Hilmer Report, p. 250.

interest.[159] If the access regime were viewed as merely an explication of the essential facilities doctrine, the involvement of the executive in this fundamentally legal determination would raise questions regarding the independence, objectivity and fairness of decision-making. From a hybridised perspective, instead, ministerial involvement confirms the access regime's divergence from general competition law towards quasi-regulation, and, in theory, provides a measure of democratic accountability for its inherent trade-offs.

In practice, however, the Part IIIA regime appears to have had only a limited – and perhaps declining – impact. In the two decades since its introduction, there have been just six positive declaration decisions granting access to some or all of the services requested.[160] It has been postulated that the mere existence of the regime, with the underlying risk that involuntary access may otherwise be imposed, has encouraged market participants to agree to private consensual arrangements.[161] Yet, recent developments at both judicial and policy-making levels suggest a reluctance to embrace an understanding of the regime that would go much beyond the parameters of the (ostensible) underlying antitrust principle, and thus apparently repudiate the idea of Part IIIA as a fully hybridised power.

First, in *Pilbara Infrastructure*,[162] the highest court in Australia adopted an interpretation of Part IIIA that firmly envisaged its application in line with conventional competition law, rather than as a more expansive tool of quasi-regulation. In particular, the High Court held that the requirement of uneconomical duplication – criterion (b) of the statutory test for declaration[163] – involves an assessment of whether duplication could potentially be 'privately profitable',[164] rather than whether the facility comprises a natural monopoly[165] or whether mandatory sharing would bring a net social benefit.[166] This interpretation would bring the operation of Part IIIA closely in line with the cautious jurisprudence of the EU's Court of Justice in *Oscar Bronner*, which, as discussed, incorporated an 'indispensability' criterion into the test for essential facilities.[167] The High

159 Marshall & Mulheron (2003b:262–3).
160 Decisions taken between November 1995 and September 2013: Productivity Commission Report, p. 15.
161 Productivity Commission Report, at pp. 14.
162 *The Pilbara Infrastructure Pty Ltd* v. *Australian Competition Tribunal* [2012] HCA 36.
163 Contained in s. 44G(2), CCA.
164 *Pilbara Infrastructure*, para. 103.
165 *Pilbara Infrastructure*, para. 79.
166 *Pilbara Infrastructure*, para. 80.
167 Case C-7/97 *Oscar Bronner*, EU:C:1998:569, para. 41.

Court moreover grounded its approach in the 'basal competition principles' underpinning the CCA,[168] firmly rooting the access regime within the established corpus of competition law.

In tandem, a government review of the operation of Part IIIA, conducted by the Productivity Commission,[169] has similarly concluded that declarations of access should be confined to exceptional circumstances.[170] The Productivity Commission determined, specifically, that access is appropriate only where there is an 'enduring lack of effective competition, due to natural monopoly', and that its main objective should be to address allocative inefficiency.[171] Any contention that Part IIIA should, alternatively, be used to address wider social and economic issues such as income distribution or environmental concerns was expressly rejected.[172] In its approach to criterion (b), the Productivity Commission diverged slightly from the private profitability test approved in *Pilbara*, which, it considered, placed inadequate emphasis on the effectiveness of prospective competition. Nonetheless, it too adopted a demanding approach, recommending that this limb should require that total foreseeable market demand for the infrastructure services over the declaration period could be met at least cost by the facility.[173] It furthermore suggested reformulation of public-interest criterion (e), to place greater emphasis on the need for access to promote, rather than merely not impede, public-interest concerns.[174]

Although the differing approaches of the High Court and Productivity Commission suggest remaining ambiguity regarding the optimal scope of Part IIIA, the general tenor of each emphasises the need for restraint, and essentially, the antitrust-focused rather than regulation-focused nature of the regime. It is unarguable that Part IIIA is formally and practically distinct from, and almost certainly more interventionist than, the conventional competition rules as contained in Part IV of the CCA, including the Section 46 prohibition. Nonetheless, it appears that, in the future, application of Part IIIA will be conditioned by much the same limiting principles that underpin, and constrain, application of Part IV. This restrictive approach can be defended in the same manner that

[168] *Pilbara Infrastructure*, para. 100.
[169] An independent research and advisory body to the Australian government.
[170] Productivity Commission Report, particularly p. 247.
[171] Productivity Commission Report, p. 7. [172] Ibid.
[173] Productivity Commission Report, p. 19.
[174] Productivity Commission Report, p. 20–1.

expansive interpretations of the essential facilities doctrine are criticised: in order to protect economic freedom and preserve investment incentives.[175] It nonetheless raises questions, on the one hand, of whether the access regime provides additional value beyond ordinary competition law, and on the other, of whether a strict adherence to an efficiency-focused approach creates risks that legitimate non-economic benefits of access might be overlooked. Self-evidently, by interpreting Part IIIA in a manner that is effectively equivalent to competition law, one incorporates the limitations of the underlying antitrust rules. Such limitations may serve to prevent the abusive or anticompetitive application of the essential facilities doctrine in the competition enforcement context, yet it is not readily apparent that such limitations are necessary or helpful, given the more closely circumscribed parameters of Part IIIA. This fascinating tension – whether (often desirable) restrictions in the antitrust context should be followed *ad nauseam* where a market regulatory instrument departs from the conventional antitrust formulation towards a hybridised approach – is reflected most obviously in the final case study to be examined.

(ii) Section 5 of the Federal Trade Commission Act

Section 5 of the Federal Trade Commission Act (§5)comprises a standalone legislative provision that would appear to provide public enforcers with a broad power of market regulation that spans the boundary between competition law and regulation. It offers an especially interesting example for our purposes, insofar as it demonstrates clearly the reasons why a hybridised approach to market control may be rejected. Despite older Supreme Court precedents that would grant *carte blanche* to the FTC in its application of §5, the textual potential for this provision to function as a hybridised mechanism has not been embraced. Moreover, contemporary debates regarding its optimal scope reflect the inherent dangers as well as the rewards of extending the antitrust rules beyond established parameters. There is an apparent consensus that, even if the scope of §5 goes beyond that of the ordinary competition rules – that is, it represents a form of 'antitrust *plus*' – the provision remains firmly within the corpus of US antitrust. We examine §5 in the context of the hybridised-power rubric insofar as its formal structure hints at its

[175] See pp. 133–5.

potential to be utilised as such, and in light of much recent reconsideration of the appropriate role for §5 as a tool for 'economic regulation'[176] that is distinct – if at all – from ordinary antitrust.

Formally, §5 FTCA might best be described as an expanded antitrust power. Located within a formal competition law rubric, §5 is a provision of general application, enforceable by a federal antitrust agency, the FTC. Yet the powers granted to the FTC under §5, if interpreted in their ordinary sense, go considerably beyond the parameters of the discrete prohibitions contained within other federal antitrust. Under §5(1) FTCA, '[u]nfair methods of competition in or affecting commerce . . . are hereby declared unlawful'.[177] On its broadest interpretation, §5 could give the FTC the power to prohibit any business practice that is deemed 'unfair' – a potentially nebulous legal standard – without any need to establish monopoly power, concertation between firms, or even consumer harm.

The legislative history of §5 explains its expansive wording. The FTCA was enacted in 1914, and sought to address dissatisfaction about the perceived ineffectiveness of the Sherman Act. It was, therefore, expressly intended to be more aggressive and far reaching.[178] The statute established the FTC, and gave the agency an intentionally broad mandate under §5 to tackle market problems outside the purview of the (then restrictively interpreted) Sherman Act. If the discrete prohibitions on anticompetitive concerted and unilateral conduct contained within the Sherman Act represent the parameters of antitrust, then §5 FTCA was drafted to go *beyond* those limits, giving the FTC powers of market control that might appear closer to industrial policy tools.[179] The extent to which the scope of §5 FTCA actually expands beyond the established competition rules towards an antitrust/regulatory hybrid, however, has been a controversial question in theory and practice.

Older Supreme Court decisions granted §5 an expansive interpretation to match its wording,[180] confirming that §5 both encompasses *and* surpasses the Sherman Act.[181] The 'broad powers' of the FTC were emphasised, as 'well established with regard to trade practices which conflict with the basic policies of the Sherman and Clayton Acts even

176 Ohlhausen (2014:6–7). 177 Now 15 USC §45.

178 Hovenkamp (2011:66); Lande (2009:1); Kovacic & Winerman (2010:931); Balto (2005:1113).

179 Or even 'industrial policy on steroids': Sims (2013:3).

180 *FTC* v. *Cement Institute et al.*, 333 US 683 (1948); *FTC* v. *Brown Shoe Co.*, 384 US 316 (1966); and *FTC* v. *Sperry & Hutchinson Co.*, 405 US 233 (1972).

181 *Cement Institute*, 694.

though such practices may not actually violate these laws'.[182] Later, even this rule of thumb – that prohibited conduct should run contrary to competition policy, even if not the strict provisions of the antitrust rules – was rejected as an absolute requirement. In assessing fairness, the FTC may take into consideration 'public values beyond simply those enshrined in the letter or encompassed in the spirit of the antitrust laws'.[183] Thus, §5 has been viewed as a potential mechanism by which to address types of anticompetitive conduct outside the discrete Sherman Act prohibitions, including oligopoly behaviour,[184] incipient breaches such as invitations to collude,[185] or conduct that would constitute an abuse of dominance under Article 102 TFEU but that fails to satisfy the market-share threshold or falls outside the established categories of monopolisation under Sherman Act, §2.[186] On its face, §5 appears to fit neatly within the rubric of hybridisation, bringing antitrust towards the realms of more interventionist regulation.

Nonetheless, the more permissive approach to alleged anticompetitive conduct adopted by US courts in recent decades renders these older cases somewhat suspect.[187] Subsequent lower court decisions view §5 restrictively,[188] while, in *California Dental*, the Supreme Court declined to comment on its relationship with the Sherman Act.[189] In theory, the older rulings remain controlling, yet commentators express considerable scepticism as to whether so expansive an interpretation would survive appellate scrutiny today.[190] Contemporary readings of the Sherman Act

[182] *Brown Shoe*, 321. [183] *Sperry & Hutchinson*, 244.

[184] Hovenkamp (2011:647); Areeda & Hovenkamp (2006:at ¶302h6, p. 35); Elhauge (2008: 549).

[185] '[T]he Commission has power under § 5 to arrest trade restraints in their incipiency': *Brown Shoe*, 322; see also Hovenkamp (2011:647); Lande (2009:1); Ohlhausen (2014:18–19).

[186] Kovacic & Winerman (2010:930); Foer (2009), who similarly suggested that §5 FTCA might bridge the gap between Sherman Act, §1 and Article 101 TFEU by avoiding the sharp *per se*/rule of reason dichotomy.

[187] Kovacic & Winerman (2010:937); see also Statement of Commissioner Joshua D. Wright, 'Proposed Policy Statement Regarding Unfair Methods of Competition Under Section 5 of the Federal Trade Commission Act', published 19 June 2013 (hereafter 'Wright (2013b)'), p. 2.

[188] For example, *Boise Cascade Corp.* v. *FTC*, 637 F.2d 573 (9th Cir. 1980); *E.I. Du Pont De Nemours & Co. v. FTC*, 729 F.2d 128 (2d Cir.1984).

[189] *In California Dental Association* v. *FTC*, 526 US 756 (1999), fn. 4, considered by Hovenkamp (2011:646).

[190] Kovacic & Winerman (2010:944–5); Creighton & Krattenmaker (2009:2); Lande (2009:2); Areeda & Hovenkamp (2006:¶302h6,p. 35); and Ohlhausen (2014:17–18).

prohibit a broader range of conduct than at the time of the enactment of the FTCA, arguably lessening the need for §5 to perform its supplementary function.[191] As considered later, for many antitrust scholars such a broad interpretation is both unnecessary and undesirable,[192] because the prohibitions contained in the Sherman and Clayton Acts – including their deliberate limitations – represent the legal manifestation of efficient antitrust policy.[193]

In one sense, the scope of §5 FTCA is more restrictive than the Sherman Act: whereas the latter is enforceable by private litigants seeking damages, and the DOJ as a civil *and* a criminal offence, §5 FTCA is enforceable only by the FTC and only prospectively through 'cease-and-desist' orders, and only if a defendant breaches an order can fines be imposed. In this sense, enforcement of §5 is closer to *ex ante* regulation than typical *ex post* antitrust proceedings. Private individuals – who, unfairly or otherwise, are seen as motivated by personal profit rather than public interest – are excluded entirely. Section 5 thus plays a complementary role within US antitrust – the clearest types of anticompetitive conduct are subject to universal enforcement and heavy penalties, whereas more ambiguous conduct is prohibited prospectively and by a specialist agency[194] – through 'a mix of strategies to fully optimize the trade-off between over- and under-deterrence'.[195]

Despite the FTC's acknowledged institutional advantages in antitrust enforcement,[196] its experiences in enforcing §5 as a standalone provision – as distinct from enforcement of §5 as analogous to the Sherman or Clayton Acts prohibitions – have been described as comprising a 'bleak record' where failures outweigh successes.[197] In certain recent cases, the FTC has struggled even to agree upon and apply a consistent understanding of §5.[198] These difficulties are illustrated by several decisions concerning digital economy markets, and it may be no coincidence that problems arise in

[191] Ohlhausen (2014:5–6). [192] Areeda & Hovenkamp (2006:¶302h6, p. 35).

[193] Areeda & Hovenkamp (2006:¶302h1, p. 29); and Wright, 'What's Your Agenda?', Remarks of Commissioner Joshua D. Wright, Federal Trade Commission at the ABA Spring Meetings, Washington, DC, on 11 April 2013 (hereafter 'Wright (2013a)'), pp. 10–12.

[194] Balto (2005:1113–14).

[195] Elhauge (2008:181); also Kovacic & Winerman (2010:932); and Hovenkamp (2011:488): 'more aggressive substantive rules are appropriate when remedies are limited and the rules cannot be enforced by private parties'.

[196] See e.g. Wright (2013a), p. 12; and Wright (2013b).

[197] Kovacic & Winerman (2010:940); echoed by Wright (2013a), p. 7.

[198] Commissioner Ohlhausen has described the current FTC position as akin to 'a sea of uncertainty': see Ohlhausen (2014:3).

such sectors: on the one hand, the FTC faces novel products, novel business practices, and, potentially, novel forms of exclusion; yet on the other, technology markets are characterised by rapid innovation and apparently fierce competition, creating a risk that government intervention may be unnecessary or even counterproductive.[199] For not dissimilar reasons, we argued in Chapter 2, the European Commission, too, has made frequent use of the commitment procedure in this sector.[200]

In *N-Data*, a 3–2 majority of the FTC voted in favour of 'broadly (but appropriately) applying our unfairness authority' under §5 to accept a consent decree from a company accused of reneging on prior commitments within a technology standard-setting process. The majority viewed the §5 mandate expansively, arguing that 'unfairness' encompasses unjust, inequitable or dishonest competition, conduct contrary to good morals, deception, bad faith, fraud or oppression.[201] This approach, self-evidently, takes the §5 power considerably beyond the limits of the Sherman Act. By contrast, the minority treated §5 restrictively, as mirroring closely the established parameters of antitrust. Whilst acknowledging the expansive scope of §5 in theory, Chairmas Majoras emphasised the restraint adopted in practice, reflecting both an academic consensus about the appropriate boundaries of antitrust, and judicial views on the limits of administrative discretion.[202] For Commissioner Kovacic, the possibility of follow-on litigation premised upon novel case theories presented a particular concern. Although §5 is enforceable only by the FTC, he noted the likely spill-over effects at state level, where successful §5 enforcement might encourage plaintiff-friendly expansion of existing antitrust laws by state legislatures.[203]

The varying approaches adopted in the subsequent *Intel* and *Google* cases further confirm the unsettled and divisive nature of §5. In *Intel*, the initial complaint was framed in terms of anticompetitive monopolisation under §2 of the Sherman Act in addition to unfair methods of competition.[204] In an accompanying statement, however, Chairman Leibovitz and

199 OECD (2012). 200 See pp. 115–16.

201 Statement of the Federal Trade Commission, *In the Matter of Negotiated Data Solutions LLC*, File No. 0510094, published 23 January 2008.

202 Dissenting Statement of Chairman Majoras, *In the Matter of Negotiated Data Solutions LLC*, File No. 0510094, published 23 January 2008.

203 Dissenting Statement of Commissioner Kovacic, *In the Matter of Negotiated Data Solutions LLC*, File No. 0510094, published 23 January 2008.

204 See *In the Matter of Intel Corporation*, Docket No. 9341, Administrative Complaint issued on 16 December 2009, paras. 97–106.

Commission Rosch drew particular attention to the §5 claim, noting the FTC's 'broad authority', and its distinction from the Sherman Act.[205] Indeed, the alleged violations at issue – tying practices, fidelity rebates and refusal to deal – faced high hurdles to establish liability under the latter. When announcing the subsequent settlement, the FTC dropped any reference to monopolisation, and, instead, emphasised that §5 is 'broader than the antitrust laws' and cannot ground liability in private litigation.[206] This retreat appears to reflect both an absence of certitude regarding the contours of prohibited unilateral conduct under the Sherman Act,[207] and greater confidence and a more expansive reading of the potential parameters of the §5 power.

Google, like *N-Data*, again saw a clear division regarding the scope of §5. While the FTC chose, unanimously, to close the investigation, the Commissioners disagreed about whether the alleged behaviour might disclose a viable theory of harm. Three Commissioners considered that Google's alleged misappropriation, or 'scraping', of content from other websites could amount to an unfair method of competition, and two of those Commissioners found that restrictions on advertisers could similarly violate §5. In both instances, the FTC accepted voluntary commitments to discontinue the practices.[208] Yet Commissioners Ohlhausen and Rosch, while supporting the decision to close the investigation, were adamant that neither practice violated §2 of the Sherman Act *or* §5 FTCA. Both argued, moreover, that the driving rationale behind the enforcement of §5 is the same as the Sherman Act: namely, the prohibition of harm to competition and consumers.[209] Absent this organising force, standalone §5 cases would be 'completely adrift'.[210]

205 See Statement of Chairman Leibowitz and Commissioner Rosch, *In the Matter of Intel Corporation*, Docket No. 9341.

206 See Federal Trade Commission Press Release, 'FTC Settles Charges of Anticompetitive Conduct Against Intel', published 4 August 2010.

207 Contrast this with the approach of the European Commission, which found a clear breach of Article 102 TFEU by Intel relating to effectively the same practices: see Commission Decision of 13 May 2009 in Case COMP/C-3/37.990 – *Intel* (D(2009) 3726 final).

208 See Statement of the Federal Trade Commission Regarding Google's Search Practices, *In the Matter of Google Inc.*, FTC File Number 111–0163, published 3 January 2013, particularly fn. 2.

209 See Concurring and Dissenting Statement of Commission J. Thomas Rosch Regarding Google's Search Practices and Statement of Commission Maureen K. Ohlhausen, *In the Matter of Google Inc.*, FTC File No. 111–0163, both published 3 January 2013.

210 Statement of Commission Maureen K. Ohlhausen, *In the Matter of Google Inc.*, FTC File No. 111–0163, both published 3 January 2013, p. 2.

At its core, the disagreement here is conceptual, involving the critical question of whether §5 FTCA should be treated as a 'core' antitrust rule – and thus subject to the limitations within contemporary antitrust jurisprudence – or whether it should be expanded to a more interventionist instrument. The approaches of both the majority and minority in *N-Data* have been criticised as unduly polarised: either too narrow of an interpretation of §5 so as to render it meaningless, or too broad thus rendering it uncontrolled.[211] If we accept that §5 does not cover precisely the same ground as the Sherman Act, the question arises as to how expansively it should be interpreted; or, put another way, how far beyond the sometimes-narrow conventional rules, and in what direction, should §5 extend? At its broadest interpretation, §5 could prohibit any business conduct deemed 'unfair', without limiting factors such as any need to establish coordination, market-share requirements or consumer harm. At its narrowest, §5 would merely duplicate the established proscriptions of the Sherman Act, albeit under a vague combined formulation. Considered critically, both interpretations appear incorrect. Section 5 FTCA was expressly intended to go further than the Sherman Act, and so to interpret its ambit as congruent to the latter arguably goes against legislative intent. Yet, §5 FTCA remains situated within the wider body of antitrust, and cannot be divorced from competition policy considerations, analytical tools, or the overarching goal of consumer welfare.

Between these opposing interpretations, a variety of potential uses have been identified that go beyond the established limits of US antitrust, but fall short of a general market-wide regulatory power.[212] The most broadly accepted is in 'frontier cases', which fulfil the legal elements for a Sherman or Clayton Act violation, but where there is an absence of precedent confirming that the case theory fits within the established framework.[213] Under this approach, §5 functions as a vehicle for innovation;[214] yet this relatively narrow approach may exclude many activities that nonetheless cause consumer harm.

[211] Leary (2009:1).

[212] Cf. Ohlhausen (2014:18), querying the utility of categorisation, and arguing that the proper focus of attention is whether the particular conduct satisfies a set of *general* criteria for enforcement under §5.

[213] Leary (2009:1); Kovacic & Winerman (2010:948); Creighton & Krattenmaker (2009:3); Marshak (2011:1144–52).

[214] The controversial *Rambus* decision, overturned on appeal in *Rambus, Inc.* v. *FTC*, 522 F.3d 456 (DC Cir. 2008), would arguably have fared better as a §5 action, insofar it met

Alternatively, §5 could be used in so-called 'yes, but' cases, which meet the legal and economic requirements for a Sherman or Clayton Act claim, but which cannot be brought for policy reasons: restrictions that stem, largely, from a perceived need to restrict speculative and/or wasteful treble-damages actions (unavailable under §5).[215] This again limits the ambit of §5 to cases that satisfy the elements required under established antitrust – oligopoly conduct, for example, would remain excluded – yet represents an expansion to the extent that apparent public-policy-based restrictions could be overridden by competition concerns.[216] The benign view of public enforcement that this approach endorses has been challenged, however, on the basis that concerns regarding, for example, collateral costs of private litigation actually reflect the fundamental difficulty of accurately identifying anticompetitive conduct generally, difficulties that are faced equally by generalist judges *and* expert agencies.[217]

Finally, §5 might be used as a 'gap-filling' mechanism, deployed where there is identifiable harm to competition or consumers, but where one or more legal elements for the established antitrust prohibitions remains unsatisfied, such as absence of agreement under Sherman Act, §1, or where market shares do not reach monopoly levels under Sherman Act, §2.[218] Hovenkamp, for instance, advocated the use of §5 in such cases, but only exceptionally: where the practice appears to be anticompetitive but is not technically covered by antitrust, and the social cost of error appears small.[219] Although the rationale for gap filling is one of effectiveness, it has nonetheless been criticised. First, there is the 'fairly metaphysical' question as to what constitutes a 'gap' as such.[220] Apparent deficiencies in the coverage of antitrust might reflect deliberate political choices, and a balancing of interests between over- and under-protection. Second, there is a persistent fear that, by adopting an expansive interpretation of §5, it risks becoming 'untethered and

the legal and factual requirements of the Sherman Act but was unsupported by precedent: see Leary (2009:3).

215 Creighton & Krattenmaker (2009:3).

216 This approach might, e.g., enable the FTC to surmount the obstacles to antitrust enforcement in regulated sectors: see e.g. 'Is There Life After *Trinko* and *Credit Suisse*? The Role of Antitrust in Regulated Industries', Prepared Statement of The Federal Trade Commission before the United State House of Representatives Committee on the Judiciary Subcommittee on Courts and Competition Policy, Washington, DC, delivered on 15 June 2010, p. 14, arguing that application of §5 FTCA should permit the FTC to sidestep the 'potential strictures' of the *Trinko* and *Credit Suisse* case law.

217 Wright (2013a: 11–12).

218 Creighton & Krattenmaker (2009:3).

219 Hovenkamp (2011:647); see also Foer (2009).

220 Wright (2013a: 9).

standardless',[221] creating a potential for unbounded liability.[222] This creates problems of legality, and may call into question the underlying efficiency of the prohibited conduct and potential 'chilling effect' of erroneous proscription.

The central advantage of embracing a broad interpretation of §5 is flexibility. Echoing more general arguments considered earlier in favour of a hybridised approach to market control, such flexibility leads to increased effectiveness in addressing anticompetitive behaviour. The provision thus may enable the FTC to prohibit conduct that impacts negatively on competition, even if it falls outside the ordinary, sometimes-narrow antitrust proscriptions. A key aim of Congress, when enacting the FTCA, was to counteract 'human inventiveness' in devising novel yet technically legal forms of anticompetitive behaviour.[223] Under §5, a broad variety of market failures that cause harm to consumers can be corrected, without need for recourse to the more time-consuming, costly and intrusive mechanism of sector-specific regulation. By entrusting the enforcement of §5 to a public agency, determination of 'unfairness' is made in the general interest rather than private self-interest. Where a broader approach to §5 has been accepted, it is generally on the basis that the 'institutional comparative advantage'[224] of the FTC – a specialist antitrust agency, where only prospective remedies are available – means both that the risk of false positives is lower, and the social costs of any such errors are lower than in other areas.[225] Thus, the benefits of hybridisation can be achieved but also contained.

Yet, flexibility, insofar as it leads to vagueness in terms of the legal standard, is also one of §5's principal flaws, and thus leans against robust categorisation of the provision as a hybridised instrument. From a legality perspective, an expansive reading of §5 may be criticised because it facilitates antitrust enforcement against business behaviour that was not clearly prohibited beforehand, contrary to the principles of *nulla poena sine lege* and legal certainty.[226] Such concerns are evidently tied to a conception of §5 a source of individual liability, while the prospective nature of the penalty imposed is likely to be cold comfort to firms facing what is, effectively, retrospective penalisation. It has therefore been argued that §5 should address only anticompetitive behaviour capable

[221] Leary (2009:1). [222] Creighton & Krattenmaker (2009:7–8).
[223] Marshak (2011:1130). [224] Kovacic & Winerman (2010:947).
[225] Hovenkamp (2011:200). [226] Similarly, *see* Wright (2013b: 9–10).

of adequate differentiation from permissible behaviour.[227] In this vein, there have been prominent calls for issuance of formal guidance regarding the scope of §5 and future enforcement priorities of the FTC.[228] This would, arguably, provide a greater legal certainty for businesses while allowing the FTC to advance a perhaps more proactive vision for §5 enforcement than simply re-treading the path of the Sherman and Clayton Act prohibitions, although both the necessity and the practicality of this task has been challenged.[229]

More expansive interpretations of §5 also face opposition as potentially harmful to competition – and thus wildly counterproductive in practice – insofar as pro-competitive practices may be proscribed in error. The central notion that US antitrust represents a 'consumer welfare prescription'[230] thus finds reflection within contemporary notions about the optional structure of the prohibition.[231] The efforts to produce draft guidance on §5 reflect a degree of convergence regarding the proposition that it ought only to target behaviour that causes harm to the process of competition, yet more technical issues, such as the treatment of efficiencies, remain disputed.[232] 'Unfairness' is not so much a public-policy- or even morality-oriented concept but rather an economic one.[233] The rationale for such 'regulatory humility'[234] reflects the maxim that 'hard cases make bad law': in order to avoid the risk that over-vigorous enforcement under §5 may have unwanted negative impacts on competition many commentators would prefer to incorporate the same safeguarding elements that limit the scope of the Sherman Act itself.

Finally, expansive interpretations of §5 may create political risks: that is, the danger that a broad application of §5 will trigger legislative efforts to curtail the FTC's power.[235] If the FTC attempts to reclaim the full hybridised textual scope of its §5 power, it thus runs the dual risks that earlier expansive precedents might be overturned by contemporary courts and/or that this may trigger a legislative retrenchment insofar as current political thinking is less enthusiastic about entrusting substantial market-moulding power in the hands of government agencies.

227 Areeda & Hovenkamp (2006:¶302h3, p. 32).
228 See, e.g., Wright (2013b), and Ohlhausen (2014).
229 See, e.g., Pozen & Six (2013); Global Competition Review, *Brill questions need for and feasibility of section 5 statement*, published 21 August 2013.
230 Hovenkamp (2005:31). 231 Rosch (2009: 2); Salop (2013:5).
232 Compare, e.g., Wright (2013b) and Ohlhausen (2014). 233 Wright (2013b:5).
234 Ohlhausen (2014:8). 235 Kovacic & Winerman (2010:943); Ohlhausen (2014:18).

Current interest in the scope of §5 FTCA reflects both the claimed inadequacy of conventional antitrust in addressing the panoply of market behaviour harmful to consumer welfare, and the understandable reluctance to expand these rules within a system where enforcement is undertaken mostly by self-interested private plaintiffs seeking treble damages. It is within this context that the potential evolution of §5 to represent something akin to a hybridised power must be understood. Allowing §5 a more overt regulatory flavour would permit the FTC to exercise its expert discretion to tackle problematic markets in a more holistic and targeted manner, yet without need for recourse to wholesale sector-specific regulation. The risks of both judicial and political push-back, however, reflect more general concerns about whether even an expert body can successfully pre-empt the market mechanism, and whether redistributive choices that might be required can legitimately be entrusted to such an agency. The central (and unresolved) question might be reformulated as the extent to which the limitations of conventional antitrust should be seen as unhelpful shackles or necessary safeguards, regardless of the enforcement context. Is an expansive vision of §5 necessary because ordinary competition law is too narrow while sectoral regulation is too all-encompassing – or, conversely, would the evolution of §5 be unnecessary precisely because this conventional division of labour between competition law and regulation reflects an unavoidable balancing of the strengths and weaknesses of each? In this regard, the lessons and complications of the §5 debate have broader implications that resonate across the whole of this work.

IV. Conclusions

This chapter set itself the task of further examining the substantive relationship between competition law and economic regulation by reference to institutional factors that may condition the interrelationship between these instruments. The overarching 'golden thread' that links the case studies considered is the notion that institutions are, to a large extent, the gatekeepers for deployment of these instruments, and that, sometimes, it can be institutional dynamics as much as the nature of the market problem at issue that may determine how a market defect is addressed and why. The allocation of enforcement jurisdiction between public enforcers does not necessarily require that antitrust powers be assigned only to the antitrust agency, nor economic regulatory powers only to the sector-specific regulator. Building on work from earlier chapters, we also saw that institutional dynamics and more overtly 'political' considerations may dictate or restrict the extent and direction in which an agency exercises its powers. In setting out our overarching conclusions in the final chapter, we throw private competition enforcement into this mix, reflecting upon the extent to which the nature of the antitrust plaintiff may affect both the application of competition law and its relationship with economic regulation. Yet this chapter was not merely concerned with institutional questions of a political nature, but also with institutional structures that facilitate a more nuanced approach to the interaction of competition law and economic regulation. In this regard, we gave particular consideration to market study procedures, which provide a formalised mechanism for identifying the optimal combined application of these mechanisms to address particular market problems, as well as the concept of hybridised powers, which unite substantive elements of each within a single legal instrument. Mirroring themes throughout this work, in relation to each we identified significant benefits that can result through departure from a more rigid separation of antitrust and regulatory functions, but also certain risks, both of legal legitimacy and economic coherence, that might follow. These diverging consequences are developed in our final, concluding chapter.

6

Analysis and conclusions

Our aim, in this work, was to provide a considered yet systematic account of the parameters of the relationship between competition law and economic regulation as mechanisms for market supervision and control. In the course of the preceding chapters we thus moved from individualised assessment of these instruments as discrete mechanisms for market supervision to consider their potential overlaps, conflicts and the influence that each may exert on the other. Two opposing conceptual models, identified from the existing literature, were explored in Chapter 1, whereby competition law and regulation are envisaged as wholly distinct and mutually exclusive market control mechanisms, or conversely, as complementary iterations of the same broader category of market regulatory tools. These dichotomous conceptions, both too narrow and unyielding to convey the full complexity and extent of this relationship, represent instead the polarised potential parameters of the interface between competition law and regulation, and might, in particular, explain the competing impulses towards convergence and divergence that arise. Throughout the more complex account that followed, therefore, glimpses of both dichotomous conceptions of the interface between competition law and regulation have, at times, been discerned.

We began, separately, with the concepts of competition law and economic regulation. Competition law was conceived as a series of discrete prohibitions on anticompetitive market behaviour that aim, broadly, at protecting competitive markets and advancing consumer welfare; economic regulation was formulated more expansively, encompassing State-imposed, positive, coercive alteration of or derogation from the market mechanism in order to address market defects, yet distinguishable from regulation that pursues a predominantly 'social' aim. While the pursuit of efficiency has been recognised as a, if not *the*, central concern of most antitrust systems, regulation can legitimately pursue a much broader range of social policy goals that might, conceivably, involve complete departure from the efficiency standard. We then considered some of the conventional distinctions between the operation and effects of competition law and regulation, which reinforced our initial approach of construing these instruments as separate and distinct market-supervisory mechanisms. In the chapters that followed, however, a more complicated and interlinked relationship between these instruments emerged, which challenged the simplicity and neatness of these earlier assumptions.

Chapter 2 examined developments towards a more 'regulatory' conception of competition law, which may incorporate processes, remedies and even legal obligations that depart from the archetype of competition law sketched initially. Chapter 3 considered a roughly equivalent movement within regulation, either as part of a wholesale deregulatory agenda, through the use of 'competition for regulation' in pursuit of liberalisation, or as a search for more effective regulation, thereby exposing greater space for competition and a consequent increased need for antitrust supervision. Clear limits were seen within both chapters. Regulatory antitrust has been strongly resisted at a doctrinal level, as demonstrated by our discussion of the essential facilities doctrine and the treatment of excessive prices. Similarly, regulation remains practically indispensable in markets where structural or distributional concerns would render a strict market-oriented outcome undesirable. Cognisant of these shifts within antitrust and regulatory thinking, and also of their limitations, Chapter 4 waded further into this complicated relationship, considering the concurrent application of competition law in regulated markets. The interconnectedness of our overall account thus became apparent: while liberalisation may create space for competition law, market problems that arise in deregulated sectors may be ill-suited to conventional antitrust doctrines and enforcement mechanisms, while the continued presence of partial regulation may complicate the competition analysis. Another consideration also came to the fore in this chapter, namely the distinction between public and private enforcement of competition law, and the different motivations that drive both forms of enforcement. A paradoxical conclusion began to emerge: that the distinction between competition law and regulation may be, somehow, both untenable yet inevitable. Finally, Chapter 5 gave consideration to certain institutional issues that can inform policy decisions regarding whether to proceed by means of competition law or regulation or both.

In this final chapter, we attempt to make sense of the strands of argument and interim conclusions that have emerged thus far. A starting premise of this work was the intricate, multidimensional nature of the relationship between competition law and regulation, and consequently, the relative impossibility of defining any set, universally applicable parameters. Various broad conclusions can, nonetheless, be drawn based upon the observations of the preceding chapters. The analysis within Chapters 2 to 5 has, perhaps unsurprisingly, reaffirmed our starting assumption that the relationship between competition law and regulation is considerably more complex, and indeed ambiguous, than the unequivocal standpoints represented by the dichotomous conceptual models presented in Chapter 1. Our analysis has highlighted, in particular, the influence of policy factors rather than purely legal considerations in determining the boundaries between competition law and regulation as market-supervisory instruments, as well as their interactions. Indeed, although this work eschews political ideology, we have seen how such concerns – from social democracy to neoliberalism, from anti-federalism to populist fears regarding aggregations of private power – have tended to have a larger impact than one might think in determining the parameters of the law. Such policy, and even overtly political, considerations may arise at a legislative, executive or even judicial level. Accordingly, there is relatively limited scope for defining any precise all-encompassing theory of this relationship that can, *a priori*, predict and account for each dimension of interaction and intersection between these legal mechanisms.

Our assessment nonetheless suggests that the relationship between competition law and economic regulation is shaped, to a significant extent, by factors and impulses that are internal to these discrete mechanisms. More specifically, the particular understanding of competition law that is adopted within a jurisdiction may determine, to a large extent, the permissible parameters of this relationship. Throughout this work, we have encountered a series of antitrust policy issues – such as private enforcement or regulatory case theories – the resolution of which may advocate for or against very different conceptions of competition law in practice. Recognising the central influence of debates regarding the optimal parameters of competition law within a jurisdiction also supports our conclusion that there is no external formulation that can define, *a priori*, the association between these instruments, given that the differing visions of competition law that can be adopted have an appreciably different impact upon the competition law/regulation interface. This argument is developed and explored further in this chapter.

Finally, throughout this work several recurring themes have emerged that pose continuing challenges in terms of striking a successful balance between competition law, regulation and the market itself. These include the need to accommodate general welfare promotion with individual rights, the appropriate role for the principle of efficiency, and the balancing of democratic accountability against the risks of political interference. These issues, which are likewise considered in greater detail in this concluding chapter, may serve to provide something of a general framework by which to assess and determine the most appropriate parameters for the competition law/regulation interface in any set of circumstances. Building upon these recurrent observations, a related conclusion of this work is the need to acknowledge, and in some extent to rehabilitate, the still-vital role for economic regulation in certain circumstances in pursuing important social goals, which can include efficiency. We have argued, not controversially, that efficient markets are not a socially valuable end in themselves. Whilst it is practically possible to apply competition law in a more strategic manner in furtherance of non-market goals, this work has queried, to an extent, the wisdom and necessity of doing so in certain instances. From an antitrust perspective, the pursuit of so-called regulatory goals may cause difficulties both from an efficiency and a legitimacy perspective, given that antitrust, unlike unconventional regulation, is premised upon individual liability. From a regulatory perspective, antitrust enforcement can provide temporary respite from on-going market defects but is unlikely to provide a more permanent or comprehensive solution. The movement towards a more regulatory conception of competition law would appear to raise an obvious question: why not simply regulate, particularly where the market difficulty is of an enduring structural nature or where intervention is motivated, primarily, by the pursuit of non-market goals? The criticisms of regulation discussed in Chapter 3 may explain a certain political reluctance to regulate, but there should perhaps be greater emphasis placed on the desirability of regulatory intervention, at least in certain appropriate instances, and how this can be best achieved. In essence, in exploring the relationship between competition law and economic regulation, this work has sought to challenge the primacy afforded to the former within much contemporary discourse, and has argued, instead, that the continuing relevance of the latter should be recognised more directly, and indeed reinforced.

I. The central role of the concept of competition law

One overarching conclusion that emerges from our review of interactions between competition law and regulation is the importance of the conception of competition law that a jurisdiction adopts, in terms of shaping the parameters of the relationship between these instruments within a system. The definition of economic regulation that has formed the basis of our analysis posits a relatively expansive yet fairly constant notion of market intervention by the State, tailored to address certain types of market defects. Competition law, by contrast, has traversed a wider spectrum of what Yeung termed legal 'paradigms of liability',[1] which may shift the antitrust archetype closer to, or further from, the archetype of regulation. Given these variances within the very conception of competition law, and the ensuing consequences that such divergence can have in terms of approximation to our model of regulation, the terms of the relationship between competition law and regulation can be shaped, to a perhaps unexpected extent, by our answer to the question: 'what is competition law?'

As Chapter 1 described, antitrust regimes typically comprise a series of discrete prohibitions on forms of anticompetitive behaviour by firms. Much antitrust scholarship and case law converges around the notion that consumer welfare (sometimes reduced to bare efficiency) provides the primary goal for competition law, yet alternative objectives have been advanced in theory and pursued in practice. Three differing visions of the role for competition law within markets and society more generally, which, correspondingly, employ differing 'paradigms of liability', can be discerned. These conceptualise competition law's function as, respectively, a public wrong, a private wrong, or a regulatory tool. These alternative models are distinct but not necessarily mutually exclusive.[2] The nature and substance of the relationship *between* competition law and regulation is dependent, to a large extent, on which of these conceptions of competition law is adopted insofar as this can impact significantly on the degree of compatibility or overlap between these instruments within a legal system.

First, competition law can be construed as establishing a type of 'public wrong' against society as a whole. As discussed in Chapter 1, the economic case against monopoly points to the allocative inefficiency,

[1] Yeung (2012:319–21).

[2] The European Commission argues that public and private enforcement of competition law, which involves a mixture of punitive fines combined with private damages, should be viewed as 'complementary': see *Proposal for a Directive of the European Parliament and of the Council on certain rules governing actions for damages under national law for infringements of the competition law provisions of the Member States and of the European Union* (COM(2013)404 final), published 11 June 2013, p. 3.

deadweight loss and welfare-dissipating rent-seeking behaviour that tend to result. Arguably, all consumers suffer where there is an overall diminution in market competition. The 'moral' case against antitrust infringements focuses on the exploitation of consumers and/or equivalence to theft. By conceiving of competition violations as 'wrongs', the focus is upon the fault of the monopolising firm(s) and not merely the harm suffered. Unsurprisingly, a 'public-wrong' conception of competition law mandates a public response to breach, whether through use of administrative fines or criminal sanctions. Public enforcement demonstrates the societal interest in maintaining competitive markets by punishing infringements, thereby deterring future anticompetitive behaviour. The adverse effects of antitrust breaches, from this viewpoint, are felt on the market generally and across society, which necessitates and legitimises public enforcement.

Second, competition law might be perceived as a 'private wrong' against specific individuals. Although monopoly tends to result in allocative inefficiency, it may augment productive efficiency through a transfer of wealth from consumers to producers. Thus, the effective outcome of an antitrust infringement may be to disadvantage *specific* consumers (or, perhaps, competitors or other market actors) to the benefit of the infringing firm(s). While such an approach is, again, dependent upon the identification of harmful conduct by the defendant, the emphasis here is upon the specific losses incurred by distinct individuals rather than injury to the market more generally. This vision of competition law is, accordingly, largely premised upon private enforcement, the rationale for which is to empower individual consumers that have suffered distinct and quantifiable harms, which are attributable directly to an antitrust breach – for example, an inflated contract price following bid-rigging of a tender – to obtain compensation for losses. Private enforcement reflects a more obligations-based approach: offending firms must make good the actual losses incurred by individual victims, a requirement that prioritises reparation over punishment.[3] Nonetheless, both of the 'public-wrong' and 'private-wrong' conceptions utilise the defendant's reprehensible conduct as a necessary element to trigger application of antitrust.

Beyond this conventional two-pronged approach, which balances public fines with private damages, a third conception of antitrust

[3] Lande (2010:9).

conceives of its prohibitions in more obviously regulatory terms as a means by which to correct market defects and secure improved performance. The economic rationale for a market failure or regulatory approach to antitrust is, again, the overall suboptimal market structures or outcomes that tend to follow from competition infringements. Unlike the public-wrong approach, however, the focus of this third conceptualisation is less upon the *fault* of the infringing firm(s) and more upon the overall *harm* to the market that results. Under this rubric, competition law is more readily interventionist than where it requires the identification of bad conduct, and it tends to embrace quasi-regulatory case theories and remedies with enthusiasm. Such an approach is, in particular, more likely to base liability for unilateral conduct on the mere existence of market power rather than its misuse. A regulatory conception of competition law tends to be more readily intrusive into the sphere of private conduct, and may involve wealth-redistributive choices that fall outside the purview of conventional approaches to competition law. For this reason, public enforcement is likely to be most appropriate in such instance; however, the primary aim here is to restructure the market for greater competition going forward rather than to punish the infringer(s) and/or compensate any victims. Where, by contrast, such a regulatory approach to competition law is enforceable through private litigation, this places a powerful tool for potential market reorganisation into the hands of essentially self-interested private parties.

This threefold categorisation – of public wrongs, private wrongs and market failures – offers a non-exhaustive account of the nature, and thus the roles, of the competition prohibitions. Although these conceptions are alternative and, to some degree, vie for acceptance, they are not mutually exclusive. A competition framework may incorporate aspects of both punitive and quasi-regulatory public enforcement, alongside private enforcement, although the presence of multiple competing visions may lead to inconsistencies or even doctrinal conflicts. In Chapter 4, we saw how misgivings regarding the potential misuse of private enforcement resulted in the constriction of general liability norms within US antitrust, while, in Chapter 5, we encountered arguments that the relative modesty of the enforcement framework for §5 of the FTCA merited a more expansive substantive ambit for this provision. A contemporary challenge within EU law is the need to accommodate the demand of private enforcement with protection of public-leniency programmes, with respect to access to material held by public enforcers. Although these competing conceptualisations of the role of antitrust do not necessarily exclude each other, they may, however, require different enforcement frameworks that are difficult to accommodate together. Identifying any 'optimal' account of competition law from amongst these three competing visions is not the purpose this work, however, insofar as it necessitates, to a large extent, policy choices rather than a strictly legal assessment.

The particular vision of competition law adopted nonetheless has important ramifications in terms of the appropriate substantive content of antitrust itself. Where application of competition law results in burdensome punitive or retributive sanctions, liability ought to be grounded in personal misconduct by defendant firms. That is, a defendant should be punished or held individually responsible only for its own bad acts rather than shortcomings of the market more broadly. Regulatory theories of competition law would therefore appear to be inappropriate within the conventional law enforcement and private enforcement models of competition law. The regulatory conception of competition law provides enforcers with unusually strong powers to mould the shape and direction of markets – powers that go beyond the simple proscription of undesirable behaviour and, essentially, allow enforcers to impose their conception of a well-functioning market on market actors. Private enforcement of such powers is inappropriate given that private litigants can be expected to act only in their own self-interest rather than in the interest of general consumer welfare. Public enforcement is arguably more acceptable, yet competition adjudicators may lack democratic accountability for the policy choices inherent within such case theories. Enforcement by a politically accountable executive body is perhaps most appropriate from this perspective, yet this renders competition law almost indistinguishable from regulation, sacrificing the comparative advantages of antitrust.

From just this brief overview, it becomes readily apparent how and why the conception of competition law adopted can impact upon the contours of the relationship between antitrust and regulation. Antitrust as a tool for either law enforcement or compensating private injury – our first and second 'wrong'-based categories, which together mirror the crime/tort formulation of the Sherman Act – is far removed from the archetype of regulation, which addresses problematic markets rather than reprehensible conduct as such. In particular, 'wrong'-based conceptions require identification of individual acts of anticompetitive conduct that are attributable to defendants. To the extent that economic regulation represents an over-reaching of the market mechanism removing scope for independent anticompetitive action by private firms, it displaces the potential application of competition law, as we saw in Chapter 4. When competition law itself embraces regulatory elements, however, these distinct instruments effectively converge. Competition law is no longer distinct from regulation, but merely represents another means by which to impose essentially the same legal obligations and remedies. The existence of regulatory controls that may affect the defendant's behaviour does not bar concurrent application of competition law, under this view, insofar as the emphasis of the antitrust inquiry is focused upon the market structure rather than the defendant's conduct. The 'wrong' versus 'regulatory' accounts of competition law therefore reflect, to an extent, the more polarised substitutionary versus complementary theories of the relationship between competition law and regulation discussed in Chapter 1.

These tentative findings may help to explain the divergence between US and EU approaches to competition law and regulation that emerged in the preceding chapters. The purported rationalisation of US antitrust has resulted in a comparatively minimal conception of antitrust as public or private wrongs, involving relatively permissive substantive standards that limit intervention by both public and private enforcers. Given this approach, it is unsurprising that US law largely rejects doctrinal regulatory antitrust, although it embraces quasi-regulatory procedural tools such as consent decrees and administrative guidelines. Concurrent application of antitrust to regulated behaviour would appear to be largely impossible, an approach that chimes with US law's adherence to a strict wrong-based conception of competition law. As Chapter 4 discussed, this restrictive approach is attributable, in large part, to concerns that relate primarily to private enforcement, a model considered to be particularly vulnerable to abuse and inefficiency. Formally, however, these restrictions relate to the substance of antitrust, and therefore affect both private *and* public enforcement. A spill-over effect of sorts can be discerned between the three conceptions of competition law: a rejection of the regulatory model in the context of private enforcement can lead to contraction of general liability norms, which, in turn, restricts public agencies operating under the law-enforcement model.

Within the EU, a more interlinked approach to the relationship between competition law and regulation prevails. Despite the more recent adoption of an effects-focused approach, EU competition law continues to incorporate elements of our third, regulatory model, alongside public- and private-wrong aspects. This can be seen, most clearly, in the European Commission's strategic use of competition law to supplement liberalisation in sectors such as telecommunications and energy, where its enforcement activities have extended considerably beyond the boundaries of conventional antitrust. EU competition law has thus been invoked to remedy the adverse impact of incorrectly implemented national regulation, to provide a reinforced enforcement mechanism for domestic regulatory obligations, and even to circumvent political objections to more intensive liberalisation efforts arising at the EU level. In effect, the Commission treats competition law as essentially just another regulatory tool by which to pursue its liberalisation policy goals. This includes, almost by definition, a continual concurrent application of competition law within regulated markets. In this context, given the heavy emphasis placed upon the effectiveness of market supervision, the parallel aim found within EU competition law of assisting the development of the internal market perhaps comes to the fore. The Commission, accordingly, deploys EU competition law in a holistic manner alongside its other tools for market integration. Problems may potentially arise, however, if and when a 'competition culture' incorporating a substantial role for private enforcement – long advocated by the Commission – develops within the EU.[4] As with US antitrust, the EU law rules regarding concurrency and the permissibility of substantive regulatory case theories would appear to apply with equal force to both public and private enforcement. In contrast to the spill-over effects experienced in US antitrust, which resulted in restriction of public enforcement, the generous and generally applicable EU rules may instead facilitate excessive and potentially harmful private enforcement. It is considerably easier to defend a market-making role for the Commission, even if it lacks full political accountability, than such a role for private litigants pursuing purely private interests. This is particularly the case to the extent that regulatory conceptions of antitrust permit competition enforcers to pursue and potentially impose their own vision of well-functioning markets, incorporating into competition law more general policy choices considerably beyond the established parameters of antitrust policy.

Our reasoning might also explain the application, or lack thereof, of competition law in newly deregulated markets. Unless antitrust is clearly distinguished from regulation, the influences that motivate deregulation may also lean against application of antitrust. The deregulatory agenda of

[4] European Commission, White Paper on Damages Actions for Breach of the EC Antitrust Rules, COM(2008)165, published 2 April 2008, at p. 3.

the Reagan administration, discussed in Chapter 3, coincided with a period of retrenchment within US antitrust, whereby both courts and public enforcers turned against interventionist antitrust doctrines. By contrast, the Thatcherite government enacted a more powerful antitrust statute, the Competition Act 1980, apparently to complement its small government agenda. The critical difference between these jurisdictions lies in the nature of the existing antitrust rules that would otherwise have applied in deregulated market. At that point, the USA had a well-established antitrust framework that was, however, increasingly criticised for its regulatory leanings and a perceived lack of economic rigour. By contrast, UK competition law was in its relative infancy, and the 1980 Act marked a departure from the existing quasi-regulatory system towards an effects-based approach in line with the conventional law-enforcement model of antitrust. This otherwise unusual divergence actually supports the argument that the model of competition law adopted within a jurisdiction conditions its relationship with regulation *and* with the process of deregulation.

The role of hybridised legal powers, considered in Chapter 5, might also be explained by reference to this antitrust-centric perspective. The various hybridised approaches considered – the UK's market inquiry procedure, the access to infrastructure regime in Australia, and §5 of the FTCA in the USA – each provide a possible means by which to circumvent certain limitations within conventional competition law. Hybridisation may, for example, dispense with the need to identify individual instances of anticompetitive conduct, or provide explicit legislative support for doubtful case theories, or enable a decision-maker to impose quasi-regulatory remedies that better address competition problems. Enactment of discrete legal instruments for these purposes, distinct from the ordinary competition provisions, represents a tacit acknowledgement that competition law as such has limits. To this extent, the category of hybridised powers rejects the third, regulatory model of competition law outlined earlier, insofar as the inclusion of such powers within the generally applicable antitrust regime should, in theory, have abrogated any need for such extended powers. It might be argued, nonetheless, that, implicitly, the regulatory model of competition law provides a template of sorts for the fusion of regulation and antitrust contained within hybridised powers.

In arguing that competition law plays the decisive role in determining the boundaries of its relationship with regulation, the intention here is not to disregard the impact that economic regulation may have within a market. Nor can it be ignored that regulation, too, may take a variety of forms, ranging from conventional command-and-control rules to regulatory schemes that endeavour to work with or mimic the market mechanism to a far greater degree, thereby arguably shifting the paradigm of regulation towards a quasi-antitrust model. Yet, inherently, regulation involves a political decision to intervene in markets more proactively in pursuit of certain regulatory policy goals. By contrast, the 'wrong'-based models of competition law rely upon a defendant's reprehensible conduct to trigger application of the residually applicable antitrust rules, which might, themselves, be viewed as an oblique form of market intervention. Although regulation may take many forms, it cannot in substance adopt the residual law-enforcement model of competition law, whereas, conversely, competition law can, to an extent, adopt positive policy-focused controls that mirror regulation. So, for example, although EU telecommunications regulation utilises antitrust concepts in developing the regulatory framework, once incorporated into the telecommunications regime these concepts essentially become regulatory terms-of-art, and thus are not dispositive of competition law concerns relating to regulated conduct. In seeking to explain the different visions of the relationship between competition law and regulation that are discernible in both the literature and case law, it is most constructive to focus on the differing conceptions of competition law that may arise. In short, the extent and manner in which competition law is, itself, conceived of as a form of regulation, and applied in a manner analogous to regulatory mechanisms, has direct implications in terms of conditioning the interface between these legal instruments, at both a theoretical and a practical level.

II. Delimiting the interface between competition law and regulation: recurring issues

Thus far, this concluding chapter has endeavoured to explain how and why the particular model of antitrust adopted is central to conceptualising the interface between competition law and regulation. Yet this claim does not, in itself, account for the full complexity of this relationship. Throughout this work, various recurring tensions or concerns have arisen that, additionally, influence selection of the appropriate antitrust model as well as the ramifications that follow. These challenges encompass the accommodation of general welfare considerations with individual rights, the role for efficiency, and the need to balance democratic accountability with risks of political interference. As suggested earlier, the implication of these recurring concerns may be that economic regulation should be preferred as a means of market supervision in certain circumstances, particularly where antitrust would struggle to achieve an effective or just outcome. Yet mandating deference to regulation is certainly not the object of this exercise; instead, our aim is simply to highlight significant concerns that should, ideally, find some reflection in whatever configuration between competition law and regulation is adopted.

(i) General welfare versus *individual rights*

The first overarching concern that arises is the need to balance considerations of general social welfare against respect for the rights of individuals, an issue that has been phrased elsewhere in this work as, alternatively, the balancing of effectiveness against legitimacy. Concerns of this sort arose, *inter alia*, in Chapter 2, when we considered the legitimacy of the shift towards regulatory competition law; in Chapter 4, when we examined rule-of-law objections to the concurrent application of competition law in regulated markets; and in Chapter 5, when we assessed the appropriateness of use of so-called hybridised legal powers to circumvent restrictions within either competition law or regulation. The crux of this concern is the difficulty of accommodating two compelling yet potentially conflicting values: the desirability of correcting market defects in order to improve the general welfare of society, and the need to protect the rights of individuals from undue interference by the State (or even other private parties).

It is not disputed here that natural and legal persons may legitimately be required to modify their behaviour or structures under either an antitrust or a regulatory rubric where such obligations benefit society as a whole and are imposed in accordance with the rule of law. Difficulties might arise, however, if this final element – rule-of-law compliance – is not fully respected. As the examples discussed in the preceding chapters demonstrate, such problems arise, not infrequently, where the boundaries between the concepts of competition law and regulation become blurred. There may therefore be a borrowing or sharing of legal powers between instruments, sometimes minus incorporation of the safeguards that constrain this power in its original incarnation. Alternatively, where competition law and regulation are applied concurrently, sufficient account must be taken of the impact of each in order to avoid distortions that aggravate individual liability unjustly. In constructing an appropriate framework to govern the relationship between competition law and regulation, a proviso should be added: the rights of individuals must be recognised and adequately respected, even when acting in pursuit of broader social welfare. This links to the observation that, where the nature of market problem at issue means that competition law would struggle to provide a robust and effective solution, it may be more appropriate to deploy economic regulation (even acknowledging its many imperfections in practice) than to distort competition law to achieve a regulatory-type solution.

(ii) The role of efficiency

The second issue of more general concern is the appropriate role for the efficiency criterion within this relationship. Although the exact status of the economic concept of efficiency within the antitrust context remains disputed, efficiency plays at least a substantial role in administering 'wrong'-based conceptions of competition law in many jurisdictions. While regulation might pursue efficiency, it can also additionally or alternatively pursue a wide range of non-economic social values. Even to the extent that regulation aims at efficiency, it often does so less effectively than competition law, which can harness the efficiency-generating power of the market mechanism more readily. These differing aims and approaches to this issue may, therefore, cause difficulties when delimiting the antitrust/regulation relationship.

There is, first, a fundamental problem in terms of accommodating efficiency and alternative non-economic values within a market system. As discussed in the Chapter 1, efficient markets are considered to deliver numerous social benefits, particularly in terms of maximising societal wealth overall and fostering technical progress. Yet efficiency, as such, is not an end in itself. While a regulated market may appear inefficient when viewed from an antitrust perspective, it may deliver an optimal social outcome when non-economic goals are taken into account. In applying competition law in regulated markets, it is necessary to grapple with the risk of not merely unfair but also counterproductive outcomes, as considered in Chapter 4. Another issue is the extent to which the efficiency criterion can prompt or legitimise progress towards a more regulatory conception of competition law: that is, a departure from the wrongs-focused approach towards one that intervenes, not against bad conduct, but rather to secure the most efficient distribution. A claimed element of the shift towards competition law-as-regulation, this issue was considered in Chapter 2. While the deregulation movement posits that unencumbered markets deliver the most efficient outcomes, Chapter 3 demonstrated that this much-heralded claim may ignore the question of non-economic values, which frequently require regulation for protection. The inability of the market mechanism alone to generate an efficient outcome in circumstances where barriers to competition are of a structural nature, moreover, may result in phenomena such as 'regulation for competition' in the context of liberalisation, or even more hands-on regulatory intervention such as rate-making, where regulation becomes necessary to avoid greater inefficiency. Finally, in Chapter 5, we considered whether legal powers should adopt or depart from a straightforward efficiency model, in view of the hybridised nature of the instrument involved.

From this brief overview, it is clear that the task of delimiting the relationship between competition law and regulation requires, amongst other things, an accommodation between the principle of efficiency and non-economic values. In cases of conflict, difficult policy questions can arise regarding the extent to which efficiency and its attendant benefits should be prioritised over other social values, when the advantages of each may well accrue to different social participants. The absence of an equity component means that efficiency is an inappropriate standard against which to measure *all* economic and social activity, although it can play a significant role in terms of setting the general tenor of economic policy. To the extent that competition law has or is becoming an efficiency-oriented concern, its proscriptions should not have the final word in demarcating the acceptable parameters of market behaviour without making sufficient allowance for other social values. In this respect, any assumption that antitrust should always trump economic regulation is flawed at best. By contrast, where a market-supervisory framework departs from the core efficiency standard, there is a need to secure sufficient political accountability for the inevitable policy choices that follow, an issue that we turn to next.

(iii) *Democratic accountability* versus *political interference*

The final recurrent theme is the balancing of democratic accountability against the risks of political interference. The law enforcement model of competition law is premised upon independent decision-making by dispassionate adjudicators who are free from political interference.

Regulation, by contrast, typically involves wealth redistributive policy choices, and therefore requires a degree of political involvement in order to provide some grounding in democratic accountability for such utilitarian activity. Where competition law and regulation become intermixed, the question is whether independence or accountability is more pressing to secure legitimacy. This links to the separation-of-powers concerns that have surfaced throughout this work, that is, whether a particular legal instrument or function should lie with the executive, the legislature or the judiciary.

Independence from government can help to avoid a misuse of legal processes to further vested interests, a key criticism of the public-choice movement. Yet, almost by definition as a mark of their independence, independent adjudicators lack political accountability. In certain circumstances, such decision-makers may be empowered or required to make determinations that have wealth redistributive impacts, such as in the regulatory antitrust case theories discussed in Chapter 2. In such cases, the policy choices inherent in this decision-making therefore fall outside the reaches of the conventional mechanisms for democratic control. The further that competition law, in particular, departs from a pure law-enforcement model, moreover, the more vulnerable it becomes to the whims of politics. An example of the conflicting considerations that can arise was seen in relation to the access power of Part IIIA, discussed in Chapter 5, which is subject to an ultimate requirement of ministerial consent. While critics argue that this requirement creates scope for politically motivated misuse, proponents consider it necessary to validate the wealth-redistribution choices inherent in the access regime.

In delimiting the antitrust/regulation relationship, a challenging but important consideration is whether protection from political interference or ensuring political legitimacy for decision-making should be the overriding consideration. This concern has parallels to the debate regarding the risks posed, respectively, by excessive concentrations of private market power or of public power.[5] The link to democracy, in theory, legitimates public power; yet even democratic institutions can fall prey to corruption and abuse. A powerful judicial (or quasi-judicial) branch can minimise the risks of capture and corruption; yet, particularly in this context, litigation may be used as a strategic tool by private interests seeking to resist regulation or simply impede their rivals, and thus

[5] Giocoli (2009:759–60); see also p. 28.

exercise private market power. Another difficult question we encountered is whether political stalemate or compromise when devising an economic regulatory framework provides grounds for ameliorative antitrust enforcement; or, to put the issue rather more provocatively, should law be able to subvert democracy in the interests of efficiency? In essence, the issue is largely one of trust: whether politicians, or public administrators, or judges, or even private firms can be best trusted to identify and secure the most advantageous outcome for society, which includes a balancing of other overarching concerns – protecting the rule of law while securing effectiveness, and the importance but also the limitations of efficiency – just considered.

III. Concluding remarks

This work set itself the task of analysing, though not quite defining, the relationship between competition law and regulation. The depiction of this relationship that has emerged from our mapping exercise incorporates both harmony and dissonance. Competition law and economic regulation are distinct but overlapping, largely complementary but not infrequently in conflict. As a tool for market control, regulation tends to operate in close proximity to markets under supervision, providing detailed bespoke solutions to particular market defects. Competition law, by contrast, operates at a more removed and residual level, offering a generalised and sometimes more dynamic response to many market issues, yet one which may not provide the best solution to address specific problems. Competition enforcement may more readily avoid the risks of capture and policy myopia that can have a negative impact upon regulation, however, and which result in regulatory failure. Neither policy instrument is perfect in itself, while each can, to a limited extent, compensate for the deficiencies of the other. Returning to the AT&T example outlined in Chapter 1, for example, Wu pointed to limitations within both US telecommunications and antitrust regulation that created scope for, and indeed perhaps necessitated, a holistic approach to supervision that incorporates elements of both.[6] Within the EU context, we have seen numerous parallel deployments of competition law and economic regulation, both to solve existing market defects but also, more proactively, to build towards the development of the internal market.

[6] Wu (2010:303–13).

Even absent this integration aim, something of a general progression towards convergence between competition law and sector-specific regulation can indeed be identified in many contemporary markets: telecommunications provide a particularly clear example.[7]

It would be unwise and potentially unjust, however, to advocate an indiscriminate combined approach to market supervision through competition law and regulation. Again within the US telecommunications context, for example, Epstein conversely attacked the redundancy and conflicts that result from extensive use of both within the sector.[8] Although competition law and regulation are largely complementary and compatible, they do not impose fully equivalent legal obligations. It cannot, therefore, be presumed that antitrust and regulatory goals always coincide or that the intended market outcomes are equivalent. While this work encourages an approach to the antitrust/regulation interface that gives due recognition to the largely interrelated character of these instruments, it necessarily adds certain notes of caution, intended to preserve the integrity of the market-supervisory enterprise. In cases involving individual liability, in particular, fairness to defendants should receive a degree of priority equal to the task of solving market failures, in order to protect the legitimacy of such State coercion. Correcting 'broken' regulation directly through regulatory reform is vastly preferable to indirect revision through antitrust enforcement. The pursuit of efficiency has limits; in particular, market interventions including deregulation must afford due deference to legitimate non-economic goals. Competition law is also a tool that appears less well suited to the pursuit of values outside the established competition-policy realm. While divergence from the conventional law-enforcement model of antitrust, including through use of hybridised powers, might be justified in many circumstances, it generates attendant risks and challenges that must be addressed.

In practice, formulation of bright-line rules that delimit enduring boundaries for the relationship between competition law and regulation is probably impossible. Instead, a more flexible standard may be necessary to reflect the complex and often contradictory nature of the influences and interactions that arise between competition law and regulation in practice. While flexible standards avoid the rigidity of concrete rules, they also sacrifice legal certainty to a degree. This work has sought to

[7] Auf'mkolk (2012:152); Cave & Crowther (2005). [8] Epstein (2007:114).

increase understanding in this area, and consequently certainty, by identifying legal, economic and policy factors that have an impact upon decision-making. While our analysis may not have produced any 'right answer' as such, it nonetheless performs the necessary task of identifying the required components to be used when assessing the 'most-right' configuration of the relationship between competition law and regulation under any given circumstances. This book began with the stated aim of exploring how these instruments, separately or together, might be deployed to help markets 'fail better'; it ends with the perhaps more positive observation that, utilised in a sufficiently nuanced yet precise manner, the application of competition law and economic regulation can, on the whole, make a significant contribution to successful market performance judged both in terms of efficiency- and non-efficiency-focused goals.

BIBLIOGRAPHY

Abbott, Alden F. (2011) 'A Tale of Two Cities: Brussels, Washington, and the Assessment of Unilateral Conduct'. 56 *Antitrust Bulletin*: 103.

Ackermann, Thomas (2010) '*Vodafone*: Price Regulation as a Substitute for Intervention under Article 102 TFEU'. 1(5) *Journal of European Competition Law & Practice*: 426.

Adhar, Rex (1995) 'The Privy Council and "Light-Handed Regulation"'. 111 *Law Quarterly Review*: 217.

(2010) 'The New Zealand Electricity Industry and the Limits of Competition Law'. 18 *Utilities Law Review*: 51.

Aghion, Philippe; Bloom, Nick; Blundell, Richard; Griffith, Rachel & Howitt, Peter (2005) 'Competition and Innovation: an Inverted-U Relationship'. 120 *Quarterly Journal of Economics*: 701.

Akman, Pinar (2009) 'Searching for the Long-Lost Soul of Article 82 EC'. 29 *Oxford Journal of Legal Studies*: 267.

Allio, Lorenzo (2007) 'Better Regulation and Impact Assessment in the European Commission'. In: Kirkpatrick, Colin & Parker, David (eds.) *Regulatory Impact Assessment*. Cheltenham, UK: Edward Elgar Publishing, pp. 72–105.

Almunia, Joaquín (2012) 'Competition Enforcement in the Knowledge Economy'. In: Hawk, Barry (ed.) *International Antitrust Law and Policy: Annual Proceedings of the Fordham Competition Law Institute*. New York: Juris Publishing, pp. 1–8.

Amato, Giorgio (1997) *Antitrust and the Bounds of Power*. Oxford, UK: Hart Publishing.

American Bar Association (ABA) Section of Antitrust Law (2007) *Antitrust Law Developments*. 6th edn. Chicago, IL: ABA Publishing.

Australian Competition and Consumer Commission (ACCC) (2004) 'The Benefits of a Single Australian Energy Regulator'. Speech by Ed Willett, Commissioner, delivered 16 August 2004, available online at www.accc.gov.au/media/speeches

Andrews, Peter (2007) 'Are Market Failure Analysis and Impact Assessment Useful?'. In: Weatherill, Stephen (ed.) *Better Regulation*. Oxford, UK: Hart Publishing.

Areeda, Phillip (1990) 'Essential Facilities: An Epithet in Need of Limiting Principles'. 58 *Antitrust Law Journal*: 841.

Areeda, Philip & Hovenkamp, Herbert (2006) *Antitrust Law*. 3rd edn. New York: Aspen Publishers.

(2011) *Antitrust Law: 2011 Supplement*. Maryland: Wolters Kluwer.

Armentano, D.T. (1985) 'Efficiency, Liberty and Antitrust Policy'. 4 *Cato Journal*: 925.

Armstrong, Mark (2001) 'Access Pricing, Bypass, and Universal Service'. 91 *The American Economic Review*: 297.

Armstrong, Mark & Huck, Steffen (2011) 'Behavioral Economics as Applied to Firms: A Primer'. *Antitrust Chronicle, Competition Policy International*, Vol. 2011(1).

Armstrong, Mark & Sappington, David E.M. (2006) 'Regulation, Competition and Liberalisation'. 44(2) *Journal of Economic Literature*: 325.

Arrow, Kenneth J. (1962) 'Economic Welfare and the Allocation of Resources for Invention'. In: Nelson, Richard R. (ed.) *The Rate and Direction of Inventive Activity: Economic and Social Factors*. Princeton, NJ: Princeton University Press.

Auf'mkolk, Hendrik (2012) 'The "Feedback Effect" of Applying EU Competition Law to Regulated Industries: Doctrinal Contamination in the Case of Margin Squeeze'. 3 *Journal of European Competition Law & Practice*: 149.

Ayres, Ian & Braithwaite, John (1992) *Responsive Regulation: Transcending the Deregulation Debate*. Oxford, UK: Oxford University Press.

Baer, Bill (2014) 'Public and Private Antitrust Enforcement in the United States'. *Remarks prepared for delivery to European Competition Forum 2014*, Brussels, Belgium, 11 February 2014, available online at www.justice.gov/atr/public/speeches/index.html

Baldwin, Robert (2007) 'Better Regulation: Tensions Aboard the Enterprise'. In: Weatherill, Stephen (ed.) *Better Regulation*. Oxford, UK: Hart Publishing.

Baldwin, Robert & Black, Julia (2008) 'Really Responsive Regulation'. 71 *Modern Law Review*: 59.

Baldwin, Robert; Cave, Martin & Lodge, Martin (2011) *Understanding Regulation*. 2nd edn. Oxford, UK. Oxford University Press.

Balto, David (2005) 'Returning to the Elman Vision of the Federal Trade Commission: Reassessing the Approach to FTC Remedies'. 72 *Antitrust Law Journal*: 1113.

Barnett, Thomas O. (2009) 'Section 2 Remedies: What to do after Catching the Tiger by the Tail'. 76 *Antitrust Law Journal*: 31.

Bator, Francis M. (1958) 'The Anatomy of Market Failure'. 72(3) *Quarterly Journal of Economics*: 351.

Baumol, William J. (1977) 'On the Proper Cost Tests for Natural Monopoly in a Multiproduct Industry'. 67 *American Economic Review*: 809.

(1999) 'Having Your Cake: How to Preserve Universal-Service Cross Subsidies While Facilitating Competitive Entry'. 16 *Yale Journal on Regulation*: 1.

(2002) *The Free-Market Innovation Machine*, Princeton, NJ: Princeton University Press.

Bavasso, Antonio F. (2004) 'Electronic Communications: A New Paradigm for European Regulation'. 41 *Common Market Law Review*: 87.

Beath, John (2002) 'UK Industrial Policy: Old Tunes on New Instruments'. 18(2) *Oxford Review of Economic Policy*: 221.

Becker, Gary S. (1976) *The Economic Approach to Human Behaviour*. Chicago, IL: University of Chicago Press.

Bergeron, James H. (2001) 'Antitrust Federalism in the European Union after the Modernisation Initiative'. 48 *Antitrust Bulletin*: 513.

Black, Duncan (1948) 'On the Rationale of Group Decision-Making'. 56 *Journal of Political Economy*: 23.

Black, Julia (2001) 'Decentring Regulating: Understanding the Role of Regulation and Self-Regulation in the 'Post-Regulatory World'. *Current Legal Problems*: 103.

Blair, Roger D. & Piette, Christine A. (2005) 'The Interface of Antitrust and Regulation: *Trinko*'. 50 *Antitrust Bulletin*: 665.

Bloom, Margaret (1999) 'The Impact of the Competition Bill'. In: McCrudden, Christopher (ed.) *Regulation and Deregulation: Policy and Practice in the Utilities and Financial Services Industries*. Oxford, UK: Clarendon Press.

Bolick, Clint (1995) 'Thatcher's Revolution: Deregulation and Political Transformation'. 12 *Yale Journal on Regulation*: 527.

Bollard, Alan E. & Pickford, Michael (1995) 'New Zealand's 'Light-Handed' Approach to Utility Regulation'. 2(4) *Agenda: A Journal of Policy Analysis & Reform*: 411.

Bork, Robert H. (1966) 'Legislative Intent and the Policy of the Sherman Act'. 9 *Journal of Law & Economics*: 7.

(1978) *The Antitrust Paradox: A Policy At War With Itself*. New York: Free Press.

Bortolotti, Bernardo & Milella, Valentina (2008) 'Privatization in Western Europe'. In: Roland, Gérard (ed.) *Privatization: Successes and Failures*. New York: Columbia University Press.

Boscheck, Ralf (2009) 'The EU's Third Internal Energy Market Legislative Package: Victory of Politics over Economic Rationality'. 32 *World Competition*: 593.

Bouckaert, Jan & Verboven, Frank (2004) 'Price Squeezes in a Regulatory Environment'. 26 *Journal of Regulatory Economics*: 321.

Brandenburger, Rachel & Janssens, Thomas (2007) 'EU Telecommunications: More or Less Regulation? (Part Two)'. 3 *In-House Perspective*: 14.

Brennan, Timothy J. (2005) '*Trinko* v. Baxter: The Demise of *U.S. v. AT&T*'. 50 *Antitrust Bulletin*: 635.

(2008) 'Essential Facilities and *Trinko*: Should Antitrust and Regulation be Combined?'. 61 *Federal Communications Law Journal*: 133.

Breyer, Stephen G. (1982) *Regulation and its Reform*. Cambridge, MA: Harvard University Press.

(1987) 'Antitrust, Deregulation and the Newly Liberated Marketplace'. 75 *California Law Review*: 1005.

Brock, James W. (2006) 'Antitrust Policy and the Oligopoly Problem'. 51 *Antitrust Bulletin*: 227.

Broder, Douglas (2010) *US Antitrust Law and Enforcement: A Practice Introduction*. New York: Oxford University Press.

Brunt, Maureen (2003) *Economic Essays on Australian and New Zealand Competition Law*. The Hague, The Netherlands: Kluwer Law International.

Buchanan, James M. & Tullock, Gordon (1962) *The Calculus of Consent: Logical Foundations of Constitutional Democracy*. Ann Arbor, MI: University of Michigan Press.

Burton, John (1997) 'The Competitive Order or Ordered Competition? The 'UK Model' of Utilities Regulation in Theory and Practice'. 75 *Public Administration*: 157.

Calabresi, Guido (1980) 'About Law and Economics: A Letter to Ronald Dworkin'. 8 *Hofstra Law Review*: 553.

Calvani, Terry (1979) 'Effect of Current Developments on the Future of the Robinson-Patman Act'. 48 *Antitrust Law Journal*: 1692.

Cameron, Peter D. (2005) 'Completing the Internal Market in Energy: An Introduction to the New Legislation'. In: Cameron, Peter D. (ed.) *Legal Aspects of EU Energy Regulation*. Oxford, UK: Oxford University Press.

Camesasca, Peter D. & Van den Bergh, Roger J. (2000) 'Irreconcilable Principles? The Court of Justice Exempts Collective Labour Agreements from the Wrath of Antitrust'. 25 *European Law Review*: 492.

Campbell, Thomas J. (1985) 'The Antitrust Record of the First Reagan Administration'. 64 *Texas Law Review*: 353.

Carlton, Dennis W. (2008) 'Should "Price Squeeze" be Recognised as a Form of Anticompetitive Conduct?'. 4 *Journal of Competition Law and Economics*: 271.

Carlton, Dennis W. & Picker, Randal C. (2006) 'Antitrust and Regulation'. *John M. Olin Law and Economics Working Paper No.312*, published October 2006.

Carstensen, Peter C. (1983) 'Antitrust Law and the Paradigm of Industrial Organization'. 16 *UC Davis Law Review*: 487.

(2008) 'False Positives in Identifying Liability for Exclusionary Conduct: Conceptual Error, Business Reality and *Aspen*'. *Wisconsin Law Review*: 295.

Cavanagh, Edward D. (2010) 'The Private Antitrust Remedy: Lessons from the American Experience'. 41 *Loyola University Chicago Law Journal*: 629.

Cave, Martin & Crowther, Peter (2005) 'Pre-emptive Competition Policy Meets Regulatory Antitrust'. 26 *European Competition Law Review*: 481.

Cengiz, Firat (2011) 'Judicial Review and the Rule of Law in the EU Competition Law Regime after *Alrosa*'. 7 *European Competition Journal*: 127.

(2012) *Antitrust Federalism in the EU and the US*. Oxford, UK: Routledge.

Chapman, Nathan S. & McConnell, Michael W. (2012) 'Due Process as Separation of Powers'. 121 *Yale Law Journal*: 1672.

Cheng, Thomas K. (2012) 'How Culture May Change Assumptions in Competition Policy'. In: Lianos, Ioannis & Sokol, D. Daniel (eds.) *The Global Limits of Competition Law*. Palo Alto, CA: Stanford University Press.

Clark, John M. (1940) 'Toward a Concept of Workable Competition'. 30 *American Economic Review*: 242.

(1961) *Competition as a Dynamic Process*. Washington, DC: The Brookings Institute.

Clarke, Michael (2000) *Regulation: The Social Control of Business between Law and Politics*. London, UK: Macmillan Press.

Coase, R.H. (1937) 'The Nature of the Firm'. 3 *Economica*: 386.

(1960) 'The Problem of Social Cost'. 3 *Journal of Law and Economics*: 1.

Colander, David; Föllmer, Hans; Haas, Armin; Goldberg, Michael; Juselius, Katarina; Kirman, Alan; Lux, Thomas & Sloth, Brigitte (2009) 'The Financial Crisis and the Systemic Failure of Academic Economics', *University of Copenhagen Department of Economics Discussion Paper* 09-03.

Colley, Liam & Burnside, Sebastian (2006) 'Margin Squeeze Abuse'. 2 *European Competition Journal*: 185.

Coleman, Martin & Grenfell, Michael (1999) *The Competition Act 1998: Law and Practice*. Oxford, UK: Oxford University Press.

Connor, John M. (2010) 'The Impact of International Cartels'. In: Foer, Albert A. & Cuneo, Jonathan W. (eds.) *The International Handbook of Private Enforcement of Competition Law*. Cheltenham, UK: Edward Elgar Publishing.

Cook, Christopher J. (2006) 'Commitment Decisions: The Law and Practice under Article 9'. 29 *World Competition*: 209.

Craig, Paul P. (1997) 'Formal and Substantive Conceptions of the Rule of Law: an Analytical Framework'. *Public Law*: 467.

Crampton, Paul S. & Facey, Brian A. (2002) 'Revisiting Regulation and Deregulation Through the Lens of Competition Policy'. 25 *World Competition*: 25.

Crane, Daniel A. (2008) 'Antitrust Antifederalism'. 96 *California Law Review*: 1.

(2009a) 'Bargaining in the Shadow of Rate-Setting Courts'. 76 *Antitrust Law Journal*: 307.

(2009b) '*linkLine*'s Institutional Suspicions'. *Cato Supreme Court Review 2008–2009*: 111.

(2011) *The Institutional Structure of Antitrust Enforcement*. New York: Oxford University Press.

(2012) 'A Neo-Chicago Perspective on Antitrust Institutions'. 78 *Antitrust Law Journal*: 43.

(2013) 'Judicial Review of Anticompetitive State Action: Two Models in Comparative Perspective'. 1(2) *Journal of Antitrust Enforcement*: 418.

Creighton, Susan A. & Krattenmaker, Thomas G. (2009) 'Appropriate Role(s) for Section 5'. 8(3) *Antitrust Source*, February 2009.

Cudahy, Richard D. (2001) 'Whither Deregulation: A Look at the Portents'. 58 *New York University Annual Survey of American Law*: 155.

Dabbah, Maher M. (2010) *International and Comparative Competition Law*. Cambridge, UK: Cambridge University Press.

(2011) 'The Relationship between Competition Authorities and Sector Regulators'. 70 *Cambridge Law Journal*: 113.

Daintith, Terence (1988) 'Law as a Policy Instrument: Comparative Perspective'. In: Daintith, Terence (ed.) *Law as an Instrument of Economic Policy: Comparative and Critical Approaches*. Berlin, Germany: Walter de Gruyter.

DeBow, Michael E. (1987) 'Judicial Regulation of Industry: An Analysis of Antitrust Consent Decrees'. *University of Chicago Legal Forum*: 353.

Decker, Christopher & Gray, Harriet (2011) 'Antitrust and Arbitration in Regulated Sectors'. 7 *Competition Law International*: 7.

Del Guayo, Iñigo & Pielow, Christian (2012) 'Electricity and Gas Infrastructure Planning in the European Union'. In: Roggenkam, Martha M.; Barrera-Hernández, Lila; Zillman, Donald N. & del Guayo, Iñigo (eds.) *Energy Networks and the Law*. Oxford, UK: Oxford University Press.

Delacourt, John T. & Zywicki, Todd J. (2005) 'The FTC and State Action: Evolving Views on the Proper Role of Government'. 72 *Antitrust Law Journal*: 1075.

Delgado, Juan & Mariscal, Elisa (2014) 'Integrating Regulatory and Antitrust Powers: Does It Work? Case Studies from Spain and Mexico'. 10(1) *Competition Policy International*: 135.

Department of Trade and Industry (DTI) (2006) *Concurrent Competition Powers in Sectoral Regulation. A Report by the Department of Trade and Industry and HM Treasury*, published May 2006, URN 06/1244.

Dempsey, Paul Stephen (1989) 'Market Failure and Regulatory Failure as Catalysts for Political Change: The Choice between Imperfect Regulation and Imperfect Competition'. 46 *Washington and Lee Law Review*: 1.

Demsetz, Harold (1968) 'Why Regulate Utilities?'. 11 *Journal of Law & Economics*: 55.

Devlin, Alan (2012) 'Antitrust as Regulation'. 49 *San Diego Law Review*: 823.

Dewey, Donald (1955) 'The Common-Law Background of Antitrust Policy'. 41 *Virginia Law Review*: 759.

Dogan, Stacey L. & Lemley, Mark A. (2009) 'Antitrust Law and Regulatory Gaming'. 87 *Texas Law Review*: 685.

Douglas-Scott, Sionadh (2011) 'The European Union and Human Rights After the Lisbon Treaty'. 11 *Human Rights Law Review*: 645.

Dunne, Niamh (2014) 'Recasting Competition Concurrency under the Enterprise and Regulatory Reform Act 2013'. 77 *Modern Law Review*: 254.

Dworkin, Ronald (1980a) 'Is Wealth A Value?'. 9 *Journal of Legal Studies*: 191.

(1980b) 'Why Efficiency? A Response to Professors Calabrese and Posner'. 8 *Hofstra Law Review*: 563.

Dyzenhaus, David (2001) 'Hobbes and the Legitimacy of Law'. 20 *Law and Philosophy*: 461.

Easterbrook, Frank H. (1983) 'Antitrust and the Economics of Federalism'. 26 *Journal of Law and Economics*: 23.

(1984) 'The Limits of Antitrust'. 63 *Texas Law Review*: 1.

(1986) 'Workable Antitrust Policy'. 84 *Michigan Law Review*: 1696.

(1987) 'Justice and Contract in Consent Judgments'. *University of Chicago Legal Forum*: 19.

Economides, Nicholas (2005) 'Vertical Leverage and the Sacrifice Principle: Why the Supreme Court got *Trinko* Wrong'. 61 *New York University Annual Survey of American Law*: 379.

Einhorn, Michael A. (2001) 'Intellectual Property and Antitrust: Music Performing Rights in Broadcasting'. 24 *Columbia-VLA Journal of Law & the Arts*: 349.

Eisner, Marc Allen & Meier, Kenneth J. (1990) 'Presidential Control versus Bureaucratic Power: Explaining the Reagan Revolution in Antitrust'. 34 *American Journal of Political Science*: 269.

Ehlermann, Claus Dieter (2000) 'The Modernization of EC Antitrust Policy: a Legal and Cultural Revolution'. 37 Common Market Law Review: 537.

Elhauge, Einer (1991) 'The Scope of Antitrust Process'. 104 *Harvard Law Review*: 667.

(2008) *United States Antitrust Law and Economics*. New York: Foundation Press.

Ellis, Jane (1999) 'The National Access Regime and Rail Line Services'. 18 *Australian Mining and Petroleum Law Journal*: 127.

Engel, Christoph (1995) 'Legal Experiences of Competition Among Institutions'. In: Gerken, Lüder (ed.) *Competition Among Institutions*. London, UK: Macmillan Press, pp. 89–118.

Epstein, Richard A. (2005) 'Takings, Commons, and Associations: Why the Telecommunications Act of 1996 Misfired'. 22 *Yale Journal of Regulation*: 315.

(2007) *Antitrust Consent Decrees in Theory and Practice: Why Less is More*. Washington, DC: AEI Press.

Evans, David S. & Padilla, A. Jorge (2005) 'Excessive Prices: Using Economics to Define Administrable Legal Rules'. 1 *Journal of Competition Law & Economics*: 97.

Evans, Eric J. (2004) *Thatcher and Thatcherism*, 2nd edn. London, UK: Routledge.

Ezrachi, Ariel & Gilo, David (2009) 'Are Excessive Prices Really Self-Correcting?'. 5 *Journal of Competition Law & Economics*: 249.

(2010) 'Excessive Pricing, Entry, Assessment, and Investigation: Lessons from the *Mittal* Litigation'. 76 *Antitrust Law Journal*: 873.

Faella, Gianluca & Pardolesi, Roberto (2010) 'Squeezing Price Squeeze under EC Antitrust Law'. 6 *European Competition Journal*: 255.

Faulhaber, Gerald R. (2008) 'Will Access Regulation Work?'. 61 *Federal Communications Law Journal*: 37.

Federal Trade Commission (FTC) (2010a) *Operating Manual*, OM Release 89–1, accessed online at www.ftc.gov/foia, in August 2014.

(2010b) 'Is there Life After *Trinko* and *Credit Suisse*? The Role of Antitrust in Regulated Industries', Prepared Statement of the Federal Trade Commission Before the United State House of Representatives Committee on the Judiciary, Subcommittee on Court and Competition Policy, Washington, DC, 15 June 2010.

Feldman, Gabriel A. (2009) 'The Misuse of the Less Restrictive Alternative Inquiry in Rule of Reason Analysis'. 58 *American University Law Review*: 561.

First, Harry (1995) 'Is Antitrust "Law"?'. 10 *Antitrust*: 9.

Fiss, Owen M. (1984) 'Against Settlement'. 93 *Yale Law Journal*: 1073.

Foer, Albert A. (2001) 'The Politics of Antitrust in the United States: Public Choice and Public Choices'. 62 *University of Pittsburgh Law Review*: 475.

(2009) 'Section 5 as a Bridge toward Convergence'. 8(3) *Antitrust Source*, February 2009.

Forrester, Ian S. (2009) 'Due Process in EC Competition Cases: A Distinguished Institution with Flawed Procedures'. 34 *European Law Review*: 817.

Fox, Eleanor M. (1981) 'The Modernization of Antitrust: A New Equilibrium'. 66 *Cornell Law Review*: 1140.

(1986a) 'Consumer Beware Chicago'. 84 *Michigan Law Review*: 1714.

(1986b) 'The Politics of Law and Economics in Judicial Decision Making: Antitrust as a Window'. 61 *NYU Law Review*: 554.

(2002) 'What is Harm to Competition? Exclusionary Practices and Anticompetitive Effect'. 70 *Antitrust Law Journal*: 371.

Frankel, Lawrence M. (2008) 'Rethinking the Tunney Act: A Model for Judicial Review of Antitrust Consent Decrees'. 75 *Antitrust Law Journal*: 549.

Freyer, Tony A. (2006) *Antitrust & Global Capitalism, 1930–2004*. New York: Cambridge University Press.

Gabor, Barbara (2013) *Regulatory Competition in the Internal Market*. Cheltenham, UK: Edward Elgar Publishing.

Gal, Michal S. (2004) 'Monopoly Pricing as an Antitrust Offense in the U.S. and the E.C.: Two Systems of Belief About Monopoly?'. 49 *Antitrust Bulletin*: 343.

(2006) 'Regulation by Declaration: A Novel Regulatory Mechanism to Limit Abuse of Monopoly Power'. 2 *NYU Journal of Law and Business*: 407.

Galambos, Louis (2004) 'The Monopoly Enigma, the Reagan Administration's Antitrust Experiment, and the Global Economy'. In: Lipartito, Kenneth & Sicilia, David B. (eds.) *Constructing Corporate America*. Oxford, UK: Oxford University Press, pp. 149–67.

Gallasch, Sven (2011) '*AstraZeneca* v.the *Walker Process* – a Real EU-US Divergence or Just an Attempt to Compare Apples to Oranges?'. 7 *European Competition Journal*: 505.

Gamble, Andrew (1989) 'Privatization, Thatcherism and the British State'. 16 *Journal of Law and Society*: 1.

Gelhorn, Ernest (1975) 'An Introduction to Antitrust Economics'. *Duke Law Journal*: 2.

Geradin, Damien & Kerf, Michel (2003) *Controlling Market Power in Telecommunications: Antitrust v. Sector Specific Regulation*. Oxford, UK: Oxford University Press.

Geradin, Damien & O'Donoghue, Robert (2005) 'The Concurrent Application of Competition Law and Regulation: The Case of Margin Squeeze Abuses in the Telecommunications Sector'. 1 *Journal of Competition Law & Economics*: 355.

Gerber, David J. (1998) *Law and Competition in Twentieth Century Europe: Protecting Prometheus*. Oxford, UK: Oxford University Press.

(2010) *Global Competition: Law, Markets and Globalisation*. Oxford, UK: Oxford University Press.

Geroski, Paul A. (2005) 'The UK Market Inquiry Regime'. In: Hawk, Barry (ed.) *International Antitrust Law and Policy: Fordham Corporate Law 2004*. New York: Juris Publishing Inc.

Ghertman, Michel (2009) 'The Puzzle of Regulation, Deregulation and Reregulation'. In: Ménard, Claude & Ghertman, Michel (eds.) *Regulation, Deregulation, Reregulation: Institutional Perspectives*. Cheltenham, UK: Edward Elgar Publishing, pp. 351–370.

Giemulla, Elmar M. & Weber, Ludwig (2011) *International and EU Aviation Law: Selected Issues*. The Netherlands: Wolters Kluwer.

Ginsburg, Douglas H. & Wright, Joshua D. (2013) 'Antitrust Settlements: The Culture of Consent' *George Mason University Law and Economics Research Paper Series* 13–18.

Giocoli, Nicola (2009) 'Competition Versus Property Rights: American Antitrust Law, the Freiburg School, and the Early Years of European Competition Policy'. 5 *Journal of Competition Law & Economics*: 747.

Glachant, Jean-Michel; Dubois, Ute & Perez, Yannick (2008) 'Deregulating with No Regulator: Is the German Electricity Transmission Regime Institutionally Correct?'. 36 *Energy Policy*: 1600.

Green, Stuart T. (2004) 'Moral Ambiguity in White Collar Criminal Law'. 18 *Notre Dame Journal of Law, Ethics and Public Policy*: 501.

Grenfell, Michael (1999) 'Can Competition Law Supplant Utilities Regulation?'. In: McCrudden, Christopher (ed.) *Regulation and Deregulation: Policy and Practice in the Utilities and Financial Services Industries*. Oxford, UK: Clarendon Press, pp. 221–34.

Grout, Paul A. & Zalewska, Anna (2008) 'Measuring the Rate of Return for Competition Law'. 4 *Journal of Competition Law & Economics*: 155.

Gunningham, Neil & Grabosky, Peter N. (1998) *Smart Regulation: Designing Environmental Policy*. Oxford, UK: Clarendon Press.

Hahn, Robert W. & Litan, Robert E. (2005) 'Counting Regulatory Benefits and Costs: Lessons for the US and Europe'. 8 *Journal of International Economic Law*: 473.

Haines, Fiona & Gurney, David (2003) 'The Shadows of the Law: Contemporary Approaches to Regulation and the Problem of Regulatory Conflict'. 25 *Law and Policy*: 353.

Hancher, Leigh & de Hauteclocque, Adrien (2010) 'Manufacturing the EU Energy Markets: The Current Dynamics of Regulatory Practice'. *EUI Working Paper*, RSCAS 2010/01.

Hantke-Domas, Michael (2003) 'The Public Interest Theory of Regulation: Non-Existence or Misinterpretation?'. 15 *European Journal of Law and Economics*: 165.

Hardacre, Alan (2008) 'Better Regulation – What is at Stake?'. *EIPAscope*, 2008/2: 5–10.

Harley, Kirsten & Armstrong, Mark (2002) 'Waiting for the Convergent Regulator'. *Network Insight, RMIT University*, October 2002: 2.

Hausman, Jerry A. & Sidak, J Gregory (1999) 'A Consumer-Welfare Approach to the Mandatory Unbundling of Telecommunications Networks'. 109 *Yale Law Journal*: 417.

Hawk, Barry E. (1995) 'System Failure: Vertical Restraints and EC Competition Law'. 32 Common Market Law Review: 973.

Hawk, Barry E. & Laudati, Laraine l. (1996) 'Antitrust Federalism in the United States and Decentralization of Competition Law Enforcement in the European Union: A Comparison'. 20(1) *Fordham International law Journal*: 18.

Hay, George (2005) '*Trinko*: Going All the Way'. 50(4) *Antitrust Bulletin*: 527.

Hayek, Friedrich A. ([1944] 2009) *The Road to Serfdom*. Reprint, Abiningdon, UK: Routledge.

Heimler, Alberto (2010) 'Is a Margin Squeeze an Antitrust or a Regulatory Violation?'. 6 *Journal of Competition Law and Economics*: 879.

Hellwig, Martin (2009) 'Competition Policy and Sector-specific Regulation for Network Industries'. In: Vives, Xavier (ed.) *Competition Policy in the EU*. Oxford, UK: Oxford University Press, pp. 203–35.

Hicks, J.R. (1935) 'Annual Survey of Economic Theory: The Theory of Monopoly'. 3 *Econometrica*: 1.

Hildebrand, Doris (2002) 'The European School in EC Competition Law'. 25 *World Competition*: 3.

Hou, Liyang (2011) 'Excessive Prices within EU Competition Law'. 7 *European Competition Journal*: 47.

Hovenkamp, Herbert (1983) 'State Antitrust in the Federal Scheme'. 58(3) *Indiana Law Journal*: 375.

(2000) 'The Robinson-Patman Act and Competition: Unfinished Business'. 68 *Antitrust Law Journal*: 125.

(2001) 'Post-Chicago Antitrust: A Review And Critique'. *Columbia Business Law Review*: 257.

(2005) *The Antitrust Enterprise: Principle and Execution*. Cambridge, MA: Harvard University Press.

(2010) 'The Legal Periphery of Dominant Firm Conduct'. In: Mateus, Abel M. & Moreira, Teresa (eds.) *Competition Law and Economics: Advances in Competition Policy Enforcement in the EU and North America*. Cheltenham, UK: Edward Elgar Publishing, pp. 238–63.

(2011) *Federal Antitrust Policy: The Law of Competition and its Practice*. St. Paul, MN: West Publishing.

Howell, Bronwyn (2010) 'Politics and the Pursuit of Telecommunications Sector Efficiency in New Zealand'. 6 *Journal of Competition Law & Economics*: 253.

Huffman, Max (2012) 'Marrying Neo-Chicago with Behavioural Antitrust'. 78 *Antitrust Law Journal*: 105.

Ibáñez Colomo, Pablo (2010) 'On the Application of Competition Law as Regulation: Elements for a Theory'. 29 *Yearbook of European Law*: 261.

Indig, Tamar & Gal, Michal S. (2013) 'New Powers – New Vulnerabilities? A Critical Analysis of Market Inquiries Performed by Competition Authorities'. In: Di Porto & Drexl (eds.) *Competition Law as Regulation*. . Cheltenham, UK: Edward Elgar Publishing.

International Energy Agency (IEA) (2005) *Energy Policies of IEA Countries: Australia – 2005 Review*, OECD/IEA 2005.

(2012), *Energy Policies of IEA Countries: Australia – 2012 Review*, OECD/IEA 2012.

Jablon, Robert A.; Hegedus, Mark S. & Flynn, Sean M. (2005) 'Dispelling Myths: A Real Word Perspective on *Trinko*'. 50 *Antitrust Bulletin*: 589.

Jacob, Charles E. (1985) 'Reaganomics: The Revolution in American Political Economy'. 48 *Law & Contemporary Problems*: 7.

Jarass, Hans D. (1988) 'Regulation as an Instrument of Economic Policy'. In: Daintith, Terence (ed.) *Law as an Instrument of Economic Policy: Comparative and Critical Approaches*. Berlin, Germany: Walter de Gruyter, pp. 75–96.

Jenny, Frédéric (2012) 'Competition Authorities: Independence and Advocacy'. In: Lianos, Ioannis & Sokol, D. Daniel (eds.) *The Global Limits of Competition Law*. Palo Alto, CA: Stanford University Press, pp. 158–76.

Jones, Paul (2005) 'The Rise and Fall of American Antitrust? An International Perspective on *Trinko* and the Regulation of the Knowledge Economy'. 50 *Antitrust Bulletin*: 687.

Jones, Alison (2010) 'The Journey towards an Effects-Based Approach under Article 101 TFEU – The Case of Hardcore Restraints'. 55 *Antitrust Bulletin*: 783.

Jordan, William A. (1972) 'Producer Protection, Prior Market Structure and the Effects of Government Regulation'. 15 *Journal of Law and Economics*: 151.

Joskow, Paul L. (2008) 'Lessons Learned from Electricity Market Liberalisation'. 29 *Energy Journal*: 9.

Kahn, Alfred E. (1987) 'Deregulatory Schizophrenia'. 75 *California Law Review*: 1059.

(1988) *The Economics of Regulation: Principles and Institutions*. Cambridge, MA: The MIT Press.

(1990) 'Deregulation: Looking Backward and Looking Forward'. 7 *Yale Journal on Regulation*: 325.

Kahn, Lawrence M. (2009) 'Sports, Antitrust Enforcement and Collective Bargaining'. 54 *Antitrust Bulletin*: 857.

Kaplow, Louis (2011) 'An Economic Approach to Price-Fixing'. 77 *Antitrust Law Journal*: 343.

Kauper, Thomas E. (2008) 'Influence of Conservative Economic Analysis on the Development of the Law of Antitrust'. In: Pitofsky, Robert (ed.) *How the Chicago School Overshot the Mark*. Oxford, UK: Oxford University Press, pp. 40–50.

Keynes, J.M. (1923) *A Tract on Monetary Reform*, Royal Economic Society edition 1971. London, UK: Macmillan.

Kingston, Suzanne (2011) *Greening EU Competition Law and Policy*. Cambridge, UK: Cambridge University Press.

Kirkpatrick, Colin & Parker, David (2007) 'Regulatory Impact Assessment: An Overview'. In: Kirkpatrick, Colin & Parker, David (eds.) *Regulatory Impact Assessment*. Cheltenham, UK: Edward Elgar Publishing, pp. 1–16.

Kirkwood, John B. & Lande, Robert H. (2008) 'The Fundamental Goal of Antitrust: Protecting Consumers, Not Increasing Efficiency'. 84 *Notre Dame Law Review*: 191.

Klein, Joel I. (2000) *The Antitrust Division's International Anti-Cartel Enforcement Program*, Speech by the Assistant Attorney General, Antitrust Division, US Department of Justice, at the American Bar Association Antitrust Section Spring Meeting, Washington DC, 6 April 2000.

Klein, Michael (1998) 'Network industries'. In: Helm, Dieter & Jenkinson, Tim (eds.) *Competition in Regulated Industries*. Oxford, UK: Oxford University Press, pp. 40–76.

Klotz, Robert (2009a) 'The Application of EC Competition Law (Articles 81 and 82) in the Telecommunications Sector'. In: Koenig, Christian; Bartosch,

Andreas; Braun, Jens-Daniel & Romes, Marion (eds.) *EC Competition and Telecommunications Law*, 2nd edn. The Netherlands: Kluwer Law International BV, pp. 107–51.

Klotz, Robert (2009b) 'The Liberalisation of the EU Telecommunications Markets'. In: Koenig, Christian; Bartosch, Andreas; Braun, Jens-Daniel & Romes, Marion (eds.) *EC Competition and Telecommunications Law*, 2nd edn. The Netherlands: Kluwer Law International BV, pp. 53–105.

Kobak, James B. & Reznick, Robert P. (2004) '*Unocal, Unitherm*, and New Uncertainty'. 19 *Antitrust*: 87.

Korah, Valentine (1986) 'EEC Competition Law – Legal Form or Economic Efficiency'. 39 *Current Legal Problems*: 85.

(2000) 'Access to Essential Facilities Under the Commerce Act in the Light of Experience in Australia, the European Union and the United States'. 31 *Victoria University of Wellington Law Review*: 231.

Kolasky, William J. (2004) 'What is Competition? A Comparison of U.S. and European Perspectives'. 49 *Antitrust Bulletin*: 29.

Kovacic, William E. (1991) 'Reagan's Judicial Appointees and Antitrust in the 1990s'. 60 *Fordham Law Review*: 49.

(1995) 'Accounting for Regulation in Determining the Application of Antitrust Rules to Firms Subject to Public Utility Oversight'. 40 *Antitrust Bulletin*: 483.

(2007) 'The Intellecual DNA of Modern U.S. Competition Law for Dominant Firm Conduct: The Chicago/Harvard Double Helix'. *Columbia Business Law Review*: 1.

Kovacic, William E. & Hyman, David A. (2012) 'Competition Agency Design: What's on the Menu?'. 8 European Competition Journal: 527.

Kovacic, William E. & Shapiro, Carl (2000) 'Antitrust Policy: A Century of Economic and Legal Thinking'. 14 *Journal of Economic Perspectives*: 43.

Kovacic, William E. & Winerman, Marc (2010) 'Competition Policy and the Application of Section 5 of the Federal Trade Commission Act'. 76(3) *Antitrust Law Journal*: 929.

Krattenmaker, Thomas G. (1984) 'Implications of Deregulation for Antitrust Policy'. 53 *Antitrust Law Journal*: 211.

Kroes, Neelie (2005) *Taking Competition Seriously – Antitrust Reform in Europe* SPEECH/05/157, Speech to the International Bar Association/European Commission Conference 'Antitrust Reform in Europe: A Year in Practice', Brussels, 10 March 2005.

Krouse, Clement G; Danger, Kenneth L.; Cabolis, Christos; Carter, Tanja D.; Riddle, Jon M. & Ryan, Daniel J. (1999) 'The Bell System Divestiture: Deregulation and the Efficiency of the Operating Companies'. 42 *Journal of Law and Economics*: 61.

Krueger, Anne O. (1974) 'The Political Economy of the Rent-Seeking Society'. 64 *American Economic Review*: 291.

Laffont, Jean-Jacques & Tirole, Jean (2000) *Competition in Telecommunications.* Cambridge, MA: MIT Press.

Lafontaine, Francine & Slade, Margaret (2007) 'Vertical Integration and Firm Boundaries: The Evidence'. 45(3) *Journal of Economic Literature*: 629.

Laguna de Paz, José Carlos (2012) 'Regulation and Competition Law'. 33 *European Competition Law Review*: 77.

Lande, Robert H. (1982) 'Wealth Transfers as the Original and Primary Concern of Antitrust: The Efficiency Interpretation Challenged'. 34 *Hastings Law Journal*: 65.

(2009) 'Revitalizing Section 5 of the FTC Act Using 'Consumer Choice' Analysis'. 8(3) *Antitrust Source*, February 2009.

(2010) 'Benefits of Private Enforcement: Empirical Background'. In: Foer, Albert A. & Cuneo, Jonathan W. (eds.) *The International Handbook of Private Enforcement of Competition Law.* Cheltenham, UK: Edward Elgar Publishing, pp. 3–11.

Larouche, Pierre (2000) *Competition and Regulation in European Telecommunications.* Oxford, UK: Hart Publishing.

(2005) 'Coordination of European and Member State Regulatory Policy: Horizontal, Vertical and Transversal Aspects'. In: Geradin, Damien; Muñoz, Rodolphe & Petit, Nicholas (eds.) *Regulation Through Agencies in the EU.* Cheltenham, UK: Edward Elgar Publishing, pp. 164–79.

Leary, Thomas B. (2009) 'A Suggestion for the Revival of Section 5'. 8(3) *Antitrust Source*, February 2009.

Leslie, Christopher R. (2007) 'New Possibilities for Asserting *Walker Process* Claims'. 21 *Antitrust*: 48.

Lewis, David (ed.) (2013) *Building New Competition Regimes: Selected Essays.* Cheltenham, UK: Edward Elgar Publishing.

Lianos, Ioannis (2012) 'Competition Law Remedies: In Search of a Theory'. In: Lianos, Ioannis & Sokol, D. Daniel (eds.) *The Global Limits of Competition Law.* Palo Alto, CA: Stanford University Press, pp. 177–201.

Lipsey, Richard G. & Lancaster, Kelvin (1956) 'The General Theory of Second Best'. 24 *Review of Economic Studies*: 11.

Litvack, Sanford M. (1982) 'The Ebb and Flow of Antitrust Enforcement: The Reagan and Carter Administrations'. *Brigham Young University Law Review*: 849.

Loevinger, Lee (1966) 'Regulation and Competition as Alternatives'. 11 *Antitrust Bulletin*: 101.

Lohmann, Heiko (2006) *The German Path to Natural Gas Liberalisation: Is it a Special Case?, NG 14.* Oxford, UK: Oxford Institute for Energy Studies.

Lopatka, John E. (1984) 'The Electric Utility Price Squeeze as an Antitrust Cause of Action'. 31 *UCLA Law Review*: 563.

Loughlin, John T. (1970) 'The Little Statute that Ran Astray'. 56 *A.B.A. Journal*: 681.

Loughlin, Martin (1989) 'Law, Ideologies, and the Political-Administrative System'. 16 *Journal of Law and Society*: 22.

Louis, Frédéric & Accardo, Gabriele (2011) '*Ne Bis in Idem*, Part "*Bi*"'. 34 *World Competition*: 97.

Low, Kelvin F.K. (2009) 'The Use and Abuse of Taxonomy'. 29 *Legal Studies*: 355.

Lunney, Glynn (2010) 'Copyright Collectives and Collecting Societies: The United States Experience'. In: Gervais, Daniel. J. (ed.) *Collective Management of Copyright and Related Rights*. Alphen aan den Rijn, The Netherlands: Kluwer Law International, pp. 339–82.

Lyons, Bruce (2007) 'The Paradox of the Exclusion of Exploitative Abuse' In: *The Pros and Cons of High Prices*, published by Konkurrensverket (Swedish Competition Authority), available online at www.kkv.se, pp. 65–87.

MacCulloch, Angus (2007) 'Honesty, Morality and the Competition Offence'. 28 *European Competition Law Review*: 355.

Maddock, Rodney & Marshall, Anthony (1997) 'Access Regulation: The New Australian Model'. 6 *Utilities Policy*: 67.

Majone, Giandomenico (ed.) (1996) *Regulating Europe*. London, UK: Routledge.

(1997) 'The New European Agencies: Regulation by Information'. 4 *Journal of European Public Policy*: 262.

Malone, Farrell & Sidak, J Gregory (2007) 'Should Antitrust Consent Decrees Regulate Post-Merger Pricing?'. 3 *Journal of Competition Law and Economics*: 471.

Manoussakis, Savas (2009) 'Liberalisation of the EU Energy Market: Enough to Power Real Progress?'. 32 *World Competition*: 227.

Markham, Jesse W. (2010) 'The Supreme Court's New Implied Repeal Doctrine: Expanding Judicial Power to Rewrite Legislation Under the Ballooning Conception of "Plain Repugnancy"'. 45 *Gonzaga Law Review*: 437.

Marquis, Mel (2007) '*O2 (Germany) v. Commission* and the Exotic Mysteries of Article 81(1) EC'. 32 *European Law Review*: 29.

Marshall, Brenda (2003) 'The Resolution of Access Disputes Under Section 46 of the Trade Practices Act'. 22(1) *University of Tasmania Law Review*: 9.

Marshall, Brenda & Mulheron, Rachael (2003a) 'Access to Essential Facilities Under Section 36 of the Commerce Act 1986: Lessons from Australian Competition Law'. 9 *Canterbury Law Review*: 248.

(2003b) 'Declarations of Essential Services Under Part IIIA of the Trade Practices Act: A 'Discipline' on Access Reform'. 31 *Western Australia Law Review*: 226.

Marshak, Amy (2011) 'The Federal Trade Commission on the Frontier: Suggestions for the Use of Section 5'. 86 *New York University Law Review*: 1121.

McBarnet, Doreen & Whelan, Christopher (1999) 'Challenging the Regulators: Strategies for Resisting Control'. In: McCrudden, Christopher (ed.) *Regulation and Deregulation*. Oxford, UK: Clarendon Press, pp. 67–77.

McChesney, Fred S. & Shugart, William F. (1995). *The Causes and Consequences of Antitrust: The Public Choice Perspective*. Chicago, IL: University of Chicago Press.

McCrudden, Christopher (1990) 'Regulations and Thatcherism: Some British Observations on Instrument Choice and Administrative Law'. 40 *University of Toronto Law Journal*: 542.

McKie, James W. (1970) 'Regulation and the Free Market: the Problem of Boundaries'. 1 *Bell Journal of Economics and Management*: 6.

Melamed, A. Douglas (1995) 'Antitrust: The New Regulation'. 10 *Antitrust*: 13.

(2007) '*U.S. v Microsoft*: Lessons Learned and Issues Raised'. In: Fox, Eleanor M. & Crane, Daniel A. (eds.) *Antitrust Stories*. New York: Foundation Press, pp. 287–310.

Mengler, Thomas M. (1988) 'Consent Decree Paradigms: Models Without Meaning'. 29 *Boston College Law Review*: 291.

Mikva, Abner J. (1990) 'Deregulating through the Back Door: The Hard Way to Fight a Revolution'. 57 *University of Chicago Law Review*: 521.

Mishan, E.J. & Quah, Euston (2007) *Cost-Benefit Analysis*, 5th edn. Oxford, UK: Routledge.

Mixon, John (2010) 'Neoclassical Economics and the Erosion of Middle-Class Values: An Explanation for Economic Collapse'. 24 *Notre Dame Journal of Law, Ethics & Public Policy*: 327.

Monti, Giorgio (2001) 'The Scope of Collective Dominance under Article 82'. 38 *Common Market Law Review*: 131.

(2007) *EC Competition Law* Cambridge, UK: Cambridge University Press.

(2008) 'Managing the Intersection of Utilities Regulation and EC Competition Law'. 4 *Competition Law Review*: 121.

(2010) 'Article 82 EC: What Future for the Effects-Based Approach?'. 1 *Journal of European Competition Law and Practice*: 2.

(2012) 'Unilateral Conduct: the Search for Global Standards'. In: Ezrachi, Ariel (ed.) *Research Handbook on International Competition Law*. Cheltenham, UK: Edward Elgar Publishing, pp. 345–368.

Morgan, Bronwen & Yeung, Karen (2007) *An Introduction to Law and Regulation: Text and Materials*. Cambridge, UK: Cambridge University Press.

Möschel, Wernhard (2001) 'The Proper Scope of Government Viewed from an Ordoliberal Perspective: The Example of Competition Policy'. 157 *Journal of Institutional and Theoretical Economics*: 3.

Motta, Massimo (2004) *Competition Policy: Theory and Practice*. Cambridge, UK: Cambridge University Press.

Motta, Massimo & de Streel, Alexandre (2007) 'Excessive Pricing in Competition Law: Never Say Never?'. In: *The Pros and Cons of High Prices*, published by Konkurrensverket (Swedish Competition Authority), available online at www.kkv.se, pp. 14–46.

Muris, Timothy J. (2004) 'Clarifying the State Action and *Noerr* Exemptions'. 27 *Harvard Journal of Law & Public Policy*: 443.

Nazzini, Renato (2004) *Concurrent Proceedings in Competition Law: Procedure, Evidence and Remedies*. Oxford, UK: Oxford University Press.

(2006) 'Article 81 EC between Times Present and Times Past: A Normative Critique of "Restriction of Competition" in EU Law'. 43 *Common Market Law Review*: 497.

New, Bill (1999) 'Paternalism and Public Policy'. 15 *Economics and Philosophy*: 63.

Newbury, David (1997) 'Privatisation and Liberalisation of Network Utilities'. 41 *European Economic Review*: 357.

Newman, Donald J. (1958) 'White-Collar Crime'. 23 *Law and Contemporary Problems*: 735.

Nicolaïdes, Phedon (2005) 'Regulation of Liberalised Markets:A New Roles for the States? (or How to Induce Competition Among Regulators)'. In: Geradin, Damien; Muñoz, Rodolphe & Petit, Nicholas (eds.) *Regulation Through Agencies in the EU*. Cheltenham, UK: Edward Elgar Publishing, pp. 23–43.

Nitsche, Rainer & Wiethaus, Lars (2012) 'Competition Law in Regulated Industrics: On the Case and Scope for Intervention'. 3 *Journal of European Competition Law & Practice*: 409.

O'Donoghue, Robert (2008) 'Regulating the Regulated: *Deutsche Telekom v European Commission*'. Global Competition Policy, MAY-08 (1).

O'Donoghue, Robert & Padilla, Jorge Atilano (2006) *The Law and Economics of Article 82 EC*. Oxford, UK: Hart Publishing.

O'Donoghue, Robert & Padilla, Jorge Atilano (2013) *The Law and Economics of Article 102 TFEU*, 2nd edn. Oxford, UK: Hart Publishing.

Odudu, Okeoghene (2006) *The Boundaries of EC Competition Law: The Scope of Article 81*. Oxford, UK: Oxford University Press.

(2010) 'The Wider Concerns of Competition Law'. 30 *Oxford Journal of Legal Studies*: 599.

Ogus, Anthony (1994) *Regulation: Legal Form and Economic Theory*. Oxford, UK: Clarendon Press.

Oldale, Alison & Padilla, A. Jorge (2004) 'From State Monopoly to the 'Investment Ladder': Competition Policy and the NRF'. In: *The Pros and Cons of Antitrust in Deregulated Markets*. Stockholm: Konkurrensverket, pp. 51–77.

Ohlhausen, Maureen (2014) 'Section 5 of the FTC Act: Principles of Navigation'. 2 *Journal of Antitrust Enforcement*:1.

Olsen, Gregory & Roy, Bryony (2007) 'The New World of Proactive EC Antitrust Enforcement? Sector Inquiries by the European Commission'. 21 *Antitrust*: 82.

Orbach, Barak Y. (2011) 'The Antitrust Consumer Welfare Paradox'. 7 *Journal of Competition Law & Economics*: 133.

(2012) 'What is Regulation?'. 30 *Yale Journal on Regulation Online*, available on SSRN at http://papers.ssrn.com/sol3/papers.cfm?abstract_id=2143385

Organisation for Economic Cooperation and Development (OECD) (1997) *Regulatory Impact Analysis: Best Practices in OECD Countries*. Paris: OECD Publications.

(2001) *Restructuring Public Utilities for Competition*. Paris: OECD Publications.

(2004) *Access Pricing in Telecommunications*. Paris: OECD Publications.

(2006) *Roundtable on Competition, Patents and Innovation*, DAF/COMP(2007) 40. Paris: OECD Publications.

(2008) *Roundtable on Market Studies*, DAF/COMP(2008)34. Paris: OECD Publications.

(2010) *OECD Reviews of Regulatory Reform. Competition Policy in Australia*. Paris: OECD Publications.

(2011a) *Competition Issues in the Financial Sector: Key Findings*. Paris: OECD Publications.

(2011b) *Roundtable on Excessive Prices: Background Paper*, DAF/COMP/WP2 (2011)7/REV1. Paris: OECD Publications.

(2012) *Report on Experiences with Structural Separation*. Paris: OECD Publication.

Parker, Christine, (2012) 'Economic Rationalities of Governance and Ambiguity in the Criminalization of Cartels'. 52 *British Journal of Criminology*: 974.

Parret, Laura (2010) 'Shouldn't We Know What We are Protecting? Yes We Should! A Plea for a Solid and Comprehensive Debate about the Objectives of EU Competition Law and Policy'. 6 *European Competition Journal*: 339.

Peeperkorn, Lucas & Viertiö, Katja (2009) 'Implementing an Effects-Based Approach to Article 82'. 1/2009 *Competition Policy Newsletter*: 17.

Pelkmans, Jacques & Luchetta, Giacomo (2013) *Enjoying a Single Market for Network Industries?* Paris: Notre Europe – Jacques Delors Institute.

Peltzman, Sam (1976) 'Towards a More General Theory of Regulation'. 19 *Journal of Law and Economics*: 211.

(1989) 'The Economic Theory of Regulation after a Decade of Deregulation'. *Brooking Papers on Economic Activity: Microeconomics*.

Pena, Julian (2012) 'The Limits of Competition Law in Latin America'. In: Lianos, Ioannis & Sokol, D. Daniel (eds.), *The Global Limits of Competition Law*. Palo Alto, CA: Stanford University Press, pp. 236–51.

Pengilley, Warren (1998) 'Access to Essential Facilities: A Unique Antitrust Experiment in Australia'. 43 *Antitrust Bulletin*: 519.

Petit, Nicholas (2005) 'The Proliferation of National Regulatory Authorities alongside Competition Authorities: A Source of Jurisdictional Confusion?'. In: Geradin, Damien; Muñoz, Rodolphe & Petit, Nicholas (eds.) *Regulation*

Through Agencies in the EU. Cheltenham, UK: Edward Elgar Publishing, pp. 180–214.

Pigou, Arthur C. (1932) *The Economics of Welfare*, 4th edn. London: Macmillan & Co.

Piketty, Thomas (2014) *Capital in the Twenty-First Century*. Cambridge, MA: Harvard University Press.

Pimlott, Nick (2010) 'Concurrency and the Role of the Competition Appeal Tribunal as Supervisor of the Sectoral Regulators'. *Competition Law Journal*: 162.

Pitofsky, Robert (1979) 'The Political Content of Antitrust'. 127 *University of Pennsylvania Law Review*: 1051.

Pitofsky, Robert; Patterson, Donna & Hooks, Jonathan (2002) 'The Essential Facilities Doctrine Under U.S. Antitrust Law'. 70 *Antitrust Law Journal*: 443.

Pollitt, Michael (2008) 'The Arguments for and against Ownership Unbundling of Energy Transmission Networks'. 36(2) *Energy Policy*: 704.

Ponsoldt, James F. (1988) 'Introduction to A Retrospective Examination of the Reagan Years'. 33 *Antitrust Bull*: 201.

Posner, Richard A. (1969) 'Oligopoly and the Antitrust Laws: A Suggested Approach'. 21 *Stanford Law Review*: 1562.

(1970) 'A Statistical Study of Antitrust Enforcement'. 13 *Journal of Law & Economics* 365.

(1974) 'Theories of Economic Regulation'. 5 *Bell Journal of Economics and Management Science*: 335.

(1975) 'The Social Costs of Monopoly and Regulation'. 83 *Journal of Political Economy*: 807.

(1979) 'Utilitarianism, Economics and Legal Theory'. 8 *Journal of Legal Studies*: 103.

(1980) 'Ethical and Political Basis of Efficiency'. 8 *Hofstra Law Review*: 501.

(2001) *Antitrust Law*, 2nd edn. Chicago, IL: University of Chicago Press.

(2003) *Economic Analysis of Law*, 6th edn. New York: Aspen Publishers.

(2008) 'The Decline and Fall of AT&T: A Personal Recollection'. 61 *Federal Communications Law Journal*: 11.

(2009) *A Failure of Capitalism: The Crisis of '08 and the Descent into Depression*. Cambridge, MA: Harvard University Press.

Pozen, Sharis & Six, Anne (2013) 'Section 5 Guidelines: Fixing a Problem that Doesn't Exist?'. *CPI Antitrust Chronicle*, published September 2013.

Prosser, Tony (1997) *Law and the Regulators*. Oxford, UK: Clarendon Press.

(2004) *The Limits of Competition Law*. Oxford, UK: Oxford University Press.

(2006) 'Regulation and Social Solidarity'. 33 *Journal of Law & Society*: 364.

Przeworski, Adam (1990) *The State and the Economy under Capitalism*. Chur, Switzerland: Harwood Academic Publishers.

Rab, Suzanne (2009) 'From Ordered Competition – Towards a New Competitive Order? The Role of the UK Competition Commission at the Interface between Sector Regulation and Competition Law'. 30 *European Competition Law Review*: 505.

Reeves, Amanda P. & Stucke, Maurice E. (2011) 'Behavioural Antitrust'. 86 *Indiana Law Journal*: 1527.

Reid, Bill & Burrows, Elizabeth (1997) 'Access to Infrastructure – Potential Passages to Remorse'. 16 *Australian Mining and Petroleum Law Journal*: 212.

Richman, Barak D. & Boerner, Christopher (2006) 'A Transaction Cost Economizing Approach to Regulation: Understanding the NIMBY Problem and Improving Regulatory Responses'. 23 *Yale Journal on Regulation*: 29.

Robertson, Elbert L. (2009) 'Does Antitrust Regulation Violate the Rule of Law?'. 22 *Loyola Consumer Law Review*: 108.

Roland, Gérard (2008) 'Private and Public Ownership in Economic Theory'. In: Roland, Gérard (ed.) *Privatization: Successes and Failures*. New York: Columbia University Press, pp. 9–31.

Rosch, J. Thomas (2009) 'The FTC's Section 5 Hearings: New Standards for Unilateral Conduct?'. *Remarks of J. Thomas Rosch, Commissioner, Federal Trade Commission Before the ABA 57th Antitrust Law Section Spring Meeting*, Washington, DC, March 2009.

Rosch, J. Thomas (2011) 'Consent Decrees: Is the Public Getting its Money's Worth?'. *Remarks of Commissioner Rosch, FTC, before the XVIIIth St. Gallen International Competition Law Forum*, 7 April 2011.

Rose-Ackerman, Susan (1990) 'Defending the State: A Skeptical Look at "Regulatory Reform" in the Eighties'. 61 *University of Colorado Law Review*: 517.

Rubin, Jonathan L. (2005) 'The Truth about *Trinko*'. 50(4) Antitrust Bulletin: 725.

Salop, Steven (2013) 'Guiding Section 5: Comments on the Commissioners'. *CPI Antitrust Chronicle*, published September 2013.

Samuelson, Paul A. (1983) *Foundations of Economic Analysis*, Enlarged edn. Cambridge, MA: Harvard University Press.

Sandel, Michael (2012) *What Money Can't Buy: The Moral Limits of Markets*. London, UK: Allen Lane.

Sappington, David E.M. & Weisman, Dennis L. (2010) 'Price Cap Regulation: What Have We Learned from 25 Years of Experience in the Telecommunications Industry?'. 38 *Journal of Regulatory Economics*: 227.

Schaub, Alexander (1999) 'Modernization of EC Competition Law: Reform of Regulation No. 17'. 24 *Fordham International Law Journal*: 752.

Scherer, Frederic M. (1967) 'Market Structure and the Employment of Scientists and Engineers'. 57 *American Economic Review*: 524.

(1987) 'Antitrust, Efficiency, and Progress'. 62 *N.Y.U. Law Review*: 998.

(2008) 'Conservative Economics and Antitrust: A Variety of Influences'. In: Pitofsky, Robert (ed.) *How the Chicago School Overshot the Mark*. Oxford, UK: Oxford University Press, pp. 30–39.

Schleifer, Andrei (2005) 'Understanding Regulation'. 11 *European Financial Management*: 439.

Schumpeter, Joseph A. ([1973] 2010) *Capitalism, Socialism, Democracy*. Reprint, London, UK: Routledge Classics.

Schwartz, Louis B. (1979) '"Justice" And Other Non-Economic Goals Of Antitrust'. 127 *University of Pennsylvania Law Review*: 1076.

(1987) 'Some Additional Safeguards for the Newly Liberated Marketplace'. 75 *California Law Review*: 1049.

Schweitzer, Heike (2008) 'Commitment Decisions under Article 9 of Regulation 1/2003: The Developing EC Practice and Case Law'. *EUI Working Papers LAW* 2008/22.

Scott, Colin (ed.) (2003) *The International Library of Essays in Law and Legal Theory, Second Series*, Regulation. Aldershot, UK: Dartmouth Publishing Company.

Segal, Ilya & Whinston, Michael D. (2007) 'Antitrust in Innovative Industries'. 97 *American Economic Review*: 1703.

Selznick, Philip (1985) 'Focusing Organizational Research on Regulation'. In: Noll, Roger G. (ed.) *Regulatory Policy and the Social Sciences*. Berkley, CA: University of California Press, pp. 363–68.

Semeraro, Stephen (2003) 'Speta on Antitrust and Local Competition under the Telecommunications Act: A Comment Respecting the Accommodation of Antitrust and Telecom Regulation'. 71 *Antitrust Law Journal*: 147.

Sen, Amartya (1993) 'Markets and Freedoms: Achievements and Limitations of the Market Mechanism in Promoting Individual Freedoms'. 45 *Oxford Economic Papers*: 519.

Shelanski, Howard A. (2011) 'The Case for Rebalancing Antitrust and Regulation'. 109 *Michigan Law Review*: 683.

(2012) 'Justice Breyer, Professor Kahn and Antitrust Enforcement in Regulated Industries'. 100 *California Law Review*: 487.

Sherwin, Emily (2005) 'Legal Taxonomy'. 15 *Legal Theory*: 25.

Shughart, William F. (2000) 'The Fleeting Reagan Antitrust Revolution'. 45 *Antitrust Bulletin*: 271.

Sidak, J. Gregory (2008) 'Abolishing the Price Squeeze as a Theory of Antitrust Liability'. 4 *Journal of Competition Law & Economics*: 279.

Sims, Joe (1979) 'Two Bites at the Apple? – Double Jeopardy and the Antitrust Laws'. 48 *Antitrust Law Journal*: 1401.

(2013) 'Section 5 Guidelines: Josh Wright as the New King of Corinth?'. *CPI Antitrust Chronicle*, published September 2013.

Skitol, Robert A. (1999) 'The Shifting Sands of Antitrust Policy: Where It Has Been, Where It Is Now, Where It Will Be in its Third Century'. 9 *Cornell Journal of Law & Public Policy*: 239.

Smith, Adam ([1776] 2007) *The Wealth of Nations*, Harriman House edn. Reprint, Hampshire, UK: Harriman House.

Smith, Vincent (2004) 'Competition Concurrency between the OFT and Sector Regulators'. 12 *Utilities Policy*: 61.

Soames, Trevor (1997) 'Ground Handling Liberalization'. 3 *Journal of Air Transport Management*: 83.

Sokol, D. Daniel (2012) 'Anticompetitive Government Regulation'. In: Lianos, Ioannis & Sokol, D. Daniel (eds.) *The Global Limits of Competition Law*. Palo Alto, CA: Stanford University Press, pp. 83–98.

Soriano Garcia, José Eugenio (2010) 'The Internal Gas Market according to the Law of Competition. Provisions of the Community's Third Package'. *European Energy and Environmental Law Review*, August 2010: 175.

Speta, James B. (2003) 'Antitrust and Local Competition under the Telecommunications Act'. 71 *Antitrust Law Journal*: 99.

Spulber, Daniel F. & Yoo, Christopher S. (2007) 'Mandating Access to Telecom and the Internet: the Hidden Side of *Trinko*'. 107 *Columbia Law Review*: 1822.

Stefan, Oana (2012) *Soft Law in Court. Competition Law, State Aid and the Court of Justice of the European Union*. Alphen aan den Rijn, The Netherlands: Kluwer Law International.

Stewart, Richard B. (1983) 'Regulation in a Liberal State: The Role of Non-Commodity Values'. 92 *Yale Law Journal*: 1537.

(1988) 'Regulation and the Crisis of Legalisation in the United States'. In: Daintith, Terence (ed.) *Law as an Instrument of Economic Policy: Comparative and Critical Approaches*. Berlin, Germany: Walter de Gruyter, pp. 97–133.

(2000) 'Economic Incentives for Environmental Protection: Opportunities and Obstacles'. In: Revesz, Richard L.; Sands, Philippe & Stewart, Richard B. (eds.) *Environmental Law, the Economy and Sustainable Development: The United State, the European Union and the International Community*. Cambridge, UK: Cambridge University Press, pp. 171–244.

Stigler, George J. (1964) 'A Theory of Oligopoly'. 72 *Journal of Political Economy*: 44.

(1971) 'The Theory of Economic Regulation'. 2 *Bell Journal of Economics and Management Science*: 3.

(1985) 'The Origins of the Sherman Act'. 14 *Journal of Legal Studies*: 1.

Stiglitz, Joseph E. (2008) 'Forward'. In: Roland, Gérard (ed.) *Privatization: Successes and Failures*. New York: Columbia University Press, pp. ix–xx.

(2010) *Freefall: Free Markets and the Sinking of the Global Economy*. London, UK: Allen Lane.

Sullivan, E. Thomas & Hovenkamp, Herbert (2003) *Antitrust Law, Policy and Procedure: Cases, Materials, Problems*, 5th edn. San Francisco, CA: LexisNexis.

Sumpter, Matt; Hamlin, Ben & Mellsop, James (2010) *New Zealand Competition Law and Policy*. Auckland, New Zealand: CCH New Zealand Limited.

Sunstein, Cass (1990) *After the Rights Revolution: Reconceiving the Regulatory State*. Cambridge, MA: Harvard University Press.

(1997) *Free Markets and Social Justice*. New York: Oxford University Press.

(ed.) (2000) *Behavioral Law and Economics*. Cambridge, UK: Cambridge University Press.

Tapia, Javier & Mantzari, Despoina (2012) 'The Regulation/Competition Interaction'. *Regcom Working Paper*: 1–12.

Tardiff, Timothy J. (2010) 'Efficiency Metrics for Competition Policy in Network Industries'. 6 *Journal of Competition Law and Economics*: 957.

Temple Lang, John (2003) 'Commitment Decision under Regulation 1/2003: Legal Aspects of a New Kind of Competition Decision'. 24 *European Competition Law Review*: 347.

Thorelli, Hans B. (1954) *The Federal Antitrust Policy: Origination of an American Tradition*. Stockholm, Sweden: Kungliga Boktryckeriet P. A. Norstedt & Söner.

Tollison, Robert D. (1985) 'Public Choice and Antitrust'. 4 *Cato Journal*: 905.

Tombs, Steve (2002) 'Understanding Regulation?'. 11 *Social & Legal Studies*: 113.

Townley, Christopher (2009) *Article 81 EC and Public Policy*. Oxford, UK: Hart Publishing.

Tridimas, Takis (2006) *The General Principles of EU Law*, 2nd edn. Oxford, UK: Oxford University Press.

Turner, Donald F. (1962) 'The Definition of Agreement under the Sherman Act: Conscious Parallelism and Refusals to Deal'. 75 *Harvard Law Review*: 655.

US Department of Justice (DOJ) (2014) *Antitrust Division Manual*, 5th edn.

Varney, Christine A. (2011) 'Antitrust Immunities'. 89 *Oregon Law Review*: 775.

Veggeland, Noralv (2009) *Taming the Regulatory State*. Cheltenham, UK: Edward Elgar Publishing.

Veljanovski, Cento (2008) 'Margin Squeeze in Telecoms'. 36 *Intermedia*.

Vickers, John (1995) 'Concepts of Competition'. 47 *Oxford Economic Papers*: 1.

(2010) 'Competition Policy and Property Rights'. 120 *Economic Journal*: 375.

Viscusi, Kip W.; Harrington, Joseph E. & Vernon, John M. (2005) *Economics of Regulation and Antitrust*, 4th edn. Cambridge, MA: MIT Press.

Von Danwitz, Thomas (2006) 'Regulation and Liberalisation of the European Electricity Market – A German View'. 27 *Energy Law Journal*: 423.

Vrcek, Bojana (2010) 'Overview of Europe'. In: Foer, Albert A. & Cuneo, Jonathan W. (eds.) *The International Handbook of Private Enforcement of Competition Law*. Cheltenham, UK: Edward Elgar Publishing, pp. 277–95.

Wagner-von Papp, Florian (2012) 'Best and even Better Practices in Commitment Procedures after *Alrosa*: The Dangers of Abandoning the "Struggle for Competition Law"'. 49 *Common Market Law Review*: 929.

Wahl, Nils (2007) 'Exploitative High Prices and European Competition Law – A Personal Reflection'. In: *The Pros and Cons of High Prices*, published by

Konkurrensverket (Swedish Competition Authority), available online at www.kkv.se, pp. 47–64.

Wallsten, Scott (2006) 'Telecommunications Regulation in U.S. States: Its Rise and Impacts in the Early Twentieth Century'. AEI-Brookings Joint Center for Regulatory Studies, Working Paper 06–04, March 2006.

Weatherill, Stephen (2007) 'The Challenge of Better Regulation'. In: Weatherill, Stephen (ed.) *Better Regulation*. Oxford, UK: Hart Publishing, pp. 1–18.

(2009) 'Competence and Legitimacy'. In: Barnard, Catherine & Odudu, Okeoghene (eds.) *The Outer Limits of European Union Law*. Oxford, UK: Hart Publishing, pp. 17–34.

Weber, Joseph H. (2008) 'The Bell System Divestiture: Background, Implementation, and Outcome'. 61 *Federal Communications Law Journal*: 21.

Weber Waller, Spencer (1997) 'Market Talk: Competition Policy in America'. 22 *Law & Social Inquiry*: 435.

(1998) 'Prosecution by Regulation: The Changing Nature of Antitrust Enforcement'. 77 *Oregon Law Review*: 1383.

(2009) 'The Past, Present and Future of Monopolisation Remedies'. 76 *Antitrust Law Journal*: 11.

Weiner, Michael L. (1995) 'Antitrust and the Rise of the Regulatory Consent Decree'. 10 *Antitrust*: 4.

Weiser, Philip J. (2005) 'The Relationship of Antitrust and Regulation in a Deregulatory Era'. 50 *Antitrust Bulletin*: 549.

Wells, Celia & Quick, Oliver (2010) *Reconstructing Criminal Law: Texts and Materials*, 4th edn. Cambridge, UK: Cambridge University Press.

Werden, Gregory J. (2009) 'Remedies for Exclusionary Conduct Should Protect Competition and Preserve the Competitive Process'. 76 *Antitrust Law Journal*: 65.

Whelan, Peter (2007) 'A Principled Argument for Personal Criminal Sanctions as Punishment under EC Cartel Law'. 4 *Competition Law Review*: 7.

Whish, Richard & Bailey, David (2012) *Competition Law*, 7th edn. Oxford, UK: Oxford University Press.

Whitehouse, Lisa (2003) 'Railtrack is Dead – Long Live Network Rail? Nationalization Under the Third Way'. 30 *Journal of Law & Society*: 217.

Wiener, Jonathan B. (2006) 'Better Regulation in Europe'. *Duke Law School Legal Studies Research Paper Series*, Paper No. 130, October 2006.

Williams, Mark (2007) 'Excessive Pricing'. In: *The Pros and Cons of High Prices*, published by Konkurrensverket (Swedish Competition Authority), available online at www.kkv.se, pp. 128–53.

Williams, Robert (1990) 'Policy, Process and Power: Understanding American Bureaucracy'. In: Williams, Robert (ed.) *Explaining American Politics: Issues and Interpretations*. London, UK: Routledge, pp. 97–115.

Williamson, John (1990) 'What Washington Means by Policy Reform'. In: Williamson, John (ed.) *Latin American Adjustment: How Much Has Happened?*. Washington, DC: Institute for International Economics.

Williamson, Oliver E. (1975) *Markets and Hierarchies: Analysis and Antitrust Implications*. New York: Free Press.

(1977) 'Economies as an Antitrust Defence Revisited'. 125 *University of Pennsylvania Law Review*: 699.

(1981) 'The Economics of Organisation: The Transaction Cost Approach'. 87 *American Journal of Sociology*: 548.

Wils, Wouter P.J. (2003) 'The Principle of *Ne Bis in Idem* in EC Antitrust Enforcement: A Legal and Economic Analysis'. 26 *World Competition*: 131.

(2005) 'Is Criminalisation of EU Competition Law the Answer?'. 28 *World Competition*: 117.

(2006) 'Settlements of EU Antitrust Investigations: Commitments Decisions under Article 9 of Regulation No. 1/2003'. 29(3) *World Competition*: 345.

(2009) 'The Relationship between Public Antitrust Enforcement and Private Actions for Damages'. 32 *World Competition*: 3.

(2011) 'EU Antitrust Enforcement Powers and Procedural Rights and Guarantees: The Interplay between EU Law, National Law, the Charter of Fundamental Rights of the EU and the European Convention on Human Rights'. 34 *World Competition*: 189.

Wood, David & Baverez, Nicolas (2005) 'Sector Inquiries'. *Competition Law Insight*, 8 February 2005.

Wright, Joshua D. & Stone, Judd E. (2012) 'Misbehavioural Economics: The Case Against Behavioural Antitrust'. 33 *Cardozo Law Review*: 1517.

Wright, Joshua D. (2013a) 'What's Your Agenda?'. *Remarks of Commissioner Joshua D Wright, Federal Trade Commission at the ABA Spring Meetings*, Washington, DC, on 11 April 2013.

(2013b) 'Proposed Policy Statement Regarding Unfair Methods of Competition Under Section 5 of the Federal Trade Commission Act'. *Statement of Commission Joshua D. Wright*, published 19 June 2013.

Wu, Tim (2010) *The Master Switch: The Rise and Fall of Information Empires*. New York: Alfred A. Knopf.

Yeung, Karen (1999) 'Private Enforcement of Competition'. In: McCrudden, Christopher (ed.) *Regulation and Deregulation: Policy and Practice in the Utilities and Financial Services Industries*. Oxford, UK: Clarendon Press, pp. 37–65.

(2004) *Securing Compliance. A Principled Approach*. Oxford, UK: Hart Publishing.

(2012) 'Better Regulation, Administrative Sanctions and Constitutional Values'. 33 *Legal Studies*: 312.

INDEX

For EU product safety concerns, contact us at Calle de José Abascal, 56–1°, 28003 Madrid, Spain or eugpsr@cambridge.org.

www.ingramcontent.com/pod-product-compliance
Lightning Source LLC
LaVergne TN
LVHW011529200926
848484LV00001B/206